PRAISE FOR
John Houseman

Run-Through

"I read this book with fascination. Quite aside from its marvelous portrait of Orson Welles, I know of no other book which has made me understand the thrills and miseries of being a producer and director. I felt as if I were running the Mercury Theatre single-handed!"—*Christopher Isherwood*

"Show biz since 1934! Viewed from the top! With total recall! What a lovely book!"—*Virgil Thomson*

DISCARDED

Front and Center

Front and Center is a book crowded with great names, great films, great theatre. . . . I can think of no one who has bridged the media of theatre and films, radio and television as completely and definitely as John Houseman. He was always where the action was—the turbulent WPA Theatre and the innovative Mercury Theatre of the 30s; producer of a dozen major Hollywood films; his stint with the O.W.I. with its "Voice of America" broadcasts which were crucial to our war effort; his brushes with McCarthyism and his ultimate emergence as a star of films and TV, and as a successful author."—*Arthur Knight*

"Finally, an educated eye scanning the glory and the ecstasy of show business. Illuminating, accurate and juicy. Five hundred pages of delight."—*Billy Wilder*

"A mature, shrewd and richly enjoyable book."—*David Elliott, Chicago Sun-Times*

Final Dress

"This is the book we have been waiting for. The wittiest and most insightful and, above all, the most human part of John Houseman's saga, *Final Dress* is more than a summing up, it is a deep look into a fascinating life by a fascinating man."—*Marian Seldes*

"John Houseman's *Final Dress* is by far the most brilliant and the best of his autobiographical trilogy. It is a book everyone interested in theatre, film, or television must read."—*Howard M. Teichmann*

BOOKS BY JOHN HOUSEMAN

Final Dress
Front and Center
Run-Through

FINAL DRESS

A Memoir
by
John Houseman

A TOUCHSTONE BOOK
Published by Simon & Schuster, Inc.
NEW YORK

Copyright © 1983 by John Houseman
All rights reserved
including the right of reproduction
in whole or in part in any form
First Touchstone Edition, 1984
Published by Simon & Schuster, Inc.
Simon & Schuster Building
Rockefeller Center
1230 Avenue of the Americas
New York, New York 10020
TOUCHSTONE and colophon are registered trademarks of Simon
& Schuster, Inc.
Designed by Edith Fowler
Picture Editor: Vincent Virga
Manufactured in the United States of America
10 9 8 7 6 5 4 3 2 1
10 9 8 7 6 5 4 3 2 1 Pbk.
Library of Congress Cataloging in Publication Data
Houseman, John.
    Final dress.
    Continues: Front and center.
    1. Houseman, John.   2. Theatrical producers
and directors—United States—Biography. I. Title.
PN2287.H7A26   1983   792'.023'0924   [B]   83-423
ISBN 0-671-42031-3
ISBN 0-671-42032-1 Pbk.

*For all those
with whom I have worked
over the past fifty years.*

Contents

CONTENTS

CONTENTS

Metamorphosis

Old men forget: yet all shall be forgot,
But he'll remember, with advantages,
What feats he did that day.

SHAKESPEARE, *Henry V*

Book One

Book One

CHAPTER I

1955-1956

AMERICAN SHAKESPEARE
FESTIVAL:
KING JOHN
MEASURE FOR MEASURE
THE TAMING OF THE SHREW
THE DUCHESS OF MALFI

IN DECEMBER 1955 I left California with my family and
moved back into the house I had built nine years earlier on a
hill overlooking the Hudson at New City, New York. It was
my eighth East–West continental crossing. The first, in 1940,
followed the dissolution of my partnership with Orson
Welles; the third came a week after Pearl Harbor when I flew
east to join Robert Sherwood on the Voice of America. The
others had been escapes of one sort or another—mostly from
frustration, boredom and fear.

This, my latest excursion, may have been precipitate and
compulsive. It certainly seemed so to my wife, who had
grown accustomed to living in Southern California, where
she had just poured much time and love into making our
newly acquired house in Santa Monica a perfect home for
ourselves and our children. It was, in fact, a deliberate and

perverse decision—one of many that have determined the course of my life.

Between the ages of forty-eight and fifty-three I had produced eight motion pictures, of which four had achieved considerable success. I had also directed two plays on Broadway (both by William Shakespeare), got married, fathered two male children and achieved a professional and financial security such as I had never known. Yet when Lincoln Kirstein called me from New York late one night and asked if I would consider taking over the artistic direction of the American Shakespeare Festival in Stratford, Connecticut, for the coming season, I said yes before he had finished speaking and before I was aware of the reasons for my response. I presently discovered that they were mostly negative.

My five years with the Metro-Goldwyn-Mayer Studio in Culver City* represented the longest and most productive span of continuous employment I had ever known. Yet the fact that I was finally achieving the professional acceptance I had so long and so desperately yearned for did not prevent me, by the autumn of 1955, from becoming increasingly restless and weary of the repetitive routine of developing and supervising the writing, casting, production, editing and, finally, the merchandising of one film after another. My latest picture, *Lust for Life,* had been well received, but it had been unusually difficult to produce and had left me enervated and discontented. This may explain why I so eagerly accepted an offer I would not have considered six months earlier and why I was prepared to exchange my hard-won position in the "big time" of show business for a future that might drastically change during the twelve months of my absence.

On the positive side, besides the lure of movement and change and the irresistible attraction of risk, there was a nostalgic temptation to return to New York City and the kind of institutional theatre in which I had begun my career—first with the Federal Theatre of the WPA, then with the Mercury and, later, with Pelican Productions and the Phoenix. With the film of *Julius Caesar,* followed by theatrical performances

* See *Front and Center,* pp. 353–487 (The Lion's Roar).

of *King Lear* and *Coriolanus,* I had acquired a reputation for being consistently concerned with the professional production of Shakespeare's plays with American actors for contemporary audiences. The Stratford offer gave me a chance to add to this reputation and to move toward the remote but alluring goal of a national classical repertory of which I had been vaguely dreaming ever since Orson Welles and I had first played with the idea more than twenty years before.

At the age of fifty-four, with my ego swollen by recent victories, ambition had become the dominant and almost exclusive drive in my life. I still functioned as a chameleon, but as my self-confidence continued to grow, a more defined, personal coloration was becoming evident in my work. Whatever secret doubts I may still have felt about my creative capacity were more than offset by my confidence in my efficiency, my sense of timing (which I had developed years ago in the grain business) and my proven ability to sense and exploit the cultural modes of the day. Besides, it was my feeling that the film industry, unbeknownst to most of its opulent and complacent practitioners, was entering a period of decline, so that, in returning to the theatre for a while, I did not feel I was following an altogether altruistic course.*

After two decades of adversity and shrinkage, theatre in America was showing signs of renewed life—not so much on Broadway as throughout the rest of the country, where an appetite for living drama and new ways of satisfying it were becoming increasingly apparent. Evidence of this was to be found in the growing number of regional theatres and festivals that were springing up all over the continent. The most successful, by far, was the Shakespeare Festival at Stratford, Ontario,† which, within a few years, had completely changed the cultural face of central Canada. Others ranged from

---

* Money played no part in my decision; my fabulous MGM contract called for full remuneration even during my year's absence from California.

† Created in the early fifties, with national support, from the dreams of an obscure young Canadian native (Tom Patterson) and the professional expertise and energy of a famed British director (Tyrone Guthrie).

T. Edward Hambleton's Phoenix and Joseph Papp's free
Shakespeare in the Park in New York City to local institutions
of various kinds and sizes in Massachusetts, Ohio, Texas,
California, Oregon and elsewhere. Last but not least of these
was the recently opened American Shakespeare Festival Theatre founded by Lawrence Langner at Stratford, Connecticut.

That I had long disliked and mistrusted Lawrence Langner
and felt suspicious and ill at ease in his presence* does not
alter the historic fact that he was a man of great energy and
skill who, between World War I and his death in 1962, played
a dominant and highly constructive part in the development
of serious theatre in America. A Welsh Jew by birth and a
patent lawyer by profession, he was one of the group that
had founded the Washington Square Players (later the Theatre Guild)—the most progressive and durable producing
organization in the history of the American theatre.

Like Ulysses, Langner was a man of many devices, and the
idea of an American Shakespeare Festival was entirely his.
He had spent years of effort and much of his own money
creating it amidst general indifference. As a longtime resident of Westport he regarded Connecticut as the proper spot
for the local equivalent of Shakespeare's shrine at Stratford-
upon-Avon; it would be a place where, he hoped, "many
thousands of Americans who can't afford a trip to England
will be able to witness the finest Shakespeare productions
during the summer vacation period." His vision, printed in
The New York Times, is a revealing sample of its author's enthusiastic, often banal, but always practical thinking:

> The theatre that will be built to house Shakespeare's
> plays will be patterned after the Old Globe Theatre in
> London and will have approximately 1600 seats. It will

---

* This feeling of suspicion was mutual, I'm sure, for my experiences
with the Theatre Guild and theirs with me had been consistently
unfortunate. *Valley Forge* and *Liberty Jones,* both of which I directed
for them, were mild failures; *Five Kings,* which foundered in Philadelphia, was a costly disaster. (See *Run-Through,* pp. 418–28).

include any appropriate improvement that has been developed since, making it possible to adapt it to any kind of production—Elizabethan or modern.

It is planned that the Festival shall begin in June and run, at first, for a period of ten weeks. Then, during the winter, the Acting Company will travel on an extended tour throughout the country. The fact that plays will be produced and played during the summer and under summer conditions will make it possible, once again, to produce Shakespeare's plays in the American theatre.

The road was not easy. In 1951, as a result of Langner's incessant effort, a bill was passed by the Connecticut state legislature establishing the American Shakespeare Festival Theatre and Academy as a nonprofit, educational corporation in that state. Lewis W. Douglas, former ambassador to Great Britain, was persuaded to become national chairman of the organization. With his endorsement it was possible to secure the interest of the Rockefeller Foundation, which pledged three hundred thousand dollars, provided that an equal sum was raised from other sources. Three new names had been added to the board of trustees—Helen Menken, the well-known actress, Lincoln Kirstein, founder of the New York City Ballet, and Joseph Verner Reed, heir to a copper fortune and long a supporter of the performing arts. A visit to Paul Mellon in Washington resulted in the Old Dominion Foundation matching the Rockefeller grant. With these massive contributions, added to those received from other foundations, from individual trustees and from some three thousand members of the general public, Langner's Shakespeare Festival dream seemed on its way to realization.*

Money, however, was not the only problem the founders had to face. For months, stretching into years, a search had been under way for a suitable site in which to locate such a festival. Over a hundred locations were submitted by a committee of Connecticut real-estate agents. Finally, after months

* The gifts received ranged from two dollars to a quarter of a million (from Joseph Verner Reed) and included valuable paintings donated by Lincoln Kirstein and thirty thousand feet of magnificent Guiana teakwood from the government of the French Republic.

of cautious negotiations, with local press support, the trustees were able to announce that they had obtained ownership to four pieces of land—formerly waste lots—at Stratford, Connecticut, on the banks of the Housatonic. (Lawrence Langner explained that "*Housatonic* is the Indian for Avon.")

On October 24, 1954, ninety-three years after the foundation of the Stratford Memorial Theatre in Warwickshire and one year after the opening of Tyrone Guthrie's Stratford Festival Theatre in Ontario, ground-breaking finally took place. "With the setting sun as a spotlight and the green, russet and gold foliage of autumn as a backdrop, Miss Katharine Cornell used a gilded shovel adorned with green ribbons to turn up a section of the soil on which the original founders of the town of Stratford disembarked from England in the year 1639."*

The Festival's architect, Edwin Howard, had drafted no fewer than five separate designs for the projected building, to conform to the constantly shifting sites and changing notions of what the Festival Theatre should be, including the trustees' final decision to make it "an all-year building which could also house ballet, symphony, concerts and a wide variety of stage presentations."†

In January 1955 work on the theatre was begun in the hope of having it ready for a mid-July opening. The builder's report shows that "in snowy, very cold weather, two bulldozers moved into the lobby area, stripping and stacking topsoil that was frozen twelve inches deep." On May 15 the rooftree raising took place—attended by such notables as Walter Hampden, Ezio Pinza, Maurice Evans, Myrna Loy and Brian Aherne.

---

* Stratford was an agreeable village with a number of fine New England houses. But, for all its historical background, it was now little more than a suburb of Bridgeport—a big, ugly industrial town with a substantial foreign, largely Catholic population. Stratford had become the site of two large helicopter factories which assumed great importance during the Korean War.
† Among those designs was a "plan for the Festival Theatre to open in two directions—inward to an auditorium of 1,600 seats and, outward, to an open amphitheatre seating 2,000."

During all this activity I was living in far-off California, working on *Lust for Life* and only vaguely aware that an American Shakespeare Festival Theatre was being formed. Since I was abroad for most of that summer, what little I knew of the Festival's first season was learned from reports in the *Paris Herald Tribune*, from clippings from *The New York Times* and, later, from eyewitness accounts by some of those who were present during that first mad Stratford summer.

In celebrating the completion of his new structure, Lawrence Langner hailed it as "a triumph of our national pride, one which will mean many things to many people. To some it will mean a place where they will go to refresh their minds and spirits, to drink deeply at the eternal fountain that is Shakespeare. To others it will mean the sheer magic of the theatre brought to them by great stars in great roles in great plays."*

Two "great plays" were duly announced: *Julius Caesar* and *The Tempest*. And an artistic director was found—an Englishman, Denis Carey, from the Bristol Old Vic.† So, now, with the building almost completed and a director appointed, the trustees were left to deal with the innumerable challenges facing the founders of an American classical repertory company—"dangerous and complex problems of style and tradition, attitude and personnel"—few of which could be solved in the time available.

Among those who had been less than enthusiastic about Langner's dream of a festival was the declining dean of American theatre critics, George Jean Nathan, who had declared that "at the bottom of the current miscellaneous drive for Shakespeare theatres is simply a combination of cultural snobbery and an obvious desire to bask in some reflected glory." He further suggested to the Festival's founders that

* In another statement Langner expressed the hope that the Festival would prove "an antidote to inferior TV presentations, often involving crime and violence."
† He was appointed over the head of another Englishman, John Burrell—formerly director of London's Old Vic Company during its brilliant years with Olivier and Richardson—who earlier in the year had been put in charge of the Festival's embryonic academy.

they should "forget about the local novices and just import some English actors."

Fortunately his advice was not taken and a number of promising young American actors were engaged for the season. But it was a company that the new artistic director had not chosen and with whose work he was totally unfamiliar. Arriving late, unused to American theatre ways, this soft-spoken man was expected to put on two of the larger Shakespearean plays in a theatre that was incomplete, in sets and costumes about which he had not been consulted, harassed by a host of trustees, each with a different idea of what the productions should be like. Finally, he was expected to work on a stage that was so far from finished that it was made available to him and his actors for a pitiful total of *thirty-four* hours before opening, including two dress rehearsals punctuated by riveting and other structural interruptions.*

Nevertheless, *Julius Caesar* opened on schedule on July 12, 1955, complete with speeches and congratulatory telegrams from President Eisenhower and Winston Churchill, who hailed this newest Stratford Festival as "completing the three sides of the Triangle." It was followed on August 1 by *The Tempest* and, later in the month, by *Much Ado About Nothing*. (Performed by junior members of the company under the direction of John Burrell, this final production received the least-hostile reviews of the season.) This first Festival season closed on September 16, 1955. Two weeks later the superintendent of the building crew reported to the trustees that work on the building was now complete.

Such, briefly, had been the first troubled year of the American Shakespeare Festival at Stratford, Connecticut. It explained the nervous anxiety that I sensed in my preliminary negotiations with the Festival's trustees, and it persuaded me to impose more stringent conditions as artistic director than

---

* The U.S. correspondent of London's *Daily Telegraph* reported: "A few hours before opening, the theatre was still occupied by a small army of about a hundred carpenters, electricians, masons and plumbers—all laboring with a zeal which, no doubt, would have pleased Shakespeare himself."

I would otherwise have presumed to demand. Even after my appointment had been formally confirmed in a telegram from Joseph Reed, this vexed question of authority continued to form the subject of long contractual negotiations. Langner, that gray, tenacious Welshman, was fighting a desperate rearguard action to retain some semblance of authority over an organization that he had conceived and created. As late as January 23 my lawyer, Arnold Weissberger, found it necessary to inform him that

> Houseman has made it quite clear that there can be only one artistic head for the festival in the coming season and if he is to assume the responsibility—the very grave responsibility—of the Stratford operation *he* must be that artistic head.
>
> As one of the directors of the Theatre Guild, you have perhaps found that production by committee can be effective: as far as Stratford is concerned that is what Houseman emphatically *does not* want. He is prepared to give consideration to all reasonable suggestions; he will not refuse criticism but—and this, I repeat, is fundamental—he *must* be the ultimate person to approve or veto all major artistic decisions.

I was well aware of how painful and humiliating it must be for Langner to accept such terms, but I was sustained in my insistence by Kirstein and Reed—both of whom held Langner principally responsible for the confusion and dangerously divided authority of the previous summer.

This protracted struggle for authority added to the tension with which I approached the problem of organizing the coming season. It was aggravated by a discovery I made during the weeks following my arrival: that dealing with the management of the American Shakespeare Festival (even with my categorical contract) was like walking on swampy ground. In addition to the board of trustees,* which almost never met,

---

* In addition to Reed, Langner and Kirstein, it included such wealthy and distinguished persons as Lewis Douglas (never present); Eugene Black, head of the International Bank, and his fellow banker, George Woods; Roger Stevens; Maurice Evans (rarely present); Stanton Griffis and Irving Olds, eminent capitalists; Theresa

there was a smaller executive committee that was expected to handle immediate and urgent matters relating to the operation of the Festival. As artistic director, I was responsible to this committee, but I soon found that my dealings were almost entirely with the triumvirate of Reed, Langner and Kirstein, with occasional interventions by Helen Menken. And this, in itself, created a number of delicate problems.

I had known, when I accepted the job, that my relations with Langner would be awkward. My absolute authority over an organization that he considered his own had been wrung from him by Reed and Kirstein as the price of Reed's continued financial support of the Festival. But he had never really accepted it and I had the constant feeling that he was sitting back, waiting for me to trip and break my neck. As a result, my conversations were mostly with Lincoln Kirstein and Joe Reed.

Reed was generous, insecure, modest, conventional, eccentric, unreliable, entirely selfish and deeply dedicated—a tall, slender, elegant gentleman with a prominent nose and a passion for petit-point tapestry, of which he usually carried a frame to rehearsals and conferences together with a basket of fresh fruit from his farm in Greenwich. His personal income (derived from inherited holdings in copper mines) was reported to be in the neighborhood of one million dollars a year—of which an appreciable amount went into the haphazard backing of artistic ventures, mostly in the theatre. He had a passion for the Bard and once wrote to me that "there's not a night that passes that I don't awaken at some time around four o'clock to wrestle with Shakespeare." Yet the only theatrical opinions I ever heard him express were personal prejudices for or against certain plays, directors and actors, together with a chronic obsession about *length*. (Most of the notes I was to receive from him during rehearsals and previews were impassioned pleas for cuts and more cuts.)

Helburn and Armina Marshall, both executives of the Theatre Guild; George Stoddard, dean of New York University; a financial expert by the name of D. Crena de Iongh; Helen Menken and her millionaire husband, George Richard; Robert Carr, head of Broadway's leading firm of theatrical accountants.

Emotionally, he was divided: one side of him seemed to enjoy trouble and turmoil; the other yearned for harmony and success. He was sensitive and callous, with the combined diffidence and presumption of the very rich. Though his attitude toward me was consistently cordial and friendly, I felt that he never quite ceased to regard me as a reckless, overweening, slightly dangerous and alien figure to whom he was never quite sure he should entrust his beloved Shakespeare.

My relations with Lincoln Kirstein were of another order entirely and far more complex: they went back more than a quarter of a century to the year in which I arrived from Europe. I first met him as a teenager in his sister's house at a time when he had just apprenticed with a stained-glass maker in Boston. This was followed by four years at Harvard, where he founded and edited a brilliant literary and artistic quarterly, *Hound and Horn*. I had read his poetry and his first moving, troubled novel, and I had watched the development of the strikingly masculine Semitic beauty that had been sculpted by Lachaise and painted by Chelishev and many others.

Since then, I had followed and admired the tenacity and courage with which he pursued and finally achieved his dream of creating a great American ballet company. He loved the theatre, and he had been a close follower of our classical productions at the Federal Theatre and the Mercury, but we had never worked together because he and Orson had such dynamic and eccentric personalities that they were totally incapable of communicating on any level. My friendship with him was long-standing but remote: the close relationship I had for years with his sister Mina Curtiss (nee Kirstein)* had made any real intimacy between us impossible.

It was Lincoln who was mainly responsible for my presence with the Festival, and, throughout that year and the next, he

---

* The Kirsteins were rich, too, but in a different way from the Reeds. Their mother was heiress to a vast clothing business; their father had been a partner of Filene in Boston, one of the founders of Federated Department Stores, a friend of Justice Frankfurter and FDR and an important figure in Jewish-American affairs.

was my regular champion and loyal ally.* I was consistently impressed by his erudition and fertile intelligence. But I was well aware that Lincoln's enthusiasms and artistic opinions were subjective, arbitrary and frequently inconsistent. Within the span of an hour he would express two directly conflicting views—each with equal conviction and vehemence—depending on changes in the emotional situation in which he found himself.

Throughout our association I tried to profit from the quality of his taste and from his vast fund of ideas without being swayed by the violence of his opinions, which were often in direct opposition to my own. He accepted these denials with good grace and without apparent resentment. He never attempted to force his views on me, nor, until much later, did he use his support of me as leverage with which to try to impose his will upon me.

During my first few months with the Festival my work was done in New York. I lived with my family in New City, driving in and out across the George Washington Bridge every day in the blue secondhand jeep we had acquired soon after our return. The boys (aged two and five) overcame their amazement at the sight of snow and ice and happily accepted the House on the Hill as yet another of the constantly changing homes in which their brief lives had been spent. John Michael attended the Rudolph Steiner Day School in Spring Valley and liked it, while Sebastian crawled around the terrace whose bricks his mother and I had laid seven years earlier. The unhappy one was Joan, who hated the Eastern cold, grieved for her house in Santa Monica (which, she felt, was still haunted by the ghosts of the distinguished European intellectuals who had frequented it during the war, and

* In late December he had written to me in California: "The Festival so far is not an institution but a Summer Season run by Langner and the Theatre Guild. Improvisation, compromise and slackness is all we really go by . . . We have had a defeat at the outset and I don't want another and I don't want you put in an ambiguous position.— With love and happy, er, new, er, year, L."

where we still occasionally received foreign fan mail addressed to Greta Garbo). She did her best to adapt to our new life but received scant comfort from me—obsessed as I was with the immediate challenge of the Festival.

My New York office that spring was a bare suite in the Squibb Building, on Fifth Avenue at Fifty-seventh Street, lent to us by Roger Stevens (one of our trustees), who controlled it temporarily as part of his far-flung real-estate empire. Here, at a borrowed desk, with a single telephone, in the company of a small, red-haired, very efficient secretary named Jane Gilliland, left over from the previous year, I settled down to the task of planning a program for an organization that was badly shaken by the failure of its first season and unsure of its own future direction. For my own part, I was shuttling, almost hourly, between my familiar poles of exhilaration and terror.

Five years of successful filmmaking had given me greater self-confidence than I ever had before. For that reason I was less reckless than usual in my approach to the problems ahead and more aware of my own limitations in dealing with them. Except for my brief foray with *Coriolanus* at the Phoenix in 1953, I had been absent from the New York theatre for close to six years. Thus I found myself, from the moment of my arrival, looking around for help of all sorts in a field—classical repertory—that had lain virtually fallow in the American theatre for many years. On the technical side I was well supplied. Left over from the first year were Peter Zeisler, the Festival's production stage manager.* And, above all, there was my beloved Jean Rosenthal. In the fifteen years since we had worked together she was little changed: the cherubic child's head, framed with dark curly hair; the snub nose, the smiling lips; the strange body, perfectly formed from the waist up and almost dwarflike below. But professionally she had come a long way since she had gone out on tour with Leslie Howard's *Hamlet*, worked under Abe Feder

---

* He had been one of my more effective aides in the production of the 1948 ANTA Album.

on Federal Theatre Project 891 and accomplished superhuman tasks for Orson and me as lighting designer and technical director of the Mercury.*

In the years between, she had designed the lighting for numerous Broadway shows and for such institutions as the New York City Opera and Light Opera Companies. But her most consistent and important functions had been those of technical director and lighting designer for Martha Graham and for the New York City Ballet Company.† It was Lincoln Kirstein who had brought her into the Stratford Festival the previous year. If he hadn't, I would certainly have done so, for, with her beside me, there were no technical difficulties I did not feel confident of overcoming.

Production was still some months away, and before that I had to determine an artistic policy and devise a viable program for the coming summer season. This involved the selection and the announcement of the plays that would form our repertory; it also meant recruiting and engaging the acting company that would perform them.

To aid me in this dangerous and delicate task, I needed to find a creative and efficient associate—someone (like Jud Kinberg at MGM) in whom I had total confidence and to whom I could delegate authority during the months ahead. Such a person was hard to find: there was no one left from the Mercury days, and none of my California associates was qualified for such a job in the theatre.

Soon after my arrival, Lucy Kroll, the agent, had suggested, for the post of associate director, a young man named Jack Landau. (His biography indicated that he was from the Middle West, that he had gone to college at St. John's under Stringfellow Barr before visiting England—first as a student and then as a junior member of the staff of the Old Vic Theatre School.‡ Later, he had served as observer-assistant to Peter Brook at Stratford-upon-Avon. On his return to

* See *Run-Through*, pp. 260, 292–306.
† For whom she eventually did the lighting for a total of more than *seventy* ballets over the years.
‡ Established after the war under the joint direction of Michel Saint-Denis, George Devine and Glen Byam Shaw.

America he had become involved with a group of young actors, many of them graduates of Carnegie Tech, who, under the name "Group 20," had played two summer seasons of classics at Wellesley College in Massachusetts. In New York, he had directed successful Off-Broadway productions of *The Clandestine Marriage* and *The White Devil;* he had also designed sets for the Broadway productions of *A Phoenix Too Frequent* and *Mary Rose.* On the side, he worked as manager and part owner of a highbrow bookstore on the mezzanine of the Algonquin Hotel.) I interviewed him among many others and found him intelligent and knowledgeable. At the same time I was vaguely repelled by his somber and unappetizing appearance. He was squat, dark and sallow, with dank hair and the molelike look that very thick lenses give their wearers. Evidently he had applied to the Festival before, for in the files I came across Lincoln Kirstein's negative report on him: "too big for his boots—a poor man's Guthrie." Nevertheless I kept him on my list of candidates.

In February I had to fly to California for a sneak preview of *Lust for Life.* Soon after I returned—on a chill, rainy New England afternoon—I made my first voyage to Stratford with Lincoln Kirstein and Jean Rosenthal to look over the Festival Theatre. I found it surprisingly handsome. "Blending into the New England countryside, the stagehouse rises tall and clear above the surrounding fields. With its high, delicate lantern and its long grey surfaces of natural wood, the Festival Theatre has more in common with the local meeting-houses and tobacco barns than with the heavy timber of the Elizabethan builders."* The interior was handsome, too, but less satisfying, and I began to understand some of the problems that had confronted my luckless predecessor the previous summer. The more I looked, the more concerned I became. What I saw before me, in the elegant, teak-finished auditorium with fair to good acoustics, was (a) a proscenium opening that seemed enormous; (b) a stagehouse of fine pro-

---

* This and other technical descriptions of the Festival Theatre are taken from *The Birth of a Theatre,* by John Houseman and Jack Landau (Simon and Schuster, 1959).

portions but with a dubious relation between stage and audience; and (c) a vast, shallow forestage with connecting side stages, above which rose two tiers of Elizabethan "galleries." None of this seemed particularly suited to the sort of production I had in mind.

On my way back to New York I made it clear to Lincoln that drastic changes must be made—particularly in the relation of stage and auditorium. He did not disagree and suggested an early meeting with a young designer for whom his enthusiasm seemed unbounded.

In the meantime it was becoming urgently necessary—for many reasons, including public relations and the sale of the season's subscriptions and tickets—for me to announce my choice of plays and actors. From the start, as soon as I stopped dreaming and got down to the practical problems of the summer season, one thing had become clear: following the disappointments of the first year it would be difficult, if not impossible, to lure any established stars onto our Connecticut stage. For that reason it would be folly to attempt any of the Bard's major works—each of which carried its accumulated burden of expectations and comparisons. With *Coriolanus*, I had discovered the excitement of introducing audiences to a great but little-known Shakespeare drama. This confirmed me in my conviction that my only hope for this hazardous second season lay in the bold, imaginative production of unfamiliar, contrasting plays, performed by a vital company of young, comparatively unknown actors.

I delayed my announcement as long as possible while I devoured every obscure work in the canon—works I had never seen or had read so long ago that I had entirely forgotten them—and held endless interviews and auditions with the actors and actresses who might be playing in them.*

Holding these auditions was anxious and lonely work, and

* Occasionally, for my own education, I would ask applicants to read a scene from one of the obscure plays I was considering. I have often wondered if Fritz Weaver's phrasing of the bastard Faulconbridge's brilliant "Bias" soliloquy and Hiram Sherman's comic reading of the genial, resourceful pimp Pompey may not have influenced me in my final choice of plays.

during the long hours they lasted and in the discussions that followed I found myself turning increasingly to Jack Landau. He was keenly perceptive and I noticed that many of the young actors whom I favored had worked with him and valued him. There was still something disturbing about his dark, timid, myopic personality contrasted with his sharp, almost aggressive intellectuality. Yet no one whom I interviewed or considered for the key position of associate director had anything like his qualifications or his personal experience of repertory. We seemed to be in agreement on the nature of the company, and, with few exceptions, we saw eye to eye on individual actors. He was also the only person (besides Kirstein, whose mercurial and violent judgments were stimulating but unreliable) with whom I could frankly and seriously analyze and discuss the season's artistic and practical problems.

The day came when I could delay no longer. I had to reveal my program—first to the trustees and then, in a public announcement, to the press. The two plays I had selected and which were scheduled to open "back to back" on successive nights had only one thing in common: their complete unfamiliarity to the audience and to all but a handful of critics. Of all Shakespeare's works I doubt if any two are more unlike (in theme, in tone, in period, in acting requirements and production styles) than *King John* and *Measure for Measure*—to which I added, for later in the season, *The Taming of the Shrew*.

This choice of plays, though it shocked some of our trustees, provoked the public reaction I had hoped for: surprise, skepticism and a grudging admiration for our daring. A second press release, some days later, carried the announcement that Rouben Ter-Arutunian would design our sets and costumes and Virgil Thomson compose our music, while Jack Landau would occupy the position of associate director. Two weeks after that I announced the names of the acting company. We could boast of no single major star, but my list included such recognized talents and respected names as Arnold Moss, Kent Smith, Hiram Sherman, Norman Lloyd, Donald Harron, Nina Foch, Jacqueline Brookes, Earle

Hyman, Whitford Kane, Fritz Weaver, Bill Cottrell, John Emery, Edith Meiser, Kendall Clark and Mildred Dunnock.*

Fritz Weaver was the only repeater from the first season. The rest of the cast was gathered from diverse places, and not a few were old friends and associates. Hiram Sherman, with whom I had not worked since our first Mercury season, had made it a condition of his joining the company that we also engage his teacher and longtime companion Whitford Kane, who was terminally ill but who wanted to spend the last months of his life on the stage, doing the work he so dearly loved. I was delighted and honored to have him with us. Finally, at the last moment, Morris Carnovsky was added to our cast; he was an old companion from the Group Theatre, whose vast theatrical experience had not yet included the playing of Shakespeare. He came into my office one day and asked to join the company, but in his infinite conscientiousness he requested only small parts the first season while he faced the new acting problems involved in the speaking of Elizabethan verse.

The following Sunday found me riding my favorite hobbyhorse onto the front page of the drama section of *The New York Times:*

> For many years American acting was an honorable branch of the British theatrical tradition. Then, with the rise of native American drama, there gradually developed an unfortunate and ever-widening chasm between the classic and realistic schools of performance in this country. In the past two generations most of our best young actors have been concerned with the inner mechanics of expressing emotions—the much discussed

* Arnold Moss was an established classical actor who had played Prospero for Margaret Webster; Kent Smith had been a fine, handsome Enobarbus with Katharine Cornell; Lloyd had played Lear's Fool for me with Louis Calhern, and Nina Foch had been a strong and moving Cordelia in that same production—besides winning an Academy nomination for us in *Executive Suite.* Bill Cottrell had been with Laughton in *Galileo,* and John Emery had appeared at the Coronet in *No Exit* and at the Phoenix in *Coriolanus;* Mildred Dunnock too was a longtime friend, best known for her great performance as Mrs. Loman in *Death of a Salesman.*

"method" and its derivatives. Of late, however, there has been a growing preoccupation with a more styled and eloquent theatre, a rising impatience with the limitations of the naturalistic stage and a general desire for a freer, more fluid and more lyric communication between stage and auditorium, between the dramatic creation and its audience. . . . A season of Shakespeare's plays, if it is to justify its production, must contribute, on both sides of the footlights, to a development of that richer, more dynamic form of drama the desire for which is so evident today among American theatre-workers and audiences.

Having made this sanguine announcement, I now had the problem of the effective production of the plays I had chosen. The three works selected had the widest possible range: the crude, savage historical conflicts of *King John;* the sophisticated, equivocal morality of *Measure for Measure;* * the simple, lusty, mountebank mood of *Shrew.* For the production of three so widely different plays in repertory, a new, more flexible stage must be devised within the existing structure of the Festival Theatre—one on which it was hoped "to combine the blunt immediacy of the Elizabethan platform stage with the visual variety that lies within the depths of a dramatically lighted proscenium arch." I wanted no unit set but an open, functional stage form within which each production would be free to develop the individual style through which it could most clearly and directly communicate with a contemporary American audience.

That was my hope, and, in pursuit of it, many trips were made to Stratford that spring and summer. With the coming of spring I gradually became aware of the beauty of the Fes-

* Ours was its first professional American production in many years —and for good reason. Of Shakespeare's comedies few have had such an uneven reception and such conflicting interpretations. Some find it careless in its construction and cynical in its writing; others have endowed it with religious overtones and have equated the Duke's return with the Second Coming. For my own part, as I read and reread it that spring, I found it a dark, sophisticated and fascinating comedy in which Shakespeare used an old Boccaccio story to express his consistent detestation of excess in all its forms—excess of virtue no less than excess of vice.

31

tival site, which had eluded me in the raw grayness of my first March visit. Inside the theatre, Lincoln Kirstein, Jean Rosenthal and Jack Landau, together with our designer and two harassed stage managers, shuffled chairs, bags of nails and sticks of wood across the stage and onto planks laid over the shallow apron and the gaping orchestra pit, while I climbed to remote corners of the balcony checking the sight lines of our imaginary stage. Continuing a practice I had begun with *King Lear*, I thought of our new stage as a large, open, raked platform—running far upstage and projecting as deep into the audience as the sight lines would allow—on which the dominant element would always be the moving figure of the actor.

The main responsibility for designing and executing this scenic concept had fallen upon a slender, elegant young man with the resonant Armenian name of Rouben Ter-Arutunian.* He was born in Russia and reared in Germany; with his shaven head and the dark, liquid eyes of a doe, he resembled a figure in a Persian miniature. (More careful inspection revealed a startling pattern of concentric ridges around the base of his skull, which may have accounted for the rigid perfectionism and mulish obstinacy of his working habits.) After weeks at his drawing board—with Jean Rosenthal hovering at his side to check the technical and economic feasibility of his designs—he came up with a model that was startling in its simplicity and beauty and formed the basis of what came to be known as the "Festival Stage."

It was a "floating" architectural unit supported on thin, setback, almost invisible legs. At one stroke he had solved the double problem of closing in the vast stage and losing the hard frame of the existent proscenium arch. On either side of the stage two huge pillars were set up, each a foot square and built of the same teakwood as the interior of the building. These reduced the width of our opening and added two more "accesses" to the platform. It was one of my require-

---

* He had designed several ballets for the City Center Company, a stylish production of Rossini's *La Cenerentola* and a television version of *The Magic Flute*.

ments for our new stage that it should have the functional qualities of an Elizabethan theatre, with its great variety of playing areas and its multiplicity of exits and entrances. On Rouben's new Festival Stage there were *eighteen* of them, including six entrances from the sides, four upstage and the rest served by steps set at various angles together with ramps, counter-ramps and strategically located "traps."

The problem of "masking" such a large open area was a serious one. Rouben solved it by hanging walls of thin wooden strips, in double layers, all around the stage in a solid-seeming surface. These were made up of strips of crating, painted various shades of silvery brown, all equally spaced, one inch apart, and mounted on parallel lines of heavy canvas tape.* Altogether sixty-three such sections of strips were assembled—amounting to ten thousand square feet of wood—each rigged, like a Venetian blind, in such a way that it could move separately and independently up and down to form an infinite variety and combination of shapes that suggested gates, doors, windows, colonnades, tunnels, chambers and passageways.†

Most of the ideas for the new stage were developed on Rouben's drawing board, but many of them underwent growth and change as the result of experiments and observations on the stage itself. In fact, some of our problems were not finally resolved until we were able to see our actors on the stage during the final week of rehearsal.

Actors' Equity had allowed us six weeks for the rehearsal of our first two plays. Just before we began I went through my usual panic, aggravated by the general sense of anxiety that pervaded the Festival organization. But at the base of

---

* Though more varied and flexible, these walls bore more than a casual resemblance to the Mercury's *Shoemaker's Holiday,* of which Jean Rosenthal had also been technical director.
† In the course of work a convenient terminology was evolved. Our vast central ramped platform became "the tray," the side approaches were known as "catwalks" and the extreme downstage side extensions as the "fenders." The walls themselves were referred to as "slats," "skins," "Venetian blinds" and "orange crates."

my insecurity there was the added personal knowledge that, with all the work and excitement of organizing and administering the new season, I had made what I felt to be insufficient directorial preparation for the two obscure plays I was about to produce. As the first day of rehearsal approached, I found myself turning more and more to Jack Landau for support and counsel. Having less to lose, he seemed less appalled than I was by the perils of the program we were undertaking.*

King John was the longer, heavier and more complicated of our two productions; I began rehearsals with that—with Jack Landau as co-director—and followed it after a few days with *Measure for Measure,* on which I had a clearer and more positive point of view and which I had intended to direct by myself. But it soon became apparent that those two productions were really indivisible. Since rehearsals inevitably overlapped, with many of the company playing important parts in both plays, continuous close collaboration between Jack and myself was essential. In time this became functional and automatic, but during those first weeks it called for exceptional tact and understanding between two men (one half the age of the other) who barely knew each other and had not worked together before. In our dealing with our actors it was essential that we give the appearance of a complete unity of concept and interpretation. Above all, there must be no suggestion of rivalry.

Rouben's new stage was built in New York and moved to Stratford in sections. Now it had to be installed and lit. This was Jean Rosenthal's domain: in addition to being our lighting designer she was also our technical director, and here our long, affectionate association proved of immeasurable value. That summer—as at all other times that I worked with her—she showed amazing skill in coordinating the various conflicting elements of production; she gave Ter-Arutunian the assurance that his set would be installed in a practical but

* My own experience of repertory was limited to our inspired but erratic goings-on at the Mercury twenty years earlier.

uncompromising way, and, in spite of her feminine handicap and her diminutive size, she maintained amicable but firm authority over our stagehands—a tough crew most of whom had been imposed on us by the New Haven and local Bridgeport unions.* Similar union demands imposed upon us a permanent orchestra of no fewer than eight men, directed by a Hungarian conductor, formerly of the City Center Opera, by the name of François Jaroschy.

In the third week of June the entire company—two dozen actors, twenty student apprentices and fourteen technicians, stage managers, wardrobe women and hangers-on—moved up to Connecticut. Some were billeted in private homes, others combined to rent houses for the summer in Stratford or at Lordship nearer the beach. As artistic director I was furnished with a house for myself and my family. For part of that summer Joan, the two boys, their keeper (an oversized, efficient Scotch woman who had come with us from California), three dogs and I occupied a pleasant, conventional suburban home with a greenhouse and a garden on Main Street within walking distance of the theatre.

For our children and dogs this was yet another inexplicable change of residence. For Joan, it was one more bewildering episode in a life that was only slightly less confused than my own—beginning with her birth during World War I in a London Zeppelin raid, through a Parisian childhood (in which her playmates were the children of Picasso and of Caresse Crosby), a Jesuit education, marriage into one of the noblest families of France, a job as a model for a leading dress house through which she supported her mother and sister during the war while her husband was off driving a tank for de Gaulle, and, finally, her adventures among the Parisian Surrealists, from whom she fled to the New World—to a job

---

* For our heads of departments we could hire our own men. The first to greet me when I went backstage was Joseph Patterson, Jr., who had been with us all through our hard but wonderful times at the Mercury. It was he who, after forty-six hours of continuous lighting of *Danton's Death*, had made the theatrical column of *The New York Times* by falling headlong, in a dead faint, off our overhead switchboard at 3:45 A.M.

at the Museum of Modern Art in New York, then to California as the companion and wife of a Hollywood film producer, and now to spend the summer on the Main Street of a small Connecticut town, where she was delighted to have the company of Ann Botsford, her oldest friend in America, whom I had engaged as an additional secretary during the summer season.

Joan's reaction to New England was conditioned at first by the perpetual chill of a belated spring and by the realization that, once again, she would be living with a man who was less than half present and whose emotional crises and releases had almost no relation to her or to the children. (With her European background she found it easier to accept and sympathize with my total absorption in the dramas of theatrical production than in the endless, incomprehensible and sordid tensions of Hollywood moviemaking. But the alienation was no less complete.)

We rehearsed our first two plays for as many hours each day as Actors' Equity would allow us and then some—mostly in a large meeting room over the local hardware store, and also, for several hours each day while the stagehands were resting, on our new stage, trying to adjust to the unfamiliarity of our raised, steeply raked open platform. Then, two days before our first preview, we held a combined dress parade and technical rehearsal of *King John*. It was a memorable occasion.

To understand and to share in the emotions through which we lived during those final days of rehearsal, it is necessary to follow us into that strange vacuum chamber in which the final stages of theatrical production take place. As the days go by and the pressure rises, normal concerns fall away and, with them, all sense of proportion. What is left is an exclusive and obsessive preoccupation with this thing you have so painfully created over the past months and over which you are about to lose control. From now on, as you speed down the dark, narrow tunnel that leads to opening night, time and space lose their reality; every incident of production takes on monstrous proportions; each step forward becomes a triumph, each reverse a calamity.

For me, during that last week of June 1956, the pressure had become almost unbearable. What I was facing was not the normal risk of theatrical success or failure; it was the entire future of an enterprise in which I had become deeply involved and on which I had placed professional and emotional bets that were far beyond my means.

Rouben Ter-Arutunian, besides planning the new Festival Stage and designing the scenery for our first two productions, was also responsible for our costumes. To convey the archaic, historical tone of the play, it had been agreed that the actors in *King John* should have an oversized, "epic" appearance. Rouben fulfilled the assignment and went beyond it. The costumes he designed, particularly those of the military figures, were not only "epic"; they were gigantic!

For economic and theatrical reasons we had decided against real chain mail. In its place our warriors were encased in padded, oversized suits of armor made up of brightly painted plaques of wood, plastic and synthetic rubber. These were handsome to look at but so bulky that when the actors inside them attempted to move they suggested the inflated figure of the Michelin Man. Besides, they became so costly that they were issued only to kings, nobles and military leaders. For the rest, Rouben raided half the Army and Navy Surplus stores in New York and came out with a collection of pea jackets, padded vests, life jackets and rubber rafts which, when cut up and sewn back together into medieval uniforms, delighted him with their formidable mass.

All martial figures were supposed to wear tall leather hip boots. Since these too were far beyond our resources, only the elite received them. The lower ranks were supplied with huge gray-green rubber waders (acquired in stores specializing in fishing equipment) which rose all the way to the crotch and which proved almost impossible to work in on account of their volume and weight but even more because of the fiendish heat generated in their airless depths when the stage lights hit them.

37

On the day of our dress parade the temperature at Stratford was close to ninety at noon and had gone down only slightly by midafternoon when the company arrived at the theatre and began putting on its costumes. From where I sat in the house I became aware of some grumbling rising from the dressing rooms below, which increased as the frailer members of the cast struggled to drag themselves and their boots up the steep steps that led to the stage. However, such murmurings are habitual, and I was too preoccupied to pay much attention to them.

Instead of the usual dress parade, I had decided—for lack of time—on a run-through in costume. Early in the first act an apprentice, a stripling in his teens, suddenly collapsed. With all that rubberized material on him he made a strange soft slurping thud as he fell. Peter Zeisler, our production stage manager, appeared from backstage with an assistant and dragged him off while the run-through continued. Rouben was seated beside me taking costume notes; I gave him a questioning look, to which he responded with a shrug. The gravity of our situation was not yet apparent.

Halfway through our first military maneuver, with the embattled forces of France and England confronting each other while Jean Rosenthal checked and adjusted her light cues, that ghastly slurping thud was heard again and then repeated with increasing frequency as, one after another, singly and in pairs, the warriors of both armies began to collapse. After the seventh had gone down I glanced at Rouben. While he frowned and muttered "Amateurs" and "Sabotage," another keeled over and then another and another—including Morris Carnovsky and Stanley Bell. By the time I reached the stage there were twelve dehydrated bodies (five nobles and seven soldiers) lying on our new shining platform—some out cold, others still conscious and writhing as they struggled to tear off their boots and jackets.

I called off rehearsal and told Zeisler to give the cast a two-hour dinner break. I did not need to add that they might remove their costumes. Then I held an emergency meeting with Landau, Zeisler and Rouben to devise desperate measures. (There is a legend among survivors of that dreadful run-through that as the company stumbled downstairs to their dressing rooms they heard voices over the intercom, which had been left open. Rouben was protesting, "But, John, you said you didn't care if the actors *were* uncomfortable!" and I was indignantly denying it.) When the cast returned from their long dinner they discovered that their boots and jackets had been punched, pierced, gouged and lacerated to permit the passage of air and the removal of several hundred pounds of cotton padding. During the next few days many additional rents and punctures appeared— most of them made by the actors themselves. By the time we opened, our soldiers had a ragged, thoroughly "medieval" and "epic" appearance and the fainting rate was down to one or two a week.

Except for the costumes, Rouben's scenic conception for *King John* proved handsome and functional. To the accompaniment of Virgil Thomson's somber military fanfares, the tall wooden walls rose and fell in constantly changing shapes and openings that formed a dark, impressive background for the groupings of our actors and permitted the action to move, without delays or laborious scene shifts, through the play's grim world of castles, walled towns, camps, battlefields, seacoasts and dungeons to its tragic climax in the orchard where the wretched King lies dying in agony to the muffled booming of an abbey bell.

The actors soon adjusted to the novelty of the steeply raked stage, but the costumes continued to bother them. A few were able to adjust: Edith Meiser as Queen Elinor and Fritz Weaver as the bastard Faulconbridge made a virtue of their "epic" garments. They were exceptions: Arnold Moss, as the King of France, seemed overwhelmed by his massive blue-and-white helmet and armor, and Morris Carnovsky never quite overcame the size and weight of his green rubber boots. But it was John Emery who suffered most. I recalled how fine and dangerous he had looked in *Coriolanus* as the Volscian warrior Aufidius. Now his awkward armor and oversized royal crown had the effect of diminishing him rather than

39

building him up; torn between reality and the "epic" style imposed upon him, he seemed ill at ease and hysterical rather than tragic in the overblown role of the King.

Our previews were played to small audiences. Those members of the board who attended were noncommittal. Lincoln, full of enthusiasm for Rouben's work, was the most encouraging. Langner sat gray and silent. Joseph Reed seemed concerned mainly with our length and with the hour at which his Greenwich neighbors would get back home.

So finally and painfully, we came to our opening night. Following the example set by Stratford, Ontario, it had become the accepted habit of festivals to open the season's first two shows "back to back" on successive nights. The New York critics (unwilling to make the journey twice) arrived in the afternoon and were dined and wined before attending the first play. They wrote their reviews on the premises (in a small historic house down by the water which was put at their disposal, together with typewriters, stationery and telephones), phoned them in to New York in time for the final edition, and then went to bed and rested until the following evening, when they covered the second show before departing. This was rough on the company and the crew and often resulted in productions being reviewed before they had a chance to shake down. But it did substantially improve the odds of our getting one or more quotable reviews from a first-string critic at the start of the season.

I had always known (and it had become daily more evident during rehearsal) that *King John*'s chances of receiving general praise were slim indeed. I had undertaken it, in a calculated risk, as the first half of a double bill, figuring that to follow this crude and savage historical tragedy with a sophisticated comedy like *Measure for Measure* would form an impressive contrast and would offer convincing proof of the range and versatility of our new Festival Company. Now this elaborate and risky strategy was about to be put to the test.

The North American festival season had opened on June 20 in Ontario with a production of *Henry V*. The two leading New York critics had found it "stunning" and "wonderfully graphic." "Everything about this *Henry V* is penetrating and exuberant," wrote Brooks Atkinson in *The New York Times,* and he went on to praise "the expression of bold characters and stirring events."

No such enthusiasm greeted our production of *King John* when it opened a week later in Connecticut. Our notices, as relayed to us on the phone at dawn of the following day, were fair to poor. Locally the *New Haven Register* reported that "Stratford on the Housatonic has taken a long step toward its proclaimed goal by transforming an obscure and episodic tragedy into a vibrant, rich and rewarding dramatic experience," but most of the New York press found *King John* long, obscure and quite dull. This did not surprise me. What did disappoint and alarm me were the reactions of the two critics whose approval and support I needed to rehabilitate the Festival. Brooks Atkinson did his best for us:

> The Shakespeare Festival has taken a new lease on life. The production of *King John* which opened last evening is not entirely satisfactory but the director's approach is enterprising and encouraging. To most of us *King John* is a new play. Votaries of Shakespeare will be grateful for an opportunity to add a rarely acted drama to their experience. . . . Although the performance is intelligent it somehow lacks the tension and the inner pressure of passionate theatre.

He was favorably impressed by some of our younger and lesser actors. He found Fritz Weaver's performance as the Bastard "witty, agile and wholly alive"; he approved of Don Harron's Dauphin and Earle Hyman's Melun. The best performance, in his opinion, was that of Hiram Sherman, who "makes something tender and moving out of the scene in which he is to burn out the eyes of the little prince." And he concluded that "while *King John* is a vast improvement over the productions of last year, the performance is not yet all of one piece and is somehow lacking in gusto and glow."

Walter Kerr of the *Herald Tribune* held a similar view:

> The first bold image in the American Shakespeare Festival's *King John* is a bit misleading. The curtain rises on a series of towering shutters stretching to the heavens.

Within seconds a sweeping cavalcade of royalty is plunging up from a deep pit at stage center and swirling headlong to the edge of the newly extended apron. It is as though an old and unfamiliar play was going to be hurled at us like a warhorse returning to battle after its long, idle years on the library shelf. It also looks, for a short while, as though director John Houseman were out to erase the staid and ritualistic impression left by the Connecticut theatre's initial season. But instead of pursuing that first fire-brand entrance and charging the play with a breakneck pace, Mr. Houseman abruptly changes his course and settles down to a stately, measured, politely intoned recital of England's political woes. It is possible to understand and sympathize but the results are, to be generous about it, decidedly mixed.

He too distributed what praise he had among the company's "younger and better actors."

The Stratford authorities are beginning to find the nucleus of a young, vigorous, well-spoken company. But the salvo that will announce the contemporary American theatre's coming of age in its long bout with Shakespeare has yet to be fired.

I read our reviews carefully when they arrived.* The critics did not detest us as they had detested the productions of the previous year. But their reviews were not calculated to send people stampeding toward our box office—and, without a substantial audience, Stratford on the Housatonic was unlikely to last out the summer. So now our survival hung precariously on the fate of *Measure for Measure,* which the crew had set up during the night and which was about to open in

---

* In the course of this history I shall find myself falling once again into a practice of which some have complained: the extensive quotation of reviews. There is no way out. Critical reaction is part of the theatrical process; after so many weeks of work, misery and creative excitement, the proof of the pudding is with the press, and the only objective reactions available (besides the box office) are those of the critics, whose opinions I have tried to quote here as honestly and with as little self-service as possible.

a few hours. It was a frail vessel into which to pour so much hope.

Our schedule for that fateful Saturday called for a technical rehearsal in the morning, a final run-through with lights, scenery and costumes at 1:30 P.M. and a 7:30 opening. Though the crew was dead on its feet, the changeover and the morning's technical rehearsal had gone smoothly. Seated next to Jean Rosenthal in the auditorium as she called and checked her light cues, I found myself marveling at the changes our stage had undergone since the night before. For *King John,* our hanging "slats" had been used as vast, dark surfaces—the somber walls of fortresses and dungeons and the stormy backgrounds of battles and midnight slayings. The same slats—with the addition of a great chandelier, crimson draperies, garish lighted windows, prison bars and the shadows of trees—were now illuminated to suggest the ducal palace, streets, a brothel, a jail and the public gardens of Vienna under the Hapsburgs. As in *John* there was a minimum use of furniture, but our props included a portable desk, chains and manacles, the Duke's shooting stick, festoons of flags for the finale, a leather hatbox capable of holding a severed head, a bird cage, a broom, a dead fish, two pedigreed wolfhounds and two oblong wooden boxes that served as benches and a headsman's block.

Our actors had been called for twelve-thirty. As they straggled into the basement they were tense and gloomy from reading the New York papers which had reached Stratford during the morning. While they were getting into their costumes (lighter and more colorful than those of the previous night) the crew returned from lunch and Jeannie had them check a few final focuses. The thirty-two-foot ladder was dragged up onto the stage and set up on the slanting surface of Rouben's platform. When it was steadied, Joe Patterson, our head electrician, clambered up it; with his legs wrapped tightly around its swaying upper extension, he reached out perilously for the instruments hanging high up inside the proscenium and adjusted them to Rosenthal's specifications. When he was done there were still a few minutes left before we let the audience into the house—just enough time to slip a crimson velvet sheath over the bare wires that held up the main chandelier in the ducal palace.

While "half hour" was being called over the intercom, an electrician, a burly middle-aged local grip, started up the ladder; halfway he turned and the red sheath was handed up to him. Dragging it up behind him, he went on up to the top and reached out to slip it over the wires. He had miscalculated the distance and couldn't quite reach it. Instead of having the ladder moved, he shifted his weight, reached far out for the hanging wires, slipped and lost his balance. We saw it happen; he hung in the air for a moment while the sheath, like a long, writhing, crimson snake, fell out of his hand to the floor. A fraction of a second later his body followed it down. It took him a long time to fall those thirty-two feet, and he landed on his buttocks and the small of his back with a grunt and a dull, hollow sound.

There, for two or three seconds, he lay quite still. Then the men who had been holding the ladder ran forward to where he lay. He stirred. He wasn't dead. Spread-eagled on the floor on his back he looked older and heavier than he had in the air. As someone ran to telephone for an ambulance he moved slightly—first an arm, then one leg—till Joe Patterson ordered him to stay still. Down in the basement, over the intercom, the actors had heard the sound of the fall and the sudden silence that followed. Some of them came up, half dressed, and now they stood on the "catwalk" in shock, staring at the body.

As I stood there, beside Joe and Rosenthal, looking down at the dark, motionless form and hoping desperately that he was not seriously hurt, my thoughts were less for the injured man than for myself and the Festival. With that hollow thud, my last hope had been shattered. Tired and enervated as they were, the crew would not go back to work—certainly not until a report had been received from the hospital. And by that time it would be too late and the final dress rehearsal would have to be canceled. Without it, that evening's opening performance would be a shambles.

I could cancel that too, invoking the accident as an excuse.

In that case the first-string critics would go home (there was no hope of holding them for a third night) and their judgment of our season would be based entirely on their dubious appraisal of *King John*. In that case the Festival was down the drain.

All this had taken half a minute or less. And then suddenly something happened. As I watched in amazement, Joe Patterson got up from beside the still-motionless body, gave Jean Rosenthal a quick, knowing look, nodded and walked briskly over to the foot of the ladder, where the red velvet sheath had dropped and was coiled on the floor. He picked it up and started to climb. When he was halfway up the ladder he paused and called sharply to the crew to come over and steady it. The men, grouped around their injured comrade, hesitated, then, obeying his order, moved forward to the base of the ladder and held it firm. High above them, with his legs wrapped tightly around the top rung while he strained to slide the long sheath over the wires, Patterson continued to issue orders for the coming run-through. Again the men hesitated, then moved at his bidding. By the time he was down and the ladder was dragged off the stage, the paralysis was over and morale had been restored. I heard Zeisler's voice over the intercom, calling to his actors to get off the stage and finish dressing. A moment later "Fifteen minutes" was called.

Jean Rosenthal was still checking light cues with her boardmen when the house was opened to the two or three hundred people who had been waiting in the lobby. They were mostly workers from the local helicopter plants, offices and hospitals who had been invited at the last moment to supply some sort of audience for our dress rehearsal. As the actors, now in full costume, began to file quietly up the stairs for the opening scene, they were delayed for a moment while paramedics carried the injured man past them down to the waiting ambulance. Whatever his internal injuries might be, it was fairly clear by now that no limbs had been broken.*

* Nor were there any serious internal injuries. He was back at work within a week, shaken but unharmed.

Measure for Measure opened with a fanfare of hunting horns as a small procession of red-coated retainers appeared at the head of the stairs, carrying the departing Duke's belongings to the carriages waiting below. Down the scarlet stairs came footmen with a large bird cage, a gun case, fishing rods, lots of expensive luggage and, finally, two magnificent wolfhounds tugging at the leash. As Arnold Moss (in an Inverness cape) and Stanley Bell (in a stovepipe hat) followed them onstage, they got weak applause from the small audience.

That afternoon's run-through was tense, slow and labored —a perfect preparation for the whirling action of that evening's opening, when it was as though all the frustrations of *King John* and all the adrenalin accumulated during the near-tragedy of the afternoon had been suddenly released into a performance that went far beyond anything that had been seen in rehearsal.

It was the first time the play had been played before a real audience, and their delighted reaction made it clear that we had found the right formula for this equivocal play. There was prolonged applause, but that did not prevent the critics —who scuttled silently up the aisle, concerned only with not getting caught in the departing crowd—from looking blank and mysterious as they followed Ben Washer, our press agent, toward the building down by the water where they would be writing their reviews.

At the opening-night party which was given in the main lobby of the theatre (under the eye of Van Soest's celebrated portrait of the Bard that had been presented to the Festival by Lincoln Kirstein) spirits were high. Everyone was exhausted and so eager to relax after the exhilaration of the recent performance that the dubious reviews of *King John* were forgotten.

Then, just after midnight, when the gaiety was at its height, the second dramatic event of the day occurred. When Ben Washer arrived at the party (after taking care of the critics, helping them to make their telephone connections and conducting them to their cars) he reported that Brooks Atkinson (who wrote his reviews in longhand) had been the last to leave and had apologized for taking so long. After he had finally driven off, Ben had gone back into the house to lock up. On an impulse he had glanced into the wastebasket beneath the desk where Atkinson had been writing. In it he had found a small, dark, crumpled ball of carbon paper which he now handed to me.

I snatched it and ran with it to my office, followed by Landau and a secretary hastily plucked from the party. By holding the creased carbon up against the light, we were just able to make out what, it now appeared, was the first page of Atkinson's handwritten review for *The New York Times*.

It took some time to decipher and for the secretary to type. When it was done I rushed out, broke up the party and read it out loud:

A Lovely Rollicking Farce at Stratford

To play *Measure for Measure* in modern dress as the American Shakespeare Festival did last evening is to accomplish two things that are not in the rule book. A complicated harum-scarum plot becomes simple and clear. An acrid comedy becomes amiable and pleasant. Add something else to these attractive dividends: the company plays *Measure for Measure* with elegance, humor and harmony. Shakespeare's bitterest comedy has never seemed so delightful and the acting on the Stratford stage has never seemed so accomplished. I urge you to hurry—

That's all there was, but it was enough. The cheering and the huzzahs went on and on. Though there was a matinee of *Measure* the next afternoon, no one went to bed before dawn, waiting for the phone calls to come through from New York with the rest of the reviews. Almost all were good; some were raves—including the rest of Brooks Atkinson's in the *Times*. No wonder it had taken him so long to write it! In his rapturous report he had compliments for everyone: for the directors, "who have made an utterly beguiling production"; for Rouben Ter-Arutunian, "whose lattice-work which seemed of little use in *King John* now is a fantastically adaptable affair" and "whose choice of nineteenth century cos-

47

tumes is inspired: there is nothing like seeing Shakespeare played in a brown derby"; for the "inspired lighting of Jean Rosenthal," who "pours light through the lattice-work with a skill that might be labelled virtuosity"; for Virgil Thomson's "carnival music."* But it was the acting "for which this column would like to express its main gratitude and enthusiasm; as the hangman and his assistant, Whitford Kane and Hiram Sherman are extraordinarily funny and, as the Warden, Morris Carnovsky whisks the head of a deceased bandit out of prison in a hatbox with hilarious craft." He commended "the benevolent comedy" of Arnold Moss's Duke; the charm of Nina Foch's Isabella set against Kent Smith's moral torment as Angelo; the beauty and freshness of Jacqueline Brookes and Sylvia Short as Juliet and Mariana; the enjoyable pomposity of William Cottrell as the Constable, and the wildness of Pernell Roberts as his drunken prisoner; the quizzical humor of Stanley Bell's Escalus; the perfection of Donald Harron's Claudio and, finally, "the wonderful mountebankery of Norman Lloyd's Lucio who, with his skinny trousers and skinny walking stick, is the embodiment of a tout."

In conclusion he described *Measure for Measure* as "a particularly winning piece of theatre—lightly devised, ingeniously staged, played lightly. It deserves a hundred and one performances in this inviting theatre on the Housatonic River." †

Not all our reviews were that rhapsodic, but, almost without exception, they were good for the box office. Even *Variety*, that pragmatic organ of showbiz, gave us high marks for entertainment and for "a leering humor reminiscent of *The Threepenny Opera*."

What reservations there were came predictably from Cath-

---

* True to his precept of T.T.T. ("Tunes Take Time"), Virgil had written a delicious, syncopated version of "Take, oh take, those lips away"—variations of which (besides a few fanfares for hunting horns) made up most of his score.

† It was typical of Atkinson's methods as the all-powerful critic for *The New York Times* that, having been disappointed by *King John* and feeling obliged to give us a mediocre notice (the effects of which he was fully aware of), he should now repair the damage with this superlative review of *Measure for Measure*.

olic critics who regretted the absence of the mystical undertones I had deliberately avoided. Walter Kerr, in the *Tribune*, conceded that "this production does wonders for the low comics: Norman Lloyd's Lucio, in particular, is nimble, cheerful and disreputably winning—a blend of something out of Dickens and Damon Runyon." But he had reservations about our three principals, with "their puzzling, tormented, poetic complexity":

> The production captures brilliantly the cynicism, the mocking laughter and the frankly bawdy quality of this cryptic play. But it does seem to me that, in the process of keeping *Measure for Measure* highly entertaining, some of the sardonic bitterness has been lost along with the disillusion and the sadness.

The fact remains that on the night of June 27, 1956, the tide turned for the American Shakespeare Festival Theatre at Stratford, Connecticut. Attendance remained spotty over the Fourth of July, then built gradually through July and August, when *The Taming of the Shrew* was added to the repertory and the number of performances of *King John* was reduced. By the end of August, standing room only was habitual on weekends.

But even more important than the box-office figures was the new image that the Festival was assuming in the eyes of the public and the press:

> Shakespeare on the Housatonic is looking up.

> The Shakespeare Festival Theatre is happily coming to justify the high hopes of its founders.

> It looks as though the American Shakespeare Festival is finally swinging.

These were typical leads of articles that appeared about us during the final weeks of the season, culminating in an editorial in *Life* that accompanied a five-page picture spread showing a gaudy parade of "trollops, petty crooks, woeful lovers and corrupt officials."

After a limping start last year, the company this summer has hit its stride and Stratford on the Housatonic has established itself as the perfect place for enjoying Shakespeare. Inside the theatre it offers good acting and excellent productions. Outside it gives patrons a riverside promenade.

Personal opinions were expressed in letters that arrived during the following weeks. From Dr. Koekeritz, Yale's expert on Elizabethan pronunciation, came a sharp admonition that Provost is not pronounced "proevoest" but "with a short 'o' as in 'bishop.' " From Philip Johnson, the celebrated architect: "Thank you for an unbelievable evening. Such staging, such lighting, such sets! The best since the Mercury! Thanks for renewing my faith in the theatre." From Margaret Webster* (in a letter written in mid-Atlantic to Joseph Reed):

> It can't be done this way! I believe that with my soul! This production is ingenious (fairly, not *very*), amusing in a Café Society way, full of sincere effort and clever (I'd say "clever-clever") ideas. If, as I suspect, the object of the exercise was to please Brooks Atkinson it succeeded admirably. But what pleases the *New York Times* is not, I repeat *not*, what is going to reach the hearts and fire the imaginations of your audience.
>
> If Shakespeare is to be done without any glamor at all (I don't even speak of grandeur or soul), there really is no point. If it is to belittle, descend and condescend, snigger up its sleeve and refuse the colour and the music, the heights and the depths, the breadth and the glory— for God's sake, call it a day and STOP!

Our third show, *The Taming of the Shrew,* had been selected as a concession to conventional programming. When I first announced it I was not at all sure it would ever reach the stage. But after the success of *Measure* and with the steady growth of our audiences, its immediate production became a necessity—one that caught me unprepared. Neither Landau

* Actress and director, best known in the U.S. for her direction of *Othello* with Paul Robeson, José Ferrer and Uta Hagen and for her direction of Maurice Evans in *Hamlet, Macbeth, Henry IV,* etc.

nor I was eager to direct it; we were both exhausted and felt that to make *Shrew* viable, a fresh, entirely new energy was needed. On the other hand, it would be unwise and dangerous to inject into our repertory situation (with our actors giving eight performances a week) an outside director unacquainted with the company and its emotional makeup. There was only one man who fitted our requirements, and that was my close friend and former associate Norman Lloyd, who had scored so brilliantly as Lucio in *Measure,* who had worked with many of our actors before, and whose early vaudeville background made him the perfect director to galvanize an old chestnut into new, comic theatrical life.

Professionally, Lloyd was a prickly fellow. In offering him the job I made no bones about the difficulties. He had only three weeks' rehearsal, which, under repertory conditions, meant a little over a hundred hours before the first preview. And, because of our financial situation, he would be limited to a minimum of production. He accepted, and we sat around for several nights cutting and editing the text and making the decision of whether to use or eliminate the so-called "induction," with Christopher Sly. Norman decided to keep him in and we offered the part to Hiram Sherman, who turned us down.* Norman then suggested an actor from the outside, Mike Kellin, whose rough but sincere comic quality would be valuable in the role of the disreputable alcoholic tinker.

The rest of the cast came from within the company. It was our largest yet—thirty-six in all, students included—and it marked the first appearance as actors of several youthful apprentices who, until now, had been no more than bodies in rubber boots or butlers' uniforms. Now a number of them appeared as Petruchio's rambunctious servants, under the command of Morris Carnovsky's tyrannical and frantic Gru-

---

* Casting, except for parts specifically mentioned in contracts, was done by mutual consent. Sherman, having appeared in two productions, was justified in turning down a third. Whitford Kane, though desperately ill, insisted on appearing in all three plays—as a defiant citizen of Angiers in *John,* as Abhorson the comic hangman in *Measure* and, finally, in the double roles of First Player and Vincentio in *Shrew.*

mio. (They were an astonishing group; their average age was around sixteen, and several of them have since become well known in show business—Peter Bogdanovich and Michael Lindsay-Hogg as directors, René Auberjonois as an actor and David Milton as a writer.)

For the leads we cast Nina Foch* as Kate; portly Pat Hines as Baptista; "macho" Pernell Roberts as Petruchio; Donald Harron as Lucentio; Fritz Weaver, brilliantly transformed into the aging, avaricious Gremio; a promoted apprentice, Barbara Lord, as Bianca.

Regarding production, we had neither the time nor the money to be anything but simple. On Rouben's Festival platform, surrounded by his walls of slats, an open playing area was created within which a company of traveling actors could set up their pickets in the courtyard of a provincial manor, overlooked by a balcony in which Sly was installed and from which he could peer down on and occasionally intervene in the turbulent wooing of Baptista's daughters. Rouben was off doing a ballet in Europe, and I turned to Dorothy Jeakins (who had done my costumes for *Lear* and *Coriolanus*) to design a color scheme that would include the costumes of our ragtag troupe and the flags and banners with which they staked out their playing area.

There is something special about working in a repertory situation with actors who, in the ten preceding weeks, have come through the stress and hardships of overlapping productions. Norman took full advantage of this. His rehearsals were relaxed, cheerful and improvisatory. Within Shakespeare's loose, farcical structure he developed a whole series of timeless gags and routines to which the actors brought many of their own suggestions of character and behavior. Nina, in particular, added her own conception of Kate's feelings for Petruchio during their rowdy but affectionate wooing. Her treatment of the sun and moon scene on the highway was both comic and touching. Music, in the absence

---

* I had offered the part to Kim Stanley, but she was interested only in playing Juliet.

of Virgil Thomson, was composed by a young man by the name of Irwin Bazelon.*

We opened with a matinee on August 5 in a relaxed summer atmosphere. Our reviews, mostly from second-stringers, were excellent. Douglas Watt of the *New York Daily News* reported that Norman Lloyd had staged the work "like the superior vaudeville it is, using stylized and comic actors' patterns and resorting to incongruous sound effects as when the miserly Gremio enumerates his worldly goods to Bianca's father to the accompaniment of an offstage cash register."† Arthur Gelb of the *Times* was enchanted by the "inspired madness" of the production and declared that it would have surprised no one if Harpo Marx had suddenly been lowered from the ceiling on a rope.

The only first-stringer to cover us was Richard Watts of the *Post* (recently returned from his annual summer visit to Ireland):

> By this time *The Taming of the Shrew* requires a lot of showmanship if it is to be amusing and this is exactly what it receives at Stratford. Norman Lloyd has thought up a seemingly endless series of gags and I thought almost all of them were amazingly funny.... It's quite amazing to note what a good, rowdy farce the old play can be when done with really comic imagination.

With full houses and no more productions to worry about, life was leisurely and agreeable on the banks of the Housatonic. It had been a good season: the weather was beautiful, morale was high, and I was becoming visible, occasionally, to my wife and children! It was still necessary, from time to time, to hold rehearsals to maintain the quality of the shows —especially *King John*. And, as the season wore on, a number

* He has become known, since then, both as a serious composer and as an expert in the creation of singing commercials.
† One of our apprentices' functions was to go out each evening before the show and capture a number of the big moths that flew out of Gremio's ledgers when he opened them to figure out Bianca's dowry.

of replacements had to be made as members of the cast left to go into rehearsals for the new Broadway season.*

My own contract with Stratford ran through to the middle of September, but I was not due back in Culver City until the end of the year. Meanwhile, I had been so immersed in the affairs of the Festival for the past nine months that I had barely glanced at the synopses, treatments and scripts for future pictures that had been sent to me from the Coast. My only contact with the studio had been to ask them to arrange a special pre-opening running of *Lust for Life*. This took place in the local movie theatre one Sunday morning for the entertainment of the Festival Company, students and staff a week before its opening in Manhattan.

Around the middle of August, over a lobster lunch with Lincoln Kirstein and Joseph Reed, I talked about the Stratford situation and about my own plans. I made it clear that my contract with Metro-Goldwyn-Mayer had four more years to run, but I did give them my very definite views on the future of the Festival and repeated these in a letter I presently sent to Reed with a copy to Lincoln:

> Many of your Trustees, and even a few of the Executive Committee, continue to think of Stratford as a superior summer theatre conveniently accessible to Greenwich, Westport and the better parts of Fairfield County. Is that enough?
>
> After all the work and hopes we've put into this venture, is it to be no more than a summer operation to be booked, as shrewdly as possible, year after year? Is that really all you want?†

---

* Kent Smith was replaced by Kendall Clark, and Mildred Dunnock by Jacqueline Brookes, who demonstrated that the widowed Queen's bereavement over the murder of her only son seemed even more poignant when played by a younger woman.

† Similar questions were being asked in the press; e.g., an editorial in the *Christian Science Monitor:* "Viewed in terms of the Stratford Festival's future, this season raises standards, hopes—and problems. The problems center around the need to begin next season at the plateau on which this season has ended. An immense contribution would be made to a neglected area of theatrical art in this country if

Then, just before Labor Day, with the Festival in its final week, I read in *The New York Times* one morning that there had been a blowup at the MGM Studio and that Dore Schary was out as head of production in Culver City. I immediately called my agents, who confirmed the news.

So now (as so often in my life) everything was suddenly changed. My position as a successful MGM producer had been based on my collaboration and understanding with Dore Schary. With him gone, I would be the lame-duck survivor of a discredited regime: I would be at the mercy of the mafia on the third floor and of whatever new executive they brought in to run the studio. I remembered my bad times at RKO and shuddered and took another look at my future.

With my disciplined opportunism, I had not allowed myself to think of continuing with the Festival—no matter how much the idea might have tempted me. Now I began to think of little else. And, almost immediately, my mind was made up. By leaving MGM I would be giving up an unusually favorable contract, but I had no feeling that I would be doing anything wrong or foolish. Aside from my deep distrust of the new management, I had a strong, instinctive revulsion against returning to California at this time. I had already proved (to myself and to the world) that I was capable of producing a string of successful and significant films.* If I went back now and even if I were lucky enough to adjust to the new regime, I would be repeating something I had already accomplished. To stay in the East and to create the first American classical repertory company seemed in every way a more exciting prospect. The enormous drop in income which it entailed played almost no part in my thinking: my behavior about money has always been insane and irrational.

I called Lincoln Kirstein and informed him under an oath

---

the means were created whereby at least a nucleus of the Festival's ensemble could maintain its entity over an extended period. Progress at Stratford this season should encourage the Festival's trustees, backers and well-wishers to work for such a desirable consummation."

* *Lust for Life* had just opened successfully in New York. See *Front and Center*, p. 482.

of secrecy that, in certain conditions, it might be possible for me to continue as artistic director of the American Shakespeare Festival Theatre and Academy. Within a few hours I received the predictable call from Joseph Reed, and a series of protracted and convoluted negotiations began that went on for several weeks during which I lived in New City, watching the trees change their color, driving into town for occasional, discursive lunches with Joe Reed in the course of which I became more than ever aware of the astonishing ambivalence of the man.

I knew that he was grateful and proud of what had been accomplished during my first Stratford season.* I also believed that he shared my view of the Festival as the first step in the formation of a national repertory company—up to a point. At the same time I knew that I frightened him, personally and professionally, and that he regarded me with mixed feelings of admiration and mistrust—as a brilliant but dangerous operator to whom he was reluctant to entrust his beloved Shakespeare for the three years that I was now demanding as the minimum term of my new contract.

Finally, late in September, I had to break the news to my poor wife that she would be spending the next three years on the Eastern seaboard. Lawyers were summoned and an agreement was drawn up appointing me artistic director (with Jack Landau as my associate) for the next three Festival seasons, with the same authority as I had demanded and obtained in my first contract. And though I could obtain no specific assurance that the Festival would become a year-round operation, it was agreed (1) that the following summer season would be extended into September; (2) that the company would be sent out on some form of national tour during the winter of 1957–58; and, more immediately, (3) that two

---

* I have in my files a collection of notes and letters received over the months. They are complimentary to the point of embarrassment—including one written during a visit to Warwickshire: "I now know that Stratford, Conn., has been *blessed* by the presence of John Houseman. . . . He has given our productions every bit as much cohesion and style as one finds here at S-on-Avon and he has invested our plays with infinitely more tautness and vitality."

plays from the current repertory would be presented by the Festival Company in New York, if possible, during the winter of 1956–57.

Throughout these negotiations I had used my MGM film contract as leverage for a quick decision. Now, on October 16, a telegram was sent to my agents in California: "John Houseman authorizes you to negotiate a settlement of his contract with MGM on the best possible terms preserving his right to whatever money is now owed him and whatever additional payment you may negotiate."

No "additional payment" was ever received, and I did not insist on it. For, by now, I was in a great hurry to abrogate my MGM contract—not only because of Stratford, but for another reason altogether.

One day early in October, I had received a luncheon invitation from an old friend. Louis Cowan and I had been together in the upper echelon of the Overseas Branch of the Office of War Information, where one of his functions had been that of coordinator between the OWI and the Army for the short-wave broadcasting of such worldwide programs to the armed forces as *News from Home, Yankee Swing Drive, G.I. Jive,* etc. He had also functioned, at Bob Sherwood's personal request, as our representative in the negotiations that were constantly taking place between the Voice of America, the networks and the unions.

In private life, before the war, Cowan had been a successful producer of commercial radio and, before that, a public-relations expert specializing in big-time religious groups, regardless of faith or denomination. He had begun life with money, then augmented that by marrying an intelligent and dedicated girl who also happened to be an heiress to the third-largest mail-order business in the country. While still quite young he had conceived, organized and brilliantly exploited a lucrative radio show known as *Quiz Kids.* After the war Cowan had returned to the mass media and the increasingly prosperous *Quiz Kids.* We remained friends throughout the late forties, and once we almost went into business together. That scheme fell through, but we kept in touch while I made films in Hollywood and he expanded and transferred to television his string of successful quiz shows that culminated in *The $64,000 Question*. As a result, in the mid-fifties, he was offered and accepted the presidency of CBS-TV, to whose annual profits his shows had greatly contributed.

Like many of his kind, Cowan combined a sincere yearning for better things with a shrewd, irresistible appetite for making money.* Over lunch he started to tell me, somewhat mysteriously, about a prestigious new television show the network was contemplating. It was to be called *The Seven Lively Arts*—using the name of Gilbert Seldes' book that had been a cultural landmark of the twenties. It would be launched as a "sustaining" show along the lines of *Omnibus,* but it would surely find sponsors and become part of the regular commercial programming that made CBS the country's leading TV network.

Cowan was vague but enthusiastic. Then, over dessert, he came to the point. He suggested that since (as he put it) I was "ass-deep in culture," I might be the man they were looking for to produce this ambitious new show. I rose to the bait, and within a few days I had met with Hubbell Robinson, CBS vice-president in charge of production, and with William Paley, the president, himself. The more they talked, the more excited I became.

Three weeks later, following a number of conferences between CBS "business affairs" and my agent, the Music Corporation of America, a deal was concluded—for more money than I had ever made before—contingent upon the cancellation of my MGM contract, which I had once again used as a weapon in our negotiations.

In a symbolic move, to confirm my continued presence in the East, and as a conciliatory gesture toward Joan, who loved

* As he grew older and his health deteriorated, the former gradually became dominant. He became a publisher, a professor at Columbia University's School of Journalism and an important figure in the administration of the DuPont–Columbia Awards for TV and Radio Journalism.

the sea, I bought a handsome beach lot at Truro, on Cape Cod, to be used as a retreat during the coming summers.*

No one seemed to question my ability to run the American Shakespeare Festival and the *Seven Lively Arts* program at the same time, and I was careful not to raise the point with either organization. As a result, by mid-November, with my two new contracts duly signed, I began the double duty of assembling the nucleus of an organization capable of conceiving, preparing and broadcasting twenty-six original hour-long television shows during the winter of 1957–58 while vigorously pursuing the plan I had laid out in my new Stratford agreement: that two of the Festival's productions be presented during the 1956–57 winter season in New York City.

The first person I approached on the subject was my old friend T. Edward Hambleton, who, with Norris Houghton, had founded the Phoenix Theatre three years earlier. I had been involved with them from the beginning as the director of *Coriolanus,* their first classical production.† Since then the Phoenix had made regular and important contributions to New York's theatrical scene, and I was delighted to propose to them a scheme that I felt would benefit both their organization and mine.

In my eagerness to find a New York outlet for our Festival productions, I proposed to "T." and Norrie that the Phoenix become our regular host for two months each winter, beginning with a revival of the two comedies that had been so well received in Stratford the previous summer. The Phoenix, on its part, welcomed this chance to present two classical productions of which its program was in dire need and for which the main costs had already been paid. Dates were fixed—for January and February 1957.

I had only one basic disagreement with the Phoenix: I

---

* Blueprints for a family beach house were drawn up by the well-known architect Eliot Noyes, but it was never built. Five years later, just before the great real-estate boom on Cape Cod, I sold the lot to pay for our new house in Malibu.
† See *Front and Center,* p. 435.

wished to present our two comedies in repertory; T. and Norris objected that they were already committed to a series of limited runs and that the whole fabric of their subscription system would be disrupted by a repertory schedule. I gave in and I have always regretted it.

Though more than three months had passed since our final performance in Stratford, most of the original cast of *Measure* were still available.* Rehearsals were once again conducted jointly by Landau and myself; the "slats" were trucked down from Connecticut and a simpler and smaller version of our Ter-Arutunian "tray" was constructed on the stage of the Phoenix. Some of the "floating" effect was lost and the use of ramps and traps was somewhat restricted but the essential, functional quality of the Festival Stage was retained.

We opened with *Measure for Measure* on January 22. (As an added attraction, a small orchestra, in red jackets, played Viennese waltzes of the period, selected by Virgil Thomson, in the lobby before the show and during intermission.) Our reviews were even better than they had been at Stratford: "Bard Has 'em Howling at Phoenix"; "Bard Triumphs at Phoenix"; "*Measure* Never Had It So Good." *Variety* declared that "the collaboration of Stratford and the Phoenix" was "a fortunate development for local legit-goers," while the *Daily News* reported: "Shakespeare's version of *Guys and Dolls* is a lusty, busty smash in every department."

Most of the first-string critics came and saw it a second time. Brooks Atkinson repeated his encomium: "We are not likely to have a better *Measure for Measure* in the foreseeable future." So did Watts of the *Post:* "Brilliantly entertaining, humorous, cynical, ironic and brightly bawdy, it is one of the finest, freshest and most imaginative presentations of the Bard in recent theatrical history."

Two months earlier, New York had seen Tyrone Guthrie's *Troilus and Cressida*. Since both were conceived in some form of "modern dress," it was inevitable that comparisons should

---

* New cast members included Richard Waring as Angelo, Nancy Wickwire as Mariana, Richard Easton replacing Harron, a fellow Canadian, as Claudio and Ellis Rabb, in his first appearance with the company, as Froth.

be made. Most of them were in our favor, but what pleased me most was a handwritten note I received from the only American drama critic whose opinions I had long held in respect. Stark Young, who was ill and no longer reviewing, had driven up to Stratford to see *The Taming of the Shrew,* of which he approved (though he chided me for our non-Italianate pronunciation of Petruchio). Now:

> Here is another song of praise.... You make the Old Vic *Troilus and Cressida* look very second-rate—better speech, a more genuine wit based on Shakespeare's lines and intentions and good readings that are always clear to hear....

Measure for Measure played out its three weeks to fine business. It was the high point of the American Shakespeare Festival's relations with New York City—that year or ever.

The Taming of the Shrew, which opened on February 20, "scored with four aisle-sitters," according to *Variety,* but I felt that something had gone wrong. The modified Festival Stage did not work as well as it had for *Measure;* Fritz Weaver was badly missed as Gremio; Norman Lloyd, our director, was involved in another production and was forced to quit halfway through rehearsal. But, worst of all, our Petruchio—who had been so virile and forceful in Connecticut—was now involved in a disturbing marital situation that seemed to deprive him of the male energy that is essential for the role. To offset his failure, Nina Foch, who had been a lovely, proud but touching Kate, now began to force her part to the point where their courtship squabbles became harsh and irritating.

Brooks Atkinson—who had not seen *Shrew* in Stratford—true to his habit of chastening those whom he had praised, found it "over-directed and tedious" and suggested that "the taming of the director would be the first step toward taming this Shrew."

Overall it was a letdown for which I blamed myself and my failure to insist on repertory—thus defeating the main purpose of our New York season. Instead of being judged as the unified effort of a young, developing classical acting company, our plays had been treated as two separate entries in the Broadway Sweepstakes—one a winner, one a loser.

Undaunted, within a week of the opening of *Shrew,* we were deep in rehearsal of a third show: Webster's *Duchess of Malfi,* directed by Landau, produced by me and financed and presented by the Phoenix. Though the production had no formal connection with Stratford, it did in fact employ many members of our Festival Company, including beautiful and touching Jacqueline Brookes in the name part and Earle Hyman as her doomed lover. New faces were those of Joseph Wiseman as the Duke turned werewolf, Hurd Hatfield as his murderous brother the Cardinal, Jan Farrand as his harlot mistress. It received mixed, generally respectful notices but, not being on subscription, did quite disappointing business.

So ended our first and only combined Phoenix-Festival season and my first year as artistic director of the American Shakespeare Festival Theatre.

CHAPTER II

1957

AMERICAN SHAKESPEARE
FESTIVAL:
OTHELLO
THE MERCHANT OF VENICE
MUCH ADO ABOUT NOTHING

LOOKING BACK, I am amazed at my ability to keep so many balls in the air at one time. Through the spring of 1957, besides my Phoenix activities, my days were divided between the long-term preparation of my second Stratford season and the setting up of an organization capable of producing the Columbia Broadcasting System's most highly publicized television series of the coming season.

Soon after the turn of the year, I had begun to spend part of every day in the long, low red-brick building on the corner of Fifty-seventh Street and Tenth Avenue which CBS had taken over for its rapidly expanding television operations. (It was known as the "Cow Barn"—for good reason. Until recently it had been a huge midtown dairy; our offices, for all their coats of fresh paint, were still fragrant with the smells of our bovine predecessors.)

As I set about assembling a staff, I discovered that I was

not the first to have been assigned to *The Seven Lively Arts*. Robert Herridge, a rising TV writer-director with the handsome head of a Greek athlete and a passionate enthusiasm for "live" dramatic television, had been on the project since the previous fall under the impression that he was to be its producer. (For this reason my relations with him, though personally amicable, remained professionally strained throughout the life of the program.) He continued to function as head of our "live" drama unit, which produced its share of our most successful shows. Also already at work were two bright Princeton boys—Charles Schultz and "Bo" Goldman, a charming, overweight young man whose wife sent him to work filled with "Tiger's Milk" every morning and who, years later, emerged as one of the film industry's most successful scriptwriters.*

In my own state of insecurity at entering yet another medium with which I was entirely unfamiliar, I was inclined to turn for help to former associates. My first choice for our general manager in charge of production was Palmer Williams, who had performed that function under horrendous circumstances for Media Productions. He was now deeply involved with Ed Murrow and Fred Friendly as production manager of *Person to Person,* but he helped me to recruit a number of the people whom I subsequently used on the show. Among these was "Shad" Northshield, a man dedicated to the recording of humane documentary material, whom I made head of our film unit.†

Finally, since I had every intention of producing a number of shows myself, I called Jud Kinberg in California and invited him to join me. We had worked well together at MGM and he was accustomed to functioning under my supervision with considerable latitude and responsibility of his own. He

* After working for years, with moderate success, on the books of musicals, he broke through with the screenplay of *One Flew over the Cuckoo's Nest.*
† He had made a fine documentary about American Indian life; later he made a much-admired film about the children of Northern Ireland caught in the fratricidal strife of their elders. He also became head of the CBS *Sunday Show.*

too had been uprooted by Schary's sudden departure, and he welcomed a chance to move into a new field.

So, slowly, an organization was beginning to develop around this vast, nebulous program of which no one had a clear conception of what it should be—except that it must be original, entertaining, prestigious and, if possible, popular. With so much lead time (*The Seven Lively Arts* was not scheduled to go on the air until November 1957) my approach to our problem was leisurely and discursive. Dozens of projects were considered during long staff meetings in the Cow Barn and with Hubbell Robinson and his assistant, Harry Ommerle, over martinis at Louis & Armand's. Unlike *Omnibus*, which, with a few exceptions, had been what its name implied, a magazine of the air, it was agreed that each one of our shows would be devoted to one single subject with no limitations as to form, style or subject matter. This permitted the use of "live" drama, film, documentary, music or dance —or all of them combined.

To develop a program out of these variegated possibilities became my summer's assignment.

Much of my energy, in the meantime, continued to be devoted to Shakespeare and the Festival. Fortunately the distance between my two offices was a short one: they were both on Tenth Avenue—one at Fifty-seventh, the other at Sixty-third, where the ASFTA's New York operation was now housed in an industrial building in what, before the erection of Lincoln Center, was one of the toughest and most run-down slums in Manhattan. Here, on two crowded floors, we conducted our multiple activities: casting, publicity, promotion and the acting school, which, during the coming year, under Jack Landau's direction, began to acquire a measure of quality and consistency. (Our visiting lecturers included Michael Redgrave, John Gielgud, Harold Clurman and, above all, Michel Saint-Denis. In fact, our students were the first to hear the four brilliant talks* he later combined to

* "Classical Theatre and Modern Realism," "Style and Stylization," "Directing and Theatrical Design," "Theatre Training."

form his book *Theatre: The Rediscovery of Style,* which, ten years later, became an essential element in the curriculum of the newly formed Drama Division of the Juilliard School.)

But my most intense personal activity went into the programming, casting and preparation of my second Stratford summer season. It was desirable to announce our repertory as early as possible. Yet it was dangerous to announce plays before we were sure we had the cast to perform them. I had announced *Hamlet* under the firm impression that Fritz Weaver was eager to parlay his successes as Casca and Faulconbridge into a starring appearance as the gloomy Dane. When his agent informed us that, for personal reasons, Fritz would not be coming up to Connecticut that summer, I was left with egg on my face, some disappointed subscribers and a gaping hole in our repertory.

True to his determination to see stars on the Stratford stage, Langner had made approaches to a number of eminent American actors during the winter. Several had expressed interest but discovered conflicts. I was not surprised or disappointed; I continued to believe that our most important task was the development of the company and that we must eventually create our own stars through the performances they gave on our stage. On the other hand, I realized that, as a Shakespeare festival, we could no longer avoid presenting at least one of the major tragedies each season. But how to cast it? We had no Hamlet now in the company, no Macbeth and no Lear.* We did, however, have an Othello.

Earle Hyman had played the Moor twice in New York.† Now, after a lapse of time, since he was a charter member of our Festival Company, it was good repertory policy to let him play it once again on a bigger stage, with a stronger company and a larger audience. As it happened, an excellent Iago was available.

* Or so it seemed. Carnovsky played it five years later and proved to be one of the most impressive Lears of his generation.
† Since Paul Robeson first did it in London it has become habitual in this country for a black actor to play the Moor. (I know of one Shakespeare festival in the West that was picketed for casting a white man in the role.)

Alfred Drake was an actor with whom I had worked twice before—in *Joy to the World* and *Beggar's Holiday*.* Neither production had been a triumph, but I continued to have great faith in him as an actor and I knew how eager he was to get out of musical theatre into classical acting, for which he was thoroughly trained. I asked him if he would like to play Iago; he said yes and asked what his other part would be. While I was preparing to answer him, something happened that caused our whole summer's repertory to fall suddenly into place.

Lawrence Langner was a man of amazing tenacity, for which, in his long theatrical career, he had been frequently rewarded. He had never fully accepted Kate Hepburn's inability to appear in Stratford that summer. Early in March, when he called her for the umpteenth time, she told him that things had changed and that she might possibly be able to join us—on condition that she appear, in repertory, in two plays. For the first, she suggested *The Merchant of Venice,* which she had previously played with the Old Vic Company on its Australian tour.

This might have been an awkward request, since, following the horrors of the Holocaust, the *Merchant* had been rigidly excluded from the American theatre as anti-Semitic. What altered the situation for us was that, during the final weeks of the previous season, we had placed a questionnaire in our program listing eight of Shakespeare's plays and asking the audiences to number them in the order of their preference. To everyone's intense surprise the leader (ahead of *Hamlet, Much Ado About Nothing* and *Midsummer Night's Dream*) had been *The Merchant of Venice*. This poll, which we had taken mainly as a public-relations gesture, now enabled us to accede to Miss Hepburn's request; it also allowed us to offer a member of our own company the best part he had ever played. If there was one actor in America physically and mentally capable of playing Shylock as an understandable and tragic rather than a hateful or grotesque figure, it was Morris Carnovsky, who had served his classical apprenticeship with us

* See *Front and Center,* pp. 191 and 220.

the previous season and who was now ready to take on one of the greatest roles in the canon.

Things were looking up, but one further decision remained to be made. Both Kate and Alfred had made it a condition of their coming to Stratford that they each appear in *two* plays. Since we now had in our company a lively Beatrice and an eloquent Benedick, it did not take me long to decide what our third production would be.

So, finally, we proudly announced our repertory for the American Shakespeare Festival's 1957 season: *Othello, The Merchant of Venice* and *Much Ado About Nothing*. And we were able, in our brochures and advertisements, to blazon the names of our two bright stars, Hepburn and Drake. Langner and most of the board were elated, but, in a piece I wrote following our announcement, I found it necessary to restate the basic principle on which I was running the Festival:

> After so much talk about a permanent company, let no one suppose that our decision to engage two stars of such magnitude was taken lightly. We are very proud of our young troupe and of its first year's achievements. By the end of this summer more than half the company will have worked and performed together in no less than seven major classical productions with consecutive employment for eleven out of fifteen months. . . . Both Miss Hepburn and Mr. Drake made it a condition of their coming to Stratford that they appear in two plays in the repertory. It was a welcome confirmation of our own conviction that our best hope of survival and growth lies in our continued and firm adherence to the practice of repertory by a permanent acting company.

In fact, the problem of integrating stars with the company was a serious and delicate one. Alfred Drake appreciated the fact that in offering him two such varied roles as Iago and Benedick I was showing my faith in him as a dramatic actor. He became a dedicated and committed member of the Festival Company—though he was never quite one of them.

Katharine Hepburn was another kettle of fish. I had known her long but not well. I had first laid eyes on her more than a quarter of a century earlier on the stage of the Berkshire Playhouse at Stockbridge, Massachusetts, and I had instantly sensed that she was a star.* I had met her many times since, on both coasts, and worked with her in radio on *The Mercury on the Air* when she played opposite Joseph Cotten in *A Farewell to Arms.* My first reaction to the news that Langner had lured her to Stratford for the summer was a mixed one. Unquestionably her name would be of value in building up our audience and establishing our identity in the minds of the general public. But at what cost to the morale of the company? She was known to be opinionated, willful and domineering, and she had Langner under her thumb. Besides, she had already played Portia with the Old Vic under conditions that were utterly different from ours.

(If I had been entirely honest with myself I might have admitted that my feelings about Kate were on two levels. There was the reservation about stars which I expressed publicly in the *Times,* and there was another, secret and less creditable emotion: the fear that Kate's powerful and glamorous presence might threaten the paternalistic leadership that I had worked so hard to establish within the company over the past year.)

Following our first long interview with her in the living room of her small house in Turtle Bay, Jack Landau and I spent hours in earnest consultation as to how to deal with this magnetic personality without endangering the style of our production or the morale of our young company. Since Kate had commitments that would delay the start of *Merchant* rehearsals by two and a half weeks, we would not be able to open the season, this year, with our first two productions back to back, on successive nights. We decided that I would start with *Othello* while Landau took on *Merchant.* Later in the season we would co-direct *Much Ado.* And we devised the following strategy: Jack would do his best to adjust his own general production scheme to the very specific and somewhat old-fashioned romantic notions that Miss Hepburn had brought

* "I watched a very young, inexperienced girl with a wide mouth, wonderful bones and an impossible voice take over the stage."— *Run-Through,* p. 79.

over from her previous performance of *Merchant*. Throughout rehearsals I would hover in the background as the heavy. Anytime Jack felt he needed support he would alert me and I would appear and throw my weight around as artistic director of the Festival.

By and large this strategy worked, though it did not take into account Kate's overwhelming charm and the fact that within two days of the start of rehearsal not only Landau but most of the company had fallen completely and unresistingly under her spell. Kate, on her part, soon came to appreciate the quality of the company and Jack's very evident taste and talent.

All this was still some weeks in the future. Soon after our first meeting, Miss Hepburn flew back to California and I went into rehearsal with *Othello,* for which—as my first solo effort as director for the Festival—I had conscientiously prepared myself. During the spring I had been asked by the Laurel Press to write one of the introductions to its new paperback edition of Shakespeare's plays. I selected *Othello.* By having to organize my ideas sufficiently to write them down, I found myself analyzing the characters and relationships of the four principal characters with more depth and imagination than I have done for any other piece I have directed.* And here there was a danger—as I presently discovered. What happens in a stage performance is, finally, the sum of three elements: the text, the individual and collective qualities of the actors, and the ability of the director to adapt these personal qualities to his own conception of the drama. The gap that eventually yawned between my essay and my production was due, in part, to my predictable failure to get the actors to adjust their living personalities to the actions and attitudes I had too firmly set for them on paper.

---

* As part of my preparation I carefully read the two hundred pages of notes made by Stanislavsky for the Moscow Art Theatre production of *Othello* that never happened. That I got so little from it was due, I believe, to the fact that the text he was so conscientiously preparing to direct was a translation *in prose.* Consequently all of his analyses and conceptions of scenes remained rooted in realism rather than in the heightened, poetic drama of Shakespeare's verse.

In this production of *Othello,* I ran into one unpredictable problem. Our Moor, Earle Hyman, had played the part twice before and had been much admired, especially for his last appearance at Jan Huss House in New York. I had not seen it, but it had been described to me as a somewhat immature but violent and whirling performance. I had assumed that he would now be able to deepen and extend this youthful ardor; I was mistaken. In the three years that had passed since his last appearance as Othello he had become more sophisticated; he had traveled, met with celebrated European actors, studied with a female voice teacher who, while purifying his speech, had added a measure of affectation to it. He was, in fact, in the intermediary stage between the natural actor he had once been and the accomplished, conscious performer he later became.

There was another factor—one with which I failed to cope until it was too late. Off-Broadway, Hyman had been surrounded by actors whom he dominated. Here the situation was reversed by the presence of Alfred Drake, who had the stage presence and self-confidence of an established star; he also had a superb baritone voice—richer, more powerful and far better trained than Earle's. If there is one quality that is absolutely essential for an effective performance as Othello it is the ability to dominate the stage at all times. (This can be achieved physically or vocally—preferably both, as it was by Paul Robeson.) That summer Hyman did not have it—and he knew it. He might have achieved it by the sheer intensity of his passion, but psychologically, at this moment of his life, he was not capable of it. For all his fine, tall figure and the striking costumes Ter-Arutunian created for him, it was Iago to whom you gave your attention when he and Othello were on the stage together.

As a director I did what I could to redress the balance. I should have done more. I knew that Hyman was going through hell, and I was torn between pity and an exasperation that made it difficult for me to help him. Then, at this most critical stage of our rehearsals, something happened in my own life that temporarily diverted and absorbed my attention.

One day in mid-June, late in the afternoon, I broke rehearsal for a brief rest. When I walked into my office one of our volunteers informed me that my wife had called from New City and, on being told that it was impossible to disturb me, had left a message: "When you see him, please tell him his house is on fire."

I rushed to the phone, dialed and heard no ring at the other end. I called our neighbors the Poors, where I got a ring but no answer.

There was no more rehearsal that day. My jeep was downstairs, and as I approached New City along Route 304 I thought I saw smoke on my hill. There were a number of cars in the right-of-way and several fire trucks at the top of my driveway—also a number of neighbors seated on the hillside with bottles of liquor that I recognized as ours, staring with pleasurable excitement at the outside of my burning house. With its two-foot-thick walls it seemed almost undamaged—except that all the large downstairs windows were broken and gaping. Inside, dim in the smoke and steam, firemen (among them the local butcher's assistant) were walking about smashing things and tearing down bits of smoldering material. What I remember most clearly was the awful stench of burning that filled the house. I asked for my wife and children and was told they were safe. Joan had driven off with them to spare them the sight of their ruined home and to spend the night with their nurse, who lived nearby.

Presently the firemen drove off down the hill, followed after a while by the last of the neighbors, leaving empty bottles behind and carrying with them the food they had found in the refrigerator. (Later, they complained that it was tainted with smoke and inedible.)

While I waited for Joan to return I set about appraising the damage. One of the firemen had left me a flashlight, with which, in the gathering gloom, I made my eerie rounds of the house I had built, which was now filled with festoons of what seemed like unusually heavy cobwebs. The second floor, including the children's quarters, was only slightly damaged, but our huge, beautiful kitchen was a burned-out shell, with blackened walls and fragments of charcoal and twisted wires where the cabinets and electric burners had been. (The massive table on which we took our meals was half eaten by the flames, and on it I noticed a strange, dark-gray pool—all that remained of the telephone, which had liquefied in the intense heat and now lay, as in a Dali painting, dripping over the edge of the table.) Elsewhere the damage seemed to be mostly from heat and smoke. Structurally, there was nothing to burn, but the great stone walls—together with carpets, furniture and pictures—were covered from floor to ceiling with a dark, corrosive grime and those awful gray, greasy cobwebs. And as the house cooled off the stench got steadily worse.

Presently I became aware of the sound of a car coming up the hill and the glare of headlights in the drive. It was my wife, entirely blackened with soot. As was her wont in a crisis, she was amazingly calm as she gave me a full, lucid account of the disaster. It was the nurse's day off, and, after spending part of the afternoon trying on summer clothes, packing and making ready for the family's imminent migration to Stratford, Joan had begun the evening ritual of preparing the boys (aged six and three) for supper and bed. She had received and granted their urgent request for *pommes frites* that she was in the habit of deep-frying for them, as a special treat, on Nurse's night off, in a deep, heavy iron skillet. Leaving both of them in the bathtub, she had come down to the kitchen to start their supper when loud, hilarious screams were heard from above, augmented by the wild barking of two dachshunds and a poodle. She ran up the narrow cantilevered circular stairs (the only staircase in the house), ordered the boys out of the tub and told them to dry themselves and put on their pajamas and robes. She was about to return to the kitchen when the phone rang. She answered it upstairs in the bedroom. It was a call from a neighbor with a problem, and it was several minutes before she could dispose of her. When she got back downstairs she found that the oil in the skillet had caught fire.

One of Henry Poor's minor errors in the construction of the House on the Hill had been the placing of a row of wooden kitchen cabinets directly over the counter with the electric burners. Now, as the flames rose from the burning oil, they licked at the base of the cabinets, and they too began to burn. Joan tried to tamp out the flames with kitchen towels and then with the tablecloth. Failing in that, with considerable courage, she picked up the flaming skillet and carried it over to the sink. Too late. The flames continued to spread from one cabinet to another till the whole wall seemed to be on fire.

Joan went to the phone and called the Fire Department. Then, turning, she saw that the kitchen was now filled with smoke, which was also beginning to make its way up the stairs. She ran through it up to the second floor, grabbed the half-dried children, rushed them through the thickening murk down the narrow stairs and, literally, hurled them out the front door into the yard. She came back, made a futile attempt to reenter the flaming kitchen, then ran back upstairs in search of the howling dogs, whom she found cowering in a far corner, and half dragged, half carried them down the stairs and into the yard, where they and the children settled down to watch the show and to await the coming of the Fire Department.

After driving the two and a half miles from New City through Zukor Lane, past the golf course and along South Mountain Road, the first fire truck to reach my driveway found the turn blocked by the trunk of a large tree. After several minutes of backing and filling, the firemen drove on half a mile toward Centenary, made their turn around the country store and came back for another approach. This time they made it.

By the time they reached the top of the steep hill, the windows had burst from the heat and the kitchen was like a furnace. They did their best, but our water on the hill came from an artesian well a quarter of a mile down the road. It was the best drinking water in the world, but its pressure was insufficient for their pumps. (Later, when the damage was finally assessed, it turned out that most of it was due to steam damage caused by the trickle of water the heroic firemen dribbled over the burning embers of the declining fire.)

When Joan had finished her story we made a tour of the

house together. There was nothing more we could do that night, and the stench was becoming unbearable. Joan went upstairs, ran a bath with water that was still warm and came down dressed entirely in white. We stopped at the local inn for champagne and dinner. Then she drove off to spend the night with the children, and I drove back to town. Three days later we met in Stratford and moved into the large, ugly but convenient house which Joe Reed had recently acquired for the Festival and which Joan and I occupied this and the following summer.

The weeks that followed were filled with meetings, depositions and negotiations with the insurance company and its agents. They came through handsomely, but the house, with sundry improvements, was not ready for occupancy until late in the fall, by which time we had all moved into a New York apartment. "The day Joan burned down the house" continued, for years to come, to occupy a traumatic place in the family annals.

It was a pleasure, on arriving in Stratford in mid-June, to discover that the advance sale of tickets (subscription and single) was immeasurably greater than that of the previous year. This was due in part to the success of our 1956 season, in part to our announced program of more familiar and popular plays, but, above all, to the well-advertised presence of Katharine Hepburn and Alfred Drake.

There were a number of staff changes from the previous year: Peter Zeisler had left us to go to work with Tyrone Guthrie in Minneapolis; his place as production manager was taken by Bernard Gersten. Our new general manager was Morton Gottlieb and our press representative was Frank Goodman, who had been with me first at the Federal Theatre and then at the Mercury. Virgil Thomson was once again our musical director, with a voluble Hungarian, François Jaroschy, once more in the pit. Jean Rosenthal remained our lighting designer and technical director, with Tharon Musser as her production manager and lighting associate.

Physically the Festival Stage had undergone additions and improvements. My basic aesthetic intention was to retain our stage's identity without letting it become monotonous and to gain added speed and variety in our scenic movements without loss of simplicity and strength. Added platforms and new "machinery" were devised which would move scenery and furniture (and even actors) up and down the stage without human intervention and which would, at the same time, solve the spatial problem of the Elizabethan "inner stage." Thus, rapid and striking transformations could be effected in full sight of the audience. (The council chamber in the first act of *Othello* became the exterior of the fort in Cyprus with no more delay than it took to make the light change from the gloom of the Doge's Palace to the stormy brilliance of the Mediterranean sky.)

The fact that this new "machinery" worked admirably and looked beautiful was only partial consolation for the troubled course of *Othello*. As we approached opening night, our Moor's depression, far from lifting, reached panic proportions; his mental distress was transformed into physical failure. On June 21, after our first preview, I received a telegram from Westport:

DEAR BOY SAW THE SHOW LAST NIGHT COULDN'T UNDER-
STAND HYMAN IT WILL BE TRAGIC IF YOU DON'T ASK HIM TO
USE HIS LIPS MORE IN SPEAKING INSTEAD OF GUTTURAL
TONES REGARDS.

LANGNER

I did not reply, for during our final preview, Hyman's voice had really begun to go. The local doctor diagnosed it as laryngitis, for which he could give only minor relief. At our last preview he was almost inaudible, and I sat up half the night with Jack Landau and Frank Goodman going over our alternatives—all of which were unsatisfactory. One was to postpone the opening while Earle recovered his voice. (This represented a financial disaster and a possibly serious loss of goodwill.) Another was to open on schedule but to head off the critics and try to persuade them to come to a later performance. (This too was dangerous, for with so many other festivals opening it was doubtful if we could ever get the first-string critics to return.) The third—the one I chose—was to open anyway and hope that Hyman's evident vocal distress would divert the critics' attention from his lack of power in the role of Othello.

Early on the morning of June 22 one of our stage managers drove Hyman to New York to visit the country's leading throat specialist, who, as expected, forbade him to open his mouth for a week. Under protest, he gave him emergency treatment, and that evening we opened with an Othello who was muted but audible through the first half of the play.

The reviews were about as expected. According to the *Times:*

> The third season of the American Shakespeare Festival has begun with a shining, immaculate production but a thin performance of Othello. As far as it goes the acting is intelligent and agreeable; Earle Hyman, an able actor, has played Othello long enough to know the part thoroughly, but it is an Othello without depth. . . . Alfred Drake reveals himself as a fine classical actor with a majestic presence and a bigness of performance; he plays Iago with grace, irony and fluency. Richard Waring conveys both the modesty and the panache that makes Cassio such a winning member of the human race. Dressed in gorgeous costumes, Jacqueline Brookes expresses the pride, breeding and womanly guile of Desdemona, and there's a particularly spirited, candid Emilia by Sada Thompson. What is missing?

Atkinson answered his own question the following Sunday when he wrote of "a fine but lopsided presentation in which Iago is so splendidly acted that our sympathy is with him rather than with the dull Othello," whose performance he described as "more like a chronicle in small beer than a bath in steepdown gulfs of liquid fire."

Another found it "a shock to compare his first Othello with his present performance." And Walter Kerr, after reminding his readers of Hyman's earlier performance, where he "writhed and flashed his way through a tempest of suspicion," now found him "strangling with an inner turbulence that refuses to surface. The result is that we watch the machinations of Iago with a tittering connivance that is almost approval."

Due to Miss Hepburn's late arrival, *Merchant* was not set to open till July 10. Thus we found ourselves forced to present *Othello* by itself, eight times a week, for two and a half weeks. This ordeal, which might have proved fatal, had a salutary effect on our Othello. Once the opening and the poor reviews were past, his voice and his courage slowly returned and his performance took on some of its former quality. Seeing him later in the season, John Gassner compared him with another Othello:

> Mr. Hyman actually gives more of a performance than did Paul Robeson, the most memorable Moor of our times. . . . Despite an impressive appearance, his personality seemed mercurial and nervous, whereas Robeson brought to the role a monolithic grandeur. Everybody I spoke to tried to explain Hyman's Othello; nobody tried to explain Robeson's—and nobody had to.

For my own part, though I was disappointed in the outcome of *Othello*, I had enjoyed working on it, particularly with Alfred Drake and Sada Thompson, whose Emilia was the most intelligently plotted and brilliantly executed I have ever seen—from the complacent pander of the early scenes to the unleashed, righteous fury of her ending.

This hiatus between our two openings gave me the first breathing space I had that year, and I took full advantage of it. Our home life was pleasant that summer in Joe Reed's spacious, ugly house with its large backyard, in which we gave opening-night parties and where Joan presently resumed the Sunday lunches for which she had become famed in California. And she began to make friends in the company. She spent time in the dressing rooms and paid visits, in her little red convertible Volkswagen, to the girls' dormitory (whose inmates, that summer, included Jackie Brookes, Sada Thompson and Olive Deering) and, farther afield, to the house in Lordship that housed Richard Easton and, later, Ellis Rabb, both of whom became her lasting cronies.

Our boys too seemed to be having a good time. Michael
went off every morning to his day camp; Sebastian, under
the guard of his keeper, showed off his angelic golden locks
all over the Festival grounds till finally, in exasperation, his
mother had them shorn off. I made regular trips to New
York to the Cow Barn on Fifty-seventh Street to watch over
the growth of *The Seven Lively Arts,* and Joan drove down
occasionally to supervise the repairs to the House on the Hill
and to furnish the small apartment we had taken on East
Sixty-fourth Street in preparation for my double duties during the fall and winter.

(It was a great summer for injections. Early in the season
there was a mild hepatitis scare, and gamma globulin was
administered to the entire company amid cries of pain. Other
shots were the Salk polio vaccine that had recently become
available and of which the doctor urged the company to take
advantage.)*

Rehearsing *Merchant* while playing *Othello* eight times a
week did not leave members of the company much leisure,
but they seemed to find time for swimming, sunbathing,
shopping, lovemaking and some social intercourse, most of
which took place late at night after the show in the back room
of a depressing bar known as Ryan's—frequented more by
Joan than by me. If the tone of the summer was generally
more relaxed and playful than that of the previous year, this
was due mainly to the influence of Miss Hepburn, who arrived during the last week of our *Othello* rehearsals. Though
she remained fairly separate, her presence in our midst was
pervasive and inescapable.

When she had agreed to come to Stratford for the summer,
Langner had offered her a number of historic houses. She
chose instead a red broken-down fisherman's shack built out
over the Housatonic River, which, at that point, swollen by

* This gave rise to an agonizing conflict in the mind of one female
member of the company. Word had gone out that these polio shots
were of dubious value to adults over the age of forty. This lady, who
was terrified of injections, spent anguished days trying to decide
which was worse—to admit her true age or submit to the dreaded
shot.

the tides, runs wide and strong into Long Island Sound. Having spent some of her own money making it habitable, she moved into this cramped dwelling while Phyllis Wilbourne, her companion and secretary, occupied a room with a local family across the road. Here Kate lived alone all summer except for occasional visits from her brother and her own rare forays into New York or to visit her family in Connecticut. According to a reporter who wrote a piece about her for a national magazine:

> She sleeps in a screened-in porch where, early in the morning she hears the birds call from a marsh across the river and underneath her the water laps gently at the pilings. The other day she spied a white heron. She has a red outboard motorboat. Recently when the wind gauge was registering seventy miles an hour in gusts, she was in her boat getting drenched by the water and revelling in it.

In her contacts with the company Kate was friendly but wholly professional. She had her favorites, but her favors were bestowed, generally, only on those whose work or character she respected. She admired audacity and strength in others; any show of weakness or fear or undue complication brought out the worst in her. She was opinionated and bossy, and in her determination to have her way she used charm and the pressure of her prestige in equal proportions. Landau, who fell instantly and totally under her spell, was putty in her strong, slender hands. Even Rouben, with his artistic integrity and mulish obstinacy, was swayed in his scenic designs for *Merchant* by her romantic and somewhat old-fashioned conception of the play.

But where Kate's influence was really decisive was in the matter of morale. Here she proved an unqualified asset. The conscientiousness of her professional behavior, the fact that, from the first day of rehearsal, she was line-perfect, the first to arrive and the last to leave, a model of dedicated and concentrated energy—all this had a salutary effect on members of the company, who (though some of them may have questioned her presence in the beginning) now derived com-

1 2

Lawrence Langner (2) and his dream, the American Shakespeare Festival Theatre (1) at Stratford, Connecticut. Our benefactor, Joseph Vernor Reed (3), left. (4) The stage house under construction.

3

4

GORLANOFF STUDIO: MILA

5

(5) Rehearsing the 1956 season of ASFTA. Second from left, Jack Landau; seated, Arnold Moss. Ter-Arutunian's "epic" costumes (6) for *King John*, and (7) the "slats" in the background.

6

EILEEN DARBY: GRAPHIC HOUSE

7

8 9

TWO PHOTOS: FRED FEHL

10

Othello (8) with Earle Hyman, left, and Alfred Drake. (9) Jacqueline Brookes as Desdemona, left, and Sada Thompson as Emilia. (10) Norman Lloyd and J.H. during rehearsals of *The Taming of the Shrew*. Mike Kellin as Sly the Tinker (11) looking down on the wedding feast.

11

12

13

The Golden Bridge in *The Merchant of Venice* (12). Hepburn and Carnovsky in the trial scene (13).

OWEN HJERPE

(14) J.H., Kate Hepburn, Jack Landau and Lawrence Langner in 1957. (15) Hepburn and Alfred Drake in *Much Ado* on the Rio Grande.

15

17
18

(16) *Hamlet* in 1958, the Play Scene: Ellis Rabb as the Player King, foreground, and on the dais, Richard Easton (Osric), Geraldine Fitzgerald (Gertrude), Fritz Weaver (Hamlet), Morris Carnovsky (Claudius), Hiram Sherman (Polonius) and Earle Hyman (Horatio). (19) *A Winter's Tale*, a "cartoon carnival," with Dorothy Jeakins' "tarot" costumes (17 and 18).

19

A Midsummer Night's Dream. The New York Times wondered whether "in the active history of the play there has ever been a better team of comics" to play the rude mechanicals (20): William Hickey, Ellis Rabb, Will Geer, Morris Carnovsky, Severn Darden, Hiram Sherman. (21) "Good night unto you all": Richard Waring, June Havoc, Nancy Wickwire, Jack Bittner, Inga Swenson, Barbara Barrie, Richard Easton, James Olson. Designed by Thea Neu.

Sunday at 5 on channel 2
The Seven Lively Arts

the new dramatic hour featuring **JOHN CROSBY**, the noted television critic, as narrator, presents a sweeping panorama of romance in America from the fringed flappers of the Twenties to the Rock 'n' Roll passions of the Television Age.

THE CHANGING WAYS OF LOVE

by the world's most improbable, but most eager authority

S. J. PERELMAN

22

SUNDAY three prominent reporters of the American scene — S. J. Perelman, John Crosby and Mike Wallace—provide a fascinating picture of the variations in style, language and behavior of three generations of lovers, as reflected in life, literature and Hollywood. This lively exploration of the most popular of all the arts presents the great screen lovers from Valentino to Dean in selected film footage from their most famous scenes; re-creates famous romantic moments from the works of F. Scott Fitzgerald, Clifford Odets and Reginald Rose; and dramatizes the influences of the Twentieth Century on our amorous attitudes, with a cast featuring Piper Laurie, Jason Robards, Jr., Rip Torn and Dick York.

ON FUTURE SUNDAYS "The Seven Lively Arts," conceived and developed by the distinguished theatrical and motion picture producer, John Houseman, will recapture the exciting creative achievements of our time in journalism and jazz, fiction and fashions, music, painting and the dance and the popular arts of politics, sports and evangelism.

NEXT WEEK be sure to see how one of America's greatest writers developed the type of fictional hero that has made his novels famous the world over. Don't miss "The World of Nick Adams," the unique and compelling dramatization of five famous stories by Ernest Hemingway.

CBS TELEVISION NETWORK ⊚

UPI

23

24

1957–58. "The Seven Lively Arts," our opening show (22) with John Crosby (23) as narrator and Hubbell Robinson (24) as executive producer.

25

26

1959. *Romeo and Juliet*, the Capulets' ball (25)
with Richard Easton and Inga Swenson. (26)
Aline MacMahon as the Nurse. (27) Joan
and John Houseman at an opening-night
party.

27

28

1960. The Professional Theatre Group of the UCLA Extension: (28) *The Prodigal*, (29) J.H. directing, (30) Robert Ryan in *Murder in the Cathedral*.

29

30

31

32

(31) *U.S.A.* by John Dos Passos, adapted and directed by Paul Shyre, with Nina Foch, William Windom, John Astin. (32) "Madame Spivy" as Madame Pace in *Six Characters in Search of an Author.* (33) Two of the Three Sisters, Nina Foch and Pippa Scott, with Gloria Grahame as Natasha and James Joyce as the Baron.

33

34   35

1961. *All Fall Down:* (34) Brandon de Wilde and Warren Beatty; (35) William Inge at MGM during work on the script. *Two Weeks in Another Town:* (36) Vincente Minnelli, Kirk Douglas and Cyd Charisse in Rome.

36

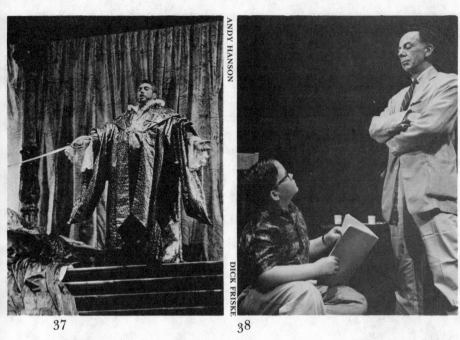

37 38

(37) Mario Del Monaco's *Otello* in Dallas. (38) Henry Jones as The Child Buyer. (39) A rehearsal of *The Iceman Cometh* by the Theatre Group, with a cast including (at either end of the table) Martin Balsam and James Dunn; also John Anderson, William Rooney, Alan Carney, Jared Barclay, June Ericson, Nina Talbot, Telly Savalas and Ed Asner.

39

40

41

1963. The Theatre Group rehearsing *Antigone* (40) with John Kerr, Joanna Barnes and Mariette Hartley as Antigone. (41) Ethel Winant. (42) *The Cool of the Day:* Jane Fonda and Peter Finch in Greece.

42

44

43   45

(43) Anne Francis with Jack Albertson as Skid in *Burlesque*. (44) Denis Deegan. (45) Morris Carnovsky making up for the opening scene of *King Lear* (46) at UCLA.

46

47

(47) J.H. with Gordon Davidson during *Lear*. (48) Sebastian
and Michael at the beach, 1964. (49) Joan bids farewell to
Malibu.

48

49

forting reassurance from their association with a major star to whom they knew they owed the exhilaration of the full and enthusiastic houses to which they found themselves playing throughout the summer.

(One personal note: Kate's long romance with Spencer Tracy was well known to the world and to the company. She spoke of him openly and always with a mingling of loyalty, tenderness and admiration. We all shared this admiration and hoped that he would presently appear among us. Several times that summer Kate joyfully announced his imminent arrival, then reported that he had been detained or prevented. Finally, during *Much Ado,* the great day came when Kate, with a young girl's enthusiasm, proclaimed that this time Spencer was really coming. His plane ticket was bought and all arrangements were made. On the evening of his arrival—carefully chosen as an *Othello* day—she drove off alone, in a state of high excitement that she made no attempt to conceal, to Kennedy Airport to meet him. Soon after she had left there was a phone call from California. Somehow, on the way to Burbank, Spencer had got lost and missed his plane. He never did appear.)

Rehearsals for *Merchant* had gone comparatively smoothly, with Landau fighting a rearguard action for some of his own ideas. What might have been a problem was avoided by the circumstance that, except for their final confrontation in court, Portia and Shylock never appear onstage together. This meant that Jack could rehearse Kate and Carnovsky separately in their own styles and with their own very different approaches to the play. Kate was present occasionally at Morris' rehearsals, but her manners were perfect and she seldom, directly or through Landau, attempted to influence or even to comment on a conception of Shylock that differed radically from the baroque manner in which Robert Helpmann had played the part on their tour of Australia. When Portia and the Jew finally did meet in the Doge's court, her very personal and surprisingly subdued rendering of the famous "Mercy" speech (in which she never acknowledged and seemed barely aware of her antagonist's presence) could not fail to affect and condition Shylock's behavior in his climactic scene. Perforce, he accepted her version and then went on to play the rest of the scene in his own way.

The Merchant of Venice opened on July 10 to mixed notices and phenomenal business. The popular press liked us. The *Mirror* announced: "The Merchant of Venice Is Great with Kate," and the veteran Chapman in the *News* pronounced it "the best production of the Festival. It is crisp, well-balanced, admirably acted and very beautiful to see." Brooks Atkinson was off on vacation, but Walter Kerr, representing the "class" press, described it as

> a great toasted marshmallow of a production, crisp and golden to look at and soft inside. The surface is burnished till it dazzles like a graceful Sunday morning pastorale. . . . Miss Hepburn is a highly giddy adolescent who has been reading far too many novels. . . . I wish I knew what she had in mind for Shakespeare's quickwitted maiden. . . .

Of her delivery of the "Mercy" speech he wrote: ". . . she so breaks it up that she seems literally to have forgotten it."

But there was one subject on which there was unanimous agreement: Carnovsky's Shylock. According to Kerr:

> There is dignity both in the person and in the performance. Mr. Carnovsky does not beg for sympathy—an approach that finally gets him more sympathy than most Shylocks. Pictorially the actor is superb: a rigid Titan as he walked into court, at all times a menace. Verbally, too, he is unfailingly clear.

Lewis Funke in the *Times* reported of Carnovsky that "he has delivered to us a performance that is a beautiful counterpoint of comedy, romance, melodrama and pathos." Henry Hewes described it as "the occasion for the best major performance in the three-year history of the Festival." Finally, John Gassner affirmed that "if ever there was a better Shylock than Carnovsky's in the entire stage history of *The Merchant of Venice*, it is not apparent to me from my personal experience or my reading," adding that "he has rendered him a completely comprehensible man capable of wringing a sympathy that Shakespeare, writing in the time he did, could hardly have intended."*

It was due in large part to Carnovsky's performance that, with the exception of one or two crank letters from persons who had not seen the show and one small demonstration outside the theatre before a performance, no serious opposition or complaint was provoked by our production of *Merchant*.

Generally admired were the Motley† costumes and Rouben's scenery, including the vast, golden Venetian bridge that spanned the stage, and our swiftly moving new "machines." But even here Kerr found cause for complaint:

> When so much filler is poured upon a stage, it is usually because someone had noticed that there is a gap to fill. When a character must be followed, flanked and flamboyantly supported by an acre of picture-book scenery, there is always the suspicion that no real character, capable of holding the stage for himself and for Shakespeare, existed in the first place. And I found, as I watched the clouds of muslin floating by, that I didn't for a minute believe that Portia existed anywhere—not even in the fairy-tale universe director Jack Landau seems deliberately to seek.

Kate took her notices in stride (she was quite accustomed to them). So did the trustees of the Festival, who found in the lines at our box office and the enthusiasm of our audiences more than sufficient compensation for a few critical reservations.

It was Kate's idea to move *Much Ado About Nothing* from fifteenth-century Italy to nineteenth-century Texas, and she supported it with a large illustrated history of the King Ranch that she presented to the directors of the Festival. There is

* He cited, as an instance, the moment when "in the midst of his grief, he breaks out in a magnificently ludicrous dance of glee. . . . This only makes the characterization more complete, and when Shylock finally leaves the court, he is an unforgettable picture of a human made small by his own malevolence."
† "Motley" at this time was the trade name for the creations of the British designer Elizabeth Montgomery.

no obvious or conventionally correct place or period for a play that contains characters with names as varied as Benedick, Leonato, Don John, Hero, Borachio, Balthazar and Dogberry. The great house with its flocks of armed and unarmed servants; the comic-opera plots and forays that motivate the action but make no sense at all; the Catholic morality surrounding the courtship of the ingenue, Hero, and the exaggerated sense of family honor; finally, the translation of Dogberry from rural constable to Texas sheriff with a gaudy star on his chest: these all made perfect sense on the banks of the Rio Grande, not to mention the picturesque military and civil costumes that Rouben could now design for us. (The girls in their mantillas were ravishing; in their tight embroidered pants and jackets, our men looked like a troupe of sexy bullfighters.)*

For *Othello*, Virgil Thomson had composed some Venetian fanfares and military flourishes and a nice version of "Willow, Willow," and he had followed Kate's romantic mood in the Belmont scenes of the *Merchant*. Now (with the exception of one lovely serenade specially composed for our countertenor Russell Oberlin) Virgil went Pop-Hispanic, with only slightly disguised versions of "La Cucaracha" and "Golondrina," performed with gusto by our Connecticut musicians under the direction of their Hungarian conductor.

For scenery we used yet another variation of Rouben's basic set. Upstage center stood a solid two-story hacienda with an overhanging red-tile roof; this was related to the familiar wooden walls of the Festival Stage by the fact that it too was entirely built of those same "slats," but surfaced in stucco and

---

* In an "ad hominem" critique of our season Eric Bentley included some pertinent observations on the subject of style in Shakespearean production. After citing the "healthy influence exerted by the Mercury's modern-dress *Julius Caesar* in wiping away the stale conventions of nineteenth century production," he pointed out that the "stalwarts of that movement are today in a very powerful position; they are the revolutionary party become the government. Like all such parties they propose to go on being revolutionary—that is, to adhere to what was revolutionary in their youth. . . . They consider the stylistic problem solved; the only problem now being how to bring their work before ever larger audiences."

painted white. No house curtain was used. In its place stood two sections of wall seven feet high, also built of stuccoed slats and pushed on and off in telescoping slabs by a swarm of barefooted, strawhatted peons.* This gave us an exciting opening for the play: As Don Pedro's army, with Benedick and Claudio at its head, marched down the aisle and then onstage to a martial version of "La Cucaracha," these great gates swung open, revealing the courtyard of the *estancia*, its steps and galleries crowded with cheering, flower-tossing ladies—among them Hero and Beatrice.

For the first time in almost a year Jack Landau and I were back to co-directing. It was a relief not to be carrying the entire burden of such an elaborate production, staged, of necessity, in such a limited number of work hours. Fortunately, *Much Ado* is broken up into parts that we were able to rehearse separately, including the comedy scenes and the tempestuous wooing of Beatrice and Benedick which forms the heart of the play and requires many hours of private and intimate rehearsal. And here we ran into one rather curious and unpredictable complication—one that related to the personalities of our two stars and to our own status as their respective trainers.

Landau was Hepburn's champion. The two of them had established an unequal but workable partnership during *Merchant* that was about to be disturbed by my appearance on the scene. (My own relations with Kate were amicable but wary. I was not convinced that, after *Othello,* she entirely trusted me as a director, while she, on her part, must have sensed that my admiration of her performance as Portia was not unqualified.)

Drake, on the other hand, was my boy. Benedick should have been a cinch for him, but now it was his turn to run into a personal problem which I found myself called upon to resolve. Under the skilled and attractive personality that had permitted him to score in such varied parts as Curley, Petru-

---

* For the most part these were student-apprentices. Among those who later grew more or less famous in one way or another were Dick Cavett, Conrad Bromberg, James Cahill and Michael Lindsay-Hogg.

chio and the beggar in *Kismet* there beat the heart of a proud and ardent Italian baritone. In all his appearances since *Oklahoma* he had been top banana; in the best tradition of the musical stage, it had been his habit, whenever possible, to extend his romantic stage association with his current leading lady into real life. I am sure that he cherished no serious hope of adding Miss Hepburn to his conquests, but he did, I suspect, entertain visions of a gallant, glamorous stage relationship with his fellow star.

Kate's idea of fun was altogether different. She loved a fight, a contest of wills, a form of mental Indian wrestling in which her regard for her antagonist varied in direct proportion to the energy with which he returned her assaults. With her Benedick, she may have felt that such backstage sparring would add spice and vitality to their stormy onstage courtship. When Drake stubbornly refused her challenge, she pressed her mocking provocations, hoping to sting him into some kind of suitable masculine retort. Alfred refused to play her game and made it clear that he found her behavior unfeminine and unprofessional.

These one-sided skirmishes extended into rehearsal. In their scenes together Drake was a polished, witty, somewhat conventional and slightly pompous wooer; Kate countered with readings that were so outrageous and bits of mischief so brash and unexpected that they threw him off balance—as she intended them to. And she laughed at him in front of the company.

It was not until I went downstairs after one such scene that I became fully aware of the gravity of the situation. Kate, whose dressing room I visited first, was weary but exhilarated —like an athlete after a stiff contest in which she felt herself the winner. When I went to Alfred's room he handed me his resignation from the cast of *Much Ado*. I reminded him that he had a contract; he declared that he refused to work with that bitch.

That storm blew over presently and Kate tempered her aggressions. But she and Alfred never entirely forgave each other. Onstage they finally became an accomplished, humorous and attractive couple, but they never quite formed the team they might have been.

Otherwise rehearsals went swimmingly. We were pleased with our cast and the new members of the company—Lois Nettleton, Richard Waring and Larry Gates. And once again, working feverishly to get the show ready in the insufficient time at our disposal, we all benefited from Kate's enthusiastic, schoolgirl, busybody and seemingly inexhaustible energy. Her eyes were painfully infected from diving into the polluted waters of a Venetian canal during the making of *Summertime*, her latest movie. But this did not stop her. She hardly ever left the theatre, and her nose was in everything, from costumes to dance steps (set by John Butler and amended by Katharine Hepburn). She was bursting with ideas, some very good and some terrible. In fact, quite a bit of Landau's time and mine, during those three frantic weeks, was taken up with moderating or discarding some of her more outrageous inventions—for herself and for almost everyone else in the cast.

In working with her, I made a fascinating discovery about star quality in general and hers in particular. Kate had learned—instinctively or, more likely, at the knee of Constance Collier, who had been her coach for many years—that stardom is achieved through beauty, intelligence, courage and energy but, above all, through the bravura that an audience comes to expect from its favorite performers. In every star role there are one or more opportunities for such peaks. If not, they must be created—as they were, in different ways, by Duse, Bernhardt, Terry and all the others.

In every performance I have seen of Katharine Hepburn's, including the two she gave for us at Stratford that summer, such peaks occurred—carefully planned and deliberately executed. In *Merchant* there were two. One was her delivery of the great "Mercy" speech. An aria was expected of her. Instead she decided to surprise her audience with a delivery so subdued that, according to one critic, she sounded "as though she were dictating a letter to a terribly efficient secretary." It was a disaster, but it caused a lot of talk. The other was her first entrance in Belmont, which, according to the Bard, calls for two ladies to enter the stage in quiet conversation. Kate decided otherwise:

> A Chinese bungalow rolls silently forward on the dimlit stage. It has barely come to a stop when the door bursts open and Miss Hepburn appears in the brilliantly lit portal. . . . Ravishing to look at in her undernourished way, she swoops around the stage and, at last, falls into a pool of satin on the floor . . .

to rapturous applause.

In *Much Ado* Miss Hepburn selected Hero's abortive wedding as her great moment. It is a justly celebrated reversal scene in which the frivolous Beatrice turns suddenly serious and demands of her lover that he kill Claudio, her cousin's betrayer. Kate played it as grand tragedy—raging, kicking hassocks around, and howling like a banshee. It was hysterical, insincere, embarrassing and utterly unbelievable, but it shook up the audience and confirmed her star status.

With this one exception I loved her Beatrice: she was quick, brilliant, delicious to look at and almost entirely sexless. I had the feeling that in this respect she was truer to the intention of the Bard than many of her more voluptuous sisters and that she came far closer than they did to the way in which Beatrice must have been played by a boy actor in Shakespeare's own company.

Much Ado About Nothing opened on August 8 to enthusiastic houses and fine reviews. Brooks Atkinson, back from vacation, felt that the transference of the play to the American Southwest was "not only shrewd but fresh and joyous and admirably suited to the personality of our leading lady."

> Miss Hepburn is an extraordinary star, an actress who commands our audience with glamor and personal magnetism. She is beautiful, debonair, piquant, with a modern personality. Her lovely-looking and humorous-minded Beatrice is one of her best characterizations, and the Benedick who has been snared into loving this sharp-

tongued hoyden is one of Mr. Drake's finest jobs. He is, by turns, sharp, ironic, lightly philosophic, a man who protests his devotion to bachelorhood too much to be believed. . . . His Benedick gives us the ironic experience of the play.

Of the rest of our "spirited cast" he reported that they performed "with gaiety and lightness."*

As a result, our season was extended, by popular demand, for one week beyond its announced closing date of September 7. On the following Sunday, in his "News on the Rialto" column in *The New York Times,* Lewis Funke observed:

There are few satisfactions in the theatre equal to that of playing on a winning team. That satisfaction in overflowing measure came to those connected with the American Shakespeare Theatre Festival this season. This afternoon the final curtain falls at Stratford on what has been a most triumphal season. . . . The last seven weeks were played to one hundred percent of capacity to a total of over one hundred and fifty thousand people during the season.†

Beyond these statistics there was another, deeper satisfaction—the sense of pride and the intoxicating pleasure which swept over me each time I stood or sat in the back of that crowded house and breathed the heady atmosphere of those sold-out performances.

It was not a typical theatre audience. No questionnaires

* Dr. Koekeritz of Yale gave us limited approval: "It is unorthodox, of course, but I'm sure Shakespeare would have enjoyed it if he could have seen it. But he would have been as shocked as I was when I heard Messína consistently mispronounced as Méssina. The stress is on the middle syllable; the 'i' is pronounced as in 'machine.' "

† According to *Variety,* "the twelve-week season—which included 48 showings of *Othello,* 35 of the *Merchant* and 25 of the belatedly installed *Much Ado*—showed a total box-office gross of more than double our 1956 figure, with an operating profit of $170,000. After paying off production costs this shows a net profit for the summer of around $10,000." However, counting our year-round operating expenses, mortgage payments on the theatre and other fixed charges, this still represented an annual deficit of over a quarter of a million dollars.

were passed out that season, but it was my impression that for many of our audience this was the only live theatrical production they had seen in recent months, and that for more than two thirds of them it was the first professional performance of a Shakespearean play they had ever attended. This made their reactions particularly interesting—and rewarding.

Without question, many of them were confused. Yet, surprisingly, after the first few bewildering moments, they never seemed bored. And when the long show was over and they walked out into the open air toward their cars and waiting buses, I felt confident that they were leaving our theatre richer than when they entered. For close to three hours they had been exposed to language which, even if they understood only part of it, could not fail to impress them with its power and beauty; they had met striking (and sometimes familiar) characters engaged in conflicts that were no less violent and relationships that were no less moving and empathic than those they were used to viewing in their local movie theatres or on the screens of their newly acquired television sets. Love, death, ambition, politics, fights, dance music, colorful costumes, jokes, moral judgments and even, occasionally, philosophy—all these elements were offered as part of the dramatic action. Add to this the exhilarating sense, on both sides of the footlights, of having been touched—across the gulf of three and a half centuries—by genius.

These fantasies did much to compensate us for the grueling labor, the hopes and terrors, dreams, hugger-mugger and compromises that went into the long-term planning and arduous execution of each successive Festival season.

More concrete and satisfying was the encouragement we continued to receive in the press. John Gassner, in his summation of the theatrical year, described ours as "the best repertory company we have had in the United States since 1926 when the Theatre Guild had its short-lived Acting Company," and went on to raise what, to me, was still the critical issue:

The difficulties of maintaining a permanent company for a three-month season each year are enormous. But, when the results prove as good as they did during the past season, one's appetite for a year-round repertory theatre is whetted.

CHAPTER III

1957-1958

THE SEVEN LIVELY ARTS

FOR SEVERAL MONTHS I had been dividing my time unevenly between the Festival Theatre and the CBS Cow Barn on West Fifty-seventh Street, where I was trying to crank up the vast machinery required to get *The Seven Lively Arts* off the ground. This meant hours of driving, several times a week, at odd times of the day and night, between Stratford and Manhattan, along the lovely but narrow Merritt Parkway, trying to give the impression to each of my employers that I was exclusively theirs.

Following the windup of our 1957 Stratford season, my time was increasingly devoted to preparations for *The Seven Lively Arts*. We were not scheduled to go on the air until early November, but in the mass media the weeks have a way of racing by, and suddenly our opening broadcast seemed to be just around the corner.

Much of my shuttling, that fall, was between the Cow Barn

and the executive offices of the Columbia Broadcasting System on Madison, where Hubbell Robinson reigned as vice-president in charge of production. I had known him for years; first, as an agency man and husband of Terry Lewis, with whom I had written Lipton Tea weekly radio dramas for Helen Hayes. From there he had gone over to CBS as head of radio production and, after the war, into television, where, with William Paley's support, he had established himself as one of the most potent executives of what is remembered as the Golden Age of Television.

He had come up the hard way, through the advertising business, and his uniform was still that of an agency man— the tight, well-tailored dark suits; the sober, sincere ties; the bowler hat; and, above all, the set, emotionless look that (together with the unusually dark-red coloring of his face) had earned him the nickname of "the Wooden Indian."

He had a reputation for toughness that he worked hard to maintain, but I always found him intelligent, sensitive and far more cultivated than he chose to appear—with a special passion for firemen's helmets, of which he had a fine collection, and for the military history of the American Civil War. Above all I remember him for the unusual loyalty with which he treated his associates, including myself, even under the most trying circumstances.

A number of subjects had been selected for *The Seven Lively Arts* during the spring and summer, and the slow work of developing them was under way. Robert Herridge was far advanced on his Hemingway project, and Northshield had spent time in the Deep South, shooting footage of some primitive revivalists he had discovered. Most of my own energy, from now on, was devoted to assembling and shaping material for "The Changing Ways of Love," which had been set as our opening show.

It was an unusually dense and complicated show—Hubbell's idea of a flashy opener. I had made no serious attempt to talk him out of it. It was, at first sight, a provocative notion. It was also a dangerous one with which to start a series that was, in itself, suspect and controversial. This, perhaps, is what attracted me to it and why I assigned it to my former

Hollywood associate, Jud Kinberg, with every intention of working closely on it myself.

The idea, vaguely outlined by Hubbell, and developed over the summer by Kinberg and myself with numerous outside suggestions, was to investigate the changing sexual, social, romantic and sentimental taste patterns of American men and women over the past thirty years, as revealed and exploited through the media of theatre, film, songs, dance, radio and, finally, television.

Right there we made our first grievous error. By cramming so many forms and styles into a fifty-three-minute show we made it almost impossible to maintain any style at all. And, in our growing enthusiasm for our disparate material, we continued to add to it till our accumulated elements ended by confusing and canceling one another.

"The Changing Ways of Love," as we conceived it, was to be divided into three acts: (1) the Jazz Age of the booming twenties, (2) the Great Depression, (3) World War II and its aftermath.

Besides our master of ceremonies, each section would have a different, specialized narrator who would review and illustrate the characteristic social and erotic modes of the period. And each would contain a dramatized boy-and-girl scene by a well-known author, typical of the sexual-emotional confrontations of the time.

In theory it all seemed lively and fascinating. It still does. Unfortunately, almost no one connected with "The Changing Ways of Love" had the slightest experience with "live" television. In my arrogant assumption that I could move freely from medium to medium I chose to ignore the fact that live television was a highly specialized form of dramatic communication. As practiced by the bright young men who were producing and directing weekly shows such as *Climax, Studio One, Philco Playhouse* and *Playhouse 90,* it had its own rules and its own aesthetic virtues and limitations of which Kinberg and I knew almost nothing. As a result, our entire concept of "The Changing Ways of Love" was based on the assumption that what was essentially a live show could be directed and edited as though it were a film. This was an error. The post-facto editing that is achieved by a filmmaker at his Moviola is quite different from the instant selections that must be made by the director in a TV control room from three or four simultaneous images he sees on his monitors. There is an irrevocable immediacy about live television that could not survive the conditions we were trying to impose on it.

Throughout the TV world at the time there was a sharp schism between the users of film and the practitioners of live television. Within two years, the introduction of videotape would change much of that, but in 1957 there was still what amounted to a caste system within which the users of electronic cameras considered themselves a much advanced and superior group, engaged in a purer and more legitimate activity than the users of film, for whom the TV tube was merely an extension of the motion-picture screen. Within our organization the former were represented by Robert Herridge—originally from the theatre and now a fanatical purist for live television drama. In that capacity he must have looked on our projected potpourri of film, still photography, documentary, cartoons and live TV with a mixture of artistic outrage and the hopeful expectation that such a hybrid contraption would crash ignominiously on its first flight.

The first cloud in the future of *The Seven Lively Arts* appeared late in the summer when, TV having run into what was known as a "soft" market, no commercial sponsor had yet come forward to pick up the bill. In theory, ours was a prestige show which the network was prepared to carry as a "sustaining" program; in fact the absence of sponsors created a nervousness that, in spite of Hubbell's consistent executive calm, added a disagreeable element of uncertainty to our preparations. Then, three months before we went on the air, the network suddenly announced that the number of our projected shows had been reduced from twenty-six to sixteen.

In the circumstances, the selection of our master of ceremonies assumed a vital importance. *Omnibus*, the only similar show on television, had been greatly aided by the presence, intelligence and urbane delivery of Alistair Cooke, the

Manchester Guardian's lively and knowledgeable U.S. correspondent.* CBS set its sights higher; it wanted a big "name."

Gilbert Seldes, author of the famous book whose title we were using, had been ruled out by the authorities as abrasive and unphotogenic. Another candidate was Clifton Fadiman, a dual celebrity as book reviewer for *The New Yorker* and the smooth m.c. of the successful and long-running *Information Please* television program. It was a safe but conventional choice, and the network's best brains soon came up with a far flashier suggestion.

Nineteen fifty-seven and 'fifty-eight were the years in which the quiz shows reached the peak of their popularity. The most successful of these pseudointellectual contests was *Twenty-One,* on which a young scholar named Charles Van Doren had recently emerged to win the hearts of the entire nation. He had everything in his favor—youth, looks, distinction, erudition and a name that was widely known among educated persons. He was even sexy in a scholarly way. By midsummer (after epic struggles in which he defeated a sophisticated jockey and a well-informed but unlikable professor) his winnings exceeded one hundred thousand dollars and he had made the cover of *Time.* At this point it occurred to Hubbell and the network that Charles Van Doren would make the perfect master of ceremonies for *The Seven Lively Arts.* For my own part, I could think of no serious objection to him, and a luncheon in the Oak Room confirmed my favorable impression. He and I had much to talk about: I knew his father and uncle and, on the distaff side, his aunt and mother. (Dorothy Van Doren had run the English feature desk on the Voice of America.) I reported to Hubbell that I approved, and contract negotiations were begun.

Then, suddenly, the sky darkened. *Look* came out with an article suggesting that there might be skullduggery on the quiz shows, that favorite candidates were being coached and given advance notice of subjects and questions. At the slight-

* He later became an even more familiar figure as host of *Masterpiece Theatre.*

est suggestion that young Mr. Van Doren's encyclopedic knowledge might not be entirely his own, the world turned against him; enthusiasm changed to fury, admiration to contempt. Frank Hogan, New York's perennial district attorney, summoned him before a grand jury, and the nation's favorite young savant was exposed and stripped of his ill-gotten gains.*

Long before that, his contract with *The Seven Lively Arts* had been torn up and we found ourselves once again looking for a suitable interlocutor. Fadiman was no longer available and things were beginning to look grim when Hubbell had his second inspiration. He invited me to come over and share his vision. "What about John Crosby?" he asked.

Today there is no exact, contemporary counterpart of John Crosby. He belonged to the Golden Age of Television and, as critic and columnist for the *New York Herald Tribune* and its syndicate, he had established a national reputation for literate, independent and fearless reviewing of the new medium. His nearest rival was Jack Gould of the *Times;* but Gould lacked the individuality and the wit that made Crosby the terror of networks and advertisers alike.

Hubbell told me that he had got the impression, during a cocktail conversation with Crosby, that he might welcome this novel and lucrative experience. The ethics of the situation did not seem to bother anyone. I asked for a few days to think it over. I had never met Crosby and I wished to find out whether his charisma equaled his writing skill.

Before I had a chance, Hubbell called again and said he had gone ahead and made the deal. He also confirmed the fact that *The Seven Lively Arts* was now definitely scheduled to

---

* A deep lacuna in my moral sense is indicated by the fact that I was never able to work up the slightest lather of indignation over the quiz scandals. I was not in the least surprised to learn that data were being fed to the contestants; it would have amazed me if they weren't. Further, I felt that the TV public, having thoroughly enjoyed the excitement of these hyped-up contests, had no right to complain about the means by which that pleasurable excitement had been achieved.

go on the air Sundays at 4 P.M.—right in the middle of what had come to be known as the "intellectual ghetto" of television.

Crosby's highly publicized appointment got a dubious reception in the trade and in the press, where his position as the nation's number-one TV critic was viewed with envy by many of his colleagues. We met to discuss the nature of his function on the show: he would write and edit his own introductory material, speak it on the air and act as general consultant on the series. This last function was never fulfilled, for almost immediately a crisis arose which came to play a crucial part in the fate of *The Seven Lively Arts*.

John Crosby was myopic, and (though this was by no means abnormal or shameful) I felt that thick glasses would not add to his image as our forthright and jaunty master of ceremonies. I suggested that he visit an oculist and get a prescription for the new contact lenses that had recently come into general use. He agreed and the most expensive optician in the city was put to work on two pairs of contact lenses with the assurance that they would be ready long before the start of rehearsals.

With that hazard seemingly disposed of, I turned my attention to other, more urgent matters of production and script. We needed a writer capable of giving unity and style to so much disparate material. After much thought our choice had fallen on the celebrated humorist S. J. Perelman. He could not have been more cooperative and industrious, but, as we discovered too late on the air, his style was better suited to the printed page than to broadcasting, where his tone seemed consistently forced and overblown.

Another problem was casting the dramatic sections of our show. It was part of the basic form of "The Changing Ways of Love" that we should illustrate the sexual attitudes and conflicts between young lovers during our three decades in scenes by popular authors of their respective periods— F. Scott Fitzgerald, Clifford Odets and one of TV's most successful writers, Tad Mosel. Partly for budgetary reasons and also because it seemed more stylish and interesting, we decided to have the three girls' parts played by the same actress, preferably one with something of a reputation in the movies. After much long-distance conversation with reluctant agents, our choice fell on Piper Laurie. Her career in films had been flashy but brief. Despite the unfortunate name they had fastened on her in Hollywood, she had a mind and a beauty of her own that had never been properly used. On our show she proved to be a sincere, hard-working and intelligent young actress, capable of adapting herself to the very different styles of the pieces we had chosen and of the three young men with whom we teamed her.

Finally, we were faced with the need to find a director for this unusual and complex production. Our choice of Sidney Lumet was based mainly on his proven ability to handle the three dramatic scenes that made up half of our script. In this respect he fulfilled our hopes: with Laurie he was patient and sensitive; the scenes we had selected were all of the realistic, personal and emotional kind which he was well equipped to direct through his work with the Actors' Studio. Unfortunately he was far less qualified to deal with the other elements of the show—the cartoons and montages, as well as the musical and production numbers, which required a sure hand and a sense of style that, at that stage in his career, he did not possess.

By mid-October, for better or for worse, all the elements of "The Changing Ways of Love" had been assembled. I have before me the seventy-two fading yellow multigraphed pages which (except for some red-pencil cuts and slashes that were made at the last moment) represent the final version of the show on which we had labored for so many months:

ANIMATED FILM SIGNATURE: *Greek Temple*

This was a short opening animation (commissioned from my friend John Hubley* with music by Alec Wilder) that was intended to clarify our title and to indicate, briefly and graphically, that the classical arts would be supplemented on our

---

* John Hubley was one of America's most original and distinguished animators. See *Front and Center,* pp. 125 *et seq.*

show by examples of the more "lively" contemporary and popular arts listed by Gilbert Seldes. This led into the main title, followed immediately by

FILM: *Love Goddesses*

a carefully selected and edited montage of glamorous stills of the great sex figures of the twenties, over which would be heard the offscreen voice of

JOHN CROSBY

This is the face of love. Those alabaster necks, these gleaming foreheads, these voluptuous lips and sparkling eyes have quickened the pulse and stirred the libido of millions. Whether you like it or not, consciously or unconsciously, at one time or another you have patterned your behavior, your romantic manners and attitudes after one or more of these divinities. You think not? Well, just wait and see.

By this time Crosby would have appeared in the flesh; he would outline the contents of the show and introduce the first of our three interlocutors, "the well-known humorist S. J. Perelman," whose voice would be heard over brief newsreel clips of Armistice Day 1918 before he appeared in person.

PERELMAN

Historians like Will Durant and Toynbee (not Arnold Toynbee, but Fats Toynbee, a kindly, thoughtful man who grows dahlias at a saloon on East Twenty-ninth Street) all agree on one thing: if World War I didn't exactly make the world safe for democracy, it had one salutary result—it effectively broke down the barriers between men and women.

During this, a "live" fashion show of scantily clad beauties of the twenties would swirl about him as he continued:

PERELMAN

As a reformed roué more interested in sex than in sociology and statistics, I can tell you that before the First World War it had taken an average of eighteen yards of material to make a woman's dress. In the twenties it took three. This meant statistically that the woman inside the dress was now six times as available.

The fashion show was replaced by a portrait of the young Edna St. Vincent Millay, over which we would hear:

PERELMAN (*voice over*)

The poet laureate of the period was a Vassar girl named Edna St. Vincent Millay, who crystallized the revolt of her generation in the boast that she burned the candle at both ends. She extenuated her conduct, poetically if not scientifically, on the ground that it shed a lovely light.

By now the screen would be filled with a series of John Held, Jr., drawings of the mid-twenties, followed by brief "live" demonstrations of the Charleston, the Black Bottom, the Bunny Hug and other dances of the period, executed by eight dancers choreographed by John Butler. These were followed by brief film clips of celebrated "vamps"—Gloria Swanson, Nita Naldi, Clara Bow and Pola Negri—at work, followed by a scene from *The Sheik* and *The Flesh and the Devil,* all with appropriate comment from Perelman.

From these aphrodisiac images we cut to a close-up of a radio cabinet, from which would issue the "velvety, nasal wood-notes of our first radio troubador, Rudy Vallee." This would lead us back to our live dancers—four couples in evening dress, dancing cheek to cheek on the veranda of the country club which would serve as a background for our first dramatic scene.

PERELMAN (*voice over*)

As prosperity spread over the land a new type of heroine arose—aristocratic, self-destructive figures like Iris March in *The Green Hat* and Lady Brett in *The Sun Also Rises.* Capricious, well-heeled and headed full-tilt for doom, they followed the pattern of what F. Scott Fitzgerald called "The Beautiful and Damned."

By now the dancers would have disappeared, leaving a boy and a girl in evening dress alone together to play a fragment of Scott Fitzgerald's *Winter Dreams:*

> JUDY
> *(after a pause)*
> Do you mind if I weep a little?

> DEXTER
> I'm afraid I'm boring you.

> JUDY
> You're not. I like you. But I've had a terrible day. There
> was a man I cared about and this afternoon he told me
> out of a clear sky that he was as poor as a churchmouse.
> *(after a beat)*
> Does this sound horribly mundane?

Their scene ran for seven minutes and ended with Judy and
Dexter going off to make love.

> PERELMAN
> As with so many of Fitzgerald's people, they didn't get
> married and they didn't live happily ever after. Without
> any real material or psychic problems, they chose to cre-
> ate imaginary ones with which to bedevil themselves.

*During his speech a ticker-tape machine has appeared to one
side and begun to chatter quietly. It grows louder as he walks
toward it.*

> PERELMAN
> It was a wonderful world while it lasted.

*Perelman has reached the machine, which is loud now. He takes
one look at the tape and reacts in horror at what he sees.*

> FADE OUT

Such was the first act of "The Changing Ways of Love." It
was overloaded with ideas and full of energy and invention.
But when it went on the air from CBS Studio 64 at 4 P.M.
Eastern Standard Time on Sunday, November 3, 1957, a
number of things happened that had not been foreseen in
the pages of our script.

We have left John Crosby with the optometrist, being
tested for contact lenses. Delivery had been promised in time

for him to get accustomed to them before he went on the air. That promise was kept. At our first reading he appeared without his tortoiseshell glasses (a vast improvement in his public "persona"), and though he complained of some discomfort from his new lenses, they enabled him to read the script without difficulty. During the next few days, as we started to stage the show, he had no problem reading his cue cards* but continued to complain vaguely about his lenses.

On Friday, November 1, halfway through our first on-camera rehearsal and forty-nine hours before air time, Crosby demanded to speak with me in private and informed me that his lenses were driving him mad—to the point where he had decided to appear without them. I told him I thought it was a great pity but, if that's how he felt, he should go back to wearing his glasses. He said he wasn't going to do that either. He assured me that his sight was not that bad and, besides, he had a prodigious memory and was entirely confident of his ability to m.c. the show without either glasses or lenses. I was against it, but John was adamant and there was no way to sway him.

The atmosphere in the studio was tense that Sunday but not more than at most premieres of a major TV show. I was tired and nervous; Kinberg, as usual, was wallowing in anxiety and despair. Yet our dress rehearsal at noon had gone surprisingly well. Crosby as m.c. was a bit stiff, but he sounded intelligent and sincere, with a style of his own, and seemed quite capable of deciphering and/or memorizing his boob cards. At 3:55 P.M., Jud, Lumet and I retired into the control room and sat staring at the studio's electric clock as its minute hand moved toward air time. We had piles of telegrams of good wishes from both coasts.

A few seconds after four, Hubley's animation started to go out on the air. A minute and thirteen seconds later Crosby's voice was heard over our montage of goddesses. "This is the face of love," he declared.

* Also known as "boob cards," these are large sheets of cardboard held up beside or behind the camera, with the text printed in firm black lettering.

Jac Venza had done a beautiful job with his photomontage of famous beauties. When it was over we dissolved to our first close shot of Crosby in the flesh. He seemed more nervous than at dress rehearsal as he informed the nation that his name was John Crosby and that this was the opening program in a new series called *The Seven Lively Arts*. He followed this with the announcement that our first show was about love.

CROSBY

Because love is not only an art in itself but is the constant theme that runs through all the other arts. Love, theoretically, is eternal. Its objectives and techniques shouldn't change much whether you are in a penthouse or a haystack. They shouldn't, but they have. How? Let's go back to the twenties and find out. For this leg in the journey we have—

The world never found out *what* we had. For, at that moment, a ghastly thing happened. Crosby's voice stopped in midsentence and a look of abject panic came over his face. For a second or two we waited, confident that he would recover himself and go on. Instead, the face on the monitor froze; the mouth went slack, then hung open like that of a dead man. The only thing that remained alive in his sweating face were the eyes, desperately attempting to focus on the boob card that the assistant was waving in front of him. Then, as he gave up, the eyes, too, glazed into a rigid stare of utter despair.

In the control room we sat helpless and numb with horror. No one moved. Even our technical director's hands seemed frozen to the controls. (The next day, running the kinescope of the show, we clocked the time during which millions of Americans stared at the silent death mask of John Crosby. It added up to eighteen and a half seconds. It seemed like six months. And it made TV history.) Finally, like members of Sleeping Beauty's court, we sprang back to life. Orders flashed over the intercom. John Butler's dancers, warming up for their first number in a neighboring studio, were rushed onto the set. Sid Perelman, pacing nervously behind a flat, was seized and hustled before a camera which caught him in a state of bewildered alarm as Crosby's voice, partially restored, reading from a boob card that the assistant was holding directly under his nose, introduced him as "S. J. Perelman, Academy Award winner for the screenplay of *Around the World in Eighty Days* and himself a survivor of the reckless twenties." Whereupon Perelman, his glasses flashing and his voice shrill with forced gaiety, went into his act and heroically launched the first of his jokes into a void of bewilderment and despair.

PERELMAN

Historians like Will Durant and Toynbee (not Arnold Toynbee, but Fats Toynbee, a kindly, thoughtful man who grows dahlias at a saloon on East Twenty-ninth Street) . . .

In the control room we sat and let the blood flow slowly back into our bodies. We were still alive, but we were ruined and we knew it. Such a catastrophe on major network television was unprecedented and unforgivable. After such a disgrace there was only one way to go—to disappear and never come back! But, for the moment, we had no choice; we had to go on with the show and it was agony. As face after glamorous face appeared on the monitor—Swanson, Naldi, Bow, Harlow, Garbo—they all seemed to be smiling at our humiliation. The dances of the twenties were dances of death; Vallee was crooning our dirge. It was not until we were well into the erotic melancholy of *Winter Dreams* that the show finally moved back into focus.

"It was a wonderful world while it lasted," observed Perelman as the lovers went off into the dark and the busy click of the ticker tape announced to the world that the great Crash of 1929 was upon us—and that the first act of "The Changing Ways of Love" was finally and mercifully over!

A number of announcements were made during the station break. Since we still had no sponsor, most of them were "billboards" for upcoming CBS shows. During that time I ran down into the studio to restore morale, to talk to Crosby and to check on his condition. He seemed to have recovered some of his composure, or maybe he was still in shock. Still without his glasses, he looked pale but determined as he prepared for the second act.

This was simpler and tougher in tone than the first. It dealt with the Great Depression, and most of it was written and narrated by Crosby himself. "Perelman was a jazz-baby. I was a Depression-baby," he observed as he introduced the second of our live love scenes—this one from Clifford Odets' *Awake and Sing*. Moe, the small-time gangster, was played by Jason Robards, Hennie by Piper Laurie, who had just made a miraculous change of hairdo, makeup and wardrobe—from Newport to the Bronx and from the twenties to the thirties. While she and Jason were settling into the set with its unmade bed, Crosby was establishing the contrast between Fitzgerald's Judy, who "had stepped into too many cars, gone to too many dances with too many boys, been in too many places," and Odets' Hennie, "whose problem was that she'd never been anywhere and that her boys never even owned a car, so that they had to wait till the family went to the neighborhood movie to find a place to make love"—which they now proceeded to do in highly stylized Odets dialogue:

MOE

(moving toward her)

Say the word—I'll tango on a dime! Don't gimme ice when your heart's on fire!

(as Hennie struggles)

I've got enough fever to blow the whole world to hell. . . . Listen to me, Hennie! Come away! A certain place where it's moonlight and roses. We'll lay down, count stars! Hear the big ocean makin' noise. You lay under the trees. Champagne flows. . . . Baby, there's one life to live! Live it!

At the end of the scene, Crosby reappeared to explain:

Trapped by the economics of the Great Depression, Hennie's and Moe's only hope was escape—escape from the grimy realities of the world around them. And for them and millions of others the best havens of escape were the movie palaces where audiences found release from their poverty and frustration in elemental collisions between males and females:

FILM: *Edward G. Robinson hitting a dame.*
FILM: *Gable belting Barbara Stanwyck.*
FILM: *Cagney putting the grapefruit into Mae Clark's face.*

While Crosby continued his report that "among our more prosperous and respectable couples, according to the press, an equally discouraging situation prevailed," the screen was filled with a montage of James Thurber's "Battle of the Sexes," followed by a series of live male and female one-liners reflecting various forms of domestic discontent—ending with a woman on a couch. That gave Crosby his next cue:

CROSBY

Psychoanalysis was a fashionable toy of the rich in the twenties; in the thirties it became the universal panacea —for the people who could afford it. For those who couldn't—

A radio and a woman listening, a carpet-sweeper idle in her hands.

FIRST RADIO VOICE

The Romance of Helen Trent—the story of a woman who proves what so many women long to prove—that the romance of youth can exist in middle life and even beyond.

A second radio and a second woman listening idly at the sink.

SECOND RADIO VOICE

Our Gal Sunday—the story that asks the question: Can a girl from a little mining town in the West find happiness as the wife of a wealthy and titled Englishman?

A third woman listening in her bathtub.

CROSBY

The question was asked five times a week and never answered. But release from these particular tensions and anxieties came soon enough. Not from Cupid but from a somewhat unexpected source:

The image of Crosby is blotted out by a giant explosion followed by war film of German fighter planes bombing and strafing the Polish countryside.

FADE OUT

END OF ACT II.

The third act, narrated by that relentless investigator Mike Wallace, dealt with the sexual revolution brought about by World War II. John Lardner, TV critic for *The New Yorker,* recorded his moment-to-moment impressions of our show and printed them in lieu of a review:

World War II, Wallace says, has opened up new vistas in love . . . says men enjoy pinups . . . Grable . . . Lamour . . . Rita Hayworth in *Gilda* . . . Women enjoy Sinatra . . . Sinatra sings . . . 1950's dual personality and Kinsey mentioned . . . more connubial . . . Sure enough, couple in next play are married . . . Wallace speaks of courtship rites today . . . someone in film drives hotrod over cliff . . . By now no one over fifteen making love on program . . . Film of Presley . . . A voice says "deep in the ecstasies of rock-and-roll." . . . Interviews with youth . . . One boy says of Presley, "I'd like to be half what he is." And the girl says, "Naw, he's too complicated." . . . Screen-deep in teenagers but Crosby says he is now excited by the significance of *My Fair Lady* . . . maybe old-fashioned romance is coming back . . . Not likely with this mob!

At long last, by rushing the final credits, we were off the air on schedule and our ordeal was ended. Soberly we bade each other good evening and went home to wait for the worst. When I got to the apartment the phone was ringing. It was Joan in New City saying that she had enjoyed the show but wondering what had happened to Crosby. I called Hubbell. He said Mr. Paley had been disappointed but we'd do better next time. Hours later came a call from Vincente Minnelli in California to say how much he'd liked the broadcast.

Our reviews were about as expected. *Variety,* realistic as ever, pronounced the show "a lively if not entirely inspired hour. There's more to come and the final answer remains to be seen, but on the basis of this first outing CBS and the viewer have the right to be Mr. Dubious." *The New York Times* was hostile: "Romance at Random: Premiere of Seven Lively Arts Gives Confused, Inert Picture of Love."

According to Jack Gould our show "encountered the misfortune that occasionally afflicts the novice in the theatre. It dashed out on stage without first making sure it had buttoned up its culture." He added that "this love fest could have done with an extra week in New Haven."

Of the local reviews the best was Harriet van Horns. She felt that the show had "humor, pathos, vulgarity and lots of rich, foamy nostalgia. The art lay in the assembly of these elements and in the slick, knowing style of their projection." Another friend was the columnist Hy Gardner:

> I don't like to be a dissenter but I enjoyed most of the first of *The Seven Lively Arts*—when I wasn't sweating along with John Crosby . . . The format of this tricky adventure into Sunday programming is imaginative; the tongue-in-cheek documentation is delightful, the expertly edited movie-clips beguiling . . . CBS should be encouraged.

The critics' chief victim was Crosby, whose colleagues from coast to coast made no attempt to conceal their glee over his discomfiture. The kindest of them found in his "cathode baptism" comforting evidence that "critics can be human" and "should be read and not seen." They reported that "he was better at roasting than hosting," and "tense as a terrified titmouse." Others were more personal: "Crosby grunted as if in constant pain and close-ups did him few favors for they presented his face with a seemingly endless mouth which, when speaking, seemed to be pulled apart vertically by unseen strings."

One of the blessings of a television series is that it leaves you no time to brood over your failures. On the morning of November 4, sixteen hours after we had got our first show on the air, we were deep in dress rehearsals, followed by camera rehearsals, of our second—"The World of Nick

Adams." This was a loose assembly of five early stories by Ernest Hemingway, and it was Robert Herridge's answer to the hybrid complications of "Ways of Love." Directed with simplicity and feeling by Robert Mulligan, it had a fine cast of young stage actors* and earned us general approval at a time when we sorely needed it. *Variety* reported: " 'The World of Nick Adams' on *Seven Lively Arts* paid off handsomely with the aid of an excellent cast and the creation of an atmosphere faithful to the Hemingway text."

Even Crosby emerged unscathed—with little to say and plenty of time to memorize and rehearse it. In fact, we never again repeated the risks we had taken on our first show. Having resigned ourselves to an uncharismatic interlocutor, we prerecorded his material on film wherever possible; on shows where he appeared "live" we made him wear his glasses.

Our third broadcast, "The Revivalists," was the creation of Shad Northshield with the aid of the boys from Princeton— Chizz Schultz and Bo Goldman. It investigated "the behavior of those men and women, black and white, local and national, who dedicate their fanatical energy to bringing people to God." It started with some remarkable documentary footage shot by Northshield in the Deep South, where, in a broken-down barn, a black preacher, Cat-Iron Carradino, whipped his ragged congregation into a rising fever of frenzied devotion. This was followed by scenes of immersion, leading to the highly organized "healing" rituals conducted by Oral Roberts, a rising evangelist-healer, whose speech and action, according to Marya Mannes in *The Reporter,* "come dangerously close to being profane and violent exercises in mesmerism." After a glimpse of the veteran Billy Sunday, of Mahalia Jackson ("whose face seems to take on a celestial glow as she belts her way through a hymn in her Chicago church") and a brief visit to Aimee Semple McPherson and the Angelus Temple, the last third of the broadcast was devoted to the

* Eli Wallach, Steve Hill, Olive Deering, William Smithers, Vivian Nathan, Frank Silvera and William Marshall.

organization and technique of power developed by that most successful of all modern evangelists, Billy Graham.

This one too got generally good reviews. *Time* reported: "After scoring a success last week with *The World of Nick Adams,* CBS' *Seven Lively Arts* established itself as one of the season's brightest new corners with *The Revivalists.*"

But in the harsh world of network television a series is assessed by the success of its first broadcast. It takes more than a couple of good shows and favorable notices to erase the bad impression left by an unsuccessful premiere. Since ours was generally considered a disaster, we found ourselves more than once, in the months to come, replaced by football games and other network events. As a result, since commercial sponsorship was now out of the question, the total number of our shows was further reduced. From Hubbell and Cowan I never received even the faintest suggestion of a reproach, but around CBS and the industry in general I felt myself treated with nervous commiseration as the leprous creator of the season's biggest turkey.

We continued to turn out shows. Our fourth was a "filmed essay" based on E. B. White's *This Is New York,* edited by Northshield and a young writer named Andy Rooney and narrated by E. G. Marshall to music by Norman Dello Joio. The marriage of text and film was never fully realized, but it had some interesting images and some elegant prose.

Our next, produced by Jud Kinberg and written by Joseph Hyams, Hollywood correspondent of the *New York Herald Tribune,* dealt with the film industry's new tendency to make its films overseas. Our four examples were *The Ugly American,* based on the novel by Graham Greene, being shot by Joseph Mankiewicz in Thailand; *Bonjour Tristesse,* shot by Otto Preminger on the Riviera; *The Vikings,* with Kirk Douglas, being shot in Scandinavia; and *The Bridge on the River Kwai,* directed by David Lean, produced by Sam Spiegel in Ceylon.

In each case we showed some footage from the movie and an interview, on location if possible, with the director or star or producer of the film. In the process we tried to shed some light on the current Hollywood thinking at a time when the competition of television was really beginning to hurt.

It was not one of our most popular shows: some TV critics felt we were doing a series of blurbs for upcoming feature films; others felt we were painting a needlessly dark and defeatist picture of the Hollywood scene. My own feeling was that it added up to a unusually honest and prophetic appraisal of the current "sick and baffled" state of the motion-picture industry.

On the first Sunday in December Robert Herridge produced a blockbuster for us. According to *The New York Times:*

> *The Seven Lively Arts* came into its own yesterday with a brilliant and exciting program on Jazz. The spontaneity and artistry of modern music were presented with more authenticity, understanding and appreciation than television has ever managed before . . . The purest of Jazz done with distinction and dedication. . . .

Written and organized by Nat Hentoff and Whitney Balliett (of *The New Yorker*) and directed by Jack Smight, it was broadcast "live" from a gutted theatre on Ninth Avenue and Fifty-fifth Street. Hailed as a unique musical event, it became a best-selling Columbia long-playing record, and, transferred to videotape, it remains in the archives of the Museum of Broadcasting.

I remember the day we made it. I have no particular knowledge or appreciation of jazz, but in that shabby, half-finished studio there was an atmosphere of musical excitement that even I could appreciate. Historically the show was notable for being one of the last public appearances of the great Billie Holiday before her final eclipse and death. With her that afternoon was her longtime lover, Lester Young, so weakened by sickness and drugs that she had to support him as they walked to the stand.

> Miss Holiday did "Fine and Mellow." Her haunting voice was worth the hour by itself, but to watch her response to the solos of Roy Eldridge and Lester Young was almost equally electric and moving. . . .

Among the jazz giants scattered around the sound stage were Count Basie, Lionel Hampton, Teddy Wilson, Thelonious Monk, Pee Wee Russell, Vic Dickinson, Jo Jones, Jimmy Giuffre, Jim Hall, Jim Atlas and many others.

> All these musicians were gathered in a studio and simply allowed to sing and play without extraneous frills. Some chose to play while wearing their hats; others wore sweaters. The studio was cloudy with cigarette smoke. The accent was on Jazz.

Bob Herridge's next and last show was a musical devised by my friend Agnes de Mille, who had been the choreographer of the Broadway musical *Paint Your Wagon* and who continued to feel that the show contained some of Lerner and Loewe's best material. She was particularly enamored of the song "They Call the Wind Maria" and made it the basis of the show, mostly dance, that she and Herridge put together for television. It was a difficult thing to pull off on the small screen, but, brightly orchestrated by Hershy Kay, it offered some of Agnes' liveliest Americana and such brilliant dancers as Gemze de Lappe and the exquisite Sono Osato.

Another music-and-dance show was *The Nutcracker,* which was presented on the Sunday before Christmas. Through my long association with Lincoln Kirstein we were able to use the New York City Ballet's production currently performing at the City Center. For my television director I selected Charles Dubin, a man of culture and taste whose career had been grievously damaged during the witch-hunts. With utter selflessness he put his television expertise at the service of George Balanchine (who himself had learned a lot about the photographing of dancers during his sojourn with Goldwyn in Hollywood). Between them, with particular emphasis on the early children's section, followed by the girl's dream and the battle of the mice, they put on a pleasant and successful holiday broadcast which, in its final sequence, featured such ballet stars as Maria Tallchief, Diana Adams, Patricia Wilde and Eglevsky. Critical opinion was divided between those who complained that "most of the magic has been lost" in black and white and those who felt that "at last a way has been found to make ballet popular on television."

For our final show we did another one with music, "Profile

of a Composer," an experiment in televised biography covering the artistic life of the American composer and Pulitzer Prize winner Norman Dello Joio. Produced by Northshield, this involved the use of stills and film, including the sound track of Dello Joio's score for *The Battle of the Atlantic* and a live performance of one of Norman's more recent compositions.

But, before that, as our penultimate broadcast, we had presented the best TV drama I have ever been associated with: "The Blast in Centralia Number Five." This was a property I had known and loved for years. I had bought it from John Bartlow Martin, its author, soon after it appeared in *Harper's* magazine, and I had come close to making it into a film with Fred Zinnemann in 1950 just before I went to work for MGM. It was the true story of an Illinois mine disaster which everyone knew was coming and which no one—neither management nor the union nor the Bureau of Mines—made one single move to prevent.

Television was the ideal medium for the telling of such a tragedy, in which documentary reality and personal drama could be blended for overwhelming emotional effect. And we were fortunate in our collaborators. Once again, Kinberg was my producer. For our script we chose Loring Mandel, a sensitive and serious writer who has specialized, throughout his creative life, in subjects of social and political significance. Bob Markell, our staff designer, achieved an unusually successful blending of the documentary material filmed by Northshield on location and the studio sets in which the live parts of the actions were played. But the highest credit must go to our director, George Roy Hill.* With his surprising combination of imagination and showmanship, discipline and self-indulgence, Hill was one of the most interesting figures I encountered in television. To the preparation and execution of "Centralia" he contributed valuable work on the script,

* He had recently surfaced as one of TV's finest young directors with his sensational live production of an enormously complex show about the sinking of the *Titanic*. His successful flims include *Butch Cassidy and the Sundance Kid, The Sting, Slap Shot, A Little Romance* and *The World According to Garp*.

114

great skill in the conception and coordination of the production and a fine sensibility in the direction of a cast that included Maureen Stapleton and Jason Robards. It is due in large part to his creative energy that the terrible irony of the disaster, with its revelations of human weakness and fortitude, came through with such overwhelming and tragic force.

The show was a faithful dramatization of Martin's original reportage: some of it was taken verbatim from the files of the official investigation that followed the explosion. Among these documents was a historic letter written on the ninth of March 1947 by the local miners to his excellency the Governor of the State of Illinois. Known as the "save our lives" letter, it began:

Governor, this is a plea to you to save our lives, to make the Department of Mines and Minerals enforce the laws of the Number Five mine of the Centralia Coal Company before we have a dust explosion at this mine of ours just like happened in Kentucky or West Virginia . . .

We saw that letter written, mailed, received and filed away. Then we heard the voice of the narrator, quiet and unemotional:

At three twenty-six of March 25th, 1947, Centralia Mine Number Five blew up. Of one hundred forty-three men in the mine at the time of the explosion, twenty-four escaped, eight were rescued, one hundred eleven were killed.

But the show's most moving moments were not taken from the official files. They showed Martin (played by Robards) visiting the widow of one of the dead men some months after the blast. Seated under a framed hand-tinted photograph of her dead husband, Mrs. Colfax (Maureen Stapleton) reads what her man scrawled as he lay dying of gas poisoning in the darkened mine.

Sammy, Raymond, be good boys. Jake, Alvin, help Mom, please. Your father, Joe Colfax. O Lord, help me.

Overleaf he wrote:

> Goodbye, Jerry and Dan, God bless you too, boys, your
> father. Vera, Ruth, please do as your father has told you
> —listen to Mom, Joe Colfax. Goodbye. . . .

Later, in a weaker hand:

> My dear wife, goodbye. Name baby Joe so you will have
> a Joe. Love all, Dad.

Of the innumerable tributes that followed that broadcast
the one that touched me most appeared in the *St. Louis Globe-
Democrat*, in the heart of the mining country:

> There will be cries from some quarters that no good can
> come from a program that rashly reopens old conflicts.
> But as my thoughts swung back to the survivors of the
> one hundred and eleven men, somehow I had the feel-
> ing that they, as I do, regard this *Seven Lively Arts* exam-
> ination of the blast as a living memorial to its victims. I'm
> certain its vivid realism renewed the hurt of painful
> memories. But I also have a personal acquaintance with
> some mining families and will speak for them. To all who
> had a hand in CBS-TV's assessment of the *Blast in Cen-
> tralia Five*—well done, well done!

Professionally, the show was a triumph. According to *Variety:*

> *The Seven Lively Arts* came through with a fine show and
> TV journalism got a big boost. It was a forceful and
> courageous presentation that scored with its simplicity
> and pointed in a direction that has barely been explored
> by the medium . . . a masterpiece.

This was echoed in notices that poured in from all parts of
the country: "A truly great example of television at its finest."
"A tragic, memorable documentary." "A searing indictment
of government red tape, of big business, of union inertia and
of a politically appointed bureaucracy." "A raw and thrilling
page from the book of life."

There was irony in the fact that many of these reviews were
also obituaries. According to Gould of *The New York Times:*

116

The Seven Lively Arts will be remembered for this brilliant dramatization . . . It was a challenging assignment for live television and it was carried off with distinction by a happy combination of talents that captured the somber quality of the story magnificently.

What *Time* described as "the season's liveliest artistic success and its costliest financial flop" went off the air for good on the afternoon of Sunday, February 16, 1958.

There is an epilogue to this story. Some months later, when I received my invitation to the annual awards of the National Academy of Television Arts and Sciences, I declined. I was still sore from the beating we had taken and resentful over what I considered the network's craven desertion of *The Seven Lively Arts*. Early next morning I received an account of what happened from Hubbell Robinson, who, as vice-president in charge of programming for CBS, was obliged to attend.

Unlike Hollywood's Oscars, the Emmys were distributed at a dinner, with the nominees and the audience seated at tables. Hubbell and his wife, Vivienne Segal* (who did not always conform to executive protocol), were at the CBS table. Bored to tears as the long evening wore on, she announced that she was off to the little girls' room. There she met a friend, and it was some time before she returned. When she did, and as she was about to sit down, she became aware of something on the table that had not been there when she left.

"What the hell is that?" she asked.

It was, in fact, a brass object about one foot tall (a species of angel with some sort of hollow globe over its head) set on a black wooden stand. It was the National Academy of Television Arts and Sciences' award for the best new show of the 1957–58 season—and it had gone to *The Seven Lively Arts!*

* A musical-comedy star best known for her delivery of "Bewitched, Bothered and Bewildered" in *Pal Joey*.

CHAPTER IV

1958-1959

MUCH ADO *(on tour)*
HAMLET
MIDSUMMER NIGHT'S DREAM
WINTER'S TALE

FOR ALL THE SUCCESS of our 1957 Festival season, it had been followed by a period of exasperating inertia. There was talk of a limited tour (as specified in my contract), but, for lack of funds, nothing had come of it. I held discussions with Hambleton and Houghton about a second engagement in their theatre, but by the time my executive committee finally made up its mind the Phoenix winter season had been fully set. So, the Festival's only serious activity that fall was the running of our embryonic academy. This was Landau's domain, and it left me free to devote most of my time to *The Seven Lively Arts*.

I did, however, take on one outside assignment. I received an urgent call one day, followed by an agitated visit from Nate Kroll, musician, conductor and cultural entrepreneur, who begged me, as an old friend of his and hers, to look at the half-hour film he was producing with Martha Graham and her company. Shot in black and white by a director-cameraman named Peter Glushanek, it was as beautiful a piece of dance film as I had ever seen. The Martha Graham Company was at its peak, especially the women—with an amazing physical and spiritual energy that I had never seen caught in a motion picture. Filmed in leotards in a low-ceilinged dance studio, with action designed and choreographed by Martha Graham (who did not appear herself), it illustrated her essential concepts of dance together with illustrations from several of the most celebrated pieces in her repertoire. In its carefully rehearsed simplicity it had extraordinary beauty and strength.

Having lured me with the quality of his film, Kroll went on to explain that he was in terrible trouble, from which only I could save him. As conceived by Kroll, *The Dancer's World* was to alternate this company footage (with voice-over commentary by Graham) with three short, intimate scenes in which Martha herself would appear in her dressing room, discussing her ideas and feelings about her work. It was when he attempted to shoot these personal scenes that the problem arose. Martha, in her perfectionism and immeasurable vanity, was terrified at the prospect of intimate contact with an instrument (the movie camera) with which she was unfamiliar and over which she had no control. She admired Glushanek's work with the company, but when it came to her own appearance she was seized by irrational fear and categorically refused to go through with it. Finally, at Jean Rosenthal's suggestion, she mentioned my name as someone to whom she would be willing to entrust herself.

(In fact, we had been friends for over twenty years—ever since the distant days of *Panic*.* We had remained in remote but constant contact ever since—partly through Jean, who remained Graham's regular lighting director. Over the years I had followed her rising fame and attended her performances whenever possible; she, on her part, had followed my career in the theatre and, more recently, in films. This, I believe, was the determining factor in her present decision.

* In which Martha had acted as choreographer and director of the all-important crowd scenes. See *Run-Through,* p. 154.

Throughout her spiritual and creative flights, she has always retained a very practical, professional attitude toward her work. That is why she was now willing to entrust her film debut to someone in whom she had confidence and who would give her the professional security of having produced films for such accredited beauties as Lana Turner, Joan Fontaine and—among the ladies who were no longer so young—Greer Garson and Barbara Stanwyck.)

We ran the film in Martha's presence and I told her in all honesty how much I admired it and how important I felt it was for her to complete it. Then we sat down in her apartment and went over her three scenes. By contrast with the main body of the film (which was shot in work clothes), she insisted on appearing in full costume and makeup. I saw no objection to that as long as it did not inhibit directness and intimacy; I explained that I would be standing behind the camera and that she would, in fact, be talking to me. If anything went wrong, we'd stop and shoot it over. Concerning her own lighting, we would get Jean Rosenthal to work with Glushanek and make her look as good on film as she did on the stage. With all these assurances, she agreed to go ahead.

Except for my reassuring presence and a few suggestions I made about continuity, I contributed little to this remarkable film, on which I am always proud but embarrassed to find my name listed as co-director. Later, Martha's talks about the dance and about her work became an integral element of her triumphal appearances throughout the world. But there is something intense and personal about that first, frightened appearance on film that has a particularly poignant quality. And it cemented a relationship—between her and me—that has survived for another twenty-five years and weathered one major professional crisis.

Early in November the Festival was approached by Robert Dowling, head of the City Investor's Corporation, which owned a number of New York theatres. It was his idea to present *Much Ado About Nothing* with its two stars and the original Stratford Festival Company at the gala opening of his reconstructed Globe Theatre on Forty-sixth Street. This was one of New York's finest and oldest playhouses, which was being entirely renovated, backstage and front, and was expected to be ready in time for a Thanksgiving premiere.

A quick check revealed that both Hepburn and Drake were available and willing to sign for a limited engagement. So was most of the rest of the company. The trustees were delighted. So was I—but for different reasons. For them a Broadway engagement with two major stars represented the Festival's ultimate achievement: for me (though once again I saw repertory being sacrificed) it marked a further, welcome step toward a year-round operation and, ultimately, a permanent Festival Company.

One rainy day, Kate, Langner, Kirstein, Landau, Joe Reed and I were led by Mr. Dowling on a tour of his reconstructed theatre. It looked as though it had been hit by a bomb. The stage was a deep crater, the auditorium a shambles of brick and steel. Mr. Dowling conceded that talk of a Thanksgiving opening might be a bit optimistic. But Christmas was a certainty. Three weeks later he admitted that the Globe Theatre would not be ready before spring.* But by then Lawrence Langner, ever quick on his feet, had converted our Broadway engagement, with Kate's consent, into a limited Eastern tour under the joint auspices of the Theatre Guild and the Shuberts' American Theatre Society.

Since I was still at the peak of my television activity, rehearsals for the tour were conducted mostly by Jack Landau, with the energetic assistance of Miss Hepburn, who was agreeably excited at the prospect of leading her forces through the American hinterland. Except for a few scenic modifications (made necessary by some of the strange theatres into which we were booked) and the presence of fewer peon-apprentices than we had available on the banks of the Housatonic, it was the full Stratford production that opened in Philadelphia on the night of December 30 with a fancy Bryn Mawr benefit in honor of its distinguished alumna, K. Hepburn.

* In fact the theatre reopened in May 1958 with the Lunts in Dürrenmatt's *The Visit*. At that time its name was changed to the Lunt-Fontanne.

Our two weeks in the Quaker City were followed by engagements in Detroit, Cleveland, Washington and Boston. Although the tour had been organized on short notice and the company faced blizzard conditions in three of its stands, we did respectable business (between thirty and thirty-five thousand dollars a week) in cities that had not seen a major professional Shakespearean performance in years.

Kate was the major attraction, of course, though our Rio Grande productions aroused general comment— "Shakespeare at the O.K. Corral," "Bard of Avon Goes That-a-Way," "Texas a Tonic for Will," "Viva El Señor Shakespeare!," "Shakespearean Hellzapoppin," "Yippee! and Yahoo!"—but our notices were generally excellent.

In Detroit (where I addressed a gathering of Harvard Business School alumni on the economics of show business) the *Free Press* urged all those who had stayed away from Shakespeare because of the sad experience of their schooldays to give themselves the treat of turning out for a production that was "theatre magic of the highest kind." In Cleveland the critic found reason for "singing and dancing in the streets," and Boston reported that "rarely in our time has a Shakespearean comedy been done with so much honest wit."

But the real value of our tour lay in the strong and favorable impression made by the Festival Company in areas where, until now, it had been little more than a name. The *Boston Herald* raised the question "Are the American People Prepared to Accept Shakespeare?" and answered it in an editorial: "The American Shakespeare Festival Theatre answers YES and in that lies hope for the establishment of a national theatre with a style of its own."

Despite one major calamity, our brief tour was a consistently pleasant one. This was attributable, in large part, to the presence of Kate. Members of the company had grown genuinely fond of her during the summer; on the road, in her double capacity of star and scoutmistress, she gave them —particularly those who were new to touring—a sense of security and solidarity. With the possible exception of Alfred Drake—who, though he had long since found emotional solace within the company, continued to be detached and slightly sulky—they looked to her for laughs, glamor, enthusiasm and leadership.

On our longer moves Kate traveled by train with the company. For shorter jumps she used her green Rolls-Royce, which she drove herself (spelled sometimes by our stage manager, Bernie Gersten) while her chauffeur and Phyllis sat in back. On arrival Bernie would go up to her suite to help with the luggage and to install her. He reported that the first thing she did after checking in was to make two long-distance phone calls to announce her safe arrival: one to Spencer Tracy in California and one to her father in Hartford, Connecticut. Bernie said that often he was unable to tell which was which.

The final weeks of the tour were darkened by tragedy. One of the original and most beloved members of the company was a willowy Englishman by the name of Stanley Bell. Descended from a long line of English actors, he had been with us from the start, playing old Escalus in *Measure*, the Duke of Venice in *Othello*, the Prince of Arragon in *Merchant* and Don Pedro in *Much Ado*. Before the start of the tour he had expressed distress over the drafting into the U.S. Army of a Stratford apprentice with whom he had become involved and who was now being sent overseas to Germany. As the weeks went by his agitation became more acute. He shared a dressing room with Will Geer, whose reminiscences of red-baiting and witch-hunts seemed somehow to heighten Stanley's anxiety over the fate of his friend. When I flew to Cleveland for our opening there, I had a disturbing conversation with Stanley in which he seemed unable to distinguish between the FBI, the Red Menace and his own emotional crisis.

By the time the company reached Washington his state had become alarming, but since there were only a few weeks left, it was decided to try to carry him through the rest of the tour. On our last day in the capital, when he arrived at the theatre for the company's Saturday-evening performance he complained of a headache and told the stage manager he would not be going on. Kate, whom nothing escaped, flew out of her dressing room to talk to him. He was one of her favorites in the company, and she gave him what she believed to be sound, therapeutic advice. The show must go on, she reminded him, and she added that there was probably nothing wrong with him that a good lively performance would not cure. He listened to her, then went up to his dressing room to make up and put on his costume.

I was in New City that night, getting ready to leave the following day for the company's Boston opening. In the middle of the night phone calls began to come through, first from Gersten and then from the press. It seems that halfway through the long first act of *Much Ado,* during the masked ball at which Beatrice and Benedick hold their celebrated verbal duel, a male figure in an embroidered velvet suit had suddenly detached itself from the dance, moved to the edge of the stage, leaped across the narrow orchestra pit and raced up the aisle, out through the lobby, and into the street. The audience, used to actors entering and exiting through the aisles in this production, thought nothing of it as the dances continued and Don Pedro's lines were picked up by other members of the company. At the end of the scene Miss Hepburn herself appeared before the curtain and announced, "Don Pedro is ill. Please be patient."

Throughout the second act (in which the part of Don Pedro was now played by Ellis Rabb), Gersten and a number of volunteers were scouring the neighborhood in search of Stanley and his two dogs—large, devoted black retrievers who rarely left his side. It was discovered that he had gone straight from the theatre to a gas station across the street, where his dogs were patiently waiting for him in a rented car. He had used the men's toilet to change his clothes and asked the attendant to take his costume back to the theatre. Then he had driven off.

Joan was in our apartment on Sixty-fourth Street. At seven-ten the next morning, when she sleepily answered a ring at the front door, she found Stanley Bell standing there with his two dogs. He asked if he might come in for a cup of tea. There was a phone in the kitchen, from which she called me in New City and said that Stanley wanted to talk with me. He was calm but vague, and his only concern seemed to be that

I might report him to Equity. I assured him I wouldn't and asked him to wait for me. I told Joan I was on my way and to hold him there. Ten minutes later, just as I was leaving the house, she called back. While she was pouring him a second cup of tea, Stanley and his dogs had vanished.

Driving in, I ran into flurries of snow, which grew heavier as the day wore on. (It was one of the weekends on which *The Seven Lively Arts* had been preempted and I could stay in the apartment till train time to Boston.) I got two calls during the day from different parts of the city where Stanley had appeared, spent time, then left suddenly without a word. There seemed to be no logical pattern to his behavior and no way to forecast his movements. As the hours went by I was torn by doubt as to whether, for his own protection, I should alert the police. I felt it was a hateful thing to do to a friend, and I held off. Around four I got a call from a priest with a parish on the Upper East Side. He told me, in a slight Irish brogue, that a man by the name of Stanley Bell had come to him for help and that, after talking to him for a while, he had taken him over to meet another actor whom he had once been able to aid in a crisis. I was astonished to learn that the actor was Rex O'Malley, whom I had directed in *Lute Song* and whom I had not seen in years.

I called Rex, who reported that Stanley had been pretty wild for a time and had talked of going to Europe to be with a friend. He was calmer now and asleep with his dogs in a back room. He had also mentioned going up to Boston and rejoining the company. Once again I considered calling the police, but once again I held back. For by now a new crisis had arisen to aggravate the horror of that black Sunday. From Washington to Boston was an eight-hour train ride, and the company, with Kate at its head, should have arrived by late Sunday afternoon. In the extreme cold, their train had broken down and they were now marooned in Connecticut somewhere without heat or food. Around seven the news came that they were moving again and would be in Boston within a few hours. And right after that Rex called, very upset. Stanley was gone—through a back window and down the fire escape into the garden and out into the street, with his dogs. Now, finally, I called the police. That evening John Crosby was giving a party for those who had worked with him on *The Seven Lively Arts*. I went, but left early to catch my train to Boston. From the station I called the police for news of Stanley, but there was no sign of him.

I lay in a lower berth, freezing, while the train made its slow way north through the ice and snow. The conductor's best guess was that we'd be close to two hours late. We were due at seven, and at seven-fifty we were still crawling through the outskirts of Boston. But the snow had stopped.

Meantime, as I learned later, beginning soon after midnight, Joan, in New York, had been receiving call after collect call from Stanley, who had reached Boston and was roaming the icy streets, using pay phones in gas stations and hotel lobbies to call not only Joan but also Kate, who had finally arrived exhausted at her hotel, till Phyllis ordered the switchboard to cut off the phone. According to Joan, he seemed more disturbed but still rational and still worrying about Equity. Joan did her best to reassure him and urged him to meet me at the theatre and straighten things out. Around dawn the calls stopped.

I reached the Shubert sometime after 8 A.M. Monday—in time to witness a bad accident as one of our loading crew slipped on the ice in the alley and slammed his head against the side of a truck. I had just gone back inside the theatre and was standing talking with Gersten in the back of the lobby when I became aware of three men entering from the street. As they came toward us I saw that two were uniformed policemen and one a plainclothesman who held an open notebook in his hand. He asked who was in charge. I said I was. He glanced at his book and asked if I knew anyone by the name of Stanley Bell. Yes. Why? And, as an icy fear moved suddenly from my groin up into my heart: "Because he just jumped from a fourteenth-floor window in the Touraine Hotel," the man said.

They drove me across town in a police car to the morgue to identify the body. I had never seen a corpse, and I got my first sight of one that morning as Stanley Bell was rolled out on the sliding shelf of a green steel closet. He was quite limp but not as battered as I expected. Only the balding head was smashed, but it was Stanley's face I saw—mud-colored, slightly smeared with blood and looking horribly amused.

I was led next to a neighboring office, where, from a small drawer, they produced Stanley's personal effects. Seeing this strange collection of stuff that had just been emptied from the dead man's pockets was far worse, somehow, than viewing the body. There was a dirty handkerchief, a number of hundred-dollar bills, a British passport, a railroad ticket to Quebec, and a Canadian Pacific voucher for an ocean passage to Europe. Also a number of coins, car keys, a rental agreement for a car, a thick book of signed traveler's checks, an Equity card, two packs of cigarettes—one half empty, the other unopened—a pencil, a pen, a signet ring and two letters in envelopes with European stamps.

They asked did I know if he had any relatives in the country? I said that I knew he did not but that his closest friend was a famous English actress named Gladys Cooper. Then I signed some papers they shoved at me, and the cop who was driving me back to the theatre said something about a "guardian" and explained that local regulations required that a lawyer be appointed to look after the dead man's affairs. From the lobby of the Shubert I called the Theatre Guild's lawyer, explained the situation and asked him to take the necessary steps immediately. Ten minutes later he called back and said it was too late. The claim for "guardianship" had already been filed and registered.

I was given the name of the successful claimant and called him. I told him we wished to appoint our own guardian. He said that it was out of the question: under the laws of the sovereign state of Massachusetts the disposition of the body and affairs of the deceased were now entirely in his hands. When I started to yell at him he hung up on me.

Kate and I discussed the matter with the Guild's lawyer and local manager. There was nothing we could do. I was overdue at the Cow Barn in New York, but before I left Boston I had another conversation with the guardian and apologized for shouting at him. I explained that Stanley had recently mentioned to us that if anything ever happened to him he wanted his body to be cremated. The man listened in silence, then informed me that Boston was a Catholic town in which cremation was not considered a suitable form of burial. Besides, he had already acquired a beautiful plot for Mr. Bell in a local cemetery. He knew we'd all be very happy with it.

Immediately after the funeral (which Kate and most of the company attended) the guardian rendered his accounting, which included the cost of the cemetery plot and the under-taker's bill. All in all, his charges amounted to the exact amount found on Stanley's body in cash and signed traveler's checks.

Speaking of money, at the conclusion of the tour Katharine Hepburn turned over her entire accumulated salary of thirty thousand dollars to the Festival for future productions and for a scholarship to be named after Stanley Bell.

The day after the tour ended, Joan and I flew south to Varadero Beach, outside Havana, Cuba. It was a modest, popular resort where we stayed in a pension that had been discovered some years ago by the Poors. This was the last year of the Batista regime; armed military police in white helmets rode American jeeps through the streets at night, but no one paid much attention to them. As I lay in the warm sand all day, looking out to where a huge manta ray was clearly visible under the bright-blue water a hundred yards offshore, some of the winter's tension began to slide away. Then the phone started to ring, and within ten days I was back on Fifty-seventh Street presiding over the melancholy dissolution of our television organization and taking leave of the last departing members of our staff.* One of the things that had brought me back was a mysterious call from Louis Cowan inviting me to lunch at the Oak Room with him and Hubbell Robinson. I anticipated a vaguely embarrassing con-versation with congratulatory reference to "Centralia"; after that we would turn to the practical consideration of my con-tract with CBS, of which the second year's option was due to

---

* "It was the finest year I've ever had and I'm grateful to you for it. My only hope—to work together again soon," wrote Northshield.

be exercised within a few days. I expected to be told as grace-fully as possible that it would not be picked up.

Instead, over his second martini, Hubbell began to speak of his plans for the coming year for *Playhouse 90*. This was Hubbell's favorite show, the first weekly dramatic TV broad-cast ever to run for over an hour. Produced in California by Martin Manulis under Robinson's supervision, it had been on the air for two season and had won critical and public favor.

After two years and fifty-two shows Manulis was tired and had accepted an offer to produce theatrical films for 20th Century–Fox. In his place Hubbell had decided to assign the show to three producers, each to do eight broadcasts in succession. Production would be done in California with the existent staff, and Hubbell would remain executive producer to ensure continuity and to avoid duplication or repetition of material; otherwise each unit would be entirely independent and autonomous.

He told me that two producers had already been chosen: Fred Coe, a well-known TV and Broadway producer, and Herbert Brodkin, a former theatrical scenic designer who had become one of the most active and successful producers in television. The third place was now being offered to me.

It was a flattering proposal and I accepted it, provided it did not interfere with my direction of the Stratford Festival, which remained my prime obligation. This presented no problem: the eight TV shows assigned to me were the first of the 1958–59 season; they would be broadcast in the fall and early winter and would in no way conflict with my summer's Stratford activities.

Since *Playhouse 90* had its own producing and casting or-ganization in Los Angeles, the staff each producer required for his preparation in New York was comparatively small. As my temporary associate I retained Jud Kinberg, who had decided to try his luck at making films in Europe but agreed to stay with me for the rest of the summer and help me select and commission scripts for *Playhouse 90*. When he left for London, and Chizz Schultz (also of *Seven Lively Arts*) took over, all but one of our shows were in work and two were already written, approved and cast.

This left me comparatively free to devote myself to the preparation of what I felt would be a crucial summer in the history of the American Shakespeare Festival. This would be our longest season yet, with the largest company to date—and no stars.

The first step was the organization and promotion of the Festival's first school season. Beginning in late May, three weeks before the start of the regular program, we would give five midday matinees a week for students of all ages at a uniform admission price of two dollars. (Most of this would be paid by school boards and by the new state and federal grants that were becoming available for cultural activities.) Saturdays and Sundays we would give previews for the general public at normal prices.

It worked miraculously, and it was an awesome sight, on summer afternoons, to see several dozen buses with plates from four or more states lined up in our parking lot while, inside the theatre, their fifteen hundred bewildered passengers, under the partial control of their harassed teachers, were introduced to the wonders of the Bard.*

Though it gave us a lot of additional work, it was worth it. Aside from the publicity and the goodwill it brought us, it offered one serious artistic benefit. Most festival performances are exposed to the public (and to the critics) long before they are ready to be shown. The school season allowed us to shake down our productions before a most difficult audience and to restore our reassembled company to some sort of cohesive ensemble before the opening of the public season. (There was the danger that in courting reactions and getting laughs from a children's audience our actors would fall into bad habits. Most of them were aware of this and readjusted without difficulty to adult audiences during the final previews.)

My master plan called for opening the school program

---

* Since their ages ranged from ten to twenty it was not possible to tell which schools supplied the best audiences. In terms of discipline and preparation the Catholic schools seemed consistently superior.

each year with a replay of the final show of the previous season. But since *Much Ado* proved almost impossible to reassemble, we decided to open with a new production that was perfect for the occasion, *Midsummer Night's Dream*, directed by Jack Landau, to be followed by a few performances of *Hamlet*, which (since it was customary to begin the season with a tragedy) would open as our first show for the general public on June 19. Later, as in previous seasons, Jack and I would co-direct a third production, *The Winter's Tale*.

When the company met for rehearsal early in May, on the upper floor of our warehouse building on West Sixty-fifth Street, barely six weeks after the end of the *Much Ado* tour, it numbered thirty-two, of whom one third were new to the company. The new faces included Inga Swenson, Barbara Barrie, Geraldine Fitzgerald, June Havoc, John Ragin, Eulalie Noble, Severn Darden, James Olson, June Ericson and, above all, the two Nancys, Marchand and Wickwire, whom Jack and I had been wooing for some time and whose appearance as permanent members added great feminine strength to the company. Among those who had left and who now returned were Hiram Sherman, to play Polonius and Bottom, and Fritz Weaver, to play the Hamlet he had been reluctant to do the year before.*

Among our sixteen student-apprentices for the season were the usual future celebrities: Ellen Geer (who played Ophelia for Tyrone Guthrie in Minneapolis two years later); Joanna Merlin (who became casting director for Hal Prince); and two future "macho" film stars—one white, Alexander Viespi (who became known in films as Alex Cord), and one black, Raymond St. Jacques (who also acted as our fencing instructor).

There were staff changes. Morty Gottlieb had left us, un-

---

* Fitzgerald, Havoc and Weaver were on special contracts which allowed them to appear in only one play. Weaver's contract stated specifically that I would be the sole director of *Hamlet*. He had given a number of brilliant performances under Landau, but he was leery of receiving dual direction in such a subjective and complex part as Hamlet.

able to combine his duties as our general manager with his own ambitions as a Broadway producer.* Jean Rosenthal was once again our technical director, though the only credit she took was that of lighting designer, which she shared with her associate Tharon Musser. A new stage manager appeared in the person of Richard Blofson; Bernard Gersten was once again in charge as production stage manager, assisted by two unusually bright and devoted assistants, William Woodman and Gordon Davidson.†

That year Landau and I also acquired a new assistant—a twenty-year-old red-haired orphan of Irish-Polish descent named Denis Deegan. He was just out of Yale and brilliantly intelligent, with great charm and flawless taste, and he continued to work for me in various capacities for the next five years.

Rouben Ter-Arutunian was away in Europe that summer. At Kirstein's urging, we brought in David Hays‡ to design individual shows within the general framework of Rouben's Festival Stage. Virgil Thomson too had European commitments; he stayed only long enough to supervise the music he had composed for my production of Leslie Howard's *Hamlet* twenty years before.§ To fill his place, I invited my old associate Marc Blitzstein to compose our music for *Dream* and *Winter's Tale*.

Another absence, and a most regrettable one, was that of Joseph Verner Reed. His wife had long been powerful in Republican politics, and during the second Eisenhower ad-

* His productions include *Sleuth* (1970) and *Same Time Next Year* (1975).
† Both became directors of important theatres in the seventies— Woodman at the Goodman Theatre in Chicago, Davidson as my successor with the Theatre Group and later as the distinguished artistic director of the Mark Taper Forum in Los Angeles.
‡ Besides designing many Broadway productions, he was one of the founders of the National Theatre of the Deaf, of which he was for many years artistic director.
§ Because the Festival, being in a repertory situation, could afford only two bagpipers and kettledrum players instead of four, as scored, the full grandeur of the final funeral march was lost, but it was still quite impressive.

ministration the Reeds were rewarded for their financial support by the appointment of Joseph as cultural attaché to the U.S. Embassy in Paris. His going was a grievous loss to the Festival and, particularly, to me. He was my only real and reliable contact with the board, and, for all his vacillation and occasional quirks, he had been a constant, sympathetic and constructive ally. For Lincoln too, Reed's departure was a serious blow; it upset the balance of power and diminished his authority as *éminence grise* of the Festival.

To fill the vacuum of his absence, an attempt was made by Langner and the board to induce Eugene Black, head of the International Bank and a Shakespeare enthusiast, to assume a more active part in the organization. This took the form of his offering us a young man from his own staff to replace Gottlieb as general manager. His name was Thomas Noone and he had been doing public-relations work for the International Bank. I would have preferred someone with more theatrical experience, but Langner insisted that we accept Black's offer—all the more since Mr. Black was prepared to pay his entire salary.

Tom Noone, a personable, energetic, handsome young man in his mid-thirties and his three-piece suits, moved from Washington to assume his new functions. He was eager and efficient and might have become a good general manager if he hadn't stepped on a land mine soon after his arrival.

By 1958 the worst of the witch-hunting in show business was over. McCarthy was gone and people were slowly drifting back into the jobs from which they had been blacklisted during the previous decade. But the House Un-American Activities Committee, though generally discredited, refused to be liquidated. To justify its continued existence it announced a new set of hearings, this time in New York City. By now there were few "reds" left to expose, but a handful was found who had been overlooked in earlier sessions. Needless to say, they included a number of my friends—among them Joseph Papp, head of the Public Theatre, and, closer to home, Bernard Gersten, our production stage manager, and Marc Blitzstein, the Festival's chosen composer for the season.

The committee arrived in New York amid general indifference: most of those who had been subpoenaed followed the normal practice of "taking the Fifth," and after a few days the committee returned to Washington. The hearings had passed almost unnoticed, and nobody had taken them seriously. Blitzstein had already delivered his score for *Dream* and we were using it in rehearsal; he was well into *Winter's Tale*, which he was completing in Stratford—some of it on the piano in our house. As for Gersten, he clearly fell under a recent ruling by Actors' Equity which stated categorically that no Equity member could be dismissed from his job for political cause.*

By this time rehearsals were well under way and it was evident, following the first run-through, that Jack Landau's production of *A Midsummer Night's Dream* was going to be a winner. It is the perfect play for a young company and it fitted ours particularly well. In concept it was conventional but not sentimental. As described by its director, it was

> mounted in festive Elizabethan manner as a Masque performed on the occasion of some country nobleman's wedding. Theseus' palace becomes a Tudor Hall complete with tapestry, choir screen and courtly music. For the transformation into the forest, sections of the gilded wooden screen detach themselves, travel downstage and form moving bowers through which humans and fairy-folk pursue each other, while the forest itself is indicated by a Gobelin tapestry which stretches and rises till it becomes a vast, luminous background of blue-green and gold. All the characters—the human beings (the nobles with their servants and minstrels, the middle-class lovers, the rude mechanicals), as well as the fairies (Titania with her sprightly train, Oberon with his guard of tree-men, and Puck as a cross between forest fawn and mischievous schoolboy in an Eton jacket)—are essentially and unmistakably English.

Costumes were designed by Thea Neu, a highly talented young designer from Vienna who had spent time in Nazi

---

* Joe Papp, who was suspended by CBS-TV from his job as floor manager, sued the network and was finally awarded not only reinstatement but his entire salary during his suspension.

concentration camps. Her fanciful costumes brilliantly fulfilled Landau's concept, which was also carried through in
the casting and the acting. The dark, stocky solidity of Jack
Bittner's Theseus next to the "bouncing Amazon" of Nancy
Wickwire—a head taller than he, in an Elizabethan riding
habit and with flaming red hair—were in direct contrast to
the exotic, slightly lunatic quality of the fairy king and queen
as played by Richard Waring and June Havoc. Dick Easton
was an energetic and endearing Puck, and our two pairs of
lovers were handsome, athletic and sexy. But it was in the
performance of its "rude mechanicals" that the production
was outstanding: only in repertory could such a group of
eminent actors be assembled to play such parts, and only in a
permanent company could such a quality of ensemble playing be achieved. It caused Brooks Atkinson to wonder in his
review "if, in the entire history of the play, there has ever
been a better team of comics to play those roles."

Each received his share of praise:

No one should be surprised to discover that Hiram Sherman is in top form as Bottom the Weaver. As Quince,
Morris Carnovsky is a caricature of the stage director,
fatuous about the importance of his office, humorously
incompetent in solving its problems. A grinning, slow-
witted Snout by Will Geer, a stumbling, awkward falsetto
Flute by William Hickey, a Starveling by Ellis Rabb that
is long gone in iron-deficiency of the blood and a ridiculously savage lion by Severn Darden complete a cast of
incomparable drolls.

The critics were unanimous: "uproarious . . . hilarious . . .
rapturous"; "a veritable dream of entertainment"; "a beguiling fantasy of gossamer mirth and lusty slapstick"; "a dream
and a delight to the eye"; "a great comic production of a
classical comedy."

The 1958 Festival was off to a good start. Our *Hamlet* had
opened the previous night and had been well received on the
whole, though it confirmed the general rule that under fes-

tival conditions Shakespeare's comedies are consistently easier to pull off than the tragedies.

Of all the plays in the canon, the most hazardous is *Hamlet* —partly because it is the most familiar and the most encrusted with preconceptions and expectations, but also because the role of Hamlet is one in which the personality of the actor playing the Prince is inseparable from the performance of that enormously demanding part.*

Fritz Weaver had an angular, intellectual, almost secretive personality that was perfect for Hamlet's early, tormented scenes of feigned madness, but limited him in the later scenes in which, as a man, he must finally face the reality of his destiny. Also there was something tense and neurotic about Weaver himself that inhibited him from achieving the full range of Shakespeare's Elizabethan hero.

I was prepared for this, but there was one other element of the production that surprised and disturbed me. In my eagerness to enforce the repertory system I had cast Morris Carnovsky in the role of Claudius. Having done so, I realized that we had no one in the company capable of playing opposite him as Gertrude. So I invited Geraldine Fitzgerald, a friend from the Mercury days whose talent and beauty I had long admired, to come to Stratford and play the Queen to Morris' King. I did her no favor. Carnovsky (who had been so great as Shylock and was to be such a notable Lear) was a stiff, ponderous Claudius of whom it was difficult to believe that he was a covetous brother whose ambition and lust for the Queen drove him to murder Hamlet's father. Added to this, Weaver's cold intensity in the closet scene and my own inability as a director to help her to make emotional contact

---

* Of the great, consecrated performances of Hamlet, two are enshrined in theatrical history—John Barrymore's and John Gielgud's. Yet the former was received, in its day, with mixed reviews and considerable outrage that a light comedian and matinee idol should have had the audacity to undertake the world's greatest tragic role. Gielgud, for all the beauty and sensitivity of his portrayal, was never able to transcend the lyric quality of his own personality and missed some of the "man of action" aspects of the Prince of Denmark which Olivier, in his film, made the essential but not entirely convincing key to Hamlet's character.

with her son and her second husband were responsible for Geraldine's unrealized interpretation of Gertrude.*

On the whole, however, we did better with our *Hamlet* than I expected. Weaver and the production were treated with respect—if not with enthusiasm. The *Times* called him "a generous, intelligent Hamlet" and, describing him on his entrance into the throne room, said: "Tall, lean, sensitive, a little withdrawn and indecisive, he gives at this moment every indication of being the most brilliant American Hamlet of recent seasons." Atkinson found Fritz's "biting style immensely effective," but in his final judgment he found his playing lacking "in depth and width; it does not overwhelm the stage."

Atkinson had good words for most of the company, and I was particularly pleased, after Earle Hyman's previous season's defeat, to find him receiving general praise for his Horatio, whom Atkinson described as having "the presence of nobility and a voice that strikes directly at the heart."

What reservations Atkinson had were restated in his Sunday piece and related mostly to Weaver's performance, which he now described as "an intelligent, dry, striving, astonished Hamlet who lives out his life and revenge in front of us, yet remains isolated under the glaring Northern Lights of Mr. Houseman's handsome production."†

Elliot Norton of *The Boston Record* found our *Hamlet* "exciting, admirable and very deeply touching." Herbert Whittaker described it in his Toronto paper as a "rousing, visually exciting *Hamlet* . . . it is such a richly satisfying production in so many ways that one only wishes one could become more deeply involved in its central character."

On the negative side Henry Hewes asked, "What is worse

---

* She came into her own some years later when she triumphed as another mother—in *Long Day's Journey into Night.*

† In a later piece in which he compared the two current Hamlets, Plummer's in Ontario and Weaver's in Connecticut, Atkinson wrote that, though they were both played by "uncommonly gifted young actors, they were both disappointing," and attributed this in part to the fact that "speaking in spacious, passionate, high-figured verse is largely a lost art."

than a bad performance of *Hamlet?*" and replied, "An indifferent one—which is the kind the Festival is giving." Harold Clurman agreed with him: "When there is no interpretation, that is to say, specific embodiment—physical characterization and visualization with unmistakable intent—there is little point in praising or blaming actors no matter what their individual talents."

Clurman also complained that our set looked "like the bleachers in a gymnasium"—the same décor which others found impressive in its "stark splendor" and which I myself felt worked admirably for the big scenes, the battlements, the coast, the play-within-the-play and the final holocaust, but seriously damaged such intimate moments as the meeting with Ophelia and the closet scene between Hamlet and his mother.

With the double bill of *Hamlet* and *Midsummer Night's Dream,* the Festival was having its biggest season yet. We had started with a substantial advance sale, all the more gratifying since it was achieved in the absence of major stars. Attendance continued to build as we went into rehearsal with our third production. Then, suddenly, just before a sold-out matinee of *Dream,* three louts appeared on the lawn in front of the theatre carrying hand-lettered signs protesting the presence of a "red" stage manager in the Festival Company.

I was shocked but not altogether surprised. Stratford was a suburb of Bridgeport, and Bridgeport was a notoriously reactionary town which, while enjoying the financial benefits it derived from our operation, had always regarded the Festival with suspicion and some distaste. Still, I was not too disturbed. I felt sure that this picket line was temporary, that it would not affect attendance and that it would disappear after a few days. I was right about that, but I was wrong in my estimate of the harm its appearance would finally do to us.

On the afternoon the pickets first appeared, Tom Noone, our manager, was off in New York. When he returned he ran smack into them as he drove up to the theatre. He was shocked and appalled and came storming into my office. I told him to relax. I understood his agitation, particularly in the light of his boss's position as head of the International Bank, but there was nothing we could do about it except hope the louts with the signs would go away.

"Shouldn't we negotiate with them?" Noone asked.

I told him that was the last thing we should do. Whoever had sent them would demand Gersten's dismissal, and when we refused we'd be in worse shape than before.

"In that case, why don't we pay Gersten off and get rid of him?"

Again I told him no and informed him of the Equity ruling.

He went off after a while to call Washington. On his way out he ran into Lincoln Kirstein, who was in one of his dark moods. Lincoln told him not to be a horse's ass, to mind his own fucking business, and to keep his goddamned mouth shut. Didn't he know that half of our company were Communists and that if we fired Gersten all the others would quit instantly? And we'd have no season? Is that what he wanted? Noone stared at him openmouthed, and Lincoln, having achieved his dramatic effect, climbed into his car and drove off to his home in Westport for the weekend. Noone took one last, nervous look at the pickets, got into his car and drove straight to La Guardia Airport and from there to Washington to carry his alarming news to the head of the International Bank.

Lincoln had, as usual, exaggerated. But, as usual, there was truth in what he said. There were, to my certain knowledge, no fewer than *five* Fifth Amendment takers in the company, not to mention half a dozen or more "fellow travelers," of whom I was, myself, the most notorious. Bernie's firing would in fact have blown the whole Festival apart.

Eugene Black's reaction to Noone's report was predictable. He requested an emergency executive meeting of the board, which took place a few days later in a room at Yale University. Present were Langner, Helen Menken and her husband, George Richard, Lincoln Kirstein and myself; also Eugene Black with his associate George Woods.* I was able to inform

* Woods later became chairman of the board of Lincoln Center.

them that the pickets had disappeared. I also reminded them that taking the Fifth was not a criminal offense and that Actors' Equity had specifically ruled against it as cause for dismissal. Helen Menken, as a member of Equity Council, confirmed this. Eugene Black then stated his position: he loved the Festival and admired what I had accomplished, but, as public figures holding important posts with the United States government, he and Woods could not continue to be associated with an organization that was being publicly accused of harboring political subversives.

The question was raised: If Gersten were paid his full salary for the remainder of the season and let go, would that violate the Equity ruling? I repeated that I would not consider such an action. Langner, torn between his long-standing liberalism and his eagerness to keep our two bankers on the board, stayed on the fence. Then suddenly, Lincoln, either to help me or to work off his own aggressions, bitterly attacked Black and Woods for putting their own personal concerns above those of the Festival. Two days later Black and Woods tendered their resignations, thus depriving the American Shakespeare Festival Theatre and Academy of its two most potent money-raising trustees. Tom Noone returned to Washington, and we were left without an executive director for the rest of the season. But no more pickets appeared as we proceeded with our rehearsals of *The Winter's Tale*.

Each season, our third production seemed to possess some special quality of its own. *Winter's Tale* was no exception. It was the simplest yet perhaps the most sophisticated production to be mounted on the Festival Stage. It is, at best, a perplexing play, broken into two parts which, on the surface, fail to match or cohere. For this reason it was essential to find a style, both of acting and of production, that would encompass its extreme changes of mood: one sufficiently formal to give the characters their fairy-tale quality, yet not so remote from life as to negate the human emotions they undergo. A solution for this blend of ritual and reality was suggested by the ancient semipolitical, semireligious symbols of the Mediterranean tarot card pack.

The idea was Lincoln Kirstein's and it evoked an immediate response in Dorothy Jeakins' imaginative costume designs. The opposing emblems of sun and moon and the recurrent symbols of sword, cup, sheath and club gave a simple and very special aspect to the production. In this formal world of tarot myth everything became possible: the King's jealous madness, the Queen's death and resurrection, the infant Perdita's exposure on the seashore of Bohemia after her abductor has been eaten by a giant bear, even Father Time's apppearance in the center of the storm under a dripping umbrella in a wrinkled seersucker suit; all these must be made to seem poetically and dramatically credible. And they did.

We were able to cast *Winter's Tale* perfectly from within our own company. John Colicos (who had replaced Drake in the final weeks of our *Much Ado* tour) was a fervid but credible Leontes, with Ellis Rabb (wearing the platinum wig he had worn the previous year as the Player King in *Hamlet*) as his suave and faithful courtier Camillo; Will Geer* and Bill Hickey were picturesque Bohemian shepherds, father and son; Richard Easton (Florizel) and Inga Swenson (a delicious Perdita) were our young lovers; Barbara Barrie was the comic Mopsa; Earle Hyman, Autolycus; Jack Bittner, an umbrella-carrying Father Time; and Hiram Sherman, a nameless gossip. (Our seven-foot bearskin was worn by a young man who later became a celebrated male model.) But the real stars of the piece were our two Nancys—Wickwire as the loving, persecuted Queen, and Marchand as the loyal and courageous Paulina. Between them they managed to bring off the corny, miraculous final scene of the play in which the Queen's statue comes to life and which never failed to send a thrill of theatrical wonder through the house.

Winter's Tale was a joy to rehearse; our actors were tired but tuned to a fine sensibility, and our technical problems

---

* In addition to his indomitable spirit and vast experience Will Geer was the possessor of a miraculous green thumb. From a small patch in the backyard of his local inamorata he produced giant vegetables in such profusion that the entire company was supplied with fresh produce all summer long. He also laid out a Shakespearean herb garden.

(with what had become an extremely complicated piece of theatrical machinery) had been finally ironed out. The reception at our matinee opening and in our next morning's reviews clearly reflected this happy, relaxed, creative mood.

Brooks Atkinson, who had recently reviewed the same play in its Stratford, Ontario, production, found that ours better captured "the wayward, fanciful spirit of *The Winter's Tale.*" *

> The American Shakespeare Festival [he wrote] has created something that is plausible and enchanting . . . a well-designed, generally well-acted afternoon of ancient make-believe. It is wonderful to discover that *Winter's Tale* on the stage is such an exquisite and charming play.

Even Walter Kerr, our severest critic in the past, who had gone so far as to refer to us as a "cultural Howard Johnson's," was reluctantly bewitched by

> the tongue-in-cheek conceits that keep entertainment lively and the audience alert and help to give some sort of unified designs to the author's almost contemptuous blendings of saleable melodrama, pretty pastoral posturing and stock theatrical effects.
> It is really a double bill with a kind of cartoon carnival thrown in and most of the amiable fantasy that the Festival has bequeathed is disarmingly right.

When the 1958 Stratford season came to a close six weeks later, I had every reason to be satisfied—critically and materially. Business had been good in '57, with stars; without stars in '58 it was even better—by more than twenty percent. Even more satisfying was the realization that on the day we closed,

---

* This comparison was in itself a significant event. Throughout its existence the Festival Theatre had paid a price for its location in Stratford, which put us in direct competition with the two senior Stratfords—in Warwickshire and Ontario. Inevitably we were considered Johnny-come-latelies; it took four years for our Connecticut productions to achieve critical parity with those of Ontario. At the same time, the Stratford name gave us an institutional status that aroused in certain New York critics the bias that I sometimes detected in favor of the more modest, simpler and *free* open-air productions of Joe Papp's Public Theatre.

most of the Festival Company had been steadily employed for twenty out of the past twenty-seven months. Under the conditions currently prevailing in the American theatre this record was unique and astonishing.*

Finally, and most gratifying of all, there was the growing evidence that my obsessive insistence on continuity and on the necessity to create a permanent Festival Company was having its effect. *Variety* now referred to us as "the ablest classical company in the U.S.," and there was more than personal satisfaction in a piece written by Elliot Norton, dean of East Coast critics, in *The Boston Record*:

> For what he has done at Stratford, Connecticut, John Houseman deserves the respect and admiration of the American theatre-goers. In three years he has developed an acting company of great promise, he has produced several productions of genuine merit and has created at Stratford something like a national center of classical production. Even more commendable, he has done it almost without stars. He has remained loyal to his own idea that he can create a versatile American company to match the best.

This attitude was reflected beyond the press; the Festival and its company were being taken seriously by many who,

---

* We could also pride ourselves on the fact that, in our first three years, we had proved ourselves to be a full-fledged repertory company. To cite a few examples: Morris Carnovsky, who had played his first Shakespearean role with us as Salisbury in *King John*, had also played the Provost in *Measure for Measure* and Grumio in *The Taming of the Shrew;* the following year he played Antonio in *Much Ado* and a memorable Shylock in *The Merchant of Venice;* this year he was playing Claudius in *Hamlet* and Quince in *Dream;* a total of seven roles. Jack Bittner, in his two seasons with us, had played Montano in *Othello*, Tubal in *Merchant*, Borachio in *Much Ado*, the Ghost in *Hamlet*, Theseus in *Dream* and Time in *Winter's Tale*. Jacqueline Brookes, during the '56 and '57 seasons, had played Blanch and Constance in *King John*, Juliet in *Measure*, the Duchess in *The Duchess of Malfi*, Desdemona in *Othello* and Ursula in *Much Ado*. Finally, Earle Hyman had played Melun in *King John*, Antonio in *The Duchess*, the Moor in *Othello*, the Prince of Morocco in *Merchant*, Horatio in *Hamlet*, Philostrate in *Dream* and Autolycus in *Winter's Tale*.

until now, had continued to think of it as just another "summer theatre." Early in August, Lincoln Kirstein and I had met with Ed Young, who was regarded as the most influential executive working for John D. Rockefeller III on his new Lincoln Center project. We discussed in general terms a plan whereby, when the Lincoln Center Repertory Theatre was finally opened, the Festival Company would become its classical arm with two annual six-week engagements—one early and one late in the season. This meant that with fourteen weeks in Stratford, twelve weeks in New York, tours to a few major cities and two months of rehearsal, members of the Festival Company would be working for eleven months a year, with one month's vacation. Since Lincoln Center was still years from completion, all this was in the nature of a dream, but it was an attractive and encouraging one.

That summer, as I remember it, also marked a high point in the morale of our company. There is something special about theatrical comradeship, particularly among members of a group that has been together for some time. Throughout rehearsals actors, director, stage managers, designers and, to some degree, the crew are thrown together physically and emotionally. As the crisis of opening night approaches, these periods of enforced intimacy and shared anxiety become longer and more obsessive until, during the final days and nights of technical and dress rehearsals, they seem to absorb the company's entire life. (What brief breaks there are for sleep and food offer no real respite from tension.) Subjected as they are to alternating waves of anxiety and enthusiasm, there develops among members of the company a sense of mutual dependence and enforced solidarity so strong that, even after opening night and long after they have gone their separate ways, an emotional residue remains—an echo of joint effort and shared danger that is never entirely forgotten.

In repertory this feeling is heightened. A company that emerges from the ordeal of one opening and is plunged, without respite, into a second and a third such experience is forced into a state of comradeship that is closer, in many ways, than that which exists among relatives and lovers. It has nothing to do with individual likes or dislikes: it is a collective and functional intimacy similar to that which unites the men of a combat unit.

Within the Festival Company relationships varied, of course. There was the crew's feeling about the actors: a strange mixture of affection, resentment, admiration and envy. There were the actors' feelings for each other, colored by competition and by their professional judgments of each other's work. And there were the feelings that existed between directors and actors. My relationship with the company was somewhat different from Landau's. He was one of them —their contemporary and their peer, with all the assets and liabilities of that equality. My own wider responsibilities as artistic director and administrator of the Festival—not to mention my age—placed me inevitably in the position of leader and father figure, and this put a distance between us that, with few exceptions, I was neither able nor particularly anxious to bridge.

With Jack Landau, my relations continued to be not unlike those of a pilot with his co-pilot. The final decisions were mine, but for functional collaboration I counted on him continually and without reservation. I had never quite overcome my physical revulsion nor my impatience with his chronic indecision, but this did not diminish my personal affection for him nor the confidence I came to repose in his efficacy and taste after three years of facing joint problems and mutual responsibilities. A somewhat similar association existed between myself and my production stage manager, Bernard Gersten. Like Landau, he was, in a sense, an extension of myself, on whom I counted for the smooth and efficient operation of the stage and for communication with the company and the technical crew. Finally, on yet another level, there was Denis Deegan, who, as my personal assistant, was often the recipient of confidences I did not dare to discuss with the others.

But by far the closest of my working relationships was that which existed between Jean Rosenthal and myself. It went back more than twenty years and it had been tempered in the fiery furnace of the Mercury, during those awful, interminable days and nights when we sat in the theatre without sleep or respite, trying to execute the conceits of the mad boy, Orson Welles, whom we hated for his thoughtless megalomania but in whose theatrical genius we had complete and unswerving faith.

The fact that Jeannie and I had not worked together in sixteen years made no difference at all. When I returned to the theatre in 1956 we picked up exactly where we left off in 1940 during the final frenzy of *Native Son*.* Only now it was no longer Orson Welles who held us together, but a joint professional determination to make a success of the Festival Theatre at Stratford, Connecticut.

Physically she was still the curlyheaded child, just out of Yale, whom I had sent out on tour with Leslie Howard's *Hamlet*. That she was a child of surprising strength and endurance had been proved, over the years, by her long, winning battle for recognition as a lighting designer against the prejudices of Broadway managements and the male chauvinism of stagehands, in which she had proved that she was a resourceful, patient and utterly determined fighter.†

During the years of our Stratford association we found ourselves repeating the patterns of those earlier years. Once again we were spending days and nights together in a darkened theatre, slowly and painfully making our way through scene after scene, discussing effects, adjusting focuses, setting light levels and organizing transitions for the next day's run-through. Around seven in the morning, with the sunlight pouring in through the skylights in the stagehouse, we would finally quit, go to our separate homes, bathe, sleep an hour or two, eat breakfast and be back in the theatre for technical rehearsal at ten. These hours of shared exhaus-

---

* See *Run-Through*, p. 47.
† Among her many theatrical achievements was the introduction of polite behavior into rehearsals. Before her ascendancy, lighting sessions had been punctuated by exasperated howls, obscenities and curses flying between the house and the stage. Rosenthal was largely responsible for changing that; with the introduction of the intercom and an obligatory "please" in every sentence exchanged, she turned lighting sessions into a civilized, if still nerve-racking, operation.

tion and exhilaration created an intimacy between us that was far closer than if we had spent the night making love together.

During the summer of 1958, not long after the Gersten episode, my relationship with Jeannie was shaken by a tremor that was the more shocking because it came from a wholly unexpected source.

I have mentioned Jean Rosenthal's position with the New York City Ballet, whose technical director and lighting designer she had been for close to ten years, and of which she considered herself an integral and indispensable element. There had been a change of general manager a few years back, but this had in no way affected Jeannie's position nor that of her growing technical staff (almost entirely female), which she had assembled and trained over the years and of which she was the undisputed and virtually autonomous head. This and a general feeling that the girls were getting "too big for their boots" finally came to irritate the two powerful and willful men who had created the company and who resented the growth of this semi-independent female unit within an organization of which they were the consecrated and autocratic rulers. I have never known the details of the purge nor whether its first impulse came from George Balanchine or Lincoln Kirstein. The fact is that, during the latter part of the summer of 1958, they decided to break up this "regiment of women" and to replace Jean Rosenthal as technical director of the ballet with a young man who had been at Stratford for two years—first as an apprentice and then as one of our assistant stage managers.

This all happened quickly and it came as a stunning blow to Jeannie, who, for all her growing national fame as a lighting designer, still regarded the New York City Ballet Company as her home and permanent base. Yet, strangely enough (not so strangely, really, if you considered his complex and mysterious personality), it was not on Jeannie but on Lincoln that the break had the most immediate, traumatic effect. It was consistent with his intensely emotional mechanism that the grief and guilt he felt over the abrupt dismissal of someone to whom he had been so very close for so many years should be followed by feelings of embarrassment and guilt that were then transformed into revulsion and hatred. Jean's name was no longer mentioned between us, and finally it got so that he could no longer bear the sight of her; if he entered the theatre and became aware of her sitting in the darkened house or heard her voice over the intercom, he would instantly turn and leave rather than face the possibility of encountering her.

I am sure that if Lincoln had been omnipotent he would have had Jeannie banished from Stratford as well. Knowing that I would never agree to that, he allowed some of his embarrassment and anger to overflow into his relations with me. And this occurred at a time when storm clouds were gathering around my head and when I desperately needed him as an ally and confidant in the crisis that was developing between myself, Lawrence Langner and the trustees of the Festival.

The brief picketing of our theatre early that summer had been insignificant in itself. But it had started a chain reaction which, within twelve months, would threaten and eventually destroy much of what I had accomplished in Stratford over the past three years. With Reed's continued absence, followed by the resignation of Black and Woods, the Festival's financial base, which had always been shaky, suddenly crumbled. During the latter part of the season Langner had missed no opportunity of reminding me that, much as he admired my integrity, it had almost certainly wrecked the Festival. This demoralization was reflected in the meetings of the executive committee, at which our summer's successes were submerged in the deepening gloom of our fiscal situation and in my own attitude of growing hostility toward the executive committee and the trustees, who, in failing to pursue and find new sources of funding, were, in my opinion, defaulting on their obligations to the Festival and on their contract with me as artistic director.

Joseph Reed, in his sincere, persistent, garrulous and often wearisome way (not to mention his own lavish infusions of money), had managed to keep communications open between the artistic director and the trustees and, more particularly, between Lawrence Langner and myself. With his departure the gap between us continued to widen.

I knew that Lawrence had never fully accepted my total authority over a project that he had labored so long and hard to create. With Joe Reed gone and with the resignations of Black and Woods (who had made it clear that they would return when the present "red" situation had been cleared up —meaning, presumably, when Gersten was fired and I was out of the way), Langner saw a chance to recapture his theatre. My contract had one more year to run and he had no intention of seeing it renewed, if he could help it. The current financial crisis gave him the desired leverage.

This was the situation in mid-October when I left for two months to produce *Playhouse 90* in California. For the first time in three years there would be no winter activity for the Festival Company. And no program could be planned or announced for the following summer until it had been authorized by the board, which remained deadlocked and paralyzed.

I hated to leave things in such a mess, but I was glad to get away. I left Jack Landau to hold the fort on Sixty-fifth Street, and to keep alive an academy that was being starved for funds. He promised to keep me closely informed, by phone and letter, of all public or subterranean developments.

CHAPTER V

1958-1959

PLAYHOUSE 90
"DILLINGER"
ROMEO AND JULIET
THE MERRY WIVES OF WINDSOR
ALL'S WELL THAT ENDS WELL

By MID-SEPTEMBER of 1958 I had all but one of my *Playhouse 90* scripts written and ready for production. It was a variegated collection: one was a political story* concerning the personal problems of an aging U.S. senator, played by Melvyn Douglas; another dramatized the visit by a group of parents to a boys' summer camp; a third covered an episode in the Capone gang wars in Chicago; the fourth was the dramatization of a new novel by the French writer Pierre Boulle;† the fifth was a television version of Henry James's *The Wings of the Dove*. But my favorite, the one with which I intended to open my season, was an original script by Loring Mandel (who had done the Centralia story for us). He called it "Proj-

* It was adapted by David Davidson, author of *The Steeper Cliff*, the first serious postwar novel about Germany during the early years of our occupation.
† Author of *The Bridge on the River Kwai*, etc.

150

ect Immortality." Its hero was an aging scientist, a mathematical genius on the order of Einstein or Von Neumann, and its background was a university community like Princeton. Loring had been working on it for many months and had transmitted some of his enthusiasm to Frank Schaffner, the director, who was eager to put it on.

With these scripts in my suitcase I departed for California, leaving Joan and the children in our new apartment on Eighty-sixth Street and Central Park West. Both the boys were now going to the Rudolph Steiner School across the park and spending their weekends and holidays in the House on the Hill in New City. Joan was eager to get back to California but felt she should not desert the children; besides, she was displeased with me for having sold our house in Santa Monica. So she stayed on in New York, which (remembering the bad years she had spent there after her arrival from France) she still feared and hated, and compensated for that and for my absence with a brief, joyless spasm of splurging at Bergdorf-Goodman, Bendel and Saks Fifth Avenue. For my part, I rented a wing of Dorothy Jeakins' small house in Brentwood, where I was able to worry in solitude over my coming television productions.

The first few weeks of my first season with *Playhouse 90* were marked by one of the last and wildest of my habitual panics. In part, no doubt, this was a hangover from the fevers and frenzies of *The Seven Lively Arts,* but mainly it derived from my familiar "new boy" syndrome—from my sense that I was once again a beginner and an amateur among highly skilled and knowledgeable professionals.

These fears were heightened by a long-distance call I received early one morning soon after my arrival in California. It was from my friend Hubbell Robinson, who told me that, after careful consideration, "Project Immortality" had been judged unsuitable for *Playhouse 90.* When I pressed him for a reason, he said it was "too intellectual." I pointed out I had nothing to take its place. He said that didn't matter. One of my shows was being preempted, and that would put things back on schedule.

I took it hard. I called him back several times. So did Frank

Schaffner. Hubbell was regretful but adamant. I decided to resign and so informed my lawyer, Arnold Weissberger, who without too much difficulty dissuaded me from this quixotic sacrifice of one hundred thousand dollars.*

When people refer to the Golden Age of Television they are usually talking about *Playhouse 90*—described by *Time* as "the best dramatic show in television's brief history." This and other leading dramatic shows (such as *Kraft, Philco, Studio One* and *Climax*) were staffed mostly by quite young men who had grown up with the industry and who, in a few years, had attained an extraordinarily high level of technical expertise. Coordinating the work of the engineers, cameramen, designers and technical assistants were the directors, an unusually talented and dynamic group. The directorial staff of *Playhouse 90* included Arthur Penn, Frank Schaffner, John Frankenheimer and George Roy Hill, all of whom later became major motion-picture directors. (Other regulars were Robert Mulligan, Arthur Hiller, Ralph Nelson, Robert Stevens, Buzz Kulik, Boris Sagal, Fielder Cook and Sidney Lumet.) Working with them was a group of young writers (some of them from radio) who found in television drama creative opportunities that were denied them in the shrinking commercial theatre and in the highly structured film industry. Among them, week after week, they turned out a large number of shows, not all of which had quality or distinction, but which, in the aggregate, displayed a remarkable range of energy and courage—in their choice of subject matter and in the dramatic and technical skill that went into their creation. That it

* The ultimate irony occurred eight months later, long after I had produced my quota of shows and was back on the East Coast. For reasons known only to the network, *Playhouse 90* was extended that year into the summer, and there was a sudden shortage of scripts. An associate producer, Peter Kortner, remembered "Project Immortality" and resubmitted it. Hubbell, cleaning up his desk a few days before his resignation, okayed it. Broadcast on June 11, 1959, directed by Fielder Cook, with Lee Cobb as the dying scientist and Kenneth Haigh as his disciple, it was nominated by the Academy and received the Sylvania Award for the best original drama of the year.

was an ephemeral art and that these creations existed only
for the duration of the broadcast and then disappeared forever was perhaps one of the virtues and attractions of the
medium. (The invention and increasing use of videotape beginning in 1958 coincides historically with the end of the so-
called Golden Age.)*

As flagship of the leading network and the only ninety-
minute dramatic show on the air, *Playhouse 90* enjoyed special
privileges as regards budget and rehearsal time. Our normal
rehearsal schedule was sixteen days. Of those, eleven or
twelve were taken up with readings, corrections of the script
and "blocking" in a rehearsal room large enough for the sets
to be marked out on the floor with multicolored tape. These
rehearsals were attended by a scene designer and a technical
director to make sure that nothing was rehearsed that could
not be executed when the show moved into a major studio.
This move took place (depending on the size and difficulty
of the production) during the weekend preceding the Thursday broadcast. By that time our sets were already standing in
various stages of completion and actors went to work in them,
watched by lighting and camera crews. On Wednesdays, like
a dark swarm of mechanical monsters trailing hundreds of
feet of black cable behind them, the electronic cameras and
their crews moved onto the floor while the director retired
into the control room, in which, surrounded by banks of
flickering consoles and monitors, he and his technical director would start shaping and editing the show.

Thursday was a day of madness. While the second hand of
the studio clock moved relentlessly through the morning and
the early afternoon toward air time, the show, with much
shouting and rushing in and out of the control room, was
run through, "teched," then dress-rehearsed. For anyone

---

* Videotape has been with us for so long that it is hard to realize
that until 1958 there was no satisfactory method of recording the
shows that were broadcast live. A method was devised—known as a
"hot kinescope"—whereby a show was photographed on film as it
first went out on the air. It was poor in quality, but it obviated the
tedious necessity of doing each show several times for different parts
of the country.

who had not grown up in it, it was an awesome and hair-raising experience: the actors in the center, and four moving cameras, on their various mountings (including one on a tall crane), waltzing in silence around them in moves every one of which was watched and regulated by the director and his technical aides from the control room above. As each scene ended, hell broke loose; there was a sudden rush of actors from one set to another, followed by the four cameras and their troops of handlers—ready to take up their new positions and to begin a scene that within a few seconds would be going out over the air to millions of viewers. For one trained in the leisurely tempo of filmmaking, the speed and skill with which these improvisations were carried out was a constant source of amazement. Once in a while disaster struck: an actor would miss an entrance, forget his or her lines or, in desperation, resort to a four-letter word; on almost every show hovering stagehands, a mike boom or another camera would briefly appear on the electronic screen. (On one of my shows an overzealous camera operator fell among the actors from the top of his eighteen-foot crane.) But such accidents were instantly and calmly corrected.*

Most of the responsibility for the quality of the shows fell on the producer for its preparation and the director for its execution. The year I came to *Playhouse 90* was the first in which it had multiple producers, all from New York—Coe, Brodkin and myself. This arrangement would never have worked had it not been for the presence on CBS's Hollywood staff of a most unusual woman by the name of Ethel Winant. She had worked in the theatre before coming to television; her present official designation with CBS was that of casting director. In that capacity she managed to reconcile quality and imagination with the network's preoccupation with star names. But she did far more than that: as each new producer took over, she became his adviser, mediator, gadfly, conscience, fixer, little mother, and devoted and loyal associate.

* One of the virtues of videotape, when it came into general use, was that it permitted the correction of such errors. However, it also resulted in an inevitable change of rhythm and a lessening of the tension that was one of the prime assets of live television.

(To old hands like Coe and Brodkin, she was invaluable; a greenhorn like myself could not have existed without her.) In a very real sense Ethel Winant was the invisible producer of *Playhouse 90,* where, in addition to her other functions, she maintained contact and ran interference between the visiting producer and the front office—with Hubbell Robinson in New York and with the local vice-president in charge of West Coast production, who, in this case, happened to be my former boss at RKO, my successor in the affections of Miss Joan Fontaine and my associate in *Letter to an Unknown Woman,* dynamic William Dozier.

This, then, was the strange and terrifying world into which I was thrown in the fall of 1958. My first two shows were broadcast live on successive Thursdays beginning on November 27. Neither was characterized by excessive boldness, and neither turned out to be a world-shaker. But they were both competently produced and directed by Ralph Nelson and Fielder Cook respectively. Of the first, "The Return of Ansel Gibbs," I remember little * except its cast, headed by Melvyn Douglas, Mary Astor and Diana Lynn. Of my second show, about a boys' summer camp, *The New York Times* reported that "parents who give vent to their own frustrations by pushing their children into excessive competition were scathingly scored last night." But it added that the whole thing "tottered close to soap opera" and that "since 'Free Weekend' had something to say it is a pity that it did not say it better."

---

* What I do remember is that it was produced in the midst of what was known as the "plugola" scandal, when it was discovered that certain directors were engaging in the trivial but shameful malpractice of placing products, with the name of their maker prominently displayed, in such a position on the set that the cameras could not fail to include them in the scene; this applied to wines, soft drinks, perfume, coffee, children's toys, luggage and shaving cream. No money passed, but cases of the product were duly delivered to the director's home after the show. This practice, when discovered, provoked great indignation among major advertisers who were paying huge sums to promote their products in the regular commercial breaks. For several months network inspectors haunted the sets of all major dramatic shows making sure that all visible products had neutral or imaginary labels.

However, it was well received throughout the rest of the country and marked the beginning of a new career for Buddy Ebsen as one of the fathers.

With my third, "Seven Against the Wall," I had found my stride and begun to enjoy myself. It was a thoroughly immoral show, the script of which I had bought from a former FBI agent: a detailed and accurate treatment of the St. Valentine's Day Massacre in which Capone and his boys knocked off seven of Bugs Moran's henchmen in a Chicago garage. Meticulously researched and brilliantly executed, it was a perfect example of what later came to be known as "docudrama," played by actors who were unfamiliar enough to be credible and not one of whom received more than seven hundred fifty dollars for three weeks' work.* And it was directed by that great craftsman Frank Schaffner with so many sets that we had to use *two* connecting studios. Except for a gang execution in a phone booth (which, on account of the danger from flying glass, was shot ahead of time, on film) it was a live show, in which Paul Lambert as Capone, in his bloodthirsty agitation, twice used a four-letter word on the air.

Unlike "Project Immortality," this show provoked no serious objection from the network. But, for my own part, I felt it desirable to announce in an interview, "Violence is not the point of the story we are telling. Our concern is with social and economic phenomena and with underworld power in the structure of our national life." For further protection, our grim epic was narrated by that paragon of journalistic probity Eric Sevareid,† who years later told me that he had "never forgotten that experience in television."

Our press was excellent. John Crosby, who was still re-

* One of them was a middle-aged actor suffering from terminal cancer whom Ethel Winant, at his own persistent request, had cast in a minor part. He collapsed during final rehearsals but insisted on being allowed to watch the show from his hospital bed and died minutes after the character he was to have played was shot down on the screen.

† In using him we defied an unbreakable network rule that no newscaster was ever allowed to host or participate in any way in a drama. It took the personal intervention of William Paley to get him onto our show.

viewing for the *New York Herald Tribune*, wrote that it was "a gripping, unsentimental and marvelously thorough recapitulation . . . This was big, big television. There was a spaciousness to the sets, to the streets, to the size of the cast, to the very scope of the enterprise."

My next two shows were recorded in December for delayed broadcasting in early January. The first was Boulle's latest novel, *Face of a Hero*, adapted by Robert Joseph* to an American locale. Ever since *River Kwai*, Boulle's was a name to conjure with, and since John Frankenheimer was, at the moment, the hottest director on television, we were able to assemble a remarkable cast headed by film star Jack Lemmon. The show, like most of Frankenheimer's, was produced in an atmosphere of intense excitement, with great emphasis on certain "terrific" scenes at the expense of the whole. I was never quite convinced that it made sense—either then or later, when it was transferred to the New York stage. However, it was well received and had some excellent reviews. *The New York Times* described it as "the story of a small-town prosecutor who ignored the voice of his conscience. It involved an important matter of morality told in provocative terms." Among the "noteworthy portrayals" were Rip Torn as a "libertine accused of murder, James Gregory as a conscientious sheriff, Anne Meacham as a neglected bride and Henry Hull as a grieving father."

Next came a version made by Meade Roberts of Henry James's *The Wings of the Dove*. There was a general conviction that Henry James and his works were unsuited to the mass media. I did not agree; I felt that James's sensitive, sophisticated treatment of what was, in fact, a sentimental, melodramatic plot was eminently suited to dramatization on TV. Directed by Robert Stevens,† with period costumes by Doro-

---

* One of the producers of Calhern's *King Lear*, who had become a writer for television.

† According to Ethel Winant, "Robert Stevens, for all his craziness, deserves a footnote in the history of television." He created much of the technology that dominated the years of live television—the moving cameras, the intensity of close-ups, etc. He had an extraordinary instinct for what worked on that little screen.

thy Jeakins and a cast that included Dana Wynter, Isabel Jeans, Henry Daniell, Lureen Tuttle, Inga Swenson and James Donald, it received a rave in *Variety,* qualified praise elsewhere and a gratifying response from an unexpected quarter: James Thurber and Dwight MacDonald were both James enthusiasts and both were extravagant in their praise. Thurber's appeared in *The New Yorker:*

> This adaptation seemed to me closer to the James tone and closer to perfection of total production than any other dramatization I have seen . . . Miss Swenson as Milly must have been recruited by James himself from among the angels.*

MacDonald's in *Esquire:*

> The whole production was at the very highest level. It was worthy of James' great novel—moving, sensitive, exciting . . . as it is always exciting to reveal human beings in action . . . It was exactly what everyone keeps hoping, usually in vain, that television will be.

By the time *The Wings of the Dove* went on the air in early January 1959, I was back in New York. I had flown in a few days before Christmas to supervise the Christmas Day broadcast of *The Nutcracker.* The modest black-and-white version we had broadcast the previous year on *The Seven Lively Arts* had been so well received that CBS now decided to repeat it in a longer and more expensive version, on prime time and in color. Since I had to be in California until three days before the broadcast, I had asked Jack Landau to represent me in New York as associate producer. It was a thankless task, and when I arrived—just in time for dress rehearsals—I found that, unlike Charles Dubin, who the previous year had devoted his considerable talent and understanding of ballet

---

* Thurber admitted later: "Because my sight has failed I could not see Inga Swenson who played Milly and this was probably fortunate since I was told she looked as healthy as one of Thomas Hardy's milkmaids but her words fell persuasively upon the ear and she *was* the dying Milly to me."

to giving the choreographer, George Balanchine, what he wanted, Ralph Nelson, our present director, had ideas of his own as to what constituted TV entertainment. After three tense days we went on the air with a compromise. It may have been color that made the difference: *The New York Times*, which had been lukewarm the previous year, hailed the present version as a "real child's fantasy in which choreography, stagecraft and technical effects all achieved distinction."

That was the end of my season's participation in *Playhouse 90*. With the loss of "Project Immortality" the number of my shows had been reduced to six—as against eight by Coe and fifteen by Brodkin. Nevertheless, we all shared equally in the Emmy Award that *Playhouse 90* received as the best dramatic series of the year, and I was reengaged as one of its three producers for the following season.

The New York Times, in an article headed "Uphill Battle," reported that CBS claimed to have lost four million dollars in unsold advertising on the show, but added: "If *Playhouse 90* has reaffirmed one lesson in this generally distressing season it is that within TV's current ranks lie extraordinarily gifted people who can turn out programming of a most superior caliber when they are allowed to do so."

Before I retired from television for the season, I did, in fact, produce one more show for Hubbell Robinson. Following the great success of "Seven Against the Wall," Hubbell proposed that I join him in launching a new series to be known as *The Lawbreakers*. It would be a weekly show and it would record the exploits of America's leading criminals. To justify this exploitation of violence we would make clear that all our heroes had come to an awful and lamentable end— thus proving that Crime Does Not Pay. As the subject of the pilot for the series we selected the most lurid of them all, John Dillinger, and assigned David Davidson to turn the available documentary material into a fifty-two-minute television script. We filmed it in the same huge barn of a studio on First Avenue in which we had done "The Blast in Centralia" the previous year. Directed by Mel Ferber and starring Ralph Meeker, it was another outrageously immoral but exciting show. Before it was finally edited and ready for broadcasting, James Aubrey (the "Smiling Cobra") had replaced Hubbell as head of CBS-TV production. He wrote me a letter thanking me for a show that was "impressive, direct, hardhitting and powerful." Then, following the time-honored custom of jettisoning all his predecessor's product, he put the show on ice and left the exploitation of twenties crime to a rival network with a show named *The Untouchables*—one of the most lucrative and long-lasting series in the history of television.

("Dillinger" was taken out of mothballs a year later and broadcast as an isolated "special" entitled "A Year to Kill." It was sponsored by Procter and Gamble and got high ratings and good reviews. The *Times* found it "absolutely fascinating if morally a little disturbing. The bad guys get it in the end—but for close to an hour they have led a pretty glorious and adventurous life.")

"Dillinger" was a welcome diversion from the depressing and exasperating deadlock which continued in the offices of the Stratford Festival on Sixty-fifth Street. During my absence in California, Jack Landau had kept me informed by letter and telephone of what was happening—which was precisely nothing. The Gersten question had been raised once again; I was asked if I intended to renew his contract. I said I did. There was no reaction. But, for weeks after my return, the executive committee continued to withhold its authorization of our plans for the coming season.

Immediately after the making of "Dillinger" I flew to Chicago for a lecture and returned on the first scheduled run of Lockheed's new turboprop Electra. The following day, on that same flight into La Guardia, it crashed into the East River with considerable loss of life. But by then I was on my way to Washington, D.C., to appear in a theatrical symposium with Isak Dinesen, Harold Clurman and an English lady scholar whose specialty was the Elizabethan theatre audience. On the train coming back, I drafted a letter to Lincoln Kirstein which I asked him to pass on to the Festival's executive committee:

DEAR LINCOLN,

I am leaving tomorrow on a fortnight's vacation. I have hung around New York for almost a month in the hope of attending a meeting which would put an end to the state of totally suspended animation in which the Festival has wallowed for almost half a year and which is making us ridiculous among members of the press and the theatrical world. I will wait no longer.

I came east three years ago at your request and that of Joseph Reed to save the Festival from disaster. I am not willing to conduct crash operations of this kind indefinitely. In this feeling Jack Landau and I are in complete agreement. For three years we have given our energy and devotion to the Festival—with appreciable results. There is a limit to the humiliation we are able to swallow and the betrayals to which we are willing to submit.

The next morning Joan and I set out in my fabulous but deteriorating Chrysler 300 for New Orleans, where we boarded an Alcoa cruise ship that carried us in great luxury during the next ten days to Santo Domingo (to what was still known as Ciudad Trujillo) and from there to Caracas, Curaçao and Trinidad. We enjoyed the chance to be alone together, and when we got back I found two notes awaiting me. One was from the Century Association informing me that I had been elected a member. The other was an interoffice memo from Lawrence Langner: a production budget had finally been approved by the board, and we could go ahead with our plans for the summer.

Regardless of my disagreements with the board, part of Landau's and my time that winter and spring had been taken up by a project that was very close to our hearts: the writing and editing of a book, *The Birth of a Theatre,* which would give a brief but comprehensive history of the Festival organization from its conception to the present day and a full record of the company's productions since its formation. With this would go a complete collection of pictures—drawings, plans and production photographs. My friend Joseph Barnes, as senior editor at Simon and Schuster, accepted it for publication, and Helen Barrow, their brilliant book designer, determined its form. It came out as a beautiful, profusely illustrated volume of just over a hundred pages, in hardcover and paperback—of which we guaranteed a sale of twenty thousand in the theatre at the paperback price of one dollar.* It took up an enormous amount of time and work, but it was worth it as a permanent record of what had been accomplished in Stratford over the past three years.

The long-delayed budget for the 1959 summer season represented a substantial reduction in production, but this was not surprising and could not be allowed to interfere with the ambitious plans Landau and I had made for the coming season. Our belated circulars, which did not go out until March, announced a three-week school season and a program of *four* productions for the season instead of the usual three. They were *Romeo and Juliet, The Merry Wives of Windsor, All's Well That Ends Well,* and *A Midsummer Night's Dream* (repeated by popular request).

This revived *Dream* was, once again, an ideal show for the schools, and we decided to keep it in the repertory for limited performances throughout the summer. *Romeo* was a play to which I had always had an intense aversion and, though I gave in to the general clamor for its production, I was unwilling to participate in its direction. Jack Landau, who did not share my revulsion, agreed to direct it.†

For our third production Jack and I had done a lot of preparatory work on a play about which both of us had positive feelings—*Troilus and Cressida.* When we first proposed it, we met with some opposition which was soon heightened by a series of hysterical personal messages from Joe Reed in Paris in which he begged us—*"please, please, please, please, please!"*—*not* to jeopardize the future of the Festival by attempting "this most hopeless and repulsive of all Shakespeare's lesser plays." I wrote explaining that Landau and I did not agree with his estimate of the play, for which we had

* By midseason it was sold out; so was a second printing before the end of the summer.
† Of all the plays we performed for the schools *Romeo and Juliet* was the only one that regularly provoked titters and undisciplined behavior among our juvenile audiences.

devised a production that, we felt, would make it "a clear, brilliant and modern commentary on love and war. However, don't worry, Joseph—your strong feelings about *T and C* have had an overwhelming effect on us all and I assure you that you will not be disturbed by its presence on the Stratford program this summer."

To replace *Troilus* we reluctantly settled on another "lesser" but infallible piece that Jack and I would direct jointly. It too had a large cast and it would give the two Nancys another opportunity to work together as young and attractive Merry Wives of Windsor. It would also give Larry Gates, one of our most stalwart and reliable actors, a chance (failing Burl Ives, whom I had approached but who was not available) to appear as Falstaff.

For our fourth and final production I decided on *All's Well That Ends Well*, for which I had developed a fondness ever since I had seen Irene Worth play Helena in Tyrone Guthrie's first season at Stratford, Ontario. I intended to direct it myself and I felt that it was a perfect vehicle for Nancy Wickwire, of whom I found myself thinking more and more as our company's leading lady.

In all my years of personal and professional observation of actors' creative mechanisms, Nancy Wickwire stands out as an extreme example of duality. There were, literally, two Nancy Wickwires. There was the well-bred, middle-class ingenue with the attendant mother; a nice-looking medium blonde with a good figure, a fresh complexion, charming manners and an outlook on the world that conformed to the social conventions of Harrisburg, Pennsylvania, where she grew up. None of this was changed much during her sojourn at the Old Vic School in London or by her early years in the American theatre, where her appearance, her training and her evident talent made life easier for her than for most girls of her age. Still, there was something missing. Watching her on the stage (with looks that were vaguely reminiscent of a young Gertie Lawrence), one often had the feeling that something was being held back and that locked inside all that style and charm there was a wild, vulnerable, generous and reckless creature whose social and emotional inhibitions were persistent enough to dim what should have been one of the brightest stars in the American theatre.

That this other Nancy existed was evident to anyone who had ever watched her dance. It did not matter where or when or with whom; the mere action of dancing suddenly changed her into another person. Her conventionally clothed figure was transformed into the free, whirling body of a maenad— the limbs flashing, the mouth open in an ecstatic, sensual smile, the hair flying wildly about her glowing face, her eyes shining with a bright green fire.*

All's Well That Ends Well had other virtues. It offered, in the Countess of Rousillon, a good role for a distinguished elderly female visitor (one who would also play the Nurse in *Romeo*). We first approached Eva Le Gallienne, and when that didn't work I invited Aline McMahon, with whom I had a friendship that went back many years.

Sada Thompson was back with the company. So was Morris Carnovsky. Ellis Rabb was absent—deep in the throes of forming his own actors' company, the Association of Producing Artists (APA) with Rosemary Harris—but Will Geer was very much with us. So were Richard Easton and Inga Swenson, whom we cast as the star-crossed lovers of *Romeo and Juliet.*

We had spent weeks wooing Fritz Weaver to play Mercutio but gave up on receipt of a characteristic note in which he apologized for the delay but explained, "Hamlet floored me

---

* Nancy Wickwire died of cancer at forty-eight in California, having found freedom and happiness in the final years of her life. Most of her best last work was done for the American Conservatory Theatre in San Francisco, where Bill Ball, who appreciated her special quality, let her play the leading roles in a repertory which included *The House of Bernarda Alba* and *The Cherry Orchard* till within a few weeks of her death. One exceptional relic of her tragically brief career is the recording of a reading of *Under Milk Wood* she made with Dylan Thomas at New York's YMHA. It was the first public performance of the work, which the poet had still not fully completed. The final section was partly improvised, including Polly's song—which Dylan asked Nancy to sing spontaneously, without preparation or rehearsal. What she gave him was wildly beautiful and moving.

last summer and I have been trying to get back on my feet ever since."

To take his place I turned to a young man by the name of William Smithers, an active member of the Actors' Studio, who had appeared in one of our Hemingway stories for *The Seven Lively Arts*. I engaged him in an attempt to strengthen the company's roster of young, virile leading men and assigned him to Mercutio and to Bertram in *All's Well*.

Otherwise, with a few gains and a few losses, it was the same company as the previous season.* Yet somehow, as we went into rehearsal, I sensed a change. There was still a general feeling of dedication and pride but some of the buoyancy and excitement of previous years seemed to be missing.

Theatrical momentum is a mysterious force—easily interrupted and difficult to recapture. The change noted may have occurred during our enforced six months' hiatus; it may have reflected my own growing hostility to the board (though I made every effort to conceal it from the company); it may have been caused by the sense of our worsening financial situation, of which the company could not fail to be aware. Finally, it may have been due to a normal running-down of energy—in myself and in the organization. Whatever the cause, I had the distinct and disturbing feeling, for the first time in four years, that the curve of our Festival operation was no longer rising.

On the other hand, our advance sale was greater than ever, and in the excitement of preparing for the coming season much of my apprehension was dispelled. Our production budget had been cut, but by making intelligent use of our previous seasons' lavish sets I had no doubt we would get by. For costume designs for our two Italianate plays I turned once again to Dorothy Jeakins, who accepted our reduced budget on condition that she be allowed to do most of her designing at home in California.

All's Well was easy for her. She and I knew exactly what we

---

* Among our new additions was a sturdy young actor by the name of Edward Asner. Before the end of the season he had wooed and won my blond secretary, with whom he migrated to California, where, in due course, he became a major television star.

wanted. "Medieval soap opera is the catchword for this one!" she wrote, and her sketches, when they arrived, were among her most elegant—sober yet romantic and beautiful. *Romeo* proved a problem. "Quite a sweaty business!" she complained. Jack was at his most indecisive; all he seemed to have was a vague mental image of a stage with lots of white on it. "I've been dissatisfied with most of what I've done," wrote Dorothy, and when she finally arrived with her sketches she was still unhappy. (When George Balanchine came to the dress rehearsal to set the dance for the Capulets' ball, he complained that the stage looked "like washing churning around in a Laundromat.")

Austerity was the word that summer. David Hays's sets for *Romeo and Juliet* made use of what he had constructed the previous year for *Hamlet* and *Winter's Tale;* they had a somewhat barren look that fitted poorly with the romantic quality of the play. For *Merry Wives* Will Steven Armstrong designed a black-and-white set that was cartoonish and viable but undistinguished; Elizabeth Montgomery's costumes were cheerful and adequate.

My description of these productions seems to reflect some of my own vague discontent with our season. As far as *Romeo* was concerned this was matched by our strangely mixed reviews. Elliot Norton wrote that it was "swift in action, lusty and vigorous . . . In Inga Swenson it has a Juliet of thrilling loveliness." The Associated Press reported that "the triumph of Miss Swenson is shared by the company and the director Jack Landau, who has staged a colorful, visual feast."

The *Post* found it "altogether too respectful," while Brooks Atkinson described it as a "lackluster production":

> Unfortunately it puts a higher value on correctness than on vehemence and audacity. It is cool and remote; the characters seem to be separated from one another; the poetry is spoken without rapture, as if it were in bad taste for an actor to be aware of rich phrases and purple passages.

He had kind words for Aline McMahon, "who plays the Nurse with a homely humor that warms the scenes she inhabits," but found Inga Swenson "less exhilarating than she deserves to be . . . She is a lonely Juliet and Richard Easton as her Romeo is at loose ends."

Our second production, which opened on July 2, fared better. With *The Merry Wives*, the company seemed to recapture some of its energy and *joie de vivre*, and good use was made of the Festival Stage—as when the huge laundry basket, with Falstaff supposedly inside it, was hurled straight out at the audience and sank with a splash of false water into the yawning chasm of our open downstage trap.

"Vibrant Country Wives," "Rollicking Frothy Fun," "Merrily Entertaining," were our headlines the next morning. Singled out for special praise were Larry Gates's Falstaff, "who is able to give both size and touching credulity to the fat knight"; Hiram Sherman's unconventionally and comically jealous Ford; Carnovsky's maniacally Gallic Dr. Caius; Sada Thompson's young and voluptuous Mistress Quickly; and, of course, the seductive housewives played by our two Nancys.

All's Well That Ends Well went into rehearsal early in July with the relaxed efficiency that characterized the final play of each season. This most charming and lighthearted of our productions was prepared in an atmosphere of rising apprehension and ill feeling between the trustees and myself. This sense of working in a lull before the storm that threatened the future of the company seemed to draw its members together and gave the rehearsals of *All's Well* a quality of intimacy and harmony that was reflected in our production.

Nancy Wickwire was all that I had hoped: she had simplicity, clarity, beauty and a sense of passionate independence that made of Helena, instead of a lovesick ninny, a "new woman" determined to get her man, almost in the Shavian manner. Her scenes with her elders, the Countess of Rousillon (Aline McMahon), the ailing King of France (Larry Gates) and the wise, courtly Lafeu (Will Geer), were played with a combination of respect and self-confidence that was in direct contrast to her humble but relentless pursuit of her reluctant lover and her warm association with a girl of her own age, Diana (Barbara Barrie). Richard Waring, in his third season with the company, gave unusual comic credibility to Parolles, playing him not as the stock *miles gloriosus* but as an eager and inept social climber in Elizabethan society.

In my casting I had made one serious error. William Smithers had been disappointing in *Romeo and Juliet:* he had shown an inability to translate his Actors' Studio training into the performance of a bravura classic role. I had hoped that in the equivocal part of Bertram his blond, virile good looks and his own strong egotism would carry him past the emotional blocks that had ruined his Mercutio. But it soon became evident that his sulky self-love made it quite impossible to believe that Helena could ever fall in love with such a lout. I have an aversion—amounting to phobia—to changing actors in midstream. (I have always felt that a director is responsible for the actors he has chosen and that recasting during rehearsal is a lazy and disruptive practice.) So I continued to work with Smithers for another week, during which I made quite sure that his understudy, John Ragin, a talented young alumnus of Carnegie Tech who had been with us for two seasons, was up in his lines.

Our official opening was scheduled for July 31. On the night of July 29, following our first preview, I decided to make the change. The next morning I put in the understudy. It is a tribute to the cohesion and morale of the company that this violent change (all the more hateful in a group that regarded itself as an ensemble) was absorbed without complaint or trauma.

Two nights later we opened to what, next to the previous season's *Dream,* were the best reviews the company had ever received:

> Speak gratefully of the American Shakespeare Festival for staging a comedy that is seldom seen. Speak gratefully of John Houseman who—with late Gothic costumes by Dorothy Jeakins, stimulating music by Herman Chessid and with admirable actors at his disposal—has directed a limpid performance.
>
> Brooks Atkinson,
> *The New York Times*

A delightful and satisfying production . . . The delight is
in the performances and the satisfaction is in the Company's triumph in what has too often been neglected as
an impossible comedy.

Judith Crist,
Herald Tribune

Delightful entertainment. . . . The affectionate production staged with remarkable life and zest.

Jerry Walt,
News

Henry Hewes in the *Saturday Review* felt that we had filled
this unpopular play with genuine passion and hailed it as "a
fine production that encourages me more than anything that
has happened since A.S.F.T.A. first announced its five-year
plan."

Especially gratifying, coming at this particular time, was an
article in the *Toronto Telegram* which declared that, for this
season at least, any comparison with Ontario's Stratford must
surely be in Connecticut's favor. It concluded with the general observation that "in a few short years Stratford's directors have developed a style of delivery that is thoroughly
American but clear, lyrical and meaningful."

With the launching of *All's Well* in late July, our summer's
repertory was complete. Now a visitor could spend a long
weekend on the banks of the Housatonic and see four of
Shakespeare's plays in quick succession. Each evening (except
Monday) and twice a day on matinee days, the wide green
lawns that ran down to the river were crowded with couples
and families; our warning bell sent hundreds of picnickers
scurrying to dispose of the remains of their alfresco meals *
before they streamed into the air-conditioned darkness of the
Festival Theatre.

Publicly things had never been better. But behind the

* Our trashcans bore evidence of the variety of our audiences: box
lunches, hot dogs, milk cartons and soda pop were mixed with the
Heidsieck and Dom Perignon, empty jars of caviar and the carcasses
of chickens-in-aspic.

scenes, in New York, in Westport and in Stratford, sides were forming for the inevitable confrontation between the executive committee and the artistic director. With the start of rehearsals a kind of armed truce had been declared; the summer's receipts and advance sales had eased our cash-flow crisis, but, beneath the surface, personal animosities and suspicions continued to ferment and sour. What brought them to a head was the growing awareness that my four-year contract as artistic director was drawing to a close. Relations had been so strained and communication so desultory over the past nine months that the matter had never been openly or formally discussed. However, I had made it quite clear to everyone that I had no intention of continuing as director of the Festival unless I received credible and satisfactory assurances that my demands for the future would be met.

There was nothing drastic or new about these demands. Most of them had been included in the general agreement I had negotiated with Joseph Reed three years before. But Joe was no longer with us, and the Festival's financial situation had become so desperate that my conditions could no longer be accepted by the trustees with any possibility of fulfillment. I knew this and it merely exacerbated my insistence: having worked for four years to raise the Festival to its present honorable estate, I had no intention of presiding over its retreat and ultimate dissolution. Lawrence Langner, on his part, saw in my obduracy his best chance to recapture his theatre and to eliminate or, at least, to reduce the authority of an artistic director who interfered with his personal control of the organization.

The annual trustees' meeting was scheduled for mid-August, and, as that date approached, the true nature of the conflict and the composition of its opposing forces became more apparent. On Langner's side were a number of trustees, mostly from the professional theatre, who liked to be consulted on matters of policy and programming, and who had long resented what they considered my arbitrary decisions and my overbearing attitude toward them. Others were divided. Whenever they visited Stratford they were generous in their praise of our productions and voluble in their appreciation of what we had accomplished. But that did not mean that they were prepared, as trustees, to support demands which, in the Festival's present fiscal condition, they felt to be totally unrealistic. Finally, there may have been a vague general feeling that, after four years of operation under one leadership, a shake-up of some sort was desirable regardless of the consequences.

Supporting me were most of the working elements of the Festival, together with much of the press, which I had so assiduously cultivated over the past four years. I was heartened by their support, yet I knew that neither would be of much help to me in the power struggle ahead. In spite of the Festival's continued success, I was well aware that my position was weaker, in many ways, than it had been during our first two years, when Lincoln Kirstein, Joseph Reed and I had formed a solid and effective triumvirate. Now Reed was gone (together with his seemingly inexhaustible money), and his warm, eulogistic personal letters from Paris were of little value to me. Lincoln, once my staunchest supporter, had become an uncertain ally. In principle he was in favor of my plans for the Festival, but he was highly emotional: the shadow of Jean Rosenthal lay between us, and he might at any moment turn into a dangerous and unpredictable enemy. Some trustees, like Helen Menken, were still wholeheartedly behind me; but her enthusiasm was counterbalanced by the misgivings of her husband, George Richard, who, as treasurer of ASFTA, was concerned with the Festival's financial survival.

As the date for the annual meeting approached, a growing tension was perceptible throughout the Festival which I did nothing to allay. On August 6, I wrote a personal letter to each member of the company—actors, staff and crew: "There has been such a flow of rumor and so much idle chatter about the future of the Festival and of its Artistic Director that I would welcome a chance to talk to all of you personally and to tell you how things stand at this time."

They all came to my house for drinks one night after the show, and I used the occasion to read a long narrative, prepared by Landau and myself, summarizing the Festival's amazing growth over the past four years and, once again, outlining my bright hopes for the company's future. These were conditional, I pointed out, upon certain essential assurances of support by the trustees: year-round employment for the company; expansion of the repertory to include a limited number of non-Shakespearean plays; the opportunity to perform in places other than Stratford, including a regular limited season in New York City. Failing such assurances, and the creation of a "working fund" that would give the artistic director sufficient financial security to avoid having to plan each successive season in a state of stultifying and morale-destroying uncertainty, I was unwilling to continue as the Festival's artistic director.

(Even as I write, the entertainment section of the Toronto paper is filled with references to a crisis in the long-standing dispute between the board and the artistic director of the Stratford, Ontario, Festival. The situation is described as "confused," "tense" and "chaotic." "Resignation," "broken promises," "arbitrary" and "bad feelings" are words that frequently recur. With the change of a few names and details these reports describe my own situation in Connecticut twenty-one years ago; there are the same demands for financial support for the company's touring activities and the same insistence on the need for a winter home. It is the chronic problem faced by successful festivals, and, under present conditions, it is apparently an insoluble one.)

This statement was received with enthusiasm by members of the company. And it formed the basis of the memorandum I presented to the assembled trustees the following Sunday with a request that they hear it before discussing any other matters. In it I recapitulated our recent successes with audiences and critics and restated my hopes for the future. I also listed my current grievances and the way in which I felt the Festival was being "betrayed" by what I considered the board's inadequate and unimaginative methods of fund-raising.*

---

* From its beginnings, Stratford, Connecticut, suffered from the general impression that it was a personal enterprise, conceived and

I read my statement and departed, leaving behind me a disturbed, angry and puzzled group of trustees. My tone was harsh and aggressive and must have come as a disagreeable shock—especially to those casual members who knew only the pleasant things they had read in the papers and were quite unaware that a crisis was brewing on the banks of the Housatonic. Even my friends on the board must have wondered what I hoped to accomplish by forcing the issue as I did. Either I was pulling a wild and dangerous bluff or I must be too drunk with power to realize that I was jeopardizing my own future and that of an institution I had worked so hard and so successfully to create and develop.

After a quarter of a century it has become possible to view my behavior in a somewhat different perspective and to face the fact that it may not have been quite as impulsive as it seemed at the time. My wife, who has long been a passive but perceptive observer of my personal and professional manipulations, maintains that whenever she sees me growing righteously indignant she knows that I am up to something devious and complicated, and that my expressions of outrage are often nothing but a mask for my own feelings of self-reproach. According to this mechanism, what I am publicly raging against may be the very thing that I have secretly decided to bring about—with my indignation rising in direct proportion to my guilt. If she is right—and I strongly suspect that she is—what I was up to during my last months at Stratford may have been an elaborate and dubious maneuver which would permit me to abandon the Festival with a feeling of virtuous grievance.

With this, I step into a hornets' nest of unanswered and perhaps unanswerable questions. For all my enthusiasm for the Festival, my very real love of the company, my intense pride in our achievement and my deep dedication to the creation of a national classical repertory company, was I, in fact, looking for a way out? After the first exhilaration of

---

supported by a handful of rich patrons; even after Joe Reed's departure this impression persisted and made it difficult to raise money from other sources.

victory against seemingly overwhelming odds was I once again becoming bored? Had the crises of the past year—the Gersten affair and our deteriorating financial situation—merely triggered my chronic desire for change? Was I blowing up my differences with Langner and my disappointment in the trustees into a self-righteous excuse for abandoning a project that I was, in fact, beginning to find stale and unprofitable? Finally, was the exaggerated hostility I expressed toward the trustees for denying my unreasonable demands a reflection of my own guilt over my imminent betrayal of a cause to which I had so publicly committed myself?

While I sat sulking in my tent waiting for the trustees' formal reaction to my memorandum I received a number of telegrams, phone calls and personal visits all urging me not to quit. From Lincoln, not a word. From Langner an outraged personal note, accusing me of gross unfairness to himself and to the board. Then, a few days later, in his next formal move, he invited me to attend a meeting with the executive committee, in New York on August 25, at noon. I accepted but, before leaving for the city, I dictated the final version of a press release I had prepared. I gave it to Frank Goodman, our press agent, with instructions to have it mimeographed and to hold it in his office until I gave him the word to distribute it. If it came to a break, I wanted my resignation reported in *my* way—and *first*.

The meeting took place in the Theatre Guild Building on Fifty-third Street, next to the Museum of Modern Art. When I came in, Lincoln avoided my look and it was evident that, for the moment at least, his emotional winds had blown him far away from me. Langner made the first move by reproaching me, more in sorrow than in anger, for my memorandum to the trustees, which, with its intemperate and unreasonable tone, had alienated the entire membership of the board. However, in recognition of my invaluable services, he had been instructed to discuss some form of continued association. He made it clear that, in the Festival's present critical financial situation, the function of an autonomous artistic director was no longer a viable one—all the more since so much of my time during the past two years had been spent doing outside work for the mass media. I objected that such outside work was provided for in my contract and that my occasional absences had allowed Jack Landau to develop into an independent artistic force that had proved of great benefit to the Festival. Here Lincoln spoke up to say that, in his opinion, the company had deteriorated in the past year. Once more I objected, citing audience reaction and our recent reviews as evidence to the contrary. Langner then repeated the complaint that I had been consistently unreceptive to artistic suggestions, his and others': how could I expect members of a board to be supportive of an operation in which their opinions and advice were consistently and arrogantly ignored?

Finally he came to the point. He suggested a new arrangement whereby I would remain as executive producer, working in consultation with himself and the committee. This would give me time for my outside work; it would also permit us to bring in directors from the outside to stage shows under my supervision. I countered that Jack Landau and I had not been directing our shows out of pure ego but because it was dangerous, while building an ensemble, to submit its members to the trauma of an outside director whose methods, inspired though they might be, might prove disruptive of the cohesion we were determined to maintain. I also reminded him that I had, in fact, spoken with Kazan and several other well-known directors, all of whom had declined to work under the Festival's special and limiting conditions. I repeated that under no circumstances would I consider giving up the title and present authority of artistic director, nor would I head a theatrical organization in which decisions were made by a committee. And I added, rising, that I saw no point in pursuing the conversation, since my conditions for staying with the Festival had been clearly stated in my memorandum to the trustees and had not changed.

That was the end. I walked over to my office on Sixty-fifth Street and, in longhand, wrote a letter which Denis Deegan delivered in person to Langner at the Guild office:

DEAR LAWRENCE,

I have considered the Festival situation in the context of my meeting this afternoon with a fragment of the Executive Committee. It is now quite clear to me that between you and the present Artistic Director, who has raised the Festival from its low point of 1955 to its present honored position in the American theatre, no common language exists. I am therefore resigning as of the end of this week, August 30th.

Sincerely,
JOHN HOUSEMAN

While the letter was on its way, I called Frank Goodman and instructed him to send out my release immediately:

After four years as Artistic Director of the American Shakespeare Festival Theatre, John Houseman today announced his resignation. Houseman attributed his departure from Stratford to divergences with the Festival's Executive Committee over the basic policies governing the management of the Festival.

The points of disagreement include the continued failure of the Board of Trustees to provide the necessary working funds to extend the activities of the Festival on a year-round basis with national scope.

And so on, ending:

"I am therefore resigning with regret and deep gratitude to all the working members of the Festival who have so devotedly collaborated with me."

It hit the papers the next morning, together with reactions from Connecticut—"Shocked by Resignation, Stratford Cast Takes Director's Side"; "Festival Group Backs Houseman"—followed by a bitter protest from Lawrence Langner over my premature and unilateral announcement to the press.

A few days later I found two letters in my mail. One arrived by diplomatic pouch from Paris:

May I say that for me personally your resignation, if it occurs, will be a very sad occasion. . . . What you have done for Stratford is one of the outstanding theatrical jobs of the century and I would regard your leaving as a personal tragedy—one that might seriously affect my own decision about remaining with the organization if I seriously believed you were about to separate yourself from us.

It was signed "Joseph."

The other was from Lawrence:

DR. MR. HOUSEMAN,

In accepting your resignation the Board does so with regret and has requested me to formulate the expression of their gratitude for the very excellent work you have performed for the Festival. It is noted that under your direction the Festival has grown from its early beginnings to a strong cultural institution and we hope it will continue to grow along the lines laid down by its founders and yourself.

CBS was pressing me to fly out to Los Angeles to start preparing and casting my second *Playhouse 90* season. But now a deep, euphoric inertia came over me. It was not unlike what I had felt on other similar occasions: the collapse and bankruptcy of the Oceanic; the end of my first marriage; my departure from the Federal Theatre; the breakup of my partnership with Orson Welles; my decision, after five successful years, to leave MGM. Following a period of intense and consuming effort, I was left in a state of emotional exhaustion in which sadness, anger, exhilaration and a deep sense of relief were all equally present.

I sent my assistant Shirley Bernstein* off to California to get things started and hung around Stratford and New York clearing out my files, holding meetings with Landau and once, surprisingly, with Lincoln Kirstein, who was now seem-

---

* Shirley had been my assistant on *Joy to the World* in 1948 (*Front and Center*, p. 292), and I had fallen in love with her briefly in Boston and Philadelphia. With Kinberg off in England, I was now looking for an assistant for *Playhouse 90*. Shirley volunteered for the job because she wished to work with me again and for another, more urgent reason. For two years she had been a leading staff member of *The $64,000 Question*—one of the nation's most successful quiz shows, now being investigated by a grand jury in New York. She hoped that a subpoena would not follow her to California.

ingly filled with regret at my leaving. He reported that the board, in an attempt to maintain some sort of continuity for next season, was about to offer the directorship, on an interim and limited basis, to Jack Landau.

Throughout the crisis, despite pressures and temptations of various kinds, Jack had remained completely and irreproachably loyal. Now, with his usual indecision, he was waiting for me to guide him—to tell him, in case it was offered to him, whether he should accept the task of running the Festival for the coming season. I told him he must feel completely free of any obligation to me. Beyond that, I refused to advise or influence him in any way. In fact, I was divided: Landau's continued presence in Stratford was my only hope for preserving some of what had been accomplished over the past four years. On the other hand, if we both quit at once it would mean total chaos for the coming season, and, in my present mood, that too was an attractive prospect.

I made my final exit from the Festival during a Saturday matinee. William Woodman gives the following lurid report of my departure:

> You drove away during a matinee of *Merry Wives* in a thunderstorm. As you left, the ventilation flaps at the top of the stagehouse disgorged torrents of water onto the stage (it had never happened before). And the next day we heard that Lawrence Langner's house in Westport had been struck by lightning roughly at the moment you must have driven past it on the Merritt Parkway.

The following afternoon Joan and I gave a farewell party in the House on the Hill in New City. It was a highly emotional occasion, complete with speeches, tears, embraces, excoriations, dancing and a lot to drink. One car (an old white Porsche) was wrecked between Stratford and New City with no serious injuries, and Morris Carnovsky, on behalf of the company, formally presented to me a set of Shakespeare's complete works in the Nonesuch Edition. At some time in the evening Nancy Wickwire, wandering into the night to cool off between dances, plunged thirty feet over the edge of our ravine, landed against a rock, got up and returned, muddy, bleeding a little but smiling, to dance some more.

A few days after our party the family's westward migration got under way. The boys left by plane with the larger of the two poodles. I drove out in my aging Chrysler 300 weighed down with books, household effects, my seventy-nine-year-old mother and Virgil, the black dachshund. We made it in three and a half days, and my mother could not remember ever having had a better time. Joan, Denis Deegan and two more dogs followed in a secondhand blue Mercedes.

By the end of September we were all settled in a ramshackle house on the beach. Joan was glad to be back in Malibu, but indignant at having to live in a rented house instead of her own beautiful and comfortable house in Santa Monica, which I had sold without consulting her the year before. (Our apartment on Eighty-sixth Street, which she had decorated agreeably but without love, suffered the usual fate of our residences: it was rented for the duration of its lease to a succession of British actors and their wives, some of whom burned holes in and spilled drinks on our furniture and carpets.)

I discovered, soon after moving into my office at the CBS Television Center, that for the second time in a year I was working for an organization that was past its peak of success. *Playhouse 90* was no longer the network's flagship but a leaky vessel that we were trying to keep afloat. It was having trouble competing for viewers with the new prime-time favorites, of which the most sensationally successful was *The Beverly Hillbillies*. Our champion, Hubbell Robinson, was gone and, with the ascendancy of the new, sordid regime of James Aubrey, the total dominance of the air by TV "ratings" had begun. During the 1959–60 season *Playhouse 90* was no longer broadcast every Thursday night but only twice a month, and this had a dampening effect on the audience loyalty that had been one of our main assets.

We still had much the same crew and most of the same writers and directors (with the exception of Frankenheimer and Schaffner, who had moved over into films), but much of the excitement was gone. Of the network executives, only Ethel Winant, muttering sarcasms and innuendos, continued to pour all her energy, her enthusiasm and her amazing expertise into a show that she dearly loved and for which she received no formal credit.

My own first broadcast was an original by David Davidson —a melodramatic but well-written account of a fictional revolution in a Latin-American state ruled by a dictator on the model of Batista or Trujillo. With Ethel's help we collected a colorful cast that included George C. Scott, Ricardo Montalban, Marisa Pavan, Liliane Montevecchi and the well-known Mexican actor Pedro Armendariz. Under Robert Stevens' direction the show came off better than I had dared to hope.* *The New York Times* felt that "*Playhouse 90* seems off to a good start. Ricardo Montalban was fine; George C. Scott sliced his special style of doggedly florid ham. . . . Montevecchi was perfectly cast, though her big scene with Montalban put us in mind of Vilma Banky grappling with Valentino."

My next, "The Sounds of Eden," by George Bellak, was based on the kidnapping, in the mid-thirties, of a wealthy oil-company executive, who, after his ransom had been paid, was able to lead the police back to the scene of his abduction by remembering the exact times at which a mail plane had flown twice a day over the isolated shack in which he was being held. Once again I sought respectability for a lurid story by inviting an unimpeachable authority to editorialize on the evils of crime. This time we used the voice of Robert Kennedy, who had just achieved considerable fame as the Senate's special investigator of underworld activity. In a letter to John Bartlow Martin, who had recently done an extended reportage on Kennedy and Jimmy Hoffa for *The Saturday*

---

* In one sense it was a watershed in television. As written and designed, the show was so large that the sets would not fit into any one studio. At the last moment it proved necessary to tape it—around the clock, for three days—for a total of seventy-two hours. The fact that the show *could* be done entirely on tape opened the way for more complicated dramas, including the use of "locations."

Evening Post, I reported: "Your friend Bobby K. was eloquent but predictable."

My third show was George Bernard Shaw's *Misalliance.* It was not ideal television material, but, in its shortened version (as edited by Meade Roberts) and with the brilliant cast we were able to assemble, it made for a rather special and fascinating broadcast. Actually, the entire experience, including rehearsals, was more like a stage performance than a TV show. Our director was, once again, Robert Stevens, but the cast was entirely and purely theatrical—with Claire Bloom as the ingenue, Isobel Elsom as her mother, Robert Morley as the father and Patrick MacNee as the brother. Siobhan McKenna was the Polish acrobat and Kenneth Haigh the burglar, together with Rod Taylor, Robert Casper and John Williams. They all behaved in the great tradition of British actors —they quarreled, gossiped, back-bit and bitched incessantly but performed brilliantly. Our critical reception was mixed. Negative in *The New York Times:*

> *Playhouse 90* elected last night to revive Shaw's *Misalliance* and one wonders what on earth for. . . . A cast of superior players raced through its lines at breakneck speed but with scant flair and flavor.

Positive in *Variety:*

> An ideal comedy venture. It set the kind of pace, irreverence, zany twists and crackling, zestful performances that make it one of the happiest farces to hit television for a long time.

Of my final broadcast I remember nothing, except that it starred Richard Basehart. For, by then, I was deeply immersed in the negotiations that my agents were conducting on my behalf with Metro-Goldwyn-Mayer and which involved my return, after more than five years, to motion-picture production. Shortly before Christmas my deal was made: two films a year for five years with the fiction of a production company, John Houseman Productions, whose product would be financed and released by Loew's, Inc.

Then, a few days before I was due to return to Culver City, the screenwriters went out on a major strike for residual rights. The entire industry was paralyzed, and the companies invoked the *force majeure* clause which allowed them to suspend all existing contracts for the duration of the strike.

So it came about that I spent almost four months waiting for the studio to reopen and for my new film producer's contract to begin. It was the first time I had been out of work in ten years, and during this brief involuntary calm a watershed was formed that seriously affected the future course of my life.

CHAPTER VI

1959-1963

MURDER IN THE CATHEDRAL
THE THREE SISTERS
SIX CHARACTERS
IN SEARCH OF AN AUTHOR
ALL FALL DOWN
TWO WEEKS IN ANOTHER TOWN
THE ICEMAN COMETH
MEASURE FOR MEASURE
THE CHILD BUYER

WITH OUR RETURN to Malibu some of the clouds that had hung low over our lives during the past year seemed to lift. Joan was delighted to be back on the beach, and my own loathing of Southern California soon dissolved in the subtropical sunshine.

Early in December we moved into another, more agreeable and roomy house in the Malibu Colony, where Christmas and New Year's were celebrated with the customary rituals.* The boys too seemed to recover a sense of freedom and physical well-being which (except for John Michael's enchanted so-

---

* These included the pouring, on New Year's Eve, of molten lead into a pot of cold water; the resultant forms were then treated in the manner of a Rorschach test.

journ in a summer camp named Blueberry Cove in Maine) they had not generally enjoyed in the East.

We had visitors. Our new home had a guest house in the back which my mother, who was approaching eighty, occupied for several months. It had a large, sunny bedroom overlooking the ocean from which she seldom stirred before midafternoon but where she presided, amid clouds of cigarette smoke, over a court of children and dogs whom she seduced with tidbits of various sorts. In March she returned to her beloved Paris, where she was to spend the next thirteen years of her life.

Another long-term guest was Denis Deegan, who converted a potting shed at the bottom of the garden into an exiguous but livable and quite elegant studio (complete with library and crystal chandelier) where he resided as factotum and family friend while he waited to go to work as my assistant at MGM.

The first consequences of my enforced leisure were some anxiety about money and a gradual renewal of my acquaintance with my wife and family and, through them, with the person I myself had become during a decade in which I had been so wholly and perpetually absorbed in work that I had little time or energy for anything else.

I spent those months of unemployment making conscientious attempts to establish social and cultural contacts with my sons. With their merciless children's observation they recognized these tardy approaches for what they were. My evening readings were only moderately appreciated—partly due to the difficulty of finding suitable common material for auditors of such different ages. The pops concerts I organized and played on the family record player were listened to with polite but wandering attention. Family walks on the beach (in the company of two poodles, a basset hound, two dachshunds and a nervous cat) were more popular. On the rare forays on which Joan joined us, she used the occasion to introduce the boys to the salty delights of the *fruits de mer* in which the beach abounded—mussels, clams, winkles and prickly sea urchins

—which Sebastian was always the first to sight and dig up but which Joan and John Michael were the only ones to relish.*

As I began to make their acquaintance, I was surprised to discover how very different those two small persons had become during the nine and six brief years of their lives. Both were healthy and charming without apparent ill effects from their incredibly diverse genes—Spanish and Finnish-Russian combined with Nebraska Scotch-Irish on Joan's side, Alsatian-French-Jewish crossed with Welsh-Irish on mine. Both were tall, handsome and fair, though Sebastian's platinum was finally darkening, and they were passionately devoted to each other.

John Michael, the elder, was not unlike what I must have been at his age, only more secure and gregarious, with a wholly egotistical interest in people that rarely outlasted their physical presence and an aptitude for mathematical and abstract conjecture in which I had been totally deficient.

Sebastian, almost from birth, revealed astonishingly keen sensory perceptions combined with a prodigious obstinacy that kept him from conforming to normal disciplines or to any sustained effort required of him. His attendance at Malibu's Catholic school was punctuated by fearful scenes with the French-Canadian nuns who presided over the establishment, including dunce caps, handslapping with rulers, and standings-in-the-corner, all of which he suffered in defiant silence. This same defiance persisted during his grilling by the local police when he and a friend (known as "Kevin-the-Bad" to distinguish him from another local boy known as "Kevin-the-Good") were caught breaking into an unoccupied beach house where they performed mysterious rites at dead of night: the burned-out stubs of several dozen candles were

* The esoteric eating habits Michael learned from his mother stood him in good stead twenty years later when, as an anthropologist in darkest Africa, he won the confidence of his hosts the Cameroonians by sharing, without apparent revulsion, in their diet of large, meaty caterpillars.

found, set in an uneven circle, on the wooden floor of the highly flammable gazebo.*

If the boys squabbled more loudly and frequently with their mother than they did with me, it was because they were more closely and uninhibitedly involved with her. With Sebastian, in particular, Joan had similarities of temperament that led to frequent conflicts based on an intuitive sense of each other's motivations. Yet her deeper maternal feelings were for John Michael, her firstborn, who could reduce her to sudden tenderness, anxiety or suffering without the slightest awareness of what he was doing.

Overall, I failed to qualify, then or at any other time, as a concerned, effective or authoritative father. Looking back, I realize that almost every decision affecting our children's health, education and welfare (including finally, at Joan's insistence, their belated baptism) was made and executed by their mother. I am also aware that, over the years, I achieved a far closer empathy with associates and played a more effective parental role with some of my actors and students than I ever succeeded in doing with my sons. However, during those four months of idleness I did make some progress and managed to establish a remote, perplexed but mildly affectionate relationship with both of them that has persisted, without much change, to this day.

Between Joan and me it was less a matter of discovery than

---

* Fire was for years the terror of the Malibu Colony. Created as a weekend retreat in the twenties by members of the film world who could not (like Hearst or Thalberg) afford mansions in Santa Monica, it was built on a narrow strip of beach that was leased but could not be bought. As a result, most of the beach houses were flimsy wooden structures knocked together by studio carpenters. Since there was neither fire equipment nor water pressure, the Colony was regularly swept by fires that destroyed between two and ten houses at a time. Today all that is changed. The Colony has been taken over by new millionaires and rock stars whose houses are solid and sumptuous; the flimsy gazebos of yesteryear have grown into massive, pretentious bastions that contain saunas, Jacuzzis and solar-heated indoor pools. When we lived there, in the fifties and early sixties, the Colony was still a modest Garden of Eden in which dogs and children lived in blissful possession of the beach and the back road.

of recognition. After twelve years of living together we held few surprises for each other, but during my long periods of physical and emotional absence I was inclined to forget or overlook certain basic facts about my wife that never failed to startle me when, in our periods of resumed intimacy, I once again became aware of them and realized how they underlay and conditioned our close and lasting relationship.

First of all was the realization, which never failed to astound me, that, as a Jesuit-educated, though lapsed, Catholic, my wife believed in the Resurrection of the Body *(le corps glorieux)* and remained secretly and painfully convinced that in marrying me while her first husband (the French count, now a resident of Brazil) was still alive she had, in the eyes of the Church, committed a deadly sin!

Another thing I was inclined to forget was Joan's unshakable conviction, in which her mother had indoctrinated her, that all men were, by nature, irretrievably sinful and dangerous. While this did not immediately affect our relationship, it no doubt colored our life together and probably helped her to put up with some of my egomaniacal behavior more philosophically than she might otherwise have done.

But, finally, the main impact of this hiatus was on myself. I found it strange and disturbing, after so many years of furious energy, to wake up in the morning and reflect that I had no bus or subway to catch, no office or theatre or studio to drive to or immediate crisis to face, and that my principal activity during the day would be a long walk along the sand and my only worry the possibility that I might come home with oil sludge on the soles of my feet.

It was not unlike the shock one experiences at the end of a long flight or after hours of cross-country driving, when the motor is turned off and all motion suddenly ceases. What I felt in the unfamiliar stillness was neither relief nor peace but a sense of emptiness, bordering on panic. It was a lost, lonely feeling that I could share with no one—least of all with Joan, who had been the principal sufferer from the succession of frenzies that had consumed me over the past twelve years and who was infinitely relieved by my temporary inactivity.

In a world where so many of my peers were using up their lives trying to "accumulate pleasures and experiences and power and honor and knowledge and love,"* I had come to concentrate on "power and honor," to whose relentless pursuit I had been ready to sacrifice almost everything else in my life.

In my solitary walks, as I slowly unwound and caught my breath after the frantic exertions of the past decade, I found myself looking back and trying, if not to understand all that had happened to me during those busy years, then at least to achieve some awareness of the forces that had driven me to such unrelenting, egotistical activity—forces I knew to be rooted in old subconscious anxieties: the primal terror of cold and hunger aggravated by my mother's recurrent economic panics over my father's reckless speculations, and my own long-standing fears of rejection and failure.

They had taken the form, early in life, of a deep, nervous inertia that had been condemned by teachers and employers alike, under the general heading of laziness. Later this had been transformed, through ambition and terror, into the compulsive energy that had served me so well in my long battle for personal and professional survival. That struggle had ended in my favor; following *King Lear* and early in my sojourn at MGM, I had achieved the success I longed for and made my breakthrough into the big time. Following my four years with the Festival, my personal and professional reputation seemed reasonably assured; the lengthening column of my credits in *Who's Who* was finally eliminating the fear of oblivion against which my life, until now, had been an unceasing struggle.

But it was a hollow victory. Far from assuaging my fever, success seemed to aggravate it; each successive achievement was followed by a compulsive need for new risks and successes and for even more difficult and dangerous assignments, of which my ventures into television had been the latest example.

Ambition assumes many forms and strives for diverse sat-

* The phrase is Thomas Merton's.

isfactions. To me it offered belated compensations for the confusions and frustrations of my youth. To make sense of some of my actions over the past thirty years and to understand the compulsions that had increasingly taken over my life, it was necessary to go back more than half a century into another world and another time.

There was, for example, my perverse insistence (almost unique among theatre workers of my generation) on jumping around between the various media. This had begun as a form of self-protection. In my deep insecurity and cowardice I figured that if and when I failed in one venture I should have a fall-back prepared in another. With the years, this had in fact become a regular working pattern in my life. I had come to believe that I was likely to achieve my best results through the intensified effort of working on two or more projects at one time. And the more I thought about it, the clearer it became that this need to divide my energy among several unrelated and possibly conflicting activities was not a professional eccentricity but followed an emotional pattern that had been set long ago by the circumstances of my abnormal upbringing.

For many years much of my emotional energy had been spent trying to adjust to the conflicting demands of the two alien and hostile worlds which I inhabited and to each of which I was desperately anxious to belong; one was my father's materialistic, inbred French-Jewish family-dominated society, the other the harsh, alien, ritualistic British public-school system into which I had been projected by my mother at the age of seven.*

My hard-won ability to survive in these two societies was further tested when the moment arrived for me to go out into the world. On the day I read in the London *Times* that I had been awarded a major university scholarship at Trinity College, Cambridge, I realized that I must now choose between two lives that had been designed for me by two separate sets of sponsors along two equally feasible but utterly opposite and incompatible lines.

* See *Run-Through*, pp. 18 *et seq.*

On one hand, as projected by my mother and my dead father's loyal friends, there was an inherited and assured career awaiting me in the international grain business. On the other, regarded as equally desirable and inevitable by the devoted teachers who had spent years preparing me for it (and for whom my Cambridge award came as a confirmation of their faith in me), there was a distinguished future of scholarship and academic honor.

I wanted both and played along with both sides, delaying my fateful decision until it could wait no longer. Then, still unable to decide, I fell headlong between two stools and earned the undying resentment of both sides. I spent seven years resentfully but successfully engaged in the grain-export business while I continued to yearn for that other life I might have had. In the process I wasted a lot of time, but, in my discontent, I developed the muscles that enabled me, at the age of thirty, to make my reckless leap into the theatre. But by then the pattern of duality had been so firmly set that it would persist, in varying forms, to the end of my life.

In show business this duality took on a form that my associates, my agent, my lawyer and my bank manager found particularly foolish and dangerous. This was my habit of oscillating between entirely different kinds of employment: on the one hand there was the work I did for professional and financial gain (this included my years with various Hollywood studios, my terms as producer for CBS Radio and Television and the theatrical productions I directed for Broadway managements); on the other hand there was the work that involved me in some form of public service in which financial considerations played a minor part (such as my two years with the Federal Theatre of the WPA, my eighteen-month service with the Voice of America and, finally, my four years as artistic director of the American Shakespeare Festival).

My attempts to justify this incessant shuttling were greeted with incomprehension and exasperation. And no wonder. Readers of this chronicle are aware of my intense lifelong preoccupation with money; they have also observed my chronic incapacity for any sort of loyalty or patriotism. Why, then, did I persist year after year in working at slave wages for the government agencies of a country to which I owed no allegiance, or for nonprofit institutions where my rewards were far lower than what I could earn in the private sector?

In vain I tried to explain the difference in the degree and quality of gratification I derived from these two different sorts of activity. In my work for the U.S. government (with the Federal Theatre and the Voice of America) I had the exhilarating and almost mystical feeling that I was participating in some sort of historical event and contributing, alien though I was, to a significant and valuable national cause. This gave my services a unique and special value of which I felt justly proud. At Stratford my sense of accomplishment had been of a similar kind. During the four years I worked there, for all my frustrations and disappointments, I enjoyed a godlike sense of having created order out of chaos and of having succeeded, against overwhelming odds, in building an organization equal to those of other countries in the presentation of the world's greatest playwright.

Yet the true explanation of my behavior, as I came to understand it during those weeks of self-examination, was rooted, once again, in my childhood. At Clifton, where I had spent more than ten of my first twenty years, generations of boys (the dumb no less than the bright) had been brought up with a strong sense of public service. The great majority of them went into His Majesty's Navy or Army or Civil Service, at home or abroad. The rest were expected to become teachers, clergymen or professionals of various sorts. Few went into commerce or industry.*

Not being British, I found much of this patriotic instruction irrelevant. Besides, by the time I was ready to leave Clifton, the dissolution of the British Empire was well under way and it had become apparent that most of those "services" for which we were being trained were no longer required. This did not change the nature or the tone of our education; for years after I left school, I carried the burden of a deep and

* With this tradition of public service went a deep prejudice among boys and teachers alike against what was still referred to as "trade." Two major causes of my early persecutions were my "foreignness" and the impression that my parents were "stinking rich."

obscure sense of guilt over the obligations I had failed to fulfill. Much later again, when, as a longtime resident and, finally, a citizen of the United States, I chose to go to work, first for the Works Progress Administration, then for the Office of War Information, it is probable that I was belatedly and subconsciously atoning for the betrayals of my youth.

(It is worth noting that these "services" which I rendered so altruistically were, for the most part, shrewdly chosen and did more than some of my more lucrative commercial endeavors to enhance my professional reputation and to feed my growing lust for power.)

My activities during the winter of 1959–60 were not limited to parental solicitude, self-analysis or repentance. I took advantage of my leisure to catch up on my flagging correspondence. Some of it—with Joe Reed, Jean Rosenthal and Jack Landau—consisted mostly of postmortem observations on the Stratford situation. There were communications, written and answered, with Jud Kinberg in Europe; with Raymond Chandler, traveling between La Jolla and London; with the Poors in New City; with the indomitable Iris Barry, retired in Fayence in the South of France;* with Ann and Keith Botsford in Puerto Rico, where he was teaching at the university; with Virgil Thomson, Mina Curtiss and Geraldine Fitzgerald in New York; with T. Edward Hambleton, who kept me informed about the affairs of his Phoenix Theatre; and with Joseph Barnes, who had begun to press me (gently, firmly and without visible results) into recording some of my more dramatic theatrical experiences during the thirties and forties.

There was also regular clandestine intercourse with the reading department of the MGM Studio. In spite of the strike, I was receiving a steady stream of material from which I was expected to cull my future productions. Two books interested me: one was a short, neurotic novel by James Leo

---

* " 'La Bonne Fonte' is a derelict cottage, a ruined farmhouse and some abandoned acres. We've been mighty busy trying to get things in order—'we' being me and a French chap of amiable disposition, a tireless worker, agreeable companion . . ."

Herlihy, *All Fall Down*, which I found dangerous but intriguing; the other was a long book that I read in galleys, *South of the Angels*, by Jessamyn West, best known for her writing about Quakers.* This was a sprawling, dramatic history of one of Southern California's vast new suburban developments that had sprung up southeast of Los Angeles soon after the turn of the century.† Today it would surely be made into a "mini-series" on television, but I saw it then as a large-scale motion picture with an unusual background and good casting possibilities. Both these properties were optioned by the studio on my recommendation, in anticipation of my return.

Meantime I was not altogether unemployed. I spent three weeks at Universal Studio (which had been taken over by the Music Corporation of America), producing a television show for my friend Hubbell Robinson, who was currently executive producer of a major dramatic anthology known as *The Ford Star Theatre*. Based on a story by Gavin Lambert,‡ who also wrote the screenplay, "The Closed Set" was about a film star in decline. It gave me a chance to work once again, for the first time in a dozen years, with Joan Fontaine and with another figure out of my past, Agnes Moorehead. According to critic Harriet van Horne:

> John Houseman has given it a handsome production, reminiscent of *Playhouse 90,* its emphasis on character rather than action, on light and shadow and subtle suggestion . . . Mr. Lambert writes well and Miss Fontaine, who played the fading film queen, captured the now-a-kitten, now-a-tiger moodiness the author intended.

* I had worked with her once before in the mid-forties on the libretto, half prose, half verse, she had written for a musical about Audubon. It was never produced, for lack of a popular score.
† It also happened to be the childhood home and, later, the political constituency of Richard Nixon.
‡ Gavin Lambert, whose first book of short stories, *The Slide Area,* had been an instant success, was a former English film critic who, in the late forties, had brought two of my films, *They Live by Night* and *Letter to an Unknown Woman,* to the attention of British film audiences.

I was glad it went well, but the strongest impression I took away from the show was my distress at the spectacle of my friend Hubbell, once the most powerful executive in the business, being subjected to the brutalities and humiliations of a system which he no longer controlled and of which he was now just another paid employee. Barely two years had passed since he had been toppled from his exalted position as head of production for CBS-TV. Tough and experienced little street fighter though he was, he was already showing unmistakable signs of discouragement and decline. Outwardly he kept up appearances—he still wore his Madison Avenue uniform and his wooden-Indian expression—but inside I knew he was falling apart.

(His secret hobby had long been the military history of the Civil War. The walls of his New York apartment and, later, of his house in Bel-Air, were covered with books, prints and photos of its major battles. Now, on the two evenings on which he asked me to go to his house to talk about the show, after drinks and dinner and then more drinks he suddenly flung off his coat and vest, loosened his tie and produced from his desk an old and battle-stained military cap. Then, with a bayonet in one hand and a glass in the other, uttering bloodcurdling yells as he leaped over and around the scattered furniture of his living room, he would re-enact, with fierce passion and total accuracy, one or more of the most dramatic actions of the Civil War. When I left, around eleven, Hubbell was hardly aware of my going. From behind me, in his lighted house, I could hear the diminishing sounds of those great victories of long ago with which he was trying to compensate for his own present defeats.)

But my main activity that fall and winter related once again to the theatre. I had been visited in Stratford early that summer by Abbott Kaplan, head of the rapidly expanding university extension of the University of California at Los Angeles. To its innumerable subjects the extension was now adding "Living Theatre." The idea was born when a number of actors and directors, most of whom were earning a good living in films and television, had come to William Melnitz, dean of UCLA's College of Fine Arts,* and suggested that the University of California act as sponsor to a group of professionals eager to engage in the stage work of which they felt themselves deprived in Southern California. Melnitz had discussed the matter with Kenneth MacGowan, chairman of the Theatre Arts Department at UCLA.† Together, they had referred the proposal to Kaplan, whose rapidly growing Extension was ideally suited to handle such a project. A weekend meeting was held in one of the university's think tanks, and a vague general plan was drawn up for the creation of a professional theatre company on the UCLA campus.‡

In Stratford that summer, I had agreed to join the group's advisory board. I was still smarting from my frustrated attempt to bring theatre to Los Angeles in the mid-forties, and I assured Kaplan that when I came out to California to produce *Playhouse 90* in the fall I would discuss the project more fully with him. By the time I arrived in October, a local organization had been formed, known as the Professional Theatre Group of the UCLA Extension, which had already presented a short summer season of play readings: *Under Milkwood,* by Dylan Thomas; *Mother Courage,* by Bertolt Brecht; and a "world premiere" of *Sodom and Gomorrah,* by Nikos Kazantzakis. To everyone's surprise these "readings" had sold out at each of their five performances. Encouraged by this response and anxious to move into fully mounted performances, Kaplan invited me to become the Theatre Group's artistic director. I said yes as usual, with no clear notion of what was expected of me, and set about planning the first full production of the sixth theatre company in which I had found myself involved in twenty-five years.

* He had worked under Max Reinhardt in Germany and, with Kenneth MacGowan, had written books about the theatre.
† Former associate of Eugene O'Neill and Robert Edmund Jones in the creation and operation of the Provincetown Playhouse, and later, associate of Joseph Reed in the production of Jane Cowl's *Twelfth Night.* After some years as a successful film producer, he had joined UCLA's Theatre Arts Department.
‡ It was attended by Lee Strasberg, Dore Schary, Walter Wanger, Delbert Mann, Paul Newman, Anthony Quinn, Eva Marie Saint, Shelley Winters, Joanne Woodward, Robert Ryan and others.

Robert Ryan, who had played Coriolanus for me at the
Phoenix in New York six years before, had been one of the
original proponents of the Theatre Group, and it seemed
appropriate that he should appear in our first production,
for which I chose T. S. Eliot's *Murder in the Cathedral*. He was
not the ideal Archbishop. Though he had done some work
on his voice since *Coriolanus,* it remained flat and unresonant,
but, as in *Coriolanus,* his vocal weakness was offset by his
physical presence, his intelligence and his personal experience (as a member of a Black Irish family, with one sister a
nun) of the emotional problems of this profoundly Catholic
play. His clerical supporters, his tempters and his murderers,
as well as the women of Canterbury (whose lines I edited in
such a way as to create individual female characters of varying ages), were played by actors most of whom I had worked
with before.* By arrangement with the UCLA Music Department we had the use of Schoenberg Hall, a five-hundred-seat
auditorium intended for chamber music and small orchestra
concerts but ideally suited to theatrical production. The
acoustics were excellent, the stage adequate in size and depth,
with a hydraulic orchestra pit that gave us opportunities to
create levels, steps and a variety of exits and entrances. (It
remained the Theatre Group's base throughout the seven
years of its existence.) For costumes and for our unit set of
Canterbury, I turned to Dorothy Jeakins, who came through
with her usual strong, distinguished theatrical vision. The
Music Department helped with the selection and recording
of the church bells and Gregorian chants that formed our
score.

Since this would be our first full production, a number of
decisions had to be made that would affect all future operations of the Theatre Group. These were debated at length
and with some heat by a board presided over by MacGowan

---

* Richard Hale, Robert Gist, Theodore Marcuse, John Hoyt, Alan
Napier, Joseph Ruskin, Robert Casper, Stephen Joyce; on the distaff
side: Pippa Scott, Doris Lloyd, Betty Harford, Jennifer Howard and
others. Our stage manager for this and many of our subsequent
productions was Jacqueline Donnet.

and Kaplan and composed, in equal parts, of professional personalities and of members of the UCLA Theatre Arts Department, not all of whom were enthusiastic over our invasion of the campus.*

Rehearsals began the day after Christmas. It was a deliberately simple production intended to clarify Eliot's thought and to emphasize the theatrical quality of his text. It opened on January 19, 1960, to excellent reviews. Local critics called it "a masterpiece of drama" and commended Ryan for his "almost homely simplicity that points up heroism as heroics would never do."

Murder in the Cathedral played its ten scheduled performances to good houses and a total attendance of close to five thousand.† And it showed a small profit. In contrast to my artistically distinguished but financially disastrous Pelican season of 1947,‡ the Theatre Group, with its university backing and its vast Extension audience, seemed about to launch an economically viable as well as an artistically exciting program of theatre in Southern California.

Reverting to my habit of issuing manifestos, I wrote one which appeared in the *Los Angeles Times:*

> In certain respects the Theatre Group is a typical example of the new theatrical wave that is sweeping away the crumbling remains of the centralized commercial theatre in America. It was created and it has flourished in response to a growing demand for quality entertainment from an audience that is intellectually and economically equipped to enjoy it.

There were ways in which I felt the UCLA Professional Theatre Group was different from other regional theatres:

* Our "executive coordinator" was a dedicated lady by the name of Frances Inglis, who had been chief of David O. Selznick's vast secretarial staff when I went to work for him in 1941.
† One hundred forty seats were priced at four dollars, three hundred sixty at three dollars. Actors received the Equity minimum of $103.40 a week.
‡ See *Front and Center*, pp. 233 *et seq.*

I. The Group [I wrote] was formed and developed through an alliance of professional theatre people and university personnel that is unique in this country.

II. It operates in a community with an exploding population and a passionate concern with establishing a cultural identity of its own.

III. The Theatre Group is fortunate in being situated in the center of one of the Western World's great agglomerations of performing and producing talent. Many established actors still find the stage the freest and most satisfying of the theatrical arts. For them the chance to appear in the kind of play the Theatre Group puts on offers a welcome opportunity to refresh and extend themselves.

The Music Department would be reoccupying Schoenberg Hall through the spring and early summer. This gave the Theatre Group several months to prepare for its first full season and allowed me to make my long-delayed return to the film business.

The writers' strike was settled by the end of March 1960, but it took the studios time to resume their normal operation. On April 18, I drove from Malibu to Culver City and reentered the MGM Studio as a senior producer. The moment I went through the front door of the Thalberg Building I was aware of a great difference between this and the institution I had deserted five years earlier. The number of films produced had been substantially reduced; television crews were beginning to occupy many of the stages that had been devoted to feature pictures. Schary was gone; so were two of the hostile triumvirate that had ruled the third floor. My first official visit was to Sol Siegel, now in charge of production at MGM. I found him in what had been Schary's office and, before that, Louis B. Mayer's.* He was a pleasant man and an experienced filmmaker with whom I had had previous

---

* It was an ironic example of the Hollywood merry-go-round that I had, myself, supplanted this same Sol Siegel and occupied his office when I went to work for Buddy De Sylva at Paramount in 1943. (See *Front and Center*, p. 112.)

dealings on the board of the Producers' Guild. We discussed the properties the studio was acquiring for me, and he approved of the two writers I proposed to engage to work on them: John Paxton for *South of the Angels* and, for *All Fall Down*, the playwright William Inge.

I had worked with Paxton (on *The Cobweb*) and I needed his experience and his conscientious sense of structure for what I knew would be a complex and difficult screenplay. Inge had recently worked on the script for Kazan's *Splendor in the Grass;* now he was thinking of moving to California and was looking for another film to write. I had known him during the years of his Broadway fame. Recently, as his star dimmed, he had become subject to fits of discouragement amounting to melancholia, which had driven him more than once to attempts on his own life. He was eager to work on Herlihy's novel, for which we both felt he was particularly qualified.

Not long after my arrival in Culver City a third project came my way. Early one morning Irving "Swifty" Lazar, the demon agent, drove into the studio, handed Siegel the galleys of Irwin Shaw's latest novel, *Two Weeks in Another Town,* and told him it was being shown simultaneously to four studio heads and would be sold to the highest bidder by noon of the next day. Siegel gave it to the chief of his story department and, on her recommendation, acquired it the next morning at an exorbitant price. He asked me if I'd like to produce it. I read it, said yes as usual and, ignoring Shaw's repeated suggestions that he write his own screenplay, engaged Charles Schnee, with whom I had worked on *The Bad and the Beautiful,* to adapt it. That gave me three films in preparation.

On one level I felt comfortable and confident in Culver City. Following the exodus, voluntary or enforced, of so many of the old-line producers, I was installed in a second-floor suite that was even more sumptuous than the one I had occupied during my previous residence; the third floor was clear of all but one of my enemies; I was one of a handful of major producers in what was still the most prestigious studio in town.

But, on a deeper, more personal level, there was uneasiness. It was a feeling I could not define or describe, for all my recent self-examination. It was not self-doubt, for my ego was more swollen than usual; it was not fatigue, for I had not been so well rested in years. Looking back, with the added wisdom of hindsight, I have tried to identify the causes of my uneasiness.

When I first went to work for MGM in 1950 my need was desperate. I must make successful films or go under. Working under the double spur of unremitting fear and a rage to win, I had triumphed and then confirmed my victory by walking away from it. Now, five years later, I was back, secure in my reputation as an established producer. With my distaste for repetition, I made this return with some misgivings, but I needed a highly paid job, I enjoyed making films, and I hoped, after this long hiatus, to recapture the thrill and fervor of that earlier time. I never did. From the start there was something wrong with the mix—perhaps the absence of terror.

In the work of a film producer there is a particularly barren and frustrating phase that lasts anywhere from three to six months. It occurs after the subject of the film has been selected and after the writer has accepted his assignment and, following preliminary discussions, has gone off to work on his treatment or first rough draft. At such times there is nothing for the producer to do but hope and chew his nails while he waits for the writer to deliver. With three pictures in this early stage, the summer and fall of 1960 would have been an arid time for me if it had not been for my activities at the university. Under the auspices of UCLA's Theatre Department I gave two public lectures: "The Entertainers and the Entertained" and "Realism and Style." I also conducted seminars within the department on such varied subjects as "Documentary and Educational Film," "Propaganda," "The Fundamentals of Dramaturgy," and "Technical Methods and Practices in the Theatre."

The Professional Theatre Group, meanwhile, had completed its arrangements with the Music Department: except for a few recitals and concerts, Schoenberg Hall would be ours from mid-July to the end of November. This permitted us to plan and announce four productions for a total of fifty performances. To keep our budget within reasonable bounds, we had decided to alternate full productions with presentations that required a minimum of scenery and costumes. For the season's first full-scale production I chose *The Three Sisters,* which, in view of Southern California's benighted theatrical record, could still be announced as a "West Coast premiere."

Of all Chekhov's plays I felt this spoke most directly to contemporary American audiences. And it was a joy to cast. Already my instinct was carrying me in the direction of a permanent company. For the sisters we had an embarrassment of riches: I ended with Nina Foch as Masha, Pippa Scott as Irina, Betty Harford as Olga and, to everyone's surprise, Gloria Grahame as Natasha. For the all-important part of Colonel Vershinin (created by Stanislavsky himself) I made another unorthodox choice—Frank Silvera, a light-skinned black actor who had recently played King Lear for Joe Papp's Shakespeare in the Park and whose work I greatly admired. Stephen Joyce was the unfortunate Baron, Theodore Marcuse an offbeat, frightening Solyony, and Alan Napier played Tchebutykin, the doctor. Mike Kellin, who had been the tinker in our *Taming of the Shrew* at Stratford, was the tedious but touching cuckold Kulygin; William Nims played the fat, defeated brother; Hilda Plowright the old nurse, Amfisa. Working with this cast and with scenery and costumes by two former associates, Edgar Lansbury and Dorothy Jeakins, gave me as much pleasure as I have ever experienced in the theatre. It was my first direction of a Chekhov play, and it was an emotional revelation.

The Three Sisters opened late in July to wonderful reviews: "admirable," "brilliant," "excellent," "uniformly superlative," "professional theatre of a rare sort," "obligatory for civilized theatre-goers." Patterson Greene of the *Examiner* (who had been so vile to Laughton and Brecht over *Galileo*) reported that "by combining realism with poetry *The Three Sisters* has the glow of an amethyst under candlelight!"

Audiences too expressed their enthusiasm for a quality of

production and a standard of acting they had not enjoyed locally in more than a dozen years—since the days of the Actors' Lab and the Pelican. In spite of our sold-out houses we stuck to our announced schedule of twelve performances and reopened after a break of five days with "Four Comedies of Despair"—a bill of short contemporary plays,* three of them from the Theatre of the Absurd—directed by Lamont Johnson. Each performance was followed by a debate in which our actors matched their bewilderment with that of panels of local intelligentsia that included Charles Brackett, Steve Allen, Christopher Isherwood and Clifford Odets.

Feeling the need for a full-length contemporary American play, we next presented *The Prodigal,* by Jack Richardson. It was an updated version of the *Oresteia* which I had seen in New York, where I felt it had been overpraised. Our Los Angeles production was marred by faulty casting in two of the principal parts, but we got by with it and it did not seriously hurt our season.

Our final attraction was the staged reading, on successive nights, of the first two parts of Sean O'Casey's autobiography, *I Knock at the Door* and *Pictures in the Hallway,* edited and directed by Paul Shyre. Everett Sloane (a former associate from the Mercury and *Lust for Life*), wearing thick glasses and a turtleneck sweater, played O'Casey looking back over his boyhood in the Dublin slums; others in the cast were Stephen Joyce, Sandy Kenyon, Jan Sterling and Gladys Cooper.† (During the run we received a letter from O'Casey thanking the Theatre Group "for its ingenuity, courage and kindliness in allowing me to pipe and prance before Los Angeles audiences.")

* These included a mime by Samuel Beckett, *Act Without Words; The Lesson,* by Ionesco; the first American performance of Edward Albee's *Sandbox;* Tennessee Williams' *This Property Is Condemned,* played by two young black actors, Billy Allen and Al Freeman, Jr.
† Following an amazing career as a chorus girl, a candy-box beauty, a musical-comedy star and, finally, one of England's leading dramatic actresses and actress-managers, she was living in a house on Pacific Palisades from which she sallied forth for long daily walks on the beach. She appeared in several Professional Theatre Group productions.

When we closed our first full season, on November 21, 1960, we had played to more than twenty thousand paying customers and established regular attendance at Theatre Group performances by audiences that came from as far away as the San Fernando Valley and Pasadena. And, in contrast to most of the country's new institutional theatres, we had achieved the near-miracle of showing a profit of more than six thousand dollars on our year's operation.

That month the *Christian Science Monitor* described the Theatre Group as a "front runner in the new American theatre wave," and *The New York Times* reported:

NONPROFIT THEATRE TAKES ROOT IN LOS ANGELES

Two vigorous theatrical taboos—one national, the other regional—have been challenged in this vicinity. The first is that legitimate theatre and a university are about as incompatible as Greek Drama and popcorn. The second is that residents of the Los Angeles area cannot be drawn into a legitimate theatre that features serious drama unless a swimming pool and barbeque pit are included in the price of admission. Both of those superstitions have been shattered by an organization known as the Theatre Group.

At our midwinter board meeting it was decided to double the number of our performances and to open in mid-January with Pirandello's *Six Characters in Search of an Author.* I undertook to direct it, feeling that I would soon be too deeply absorbed in film production to undertake any further stage direction for a while.

By midautumn only one of my film scripts had been completed. John Paxton, who had injured his back while rebuilding one of his houses, was far from finished with *South of the Angels,* and Charles Schnee was having problems with Shaw's novel, which Lazar had been smart to sell before its reviews came out. But Inge, as a playwright, was accustomed to working fast. In less than five months he had written and made revisions on the screenplay for *All Fall Down.* I gave it to John

Frankenheimer, who immediately agreed to direct it. Simultaneously, with no effort on my part (in fact, almost against my will), I had acquired a leading man for the equivocal role of our charming but worthless young hero, "Berry-Berry."

Inge had suggested him, and Warren Beatty himself had done the rest. In an astonishing campaign of self-promotion this young man, whose only film appearance had been in a small role with Kazan in *Splendor in the Grass* and whose only other claim to fame was his fraternity to Shirley MacLaine, had managed to get pictures of himself, together with feature articles, into every major magazine in the country. Using charm, sex and unmitigated gall, he kept the country's female columnists in a tizzy.* Within a few months, before we had shot a single frame of film, he had turned a tall, nice-looking but rather awkward and completely unknown young man into one of the hottest names in the business—completely eclipsing such well-established fellow players as Eva Maria Saint, Karl Malden, Angela Lansbury† and the former child star Brandon de Wilde.‡

The front office never entirely shared my enthusiasm for *All Fall Down*. It was offbeat; it had a dubious hero, a flawed heroine, censorship problems and a tragic ending. So, before going into production, I made a special trip to New York to confer with the heads of the publicity and sales departments. I assured them that unless its release were carefully planned the company would be better off not making the film at all. It must be presented to the public in a medium-sized theatre

* His subsequent brilliant career in a series of highly successful films, as actor, director and producer, has fully justified their enthusiasm.
† Angela, whom I had wooed desultorily in the early forties, when she had just made a name for herself at MGM (as the murdered girl in *Dorian Gray* and the maid in *Gaslight*), had married, had children and suffered an eclipse in what had begun as a brilliant career. Her performance as Warren's mother in *All Fall Down* marked her first appearance in a middle-aged part and the start of a new career that led her to such triumphs as *The Manchurian Candidate*, *Auntie Mame* and *Sweeney Todd*.
‡ He achieved fame as the bespectacled little brother in *Member of the Wedding* and starred in *Hud* and other films before dying in a car crash in his twenties.

(like *Lust for Life* at the Plaza in New York) where it could build publicity and reputation before going into general release. Having obtained a definite assurance that it would be treated in that way, I returned to Culver City and put the film into production. But before we started shooting I had time to stage Pirandello's *Six Characters in Search of an Author* for the Theatre Group.

I had known and loved the play for many years and seen it performed a number of times in various parts of the world. Los Angeles, where it was still a novelty, was the ideal place in which to cast it and the perfect atmosphere in which to play it. For the father, I used Joseph Wiseman (my Edmund in *Lear*); the unhappy wife was Katharine Bard; the neurotic son, John Alderman; the angry daughter, a rising young television actress named Joanne Linville; the procuress, a nightclub "chanteuse" known as Madame Spivy. Larry Gates was the harassed director.* Between them they gave an unusually lucid and dramatic performance of Pirandello's masterpiece.

> The Theatre Group has again evoked the magic that is exclusively the theatre's.
> This mercurial play, a triple exercise in a perilous format, seems to be newly minted as the day it was written.
> Staged in excellent fashion at Schoenberg Hall, it has its high-brow implications and its "metaphysical mischievousness," but most of the time it is funny and curiously touching underneath. [Phil Scheuer, *Los Angeles Times*]

It was followed after a few weeks by Paul Shyre's version of Dos Passos' *U.S.A.*, which Paul himself directed and for which I acted as producer. Billed as a "dramatic revue" and brilliantly played on a bare stage by performers who all, sooner or later, achieved fame of one sort or another,† it was another unqualified success: "*USA* Sparked by Brilliant Acting," "*USA* Kaleidoscopic Triumph at UCLA," "*USA* Provides Engrossing Evening," "UCLA Has Winner in *USA*."

---

* A part I was to play on television fifteen years later.
† John Astin, Evans Evans, Nina Foch, Diana Lynn, William Windom.

The portrait of a nation during thirty years that Dos Passos tried to fit into a thousand pages is now being fitted into the tiny limitations of a stage . . . it is both strong and gentle, moving and thought-provoking.

So ended the first full season of the Professional Theatre Group of the UCLA Extension. We had given over one hundred performances before an audience of close to fifty thousand people. And once again, even after paying new overhead charges to the university, we showed a modest profit.

In the casting and production of *Six Characters* and *U.S.A.*, I had received welcome aid from my former associate on *Playhouse 90*, Ethel Winant, who, like almost everyone in television, was eager to move into what still seemed the freer and more prestigious field of motion pictures. For my part, with my growing list of projects at MGM, I needed someone to take over the position of production associate that Jud Kinberg had occupied so successfully in the early fifties and which Denis Deegan, for all his intelligence and taste, was still too inexperienced to fill.* In the spring of 1961, having completed her work with Rod Serling on his new supernatural television series, Ethel Winant took an extended leave of absence from the CBS Network and moved into one of the offices of my suite in Culver City. She was with me there for close to two years and during that time, without doubt, she saved my life. Of the many messes into which I got myself during my second sojourn with MGM and from which she did her best to extricate me, *All Fall Down* was the least grim. It was the only one of my three films that I enjoyed making and with which I was, finally, reasonably satisfied.

Shooting started in late spring, and within forty-eight hours John Frankenheimer and I were locked in a fearful

---

* He had been assistant stage manager in all my productions for the Theatre Group and was now preparing, on his own, in a small Beverly Hills theatre, to produce a new play by a young playwright from Arkansas named James Bridges in which he invited my wife to appear as a Venice (California) barfly.

dispute. He rushed into my office from the set after the second day's shooting and announced that my friend Angela Lansbury was "impossible," that he could not direct her and that the part must be recast immediately. I disagreed. It got to the point where he announced that if she didn't leave the picture, *he* would. I stood firm. Forty-eight hours later they had become inseparable, and he refused to make his next film, *Manchurian Candidate,* without her.

From the start, our most serious problem was young Mr. Beatty. With his angelic arrogance, his determination to emulate Marlon Brando and Jimmy Dean, and his half-baked, overzealous notions of "Method" acting, he succeeded in perplexing and antagonizing not only his fellow actors but our entire crew. While the company was on location in Key West, our veteran cameraman, Curly Lindon, became so exasperated with him that he flew a camera-bearing helicopter within a few inches of his head. And on the last day of shooting, in a secret agreement with the local police, Warren Beatty was left to languish overnight in a bare cell of the Key West jail while the company flew back to California.

Feelings about films one has made are emotional and subjective—influenced by the circumstances in which they were made, by the critical and popular success they achieved, and, finally, by the degree to which they fulfilled or failed to live up to one's expectations for them. Two of my films that I often find myself bracketing (although they were made more than a dozen years apart) are *All Fall Down* and *They Live by Night.* Both were modest, adventurous, emotional films about young people made by young directors at the start of their careers. Both looked like winners until they were sold down the river.

All Fall Down was completed in the late summer of 1961 and edited and previewed by the end of the year. Its advance reception in the trades and the magazines was encouraging. *Newsweeks*'s critic, after pointing out that "the eccentric family has had an unusually long and fruitful lineage in American Show Business," assigned *All Fall Down* to "a place of its own in between 'You Can't Take It With You' and 'Long Day's Journey into Night.'" It was reviewed in *Show* by its visiting film critic, Arthur Schlesinger, Jr.:

> To judge by *All Fall Down,* one of the best domestic movies in a decade, Hollywood at last seems to have learned its Freudian lesson so well that it no longer needs to spell it out . . . John Houseman, who has given Broadway, television and movies some of their finest hours, has put together an extraordinary production. John Frankenheimer emerges as a major director, drawing exceptional performances from his cast, particularly from Eva Marie Saint. And William Inge, who, with varying success, has been trying to write the Great American Family Drama throughout his career, has come closest to it with this sensitive adaptation of James Leo Herlihy's novel. Together they have managed to put flesh and blood around Everyfamily's closet skeletons.

After such reviews MGM's sales department seemed disposed to keep its promise: *All Fall Down* was booked into the Plaza Theatre in New York and into a handful of similarly prestigious small houses in major cities. The wisdom of this strategy was confirmed by the news that the film had been chosen, not once but twice, as the U.S. entry at the Cannes Film Festival: first by the American Motion Picture Producers' Association and then again by members of the festival's own selection committee. Then, overnight, all our well-laid plans were blown sky-high.

MGM's most ambitious picture of the year was Blasco-Ibáñez' *Four Horsemen of the Apocalypse,* in which Valentino had tangoed his way to stardom in the early twenties. It had now been remade with Glenn Ford as the young Argentine and Ingrid Thulin (Ingmar Bergman's star) in the Alice Terry role. Booked with considerable hoopla into flagship theatres all over the country, it turned out to be the year's major critical and popular disaster.

Desperately casting about for an instant substitute for its faltering monster, MGM discovered that it had only one film available, *All Fall Down*—a small, black-and-white program picture with no major stars. Prints were rushed through the

1965. Joan and Mousy-Cat (50) return to the U.S.A. (51) T. Edward
Hambleton and Ellis Rabb during their APA-Phoenix association.

51

(52) Ellis Rabb's *Pantagleize:* "It's a lovely day!"
(53) Ellis Rabb in *Escorial.*

APA-PHOENIX

apa REPERTORY COMPANY

PANTAGLEIZE   **THE SHOW-OFF**

EXIT THE KING   **THE CHERRY ORCHARD**

LYCEUM THEATRE: 45th St. E. of B'WAY. • JU 2-3877

54

(54) The APA-Phoenix New York season.

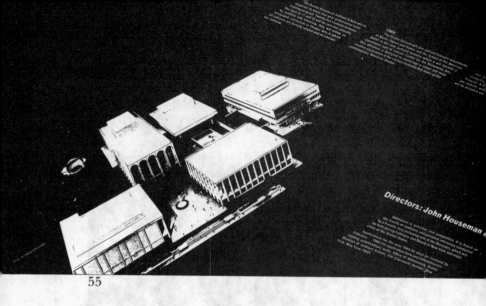

55

The Lincoln Center for the Performing Arts with the new Juilliard building on the right. The Drama Division used this for years as the cover of its brochures (55). Michel and Suria Saint-Denis (56).

56

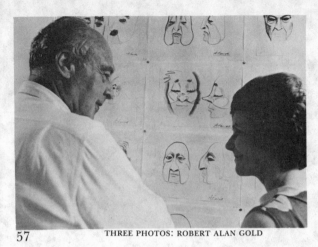

57   THREE PHOTOS: ROBERT ALAN GOLD

1968. The "Retreat" at Wykeham Rise: (57) J.H. and Elizabeth Smith; (58) Michel Saint-Denis explaining "Mask Improvisation."

58

Juilliard For Peace

59

The last and most dramatic of our mass protests (59) against the Vietnam War. (60) Patrick Hines and Christopher Walken in *The Chronicles of Hell.*

RICHARD LEE

60

61

62

(61) Marian Fenn. (62) Martha Graham making up as Clytemnestra.
(63) Jean Rosenthal at rehearsal.

63

64

(64) The Drama Division's class of 1972 preparing for its first school tour in *Scapin*. 1972. The Acting Company's first repertory season, David Ogden Stiers and Mary Lou Rosato in *The School for Scandal* (65).

65

66

67

(66) Mary Lou Rosato in *Women Beware Women*. (67) Patti LuPone and Benjamin Hendrickson in *Next Time I'll Sing to You*. (68) Reading our first great review in *The New York Times*.

68

RAIMONDO BOREA

69 70

1973–74. The Acting Company's second repertory season. *The Three Sisters* (69) with Mary Joan Negro, Patti LuPone and Mary Lou Rosato. (70) David Schramm and Leah Chandler in *Measure for Measure*. (71) Kevin Kline and Patti LuPone in *The Beggar's Opera*.

71

72

1974. The Acting Company during its third New York repertory
season (72).

73

1973. *Lord Byron* at Juilliard. (73) Left to right, Jack Larson, Virgil Thomson, J.H., Peter Mennin and Gerhard Samuels. (74) The Poets' Corner in Virgil Thomson's *Lord Byron* at Juilliard, 1972.

74

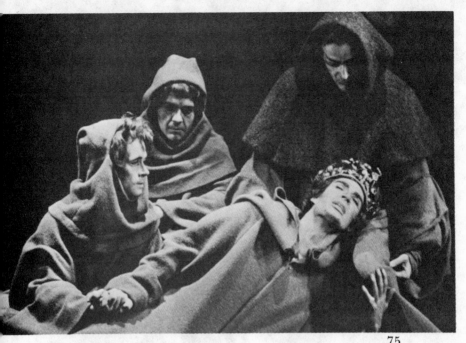

75

1973–74. (75) Ellis Rabb's production of Marlowe's *Edward II* for The Acting Company, with Norman Snow as the King. (76) The first rehearsal of *The Country Girl:* left to right, James Karen, Jason Robards, J.H., George Grizzard, Maureen Stapleton, (seated) Joe Ponazecki, Porter van Zandt.

76

(77) James Bridges and J.H. during filming of *The Paper Chase* in Toronto. (78) J.H. making his acceptance speech for the Academy Award, April 1974. (79) Bringing the Oscar to the Drama Division.

77

78

(80) May Haussmann lunching in New City at the age of 96. (81) Henry Fonda as Clarence Darrow.

79

80

81

MIKE MERRICK AND DON GREGORY PRESENT

HENRY FONDA AS
CLARENCE DARROW

A NEW PLAY BY
DAVID W. RINTELS
BASED ON "CLARENCE DARROW FOR THE DEFENSE" BY
IRVING STONE
SCENERY AND LIGHTING BY
H. R. POINDEXTER
DIRECTED BY
JOHN HOUSEMAN

A DOME PRODUCTION

SIX WEEKS ONLY! LIMITED BROADWAY ENGAGEMENT
MARCH 26 - MAY 4
HELEN HAYES THEATRE
46th Street West of Broadway · Mondays thru Saturdays at 8:00 P.M.
Wednesday & Saturday Matinees at 2:00 P.M.

82

labs, and within a few days, with no time for publicity or preparation, our sophisticated, neurotic little film was thrown into dozens of oversized movie palaces that habitually housed major spectacles and musicals in color. Inevitably it withered and died. This time the reviews were of little help: most local critics were influenced by the cavernous gloom of empty theatres and sparse and bewildered audiences. Their principal victim was Warren Beatty. *The New York Times* described him as a "disgusting young man who is virtually a cretin," "a noxious young brute who provokes a reasonable spectator to give up finally in disgust."

> Surly, sloppy, slow-witted, given to scratching himself, picking his nose and being rude beyond reason to women and muttering about how much he hates the world—this creature that Mr. Beatty gives us is a sad approximation of modern youth. *All Fall Down* is a picture that should fall on its face. But it won't.

Mr. Crowther was mistaken. It did fall flat on its face. As soon as MGM could ready another, more generally salable film, *All Fall Down* was pulled out, jettisoned and classified as a turkey.

This was my first indication that my second sojourn in Culver City might not repeat the triumphal exhilaration of the first. Show business has its own mysterious rhythms of success and failure. Personal and professional reasons may be found for those swings, but they do not fully explain the violence or the seeming inevitability of these upward and downward curves. Looking back on the first and second years of the Mercury Theatre, I had once observed that whereas in our first season we could do no wrong, in our second, no matter how hard we tried, we could do nothing right. The same was true of my second term with MGM.

I continued to work with John Paxton on the elaborate tapestry of *South of the Angels* and with Charles Schnee on the final draft of *Two Weeks in Another Town*, which was to be my next picture. An early version of the script had been mailed to Bill Holden in Kenya, but before a reply was received I had made a deal with Kirk Douglas to star in what would be

our third picture together. With Minnelli once again directing, a screenplay by Charles Schnee and production by myself, we were clearly making a calculated attempt to duplicate
the success of *The Bad and the Beautiful.*

This proved to be more of a liability than an asset. In the
years that had passed we had all undergone great personal
changes: I was no longer the frightened, desperately eager
producer I had been in 1952; Charlie Schnee, increasingly
beset by bad health and domestic troubles, was not the flexible, fresh, imaginative writer he had been nine years before;
Minnelli, grinding out film after film for MGM, had begun
to tire. Kirk, finally, was now an established major star, no
longer at that stage in his career where his intense, tireless
drive for success and recognition coincided perfectly with the
roles he was playing for us as Jonathan Shields and Vincent
Van Gogh.

But there was another, more specific reason for our failure.
In *The Bad and the Beautiful* we had dramatized a scene with
which we were all factually and emotionally familiar. Shaw's
novel, by contrast, dealt with a world which we knew mostly
by hearsay and of which we had almost no direct experience.
Unconsciously, we found ourselves drifting into a Hollywood
version of *La Dolce Vita*—without the intimate observation,
the social and human attitudes and the brilliant imagination
that had given Fellini's film such an irresistible quality. For
Minnelli, in particular, the anxiety to create an authentic yet
startling Roman film proved a dangerous preoccupation
which frequently diverted him from the dramatic flow and
personal relationships of the film he was making.

Soon after my return to Culver City I had given a confident
and rather self-satisfied interview to *The New York Times,* in
which I expatiated on the duties and responsibilities of the
producer: "Too often we see pictures that appear to be without ideas of any sort. That usually means that the picture,
during its making, has gotten away from intelligent control
and consistent development that should be supplied by the
producer." *Two Weeks in Another Town* ended as the perfect
model of a film that "got away" from "intelligent control and
consistent development."

Even our casting was curious. For our villainess, the hero's estranged but persistently destructive nymphomaniac wife, Minnelli opted for Cyd Charisse, who had danced and starred in several recent MGM musicals. Dressed to the nines in Balmain's flashiest creations, she was gorgeous to look at but never entirely convincing as the Queen of the Jet Set. Our other main sex interest was supplied by a lovely young Israeli named Dahlia Lavi in the equivocal role of an Italian girl, onto whose realistic character of a warmhearted, hungry teenage Roman whore we had grafted a conventional Hollywood ingenue. Other additions to the cast included Edward G. Robinson, Claire Trevor, George Hamilton, the rising Italian star Rosanna Schiaffino, and a close friend from the Mercury days, Stefan Schnabel.

I arrived in Europe ten days before the start of shooting. In the pleasurable agitation of my flight to Paris and then on to Rome, most of our obvious hazards were overlooked or ignored. (It was exciting, after half a century, to be living once again at the Hotel Excelsior, where I had stayed with my mother on one of her cultural excursions.) I was too preoccupied and too timid fully to enjoy the international high life of which the Douglases, Denise Minnelli and her friend Mrs. Spiegel were familiar and active participants. Instead, I spent a weekend with Nick and Betty Ray at their house on the Via Appia and made limited use of the letters Pier Pasinetti had given me to the three Balboni sisters* and others of his Italian friends. (I did some sightseeing, and I have never forgotten an afternoon in which Titina Maselli, the painter, led me on a magic round of Rome's exquisite private churches, some hardly larger than a living room.)

These were brief diversions. We spent a few pleasant days scouting locations; then, soon after the start of filming, I was submerged in a sea of trouble that put an end to all thoughts of personal pleasure. The pressure began when our first rushes came out of the lab in California and were screened in Culver City. It started with a call at dead of night from

* A remarkable trio, one of whom was married to the Italian film director Michelangelo Antonioni.

Ethel Winant. Sol Siegel had summoned her and warned her of trouble ahead: not only were we already behind schedule, but the tempo of the scenes Minnelli was shooting in Rome was deadly *slow*. In part, these complaints were justified. The Eternal City was having its insidious effect on the art student Minnelli had once been. Overwhelmed by the architectural wonders that surrounded him, he was allowing them to distract him from the none-too-solid story he was supposed to be filming. Thus our first and most important love scene (shot with masses of mobile equipment and a huge crew over an agonizing stretch of three freezing nights) ended up as little more than an instructive architectural tour of Michelangelo's Campidoglio. Things went somewhat better with our interiors, though I still recall several days of cramped and tedious shooting with Edward G. Robinson playing an endless death scene in an apartment overlooking the main fountain of the Piazza Navona.

To make up for our delays I resorted to the old producer's device of tearing whole scenes out of the script. When I called Ethel to tell her what I was doing and to request some rewrites and new transitions from Charlie Schnee, I learned that Mary Schnee had killed herself the night before under particularly awful circumstances and that there were growing rumors of Siegel's resignation.

I was abroad for less than a month, but it seemed an eternity and I was delighted to get home. Soon after our return, Minnelli and I spent two whole days, in a projection room in Culver City, viewing all our Italian footage, much of which we had never seen. Some was wonderful; some could just as well have been shot on the back lot. We still had half the film left to shoot: all the Hollywood scenes, most of the professional and personal encounters, and a number of receptions and parties of which we had already filmed the exteriors in Rome.* Back in Culver City, in the familiar atmosphere of the studio, we made up some of our lost time and added a

---

* In one of these Joan made her film debut as a very elegant and credible Italian countess. This was followed some months later by

few scenes intended to clarify and strengthen our story line. Then, in our final sequence, with several dozen carefully selected Hollywood "dress extras," Minnelli got around to shooting the Roman "orgy" to which he had been looking forward for weeks. It took four days to film, under the watchful eye of the censors of the Motion Picture Producers' Alliance,* and it ended up being so sophisticated and so oblique that three quarters of it landed on the cutting-room floor—not for obscenity but for obscurity and tedium.

The assembled film, when we finally saw it in its rough-cut, four-hour form, contained some exciting and visually beautiful (sometimes too consciously beautiful) material. But, for all its quality, it remained strangely pedestrian, with little of the invention and irony that had distinguished *The Bad and the Beautiful.* With the necessity for drastic cutting, the disagreements and resentments that had marred the final stages of our editing on *The Cobweb* were beginning to flare again when our entire situation was suddenly and drastically changed.

Sol Siegel was gone as head of production—resigned or fired. In his place there appeared a smooth fellow by the name of Bob Weitman (formerly an executive of CBS). But the real authority, it soon became evident, lay with the new head of the New York office—a certain Joe Vogel, whose entire experience had been in distribution and sales and who in his present position proved ignorant, tasteless, bigoted and hopelessly incompetent. Under the delusion that he could bring back the happy days of Louis B. Mayer's "family pictures," he set about cleaning up all existent MGM films, including ours. Full of strange notions and prejudices, he developed a most curious and almost pathological detestation of poor Cyd Charisse. As a result, when he was through with his editing (which he conducted alone with the studio's editor-in-chief in a locked projection room) most of Cyd's scenes

---

appearances as an American housewife in *Smog*—an Italian film shot by Franco Rossi in Southern California—and later with the Burtons in an unfortunate film called *The Sandpiper,* in which her voice had to be dubbed because it did not sound sufficiently American.
* Formerly known as "the Hays Office."

were gone or emasculated. Since, for better or worse, it was she who galvanized and motivated most of our battered hero's actions in the picture, her removal reduced a film that was already confused to abject nonsense.

I addressed a memo to the head of MGM's legal department:

Drastic changes have been made in *Two Weeks in Another Town*—a film of which I am the accredited producer. These changes were at no time discussed with me and in spite of my formal request, the negative has now been cut without me or my director being given a chance to view the changes. *Two Weeks* in its present form does not represent my work and I cannot permit my name to appear on it as producer.

My memo was ignored, as I knew it would be, and I continued to be billed as the producer of a film that got an almost unanimously bad press. *The New York Times* headed its review

DEGRADATION

It is well known that a class of trashy movies of a certain lush, synthetic sort is made in Rome. That is a fact of film commerce that has to be patiently endured. But when a group of top American film-makers goes all the way to Rome to make a picture about the sort of Hollywood rejects who get involved in that sort of trash, and then makes it as trashy as the worst stuff, it is time for a loud and pained complaint. . . .

In his closing paragraph Bosley Crowther rubbed salt in our wounds:

At one point snatches from a film these washed-up characters are supposed to have made when they were winning Oscars are shown. They are actually scenes from *The Bad and the Beautiful,* an interesting film about Hollywood that the Messrs. Schnee, Minnelli, Houseman and Douglas made ten years ago. There is something grim about seeing this recollection in the context of *Two Weeks in Another Town.*

This was my first film in ten years in which I had taken neither pleasure nor pride. Worse was to come. Having disposed of the studio's existent product, Mr. Vogel turned his attention to films in preparation. He sent for a synopsis of *South of the Angels,* for which I had such high hopes. John Paxton's conscientious adaptation of this massive work by a distinguished Quaker novelist contained, among its several personal stories, one episode of ardent young love, one slow death from cancer and one intense, heartbreaking adultery. Mr. Vogel decided that these made the picture "unpleasant," "immoral," "unfit for family entertainment" and unsuitable for production under the trademark of Leo the Lion.

If it had not already died a natural death, Mr. Vogel would also have liquidated the only other production left on my schedule—*The Rise and Fall of the Third Reich,* which I had announced with considerable fanfare the previous spring. In point of fact, MGM had not consulted me before making the purchase, and I never discovered what they thought they were buying—besides a current best-seller. Nevertheless, once the studio had acquired it, I conducted an aggressive campaign to have it assigned to me, on the grounds that its author, William Shirer, and its editor, Joseph Barnes, had both been close associates of mine at the Office of War Information. Having succeeded, I realized I had not the faintest notion of how to turn it into a viable film. The one good idea I had was to invite George Roy Hill (who had done such a brilliant job of combining historical reality and drama on *The Titanic* and *The Blast in Centralia Number Five*) to come and work on it. We sat together watching thousands of feet of newsreel footage, and early in 1961 Shirer, Schnee, Hill and I had lunch around the pool at the Beverly Hills Hotel to discuss the project. Some weeks later, in mid-April, before going off to direct another film on an earlier commitment, Hill handed me a long and extremely intelligent memorandum in which he outlined the various possible approaches to such a film.

By the time George Roy Hill was once again available, Schnee was dead of a heart attack (having survived his wife, Mary, by barely four months); the studio was in chaos; the market was flooded with lurid Hitler quickies; and my own enthusiasm for the project (which had never been deep or clear) had entirely evaporated.

Nineteen sixty-two and 'sixty-three were years of uncertainty and conflict during which I felt myself sliding back into many of the anxieties I thought I had left behind me forever. My situation at the studio had deteriorated and my personal life was not without problems. Joan had an operation that gave us momentary concern; Michael was off in Europe, following an invitation from my mother to spend a year in school near Paris, and Joan missed him. Sebastian, having transferred from the Sisters of Malibu to the Montessori School in Santa Monica, was in the same difficulties as before and came close to losing an eye when a neighbor's child shot at him point-blank with an air gun loaded with gravel. But my most immediate and incessant cares were material. With the purchase (almost entirely in cash) of a new house in Malibu, I found myself in a state of such constant financial difficulty that my mail was once again filled with irritated letters from my bank manager and my lawyer warning me of tragic consequences if I did not come to my senses and mend my ways.

Glumly I accepted the first reasonable offer I received for the House on the Hill in New City. Joan had never been happy there, and its sale eased my immediate financial problems, but the secret guilt and misery I suffered over the sale of the first home I had ever built, and about which I had always had such complicated emotions, added to the rising tide of my restlessness and discontent.

On the bright side, there was the pleasure we had both begun to take in our new house on the beach. No. 47 Malibu Colony was a beautiful home with which I partially made up to Joan for the loss of her beloved house in Santa Monica. She had furnished it with her usual skill—mostly with things from the House on the Hill and from the New York apartment (including hundreds of books making their third trans-

continental crossing in five years). It was a large house, and
Joan and Denis Deegan had scoured Southern California for
the pieces she still needed, chief among them a large dining-
room table to replace the one we had lost in the New City
fire. Somewhere beyond Pasadena they discovered and, for
fifty dollars, bought an old California farm table that weighed
a ton and which, in our new paneled, blue-floored dining
room, surrounded by tall straw-seated wooden-frame chairs
I brought back from Italy, allowed us to increase our Sunday
lunch parties to twelve and even sixteen. We had a number
of "regulars," but we tried, through constant infusions of
Eastern visitors and people not engaged in show business, to
keep our parties from becoming repetitive Hollywood gath-
erings. Shop talk was inevitable, but too much of it was discouraged, and, over the years, a number of artistic and
theatrical associations were formed there; a "monster" film
was shot there one weekend by Andy Warhol and his followers; several interesting love affairs started there, and at least
two international marriages, one of which has lasted to this
day.*

This was the era of "happenings," of which one of the most
memorable was the dramatic unveiling of a new portrait of
Anaïs Nin by Joan's friend the Austrian painter Renate
Druks. The event was described by James Bridges in a letter
to Virgil Thomson:

> The painting occupied one entire wall and in front of
> it were seven veils of different colors—the first pink, the
> second lavender, the rest in rainbow shades of various
> hues ... At a certain point in the festivities, three ladies,
> Joan, Anaïs and Renate, disappeared. A few minutes
> later, Joan and Renate reappeared in costume. They
> wore shortish nightgownish choir-robish affairs and no

* Built in the early forties of brick and steel by my former boss at
Paramount, Buddy De Sylva, No. 47 was generally considered the
best house in the Colony. I had bought it for what I considered the
outrageous sum of ninety-five thousand dollars. Five years later,
when life took me back to the East Coast, we sold it for one hundred
ninety-five thousand dollars. Thirteen years later, at the height of
the inflation, it was sold for close to two million dollars.

shoes as they moved to stand in front of the painting. Then John Houseman was presented with a pair of scissors and was told to stand nearby and on cue to cut the strings holding the veils. Now Anaïs herself appeared, as in the portrait, dressed in bands of black paper wrapped around and around her body. On top of the black paper dress, around her bosoms and waist were wrapped white paper bands four inches wide on which Anaïs had written the verbal accompaniment to the happening. As Anaïs slowly turned around and around, Rupert* stood beside her and read from the paper. It was all very Anaïsninish, about the two fish of the sign of Pisces, and how the positive one was favored and the negative one feared.

As the last veil fell away, suddenly, from the back of the room, there were two explosions! Gun-shots. Everyone screamed and turned to stare at Tim Crawford with a smoking revolver in his hand. Heads snapped back to the two ladies (Joan and Renate) in front of the painting. Great splotches of blood appeared on the fronts of their robes. Breasts covered with blood. It dripped to the floor. The two ladies swayed back and forth, moaning. Anaïs continued to turn. Rupert continued to read. Suddenly both ladies reached up under their robes and pulled from the Delta of Venus huge red bouquets of flowers. As Rupert read on, something about "out of death one gives birth to beauty," Renate and Joan sank to the floor with their arms around each other and expired. Applause! After which two large fish (which had been models for the painting), frozen and thawed out for the happening, were carried about the room for all to see and admire.

More solid satisfaction came from my renewed and growing involvement in the UCLA Theatre Group, which was establishing itself as the only professional theatre company in the country performing regularly within a university structure. In the community, our position was growing stronger

* Rupert Paul was the husband of Anaïs Nin and became literary executor of her work after her death.

with each new production. During my absence in Rome Lamont Johnson had produced an abrasive French comedy, *The
Egg*, by Félicien Marceau.* Described by one reviewer as
"The Heel's Progress," it was in healthy contrast to the classic
diet I'd been providing: "A wildly stimulating experience. . . .
Once again the Theatre Group has batted a home run, this
time with bases full."

It was a good opening for our new season, and though I
was still in the throes of *Two Weeks in Another Town,* I found
time and nerve to undertake the prodigious task of preparing
and directing a production of O'Neill's *The Iceman Cometh.*

To help me to meet the challenge of this titanic work, I
took on as associate director a young man from television
named Ralph Senensky, who was familiar with the play, having directed it recently in a community theatre. My own acquaintance with O'Neill's masterpiece went back more than
thirty years to the night in New York when I had seen it
wrecked at its first performance by a tragic accident of casting.† I had proposed it once to the Phoenix, but now I was
glad nothing had come of that, since Los Angeles, with its
vast pool of mature male actors, seemed to offer unique opportunities for casting. Indeed, I still believe that the company we presented on the stage of Schoenberg Hall that
winter was, with one single, special exception, the best ever
assembled to portray the inmates of Harry Hope's bar: John
Anderson as the anarchist; William Rooney and Alan Carney
as the two busted vaudevillians; Jared Barclay as the young
fink; June Ericson and Nina Talbot as the whores; and, behind the bar, Telly Savalas and his helper, Ed Asner. Finally,
I am convinced that in the history of the play there will never
be a truer, deeper and more touching interpretation of

* With a lively cast that included Carroll O'Connor, John McGiver,
Carol Rossen and, in the leading role, Don Taylor.
† In a marvelous set by Robert Edmund Jones which miraculously
combined realism and imagination, James Barton, the great vaudeville comedian, had proved incapable of remembering his lines or
his business or of comprehending the scope of the role of Harry
Hope.

Harry Hope than that given in our production by James Dunn* a few years before his death.

That left Hickey—the part that had been so magnificently played by Jason Robards in José Quintero's production at New York's Circle in the Square. After much searching I chose Martin Balsam to play the doomed, irrepressible drummer. He came through with an intelligent, sensitive and technically brilliant performance. But there was one fatal flaw in it: Balsam, no matter how hard he tried, was Jewish, not Irish.

Once again, as with Chekhov and Pirandello, I had the thrilling experience of feeling myself involved in the performance of a great work. Even with the deep cuts we made, the play was unusually long. Yet it never faltered.

> Probably the greatest play in the American language, Eugene O'Neill's *The Iceman Cometh* gets a production equal to its importance . . . It is true O'Neill with all his imperfections, his rough humor and raw tragedy . . . A great experience.

So wrote James Powers in the *Reporter;* and according to Scheuer of the *Los Angeles Times:*

> It isn't too often that you get the chance to sit through four acts and some four hours of Eugene O'Neill. Thanks to the Theatre Group for once again bringing sustenance and substance to those for whom the theatre is a meaningful and living thing.

As a result, we extended *The Iceman* for our longest run yet: twenty-two performances before over ten thousand people.

On account of my frequent absences and the inevitable overlapping of rehearsals, there were some Theatre Group

---

* James Dunn (1906–67) won an Academy Award for best supporting actor for the part of the drunken waiter in *A Tree Grows in Brooklyn.* After years in the theatre, he made fifty films and then went to television, where he starred in his own series, *It's a Great Life,* before his final triumph as Harry Hope.

productions in which I played virtually no part. Such a one was an Italian piece by Diego Fabbri, originally named *The Trial of Jesus Christ*, which had been adapted by Warner Leroy under the title *Between Two Thieves*. It was directed by Joseph Sargent and presented in a small auditorium in the Humanities Building, where it had a successful run and furnished conversation at many Beverly Hills dinner tables during the Christmas season.

As the Theatre Group moved into its third year, certain members of the board, led by Kenneth MacGowan, suggested that the time had come for us to produce a classic and, preferably, an Elizabethan play. I agreed and offered them a choice of Marlowe's *Edward II* or Shakespeare's *Measure for Measure*. The board chose *Measure*, which I presented in a reduced version of my "Hapsburg" production that had been so successful at Stratford.

I found this dark Shakespearean comedy more difficult to cast among Hollywood actors than our previous, more realistic productions. But, once again, with Ethel's help, I managed to assemble an interesting cast—our largest to date.* Once again I used Virgil's beguiling score, but our setting (which, to conform to the structural limitations of our Schoenberg stage, turned out quite unlike our original Stratford version) was designed and painted by a young California artist, Paul Matheson. "Plenty of Paprika," reported the *Los Angeles Times*, which informed its readers that

Houseman has Wiener-Schnitzeled and Arthur Schnitzlered it all over, as well as giving it the suggestion of the *Threepenny Opera*—not too implausibly since its theme is

---

* Arnold Moss repeated his performance as the wandering Duke; the Irish actor Dan O'Herlihy was the erring deputy; Geoffrey Horne was Claudio, Alan Napier Escalus, together with Alan Suess, Jacques Aubuchon, Robert Casper, Arthur Mallet and Ted Marcuse in the roles of sundry low characters and officials. The women were played by Betty Harford, Paula Prentiss and our Stratford discovery, the strawberry-blond Mariette Hartley, as Isabella. My wife, Joan, appeared as a distinguished, if somewhat exotic, abbess.

civic corruption. Its shaping is elaborate and fulfilling
. . . Miss Hartley is a revelation—remarkably warm and
womanly for one so young.

The *News* gave highest praise to Moss's "Frisky Friar" and
declared: "Bard's Darkest Play Is UCLA's Brightest Spot."

Immediately following *Measure for Measure* we presented
what may well have been the most original of our productions
so far—John Hersey's *The Child Buyer*. It was certainly the
most "relevant" of our plays, produced during the national
scientific offensive that followed the Russian sputnik's first
successful orbit in space.

Paul Shyre had done a skillful job of adapting Hersey's
dramatic narrative, and for the play's world premiere we had
assembled a wonderful cast. Gathered around the chubby,
round-faced little boy with the phenomenal IQ, and responsible in one way or another for his fate, were such veterans
as Edward Andrews, Russell Collins, Don Keefer, Mercedes
McCambridge, Kent Smith, Edith Atwater, Maxine Stuart
and William Windom, while the Mephistophelean child
buyer was brilliantly played by the gentle comedian Henry
Jones.

Attracted by the play's authorship and subject matter, *The
New York Times* sent its first-string drama critic, Howard
Taubman, across the country to see it.

No matter how little you (in New York) may have
heard about it, there is professional theatre in Southern
California, and it has an audience. Indeed, this audience
is eager, willing to make up its own mind and ready to
respond to plays that have not yet won the imprimatur
of New York.

Paul Shyre's dramatization of Hersey's *The Child Buyer*
had its world premiere here ten days ago. The public
response has been so enthusiastic that the run has been
extended and if the Theatre Group did not have certain
commitments the production might run for months.

On several grounds the public judgment is sound. *The
Child Buyer* deals with a profoundly pertinent theme for
our time—the corruption of human values. The performance observes high theatrical standards. Not many of

the world's metropolitan centers match the pool of talent available here and the actors assembled for this production are exceptional.*

This review may have helped to bring about the happy surprise we received a few weeks later when we were informed that the Theatre Group would be receiving from the Ford Foundation a grant of half a million dollars to be used toward the construction and operation of a theatre on the University of California's Los Angeles campus. According to the formal citation:

The Theatre Group has established a new pattern for a professional theatre company. Through its activities over the past three years professional theatre has been added to the community resources traditionally provided by universities.

With that our fondest hopes seemed to be realized. We had created an audience;† now we were acquiring a home. No one seriously doubted our ability to raise the rest of the money required to erect a suitable playhouse on the fine plot of land that had been allocated to us by the university. In an interview with the *Los Angeles Times* I confidently predicted that the new theatre would be ready for operation during the 1964–65 season: "With a theatre that will seat around one thousand, and by presenting up to ten plays a year, the Theatre Group hopes to establish a regular audience of around forty thousand who will be looking forward to a stimulating evening in the theatre ten times a year. Who can ask for more?"

* So exceptional that when the opportunity arose to present *The Child Buyer* in New York I passed it up on the grounds that we could never remotely approach the quality of the cast we had in Los Angeles.
† "The eagerness and enthusiasm of the Theatre Group audiences were quite remarkable. Going to the plays you had the feeling that you were attending a party. You ran into friends and intermissions were alive with spirited discussions."—Cecil Smith, *Los Angeles Times*, May 1981.

CHAPTER VII

1962-1963

THE COOL OF THE DAY
OTELLO
ANTIGONE
BURLESQUE
THE GREAT ADVENTURE

THE FORD FOUNDATION's announcement marked a peak in the fortunes of the Professional Theatre Group. For me, personally, it represented a justification of the two years of activity, which was now reported in a full-page article in *Time*—

MOONLIGHTER

John Houseman, 59, producer for Metro-Goldwyn-Mayer, is paid more than $100,000 a year. But he moonlights. After working at his other job until dawn he drives home to his beach house in the Malibu Colony, bathes, showers, breakfasts and returns to Culver City by nine A.M.

Houseman's "other job" is artistic director of Los Angeles' three-year-old Theatre Group at UCLA which presents first-rate stage productions (including a recent superb performance of *Measure for Measure*) drawing from an eager pool of movie and television actors who are willing to work for Equity minimum just to submit themselves to the sterner discipline of the stage. This discipline is measured out sternly enough by director Houseman, whose diffident and quiet manner never quite accompanies him into rehearsals—

together with a severe photograph of me directing and an incomplete, distorted bio.

Time had, as usual, overstated the case—but it was true that I was in the studio every morning before nine and seldom left before six, and that, since most of the actors in our Theatre Group productions also appeared on TV or in pictures, theatrical rehearsals usually began at 7 P.M. and continued until midnight on weekdays and all through the weekend. Thus, though most of my regular working hours were spent in Culver City, the greater and better part of my creative energy was going into my activity with the Theatre Group. It is conceivable that if I had been less concerned with the theatre I might have been more effective and successful in my filmmaking. But I doubt it.

The malaise from which I suffered each time I drove into the studio and made my way to my sumptuous second-floor corner suite went deeper than my own personal problems. It pervaded the entire industry as it finally faced the fact that television was displacing it as the world's prime instrument of dramatic communication. And it was particularly virulent at MGM, where rival factions of stockholders seemed more concerned with the disposition of the company's assets than with the creation of new motion pictures. This still didn't entirely explain my own attitude—the indifference bordering on revulsion with which I found myself facing the years of lucrative filmmaking to which my current contract and our present standard of living irrevocably condemned me.

Between 1951 and 1956 I had produced a dozen films; with few exceptions they had revolved around vital and significant subjects: *Lust for Life* had followed a creative talent to its final, tragic expression; *Executive Suite, The Bad and the Beautiful, Julius Caesar,* my abortive *Labor Story* and even the frail *Cobweb* were all concerned with the acquisition and the consequences of power. Since my return to MGM (with the exception of *The Third Reich,* which I never really intended to do, and *South of the Angels,* which I was not permitted to make) the themes of the films I had chosen to work on had been trivial and enervated—none more so than the one I was now preparing without enthusiasm or confidence.

Based on a book by a female novelist who had once written a best-seller, *The Cool of the Day* was a lugubrious story of upper-middle-class adultery. Nobody liked it. Siegel, before leaving, had advised against it; two friendly directors (Robert Wise and John Frankenheimer) had turned it down, and two experienced and intelligent screenwriters had declined my offer to adapt it. They said it was morbid—which it was. Finally I entrusted the screenplay to Meade Roberts, who had done so well with *The Wings of the Dove* and who was in no position to turn down a job. For my director, at the last moment, I chose Robert Stevens, who, for all his temperamental eccentricities, had done remarkable work for me on television.

I had persuaded the studio to acquire *The Cool of the Day* for two reasons. Both were bad. The first was an attempt to placate my agents and assuage their constant nagging over the fact that, as I completed my second year in Culver City, I had produced only two films. To ensure the extension of my contract, they kept urging me to acquire additional properties and put them into work without delay.

My second reason was more personal and reflected my growing restlessness. My Roman voyage, with all its problems, had revived my long-repressed yearning for travel. Much of the action of *The Cool of the Day* was laid in Greece; its production would involve a voyage to such places as Athens, Delphi, the Gulf of Corinth and the Peloponnesus at the best time of the year, with all expenses paid. Neither of these motivations would have been valid at another time. They might not have prevailed even now but for a special situation of which I took full advantage. As a relic of its imperial days when it dominated the European film market, MGM owned and operated a studio at Boreham Wood on the outskirts of London. It had become something of a white elephant, but it permitted MGM to use up some of its frozen European currencies and to take advantage of a subsidy devised to aid the British film industry, known as the Eady Plan.* *The Cool of the Day,* with its international cast and European locations, qualified for such benefits.

Torn between nagging doubts as to the quality of the project and my neurotic anxiety to get going, I flew to London, where I spent several days going over our budget and setting up an organization that qualified under the Eady Plan. On my return, we started to cast and discovered that, by emphasizing the attractions of our Greek locations, we were able to attract a surprisingly desirable band of stars. Our two involved couples finally consisted of Jane Fonda and Arthur Hill on the American side, Peter Finch and Angela Lansbury on the British. Later we added such fine actors as Constance Cummings and Alexander Knox.

It is almost impossible, once you get started, not to become infected with the excitement of a major film. In the weeks that preceded our departure for Europe all kinds of decisions had to be made. Among them was the problem of creating a new personality for Jane Fonda. She had scored a personal success as a teenage hoyden in *Walk on the Wild Side,* a far cry from the delicate Westchester princess she would be playing for us. Our efforts to transform her were not wholly successful. Someone (I suspect it may have been Sydney Guilaroff, the demon hair stylist of MGM, abetted by Jane herself) devised a hairdo for her that bore a close and unfortunate resemblance to Elizabeth Taylor's Cleopatra. Several such dark, helmetlike wigs were made at enormous expense, and no matter how much we fiddled with them later they completely destroyed the mobility and fascination of that expressive face. For her clothes she turned down Walter Plunkett,† one of the world's great costume designers, and chose, in his place, a fashionable designer whose elaborate creations turned out to be curiously unattractive and unconvincing.

* This involved the employment of a high percentage of British actors, technicians and office staff.
† His credits included *Little Women, Gone with the Wind, An American in Paris, Lust for Life* and many others.

Finally, as part of her transformation into a modish latter-day Camille, Jane insisted on wearing high spike heels throughout the film—even on the rocky slopes of the Parthenon.

I left for London some days ahead of the company. This time our family disruption was complete. Since John Michael was already in France, Joan flew directly to Paris, where she stayed with her mother for some weeks before joining me in Greece. Sebastian spent the first part of the summer in Puerto Rico with our friends the Botsfords and the rest of it in the Malibu Colony with our two poodles, the basset hound, the one surviving dachshund, two cats and two tortoises in the care of our devoted couple, Barbara and John. (Besides being an accomplished bass player and horseman John Martin was a mechanical wizard; from materials obtained from Howard Hughes's experimental plant where he worked, he built Sebastian a midget racing car which, in our absence, he drove daily with great skill and daring around a miniature track in the hills.)

Arriving in Boreham Wood, I was happy to encounter a few friendly faces. Robert Wise was there, producing and directing some sort of ghost story—also under the Eady Plan. With him was Marian Fenn, the wry, sharp-featured, nice-looking, intelligent young Englishwoman who had been my secretary in Culver City for a while until Charlie Schnee borrowed her to work on *Two Weeks in Another Town*. Disagreeably involved in a grotesque situation that ended with Mary Schnee's suicide, she had eagerly accepted Wise's offer to work for him in England.

At the studio I found that enough of the international prestige of *Julius Caesar* and *Lust for Life* remained to assure me of a respectful reception. It did not last long, for it soon became apparent that there was a general dislike of my script and resentment over this American invasion. To aggravate matters, within a few days of his arrival Robert Stevens, my director, succeeded in antagonizing not only the front office (which I didn't mind) but also his production designer, cameraman and assistant director—not to mention the entire

British crew with whom he would be working for the next three months.

As a break-in period for cast and crew, we had decided to film for a week at Boreham Wood before departing for Greece. It was during those first days of shooting that I discovered that Jane Fonda was currently playing Trilby to the Svengali of a young Greek comrade from the Actors' Studio, who accompanied her on the set and remained there throughout rehearsal and filming. Under his tutelage, before each take of an emotional scene Jane emitted a chilling and ear-splitting primal scream. After each take her first look was to him for approval over the heads of her director and of a perplexed Peter Finch, with whom she was playing most of her scenes.* Our first batch of rushes was greeted in Culver City with the usual flurry of disapproval: the tempo was slow; Fonda's makeup was too heavy. I ordered two of the scenes reshot and left for Greece.

The heat in Athens was overwhelming, and a heavy cloud of dust hung over the city; still, it was better than the murk of Boreham Wood. Our search for locations was conducted under the guidance of our local unit manager, a forceful, oversized, handsome Olympian female by the name of Aspa Sotirchos. Aside from the obviously impressive antiquities— the Acropolis, the shrine and theatre at Delphi, the barren grandeur of the Lion's Gate—it was the Greek countryside that impressed me. In its beauty and abject poverty it was unlike anything I had ever seen. Everywhere were the clear marks of hundreds of years of foreign occupation and

* Jane Fonda, whom I hold to be one of the outstanding women of our time, has always shown a wonderfully feminine capacity for taking on the color, the attitudes, the opinions and even the personalities of her men. During the making of our film she played the part of the dutiful Greek future daughter-in-law. This was followed, within a year, by her total transformation into the jet-set wife of Roger Vadim—the "Barbarella" period—which was succeeded before long by the social and political activism of her marriage to Tom Hayden. Simultaneously she was to transform herself, as a daughter, from Electra to Cordelia.

oppression; you could drive for miles without seeing one substantial house or estate. The sparse villages through which
we passed and where we occasionally stopped were clean and
neat, but it was the cleanliness of dire poverty and one had
the strong impression that their inhabitants had lived for
years, and were still living, on the very edge of starvation.
Over it all hung an inescapable, ever-present feeling of tragedy. Of the men I talked to in the villages and among the
members of our caravan and local crew, almost everyone
drifted back sooner or later to the events of the Second World
War when Nazis, Communists and the British under Churchill had each done their part to set these contentious and desperate people against one another. The war had been over
for eighteen years, but everywhere, close below the surface,
one could sense currents of hatred and savagery, the ran-
corous memories of that terrible civil war.* Reluctantly one
found oneself listening to stories of revenge and betrayal; of
bodies thrown at night into unmarked graves; and, in one
village, from the lips of a gentle, white-haired man over a
glass of retzina, I heard the tale of a barrel filled with eyeballs
of slaughtered compatriots.

It was in this fabulous countryside and against this tragic
background that our banal story of upper-middle-class
Anglo-American adultery was being shot and falling further
behind schedule with each successive location. Waves of disapproval reached us from the studio, but they were faint and
harmless by the time they had traveled the eight thousand
miles that separated Athens from Culver City. Ethel's personal cables and letters came regularly; they were filled with
local news and false courage, but I could sense that life must
be hell for her—left behind in the enemy camp as a hostage
and a scapegoat for all the grievances that the studio was
building up against her master:

> I miss you terribly and find that I have to get to the
> studio earlier and really discipline myself to attend to my

* In the early sixties it was generally known that a number of concentration camps were still being operated by the Royal government.

chores without the contentment and stimulus of your
presence . . . You have always charged me up and it was
all easier or at least I never realized that I had to create
a false energy in your absence. What charges *you* up? Or
do you do it all by yourself all the time?

For my own part, I was beginning to have such a good time
that it almost justified the long misery of this dreary film.
Joan had arrived in Greece, accompanied by John Michael,
who had completed his French school year; Denis Deegan,
with Ethel Winant's help, had managed to scrape together
the plane fare and he too joined us for a few days as we
moved, after ten days in Athens, westward to Delphi, where
we shot an improvised and decorative but rather silly scene
between our two lovers on the steeply rising steps of the
amphitheatre.

Years later, Joan spoke of her Greek voyage with nostalgia,
but at the time it was my impression that it disturbed and
frightened her. Partly this had to do with the devastating
heat; partly, it was her strong emotional reaction to the
immense power of those battered but still furiously
living stones. At Delphi, in the shrine in which she had asked
to be left alone for an hour, this backsliding French
Catholic claimed, in all seriousness, to have had a personal
interview with the oracle. Addressing her in French, a
woman's voice had told her that she would never find peace
(*tranquillité*) until she got rid of the anger (*rancoeur*) in her
heart.

We drank champagne to the sybil that night in an ugly
modern hotel whose windows looked down over the endless
olive groves that run sheer down to the valley and out to the
sea. We laughed about her experience, but to this day my
wife is convinced that on that sunny afternoon she recaptured some of the peace she had lost during her troubled
years of displacement.

From Delphi our adulterous lovers' flight took them into
the Peloponnesus. During our scouting expeditions we had
found the perfect vehicle in which to carry them across the
Gulf of Corinth: an improvised motor ferry (made up of two
damaged landing craft left over from World War II). The

first day we saw it, there were five or six cars aboard, some thirty passengers, and a flock of sheep being driven south to their autumn pastures. After elaborate negotiations we succeeded in chartering this ferry for one day; then we set about organizing extras and half a dozen suitable cars. We also ordered a small flock of sheep.

Now a curious and very Hellenic complication arose. When the sheep arrived at the dock and were about to be driven aboard, the young, dark, handsome gendarme who had been assigned to the company summarily forbade the sheep's embarkation. He asserted that Greeks were civilized people and accused us of wishing to portray them to the world as barbarians who knew no better than to mix men and animals. In vain we pointed out that sheep *were* regularly transported on that ferry and that we had seen them with our own eyes. Our attempts to bribe him only made matters worse. He remained adamant in defense of his country's honor and showed us, in a small official book he carried, that he was technically correct about the sheep. So the flock was paid off and sent back into the hills, while we filled the gap left by their absence with five added cars and two dozen more extras before we headed for the open waters of the gulf.

It was on this excursion, halfway across the Gulf of Corinth, that we finally came nearest to achieving our desired atmosphere of warmth and excitement. Jane took off her shoes, forgot her makeup and let the sweat run down her face. Peter Finch, after a number of ouzos, cast off the attitude of sulky boredom which he had maintained ever since it had become clear to him that Jane was not for him. The bazouki band warmed up; so did the dozen male dancers whom Aspa, our unit manager, had mobilized and who filled the deck with their slow, heavy, intense stamping dance, in which they were presently joined by Jane, Peter and my son John Michael. It was growing dark when we returned— drunk, sunburned, exhausted and very happy.

(Before leaving Delphi, Jane presented to Joan and me a marble head that had broken off some ancient classical fountain. It was shipped back, wrapped in a Greek sheepskin, to California, where it lies today among the flowers in our garden, its mouth open, staring out over the Pacific Ocean, to remind us of that strangely euphoric week.)

The music that was played that day in the Gulf of Corinth had been obtained following a curious series of negotiations conducted by Aspa on my behalf. Greek music had arrived in America with Jules Dassin's film *Never on Sunday*, whose theme song had been on the *Hit Parade* for weeks. Soon after my arrival in Athens, I had a meeting with its composer, Manos Hadjidakis—a small, dark, pudgy man with bad teeth, beautiful eyes and irresistible charm.*

I told him in French about our project; I suggested that he compose one major theme song for us and also allow us to use several of his already recorded popular tunes as "source music" in the course of the film. He agreed, but, being gentlemen, neither of us made any mention of money. Instead, we discussed the theatre and he played me the tapes of scores he had composed for a local art theatre—for Aristophanes' *Birds* and for Anouilh's version of *Antigone*. Next day I instructed Aspa to get a price from him. She returned with a figure of twenty-five thousand dollars per tune. When I objected that this figure was high, Hadjidakis took umbrage and broke off negotiations. Two days later he sent word that, rather than haggle with a man he liked and respected, he would do the whole thing for nothing!

Bewildered by these tactics, I hesitated, reluctant to believe that he meant what he said. Aspa, who had known him for years, assured me that he did and that, rather than see the job go to his rival Theodorakis, he would in fact charge us only for the mechanical cost of new recordings and the union wages of his own band of bazouki players. Our recordings were made over a period of two days—improvised mostly, without musical parts but with frequent interruptions for food and drink.†

* He was one of Greece's two outstanding musicians—both far left and both combining popular with theatrical and "serious" music.
† If we finally achieved no single equivalent of "Never on Sunday," this was not Hadjidakis' fault. For a theme song MGM later substituted a vapid ballad which, although recorded by Nat King Cole, made no perceptible dent in the U.S. music market.

We stayed in Greece for three weeks. Bright sunshine, blue skies, ouzo and the beauty of the countryside had raised our spirits and injected false optimism into our company. This was quickly dispelled on my return to the darkness of Boreham Wood.

For years I had enjoyed and benefited from the mass and power of a great studio organization. Now I was to experience it in all its brutal malignance. I was told in no uncertain terms that my film was a disaster and that the studio had only one concern—to get it finished as quickly and cheaply as possible. A new unit manager arrived to take over many of my producer's duties. On the grounds that I had proved incapable of controlling and disciplining my director, all shooting schedules were taken out of my hands. And soon after our return from Greece, MGM's chief film editor, Margaret Booth,* arrived from Culver City and made no secret of the fact that she was here to salvage a hopeless project. Everywhere I turned I faced frustration and what often seemed like deliberate humiliation.

(Lest it appear that I was suffering from persecution mania, I must explain that I was receiving covert confirmation of the studio's attitude from Marian Fenn, who, after finishing her work for Robert Wise, had been kept on by the company as secretary to our new unit manager. This put her in a position to show me copies of all cables and letters and to give me verbatim reports of transatlantic phone conversations—all detailing my shortcomings as a producer and citing new examples of my inefficiency and weakness.)

The truth is that after our return to Boreham Wood morale on the picture collapsed (partly through my own fault and partly as a result of the studio's attitude). Bob Stevens had always been "difficult," but on the short span of a TV show his eccentricities could be curbed and channeled. Now, as we went into our third month of shooting, there were times

* She had been Irving Thalberg's cutter and was credited with the editing of *Mutiny on the Bounty* and other MGM triumphs of the thirties and forties. Much as I admired her skill and experience, she and I had never seen eye to eye. In the days of my success I had been able to keep her at bay; now she moved in with a vengeance.

when he appeared to be taking leave of his senses. There was nothing I could do except change directors—and it was too late for that. For twenty years, ever since my first tentative producer's steps into *The Unseen*,* I had, for better or for worse, managed to maintain control over the style and tone of my productions. Now, suddenly, I felt utterly helpless and impotent as I watched *The Cool of the Day* drifting toward its hopeless and shameful end.

During those last horrible weeks I enjoyed two brief respites. The first was a visit, over the August bank-holiday weekend, to Rathfarnham outside Dublin, where Dorothy Jeakins was living in a small Georgian manor house that had been lent to her by Morris Graves, the American painter.† I had never been in Ireland and I spent two blissfully peaceful days in pouring rain and an odor of burning peat.

Returning to Boreham Wood, I found a new humiliation awaiting me. From my earliest days of filmmaking I had taken pride in my use of music: I had worked on good terms with Virgil Thomson, Ernst Toch, Bernard Herrmann, David Raksin, Miklós Rosza, Alex North and Aaron Copland. In England, on the advice of friends familiar with the local scene, I had selected for our main scoring (in addition to the Hadjidakis source music) a respected and experienced composer by the name of Chagrin. He was halfway through his musical sketches when he was told that since I no longer had authority over the final editing of the picture, he would be wise to discuss his musical problems with Miss Booth rather than with me.

Two days later I received a cable from George Stevens, Jr., of the U.S. Information Service in Washington. Since I was already in Europe, would I represent the United States on the jury of the Venice Film Festival? It was only a week away, and while I was weighing his offer there arrived an engraved invitation with a gold seal from Venice in which I was addressed as *"egregio"* and *"serenissimo."* That settled it. I ac-

---

* See *Front and Center*, pp. 114 *et seq.*
† I was acquainted with his bird paintings from having seen them hanging between the Renoirs and the Cézannes on the walls of Charles Laughton's house in the Pacific Palisades.

cepted with alacrity, packed my evening clothes and, abandoning my battered film, flew to Paris, where I picked up Joan, and flew on the Milan and from there to Venice. We arrived before dawn and were taken on to the Lido by boat as the sun rose.

Venice was my wife's favorite city, and she spent her days cruising between the Lido, Harry's Bar, the Biennale and the churches. I remembered it vaguely from having spent a week there as a child;* my duties with the festival kept me so busy at the Lido that I didn't get to see much of it now. We were expected to view between three and five films a day in various categories, and we attended nocturnal functions to the point of exhaustion. It was a welcome change from my life of the past three months, but, with new horrors developing daily in Boreham Wood in my absence, it was not as satisfying as it might otherwise have been. As it happened, 1962 was not a particularly brilliant festival year, and I soon found that my interest centered less on the films we were being shown than on the machinations of which the festival was the center.

I had been made aware of this during a luncheon briefing by George Stevens. He explained that the decisions of the Venice Film Festival were often more political than aesthetic and that there was an unholy alliance between the Russians and the Italians ("most of them Communists"), together with some of the French, to tip the scales against Hollywood and in favor of the Socialist countries. I resented his briefing but soon discovered for myself that the awards were unquestionably affected by political alliances and that the pressures on the jury were constant and unrelenting.

In effect, most of our awards that year were negotiated— the result of deals and compromises arrived at between the two sides of this artistic cold war in which I tried, with only partial success, to maintain an open and unprejudiced atti-

---

* My only clear recollection was of huge, blood-glutted mosquitoes which, in self-defense, I crushed in large numbers against the flowered paper with which the walls of the Hotel Danieli were decorated. The management, I remember, attempted to charge my parents several hundred lire for property damage.

tude, and in which I frequently found myself associated with Ronald Neame, Britain's representative on the jury.

I did not stay for the formal presentation of the awards. Joan flew directly from Paris to California, and I returned to the gloom of Boreham Wood. Two weeks later I too flew back to Los Angeles. (To this day I have never seen *The Cool of the Day*, and I have noticed that neither Jane Fonda nor I ever list it among the films we have made.)

Back in Malibu, with the family reunited on the beach, my melancholy lifted. And here my incurable and reprehensible habit of flitting from one medium to another once again proved invaluable. During my absence overseas a surprising variety of offers had accumulated. While I sifted them I instructed MCA to negotiate the termination of my contract with MGM as quickly and advantageously as possible.* After some maneuvering, we settled for nine months of full remuneration. But even before the deal was signed, I was at work on the first and most urgent of my new assignments—the direction of Verdi's *Otello* in Dallas, Texas.

While still in London I had received a cable from Lawrence Kelly of the Dallas Civic Opera Company asking if I'd be interested in directing an opera in early November. (Here I detected the small, firm hand of Jean Rosenthal, who was technical director and lighting designer for the Dallas Opera.) I replied affirmatively. Then, during the Venice Film Festival, my hotel room had been invaded one night by a young Italian with the sonorous name of Attilio Colonello, accompanied by two male slaves carrying an enormous model of the stage settings he had designed for *Otello*, for which Mr. Kelly had instructed him to get my approval. Two days after my return to Malibu I bought a score and started to play the album of *Otello* as recorded by Arturo Toscanini.

* A fellow producer in much the same situation as myself had recently abrogated his contract for a surprisingly large sum. When I suggested that I might get the same, my agent (whose cynical and pessimistic tone had won him the nickname of "Dr. No") soon disillusioned me. "No way!" he explained. "They don't hate you nearly as much as they hated him!"

I assumed that I had been asked to stage the opera because of my reputation as a Shakespearean director. But I was not altogether without operatic experience. I had worked with Virgil Thomson and Frederick Ashton on *Four Saints in Three Acts,* and I had staged the first performance of Stephen Vincent Benet and Douglas Moore's *The Devil and Daniel Webster,* with Fritz Reiner conducting. I was unable to read a score, but by following it attentively while listening repeatedly to a recording, I could familiarize myself sufficiently with the piece to work effectively with the conductor, singers and chorus. I found this particularly easy with *Otello* through my close acquaintance with Shakespeare's play.

It was a joyful experience, partly because it meant working once more with Gordon Davidson as stage manager and with my beloved Jean Rosenthal, and partly because Larry Kelly was a brilliant, generous, creative impresario who gave me complete freedom while furnishing me with every element I could conceivably require to achieve the best possible results, including what was, by operatic standards, lavish rehearsal time.* The sets and costumes were designed and executed in Italy in the best conventional operatic tradition; the large local chorus was conscientiously rehearsed over a period of weeks. Our cast was unusually distinguished: a rising young soprano by the name of Ligabue as Desdemona, together with not one but *two* major male stars in the persons of Mario del Monaco (the most illustrious Otello of the decade) and Ramon Vinay (who, before his voice deepened, had been Toscanini's favorite Otello) in the role of Iago.

I found Vinay especially exciting to work with—perceptive, intelligent and infinitely experienced. Del Monaco (in what, by his own count, was his 152nd performance of *Otello*) gave me no trouble at all; as long as I placed him in a position onstage (preferably on a set of steps) where he could exercise

---

* Lawrence Kelly died of cancer at the age of forty-one. First in Chicago and then in Dallas, in association with his conductor, Nicola Rescigno, he had established a remarkable record of operatic innovation. He is credited with introducing Maria Callas to this country, together with promoting first American opera appearances of Montserrat Caballe, Teresa Berganza and Joan Sutherland.

the "extensions" which he used to conceal his extremely short stature, he accepted my staging without question.

Otello has a particularly exhilarating first act. With close to two hundred people on the stage, all moving and singing their heads off at my behest, my recent defeats and humiliations were instantly and completely forgotten. My ego received a further sharp boost when, two days before opening, a cable arrived from Milan from the general manager of La Scala: "PLEASE CALL TONIGHT OR TOMORROW IF YOU HAVE POSSIBILITY TO DIRECT MOZART DON GIOVANNI AT SCALA MILAN NEXT MARCH."

It was an opera I had always yearned to do, and it broke my heart to have to tell the gentleman in French over a bad long-distance line that, due to previous commitments, it was not possible for me to accept his offer.

My stay in Dallas was marred by one trivial but disagreeable incident. On the night of our dress rehearsal in the huge, shabby Shrine Auditorium which served as Dallas' opera house, I noticed that a number of stagehands and musicians, returning from their supper break, were slipping sheets of yellow paper into their pockets or crumpling them and throwing them into the trashcans that stood by the stage door. Out of curiosity I fished one out and glanced at it. It stated in crude mimeographed type that Leonard Bernstein was a Communist and so were Copland, Blitzstein and others whose works had recently been performed in Dallas. And now, worst of all, Houseman, a NOTORIOUS RED, had been hired, over a number of more competent and patriotic Americans, to stage a work for the Civic Opera Company. "STOP SPENDING OUR MONEY ON DECLARED ENEMIES OF THE UNITED STATES." Nobody seemed to pay much attention to it, but it gave me a strange feeling about Dallas that was confirmed a year later when John Kennedy was assassinated there.

The opera was a huge success and there was a sumptuous party afterward at Neiman-Marcus, from which I went straight to the airport. Jean Rosenthal sent me the reviews, which were excellent, but by the time they arrived in Los Angeles I was already deep into my next venture.

•

I had left the UCLA Professional Theatre Group at the peak of its success with the promise of half a million dollars from the Ford Foundation and the firm prospect of a new theatre on campus the following year. By October, when I returned from abroad, the situation had deteriorated. Since we needed a small production after *The Child Buyer*, I had encouraged Paul Shyre to repeat his New York production of Strindberg's *Creditors*. This was followed, during the summer, by Frisch's *Chinese Wall*, directed by Norman Corwin, and a revival of Clifford Odets' *Rocket to the Moon*, to be directed by Odets himself and, when that fell through, by Daniel Mann. I saw none of them. *Creditors* was mildly successful. The production of *The Chinese Wall* seems to have been confused but provocative and highly successful with audiences. *Variety* described it as "an overall concoction that initially appears inane but turns into a solid treatise of significant impact." *Rocket* was generally regarded as a failure.

The progress of these productions had been reported to me in some detail by phone and letter by Ethel Winant, on whom, as my deputy (though she had no official position with the organization), much of the executive responsibility for the summer season seemed to be falling. Soon after my return I had a meeting with Kaplan and the executive committee, who proved incapable of giving me any definite information about the construction or even preliminary designs for our theatre. But they begged me to produce and direct the Theatre Group's next production. I selected Anouilh's *Antigone*, and, since Schoenberg Hall was not available, I agreed to stage it in the small amphitheatre in the Humanities Building.

*Antigone** had been in my head for some time—probably since hearing Hadjidakis' score that summer. After trying to get Joan Hackett and Phyllis Love for the name part and various male stars for Creon, I ended up with two Stratford

* In the translation made by my friend and collaborator Lewis Galantière for Katharine Cornell.

alumni, Mariette Hartley and Larry Gates. It was an austere and quite simple modern-dress production with no scenery except two blackboards, one on either side of the platform. On one was a chalk outline map of Greece and on the other the family tree of the doomed house of Atreus. For music I used the Hadjidakis tape that I acquired by cable for five hundred dollars. Costumes were once again by Jeakins.

Audiences found the play talky but relevant. It received mixed notices in the local press:

> The Theatre Group has never joined material and performance with better effect . . . In the title role Mariette Hartley ranges from girlish charm to savage ferocity.

> Anouilh's heroine is an impossible combination of St. Joan and a dockside harpy and one cannot entirely fault Miss Hartley for lack of warmth and conviction.

Our next offering, by way of contrast, was a piece of showbiz nostalgia that I remembered with pleasure from the late twenties, when Arthur Hopkins had produced it on Broadway with Hal Skelly and Barbara Stanwyck. *Burlesque* was the Theatre Group's twenty-fourth show, and its production was a capricious and unilateral decision on my part. My relations with the executive committee were deteriorating, and while I waited for the next board meeting to determine my future with the Group I decided to give our audiences a complete change of pace with this piece of vintage kitsch.

Since I knew nothing of backstage burleycue, I entrusted the production to Jack Albertson, himself an old "skuller," with Anne Francis as the girl, the rising young comic star Jimmy Hutton as Skid and a supporting crew of burlesque old-timers. The day before rehearsal Hutton got cold feet and disappeared. Rather than scrap or postpone the production, I persuaded Albertson (who was twice Jimmy's age) to step into the leading role. I wanted him to continue directing, but, as a measure of insurance, I agreed to stand by if needed.*

---

* Jack maintained that this role, which he had no intention of playing, was responsible for a whole new turn in his theatrical life. He

We had a fine, hectic time getting *Burlesque* onto the stage (The late Dr. Schoenberg must have turned in his grave at some of the sights and sounds that filled the auditorium that was so reverently dedicated to his memory.) Audiences loved it, and *Variety* reported: "It has the flavor and honesty of theatre when it was Show Biz—a mixture of hoke, sass, brass, tricks and truth, laughter and tears that made up the world of entertainment." A jazz band (led by Jack Boyle) played in the lobby during intermission, but the main attraction of the evening was the authentic burlesque show with which the show ended.

> When the baggy-pants, putty-nose comic comes on with the girls, I could have sworn I was back at the Orpheum in the twenties! . . . Suffused with the love of solid professionals, enlivened with a thousand years of theatrical experience called up in a few performances, it plays with the luminous charm of a phosphorescent valentine.

While this vulgar but cheerful entertainment was filling the theatre downstairs, more serious and far less pleasant business was being transacted in an upstairs boardroom. For months now—since shortly after the Ford Foundation's grant had been triumphantly announced—a strange silence had surrounded the Theatre Group's future. Little by little, during the fall, the truth had begun to leak. Now, finally, it came out. The project of a theatre on the campus, though formally approved by the chancellor, required the official sanction of UCLA's board of regents, of whom the most powerful was Dorothy (Buffy) Chandler, owner by marriage of the *Los Angeles Times*. It so happened that Mrs. Chandler was herself engaged in raising vast sums of money for the creation of the

---

was seen in the part of Skid by the playwright Frank Gilroy; two years later when a producer was looking for an actor to play the part of the father in *The Subject Was Roses*, Gilroy suggested Albertson. The play won a Pulitzer Prize, and Albertson, in due course, became a national star.

Los Angeles Music Center. When she learned of the Theatre Group's intention, she hit the ceiling and declared that she would countenance no university theatre plans until her own major downtown fund-raising drive was completed. And she virtually ordered Chancellor Murphy to abandon the idea of a theatre on campus until further notice.*

This was the bad news I finally received at our board meeting. I also learned that, since plans for our theatre were now indefinitely postponed, the land previously allocated to the theatre building had been reassigned to more urgent uses. The board (many of them members of the UCLA Theatre Department, which had long had ambivalent feelings about the growth of the Theatre Group) were inclined to accept this decision. Kaplan was disappointed but unwilling to raise an academic storm. I had no such scruples. With my usual tact, I accused Murphy and Kaplan of selling out to Mrs. Chandler and added that if I and other professionals had given freely of our time and talent to the development of the Theatre Group over the past three years, it was on the assumption that we were helping to create a permanent organization with its own artistic identity and its own base on campus. Now all these hopes had been shattered. If the best we could hope for was to continue to function indefinitely as "migrant mummers," dependent for acting space on the whims of the Music and Humanities Departments, then I, for one, was no longer interested!

On March 26, 1963, true to my habit of getting first to the press, I instructed the university to release the announcement of my resignation as artistic director of the Theatre Group.

The blow was a particularly painful one, coming so soon after my debacle at MGM and after what I still considered my betrayal by the American Shakespeare Festival. Once

* Considering who she was in Los Angeles, it is probable that Mrs. Chandler would have had her way in any case. What made it a certainty was the circumstance that Chancellor Murphy was about to leave the university for an important position in the Chandler organization.

again I had failed in an attempt to create a lasting theatre organization. But, once again, I was saved from complete demoralization by my ability to leap from one medium to another.

Soon after my return from London, while I was still negotiating my release from MGM, I had been approached by the National Broadcasting Company to produce a dramatic anthology for the Chrysler Corporation. When that was dropped in favor of *The Bob Hope Comedy Hour* it was replaced by another offer—from my former employers, CBS-TV.

William Paley was having second thoughts, apparently, about his treatment of Hubbell Robinson, whom he had dropped, after many years as the network's head of production, in favor of the rising hotshot James Aubrey. Now, four years later, he asked Hubbell to return to the network as executive in charge of special productions. Hubbell accepted and, for his first project, proposed a dramatic series to be known as *The Great Adventure,* which he asked me to produce. I accepted with satisfaction that was heightened by the discovery that Ethel Winant (who had returned to CBS after her two mad years with me in Culver City) was to be my associate. I flew to New York and appeared at a CBS affiliates' reception attended by Paley, Stanton, Hubbell, Aubrey and other network notables at which high hopes were expressed for the success of the new series. The next day the trades carried the announcement "John Houseman has been set to produce a new hour-long weekly dramatic series based on American history and designed to provide family entertainment that is both exciting and educational."

While researchers on both coasts were digging up material and sifting the mass of suggestions we received, I began to give out my customary interviews, outlining (not always consistently) the plans I had for *The Great Adventure.* It was, I announced, "an anthology relating to American historical events and characters . . . Our intention is to avoid the familiar giants of history." And I made the point that we would avoid the hateful term "education" but would offer instead "vivid and unpredictable drama through little-known incidents and people." I also declared that "fiction is running thin" and that "history is infinitely more exciting than any plots our writers could contrive."

I took a more realistic view of our problem in an imaginary interview I wrote for the *Los Angeles Times*:

FADE IN: *Producer's office—Dawn*

Close on Producer—a heavy-set, balding, harassed-looking man in his late fifties.

Pull back to reveal that the Producer is talking to himself.

Q

A history series on TV?

A

Uh-huh.

Q

Over the CBS Network? On prime time?

A

Uh-huh.

A pause. Then:

Q

Who plays George Washington?

A

Nobody.

Q

Lincoln? Ben Franklin? F.D.R.? Daniel Boone?

No answer.

Q

You did say this was an American history series?

A

Uh-huh.

I was assigned an office in that same huge white box, the CBS-TV Center, in which I had produced *Playhouse 90* three years earlier. Only now everything was changed. For one thing, drama had almost entirely disappeared from the network's production schedule—replaced by such successful but repulsive items as *The Beverly Hillbillies* and sundry game shows. For another, the executive personnel was now made up entirely of Aubrey appointees.

During the first few months of preparation of *The Great Adventure*, Ethel and I were left pretty much to ourselves, with occasional reminders that the series was expected to be commercially as well as critically successful. Then, one day, came the predictable but shocking news that the "Smiling Cobra" had made Hubbell Robinson's position at CBS untenable and that he had once more left the network. I grieved for him—and for myself. For this left me without allies in what (except for Ethel) I felt to be a bitterly hostile world. My dealings, from now on, were almost exclusively with Aubrey and his lieutenants—Hunt Stromberg, Jr.,* Mike Dann † and a garrulous and sinister figure with the unlikely name of Shakespeare who later became television adviser to Richard Nixon and played a significant role in the emasculation of public television.

With Robinson's going I realized that our show was doomed. I had been in the business long enough to know that executives do not welcome the success of their defeated rivals' projects. But we continued our intense preparation. By late spring we had collected roughly a dozen stories, half of them in script form, ready to shoot. Our problem was stated by Art Seidenbaum of the *Los Angeles Times:* "Can you be accurate, educational, dramatic and popular in prime time? *Yes,* says the producer."

My confidence was not shared by the executives of CBS, and increasing pressure was brought to bear to make the series more "popular"—with more fights, shootings and, if possible, sex. Meantime, by early summer we were ready to go into production. Our first show told the story of the Confederate submarine *Henley,* a miniature underwater craft driven manually by eight men which, after incredible trials and dangers, succeeded in blowing up the Union battleship

---

* For whose father I had worked briefly as a writer in 1932.
† In charge of programming. He later became president of CBS-TV —a position he occupied for several years before heading for the Children's Television Workshop.

Housatonic before itself disappearing with the loss of all hands. It was directed by Paul Stanley and featured Jackie Cooper and James MacArthur, Helen Hayes's son.

Our second was a two-parter, starring Joseph Cotten in a factual and disturbing account of the events leading up to the Indian massacre at Sand Creek, which also featured Ricardo Montalban and Miriam Colón. It was a highly dramatic if somewhat depressing story, in which Sitting Bull met death at the hands of his own people. The fourth, featuring Ruby Dee and written by James Bridges, was the story of Harriet Tubman, a black woman who played a heroic part in the Underground Railroad during the years preceding the Civil War.*

The fifth and the last of the shows I produced that summer featured Lee Marvin. It was called *Wagons to the Sea* and it was based on a true incident; written by Al Bezzerides, it described the heroic resistance by a handful of Armenian raisin growers in California's San Joaquin Valley to the economic pressures of the Southern Pacific Railroad. All five shows were filmed and eventually received good reviews and fair-to-poor ratings. But by then I was no longer around.

On July 27, more than two months before the first of our shows was due to go on the air, Hal Humphrey was writing in the *Los Angeles Times:*

> There are indications that John Houseman's troubles with *The Great Adventure* spring from his going too "long hair"—in other words, taking too much time and spending too much money for a quality which the network bosses felt would not be appreciated by an early evening audience of kids (7:30 in the East, 6:30 in the Midwest).

This was followed by an item in Ben Gross's syndicated TV column:

> A bit of a hassle appears to have developed between CBS-TV and producer John Houseman over his impending departure from *The Great Adventure* fall drama.

* It was the first of a number of shows broadcast on the same subject, and it received several national awards, including a Peabody.

He says he is leaving because of differences over the program; the network insists he is reassigned to dramatic specials and denies there is any problem with the series. CBS-TV program boss Mike Dann said yesterday, "Houseman has not quit. We're paying him $104,000 a year and we intend to pay him in full. If someone were quitting would we pay the money?"

He was right. For once, at Ethel's insistence, I had not made my big quitting gesture. As a result, the CBS Network ended by paying me one hundred four thousand dollars, spread over the next two years, for doing nothing. As for *The Great Adventure*, it stayed on the air for a few weeks after the last of my shows, then vanished without comment.

CHAPTER VIII

1963-1964

"Here I sit, on my well-kept beach, complete with wife and children and animals, waiting for lightning to strike. I have no immediate financial concerns and no projects or ambitions that go further than tomorrow morning. . . . The view, as I peer into the future, is more murky than usual; it is shrouded in mists of fatigue and boredom—made denser by a new, sobering sense of the irresistible approach of old age!"

Writing to my friend John Bartlow Martin in Santo Domingo, where he was U.S. ambassador, I was exaggerating, as usual.* But this letter, written in the early fall of 1963, accurately described my state of mind at the time. After the adrenalin of my successive crises had drained off, I had been

---

* Just as, eighteen years earlier, I had informed Mina Curtiss that I was in the "last intensive, productive phase of my life."

left with the sobering realization that the two major organizations (MGM and CBS) on which I had depended for more than a decade for rewarding and exciting employment were both closed to me for years to come. Following my two well-publicized setbacks, I feared I might be acquiring the reputation of being, at best, a troublemaker and, at worst, a loser.

I had known several such periods of decline—but never from such a height. The knowledge that I was better situated financially than I had ever been helped me to face this crisis without undue panic. But the new and chilling element that now appeared for the first time in my thinking was reflected in the final sentence of my note to John Martin.

At sixty-one I could say in all honesty that a sense of age had never played the slightest part in my planning. I had been a late starter—in my choice of work, in my emotional development and in my assumption of personal and professional responsibility. Having started late, I had so far to go and I was in such a frantic hurry to get there that I had remained quite unaware of the passage of years. (I think the death of my father of Addison's disease at forty-two may have contributed to this attitude—a feeling that I must hurry to make up, in my own life, for the lost years of that brilliant, doomed man.)

Entering my sixties with undiminished energy, I might have continued to ignore my age entirely had it not been for my recent defeats. In my newly acquired involuntary leisure I found myself facing a number of disturbing questions about my future: Was my recent succession of disappointments attributable to the normal odds of an uncertain and speculative business? ("You can't win 'em all!"). Or was it due to a gradual and imperceptible slowing down—a reduction of ambition that was normal in a man of my age but profoundly disturbing to someone who had never even considered such a possibility? In taming my ego and shedding the worst of my fears had I also lost some of my will to win?

These questions came up as I found myself considering some of my alternatives. Retirement was out of the question: I hadn't saved a penny. Show business remained my chosen field in which my accumulated reputation and the ever-growing list of my credits were such that I had little of my old terror of unemployment. What had begun to worry me was my own attitude toward my work. Previously, when I made my frequent, sometimes inane leaps from one activity to another, I made them quickly, almost thoughtlessly, with the tailwinds of fear and ambition blowing so strongly that it was all I could do to hold on. Now things were different. My spasms of despair and terror were less frequent and intense than before—but so was my libido and my blind, secret confidence in my ability to conquer the world. The tides that had raged around me for thirty years had swept me to a considerable height; but they had not prepared me for thoughts of declining productivity nor for the acceptance of such limited objectives as could be expected by a man who was entering the last quarter of his life.

It was during these months of perplexity and discouragement that I made my first weak, undirected attempts to work on the memoir of my life in the theatre that my friend Joe Barnes kept urging me to write. The little I turned out was not satisfactory, either as personal therapy or as contemporary history. The best I had been able to squeeze out of my personal probe of the past was a series of disconnected notes and reminiscences. They afforded me some nostalgic satisfaction, but they proved quite worthless when I finally came to face the real problem of turning them into a book.

This period of nervous stagnation did not last long. I was saved, as usual, by the invitations that kept coming my way. The first was a short-term job offer I received from Ann Borden, whom I had met years ago with Eleanor Roosevelt on the Voice of America, and who now asked me to take over production of an international tribute to Eleanor Roosevelt, to be held in the newly opened Philharmonic Hall at Lincoln Center under the auspices of the United Nations. It was (like most such affairs) a composite of personal loyalty and political and artistic maneuvering, in which the principal role was played by Adlai Stevenson. Reading John Bartlow Martin's biography years later, I realized that this was a bad time for Stevenson; his position as U.S. ambassador to the United Nations was full of conflicts, and his health was not of the best.

Whatever the reasons, I must report that I found him testy and vain—querulous about the amount of work that was being asked of him, yet determined to be recognized as the undisputed star of the event.

I found when I arrived in New York that many of the arrangements and commitments for the show had already been made. One part of my job was to see that the evening did not run inordinately long and to regulate traffic among the assembled politicians and musicians. The politicians included Stevenson, Madame Pandit (sister of Jawaharlal Nehru and head of the Indian delegation to the UN General Assembly), Secretary General U Thant, Ralph Bunche, Helen Gahagan Douglas, Bess Myerson and Esther Peterson; the musicians, Marian Anderson, Byron Janis, Yehudi Menuhin, Rostropovich, Leonard Bernstein and a large children's chorus. My other, more creative function was to help prepare the main event of the evening—a montage of film and photographs assembled with loving care under the title "Ubiquitous E.R.," with a text by Millard Lampell and Norman Corwin.* It took Eleanor Roosevelt from her honeymoon in Venice to scenes photographed shortly before her death. It showed her in war and peace, in innumerable places with an incredible variety of people—on boats and planes and trains, in a Puerto Rican slum, in Buckingham Palace, on a Galápagos GI chow line, with farmers in the Blue Ridge Mountains and Okies in California, with GIs under palm trees, with GIs sitting on the ground laughing, with wounded GIs, with women in Japan, with a cardinal in Brazil, with Brahman bulls in India, with students in Utrecht, with Tito, with Sukarno, with Ben-Gurion, with coal miners, with Africans, with Khrushchev, with women in Karachi, on a kibbutz, with Malayan women, with an old man in Hong Kong, with a baby . . .

This informal visual record (almost like a family album) of Mrs. Roosevelt's tireless travels proved moving to an audi-

---

* It was finally edited by myself, Gordon Davidson, my assistant, and Elinor Bunin, a brilliant graphics artist who had worked with me at CBS.

ence many of whom had known her personally. It was the climax of an evening in which (in spite of the garrulity of politicians and the chicaneries of the musical world) the memory of a great lady was kept green and an appreciable amount of money was raised for the Eleanor Roosevelt Memorial Foundation.

Another of my projects that winter came to me through Charles Eames,* who called me one day in California to ask if I would be interested in taking over a film he had agreed to make for New York's 1964 World's Fair but which he now found himself too busy to undertake. It was to be a twelve-minute film dealing with the history of immigration in the United States over the past two hundred years. I said yes, of course, and flew once again to New York to meet with representatives of the fair, of the Department of Commerce, which controlled the U.S. Federal Pavilion, where the film would be shown, and of the Franklin National Bank, which was helping to finance it. I was shown the budget, which was generous for such a short film, and I was informed that it was being made at the express request of President Kennedy to help create a favorable climate for the new immigration laws he was about to submit to Congress. Otherwise I was free to choose my own form and content.

Given the brevity of the film, the immensity of the subject and the short time at my disposal, it soon became evident that *Voyage to America* (as it came to be called) could best be told through a dramatic and imaginative arrangement of existing graphic material (photographs, drawings, cartoons and engravings), of which there was an extraordinary wealth. This

* I had known Charles and his wife, Ray, since the early forties, when they were conducting experiments with laminated-wood construction that led to Eames's revolutionary furniture designs in the late forties and fifties. From that they moved on to photography and filmmaking and into the computerized, multiscreen projection of slides and motion-picture film that won them international fame in the sixties. I had seen an early version of their multi-image projection of life in the U.S.A. which made such an impression at the Moscow World's Fair, and more recently I had, myself, appeared briefly in the film they were making for the IBM exhibit at the New York World's Fair of 1964.

would have been a perfect subject on which to work with my friend Nick Ray. But since Nick was off in Europe, I turned to three local associates: Richard McCann, film critic and West Coast correspondent for the *Christian Science Monitor;* Ben Jackson, a young filmmaker out of UCLA, of whom I had heard good things;* and Dorothy Jeakins, on whom I counted for the research and selection of authentic and unfamiliar material.

To establish a business address for "John Houseman Productions" and to take care of the paperwork involved, I rented a second-floor apartment on Beverly Glen in Westwood, across from the new synagogue. The front part was used as an office, the back as sleeping quarters for Marian Fenn, who, on a rented machine, typed the successive versions of our film, on which we made several false starts. We arrived finally at a conventional but dynamic, vaguely chronological structure that took us quickly from Virginia and Plymouth Rock to the great westward population movements and, finally, through the massive successive waves of German, Irish, Italian and Eastern European Jewish immigration that rose to more than a million souls a year in the late nineteenth and early twentieth centuries.† All this in a little over ten minutes!

McCann and I wrote most of the narration, changing it constantly to conform to Ben Jackson's dramatic requirements and to absorb the flood of new graphic material Jeakins was sending in from obscure regional sources. By early November we had assembled the draft of a script and some choice graphic material that I took east with me to submit to the Commerce Department and the White House for approval. I was lunching in the Oak Room of the Plaza Hotel, discussing a point in the script with one of Kennedy's bright young men when the news came—in whispered disbelief at

* His tragic death while still in his twenties put an end to what would most certainly have been a brilliant career in films.
† It is worth noting how little attention was paid in such a film to the Hispanic influx which twenty years later had become the dominant factor in our immigration mix.

first, then confirmed on the ticker and spreading like wildfire
—that the President had been wounded and, a moment later,
that he was dead. I remember drifting, aimless and incredulous, from table to table and then out onto Fifth Avenue,
where drivers sat frozen behind the wheels of their buses and
taxis and pedestrians stared at one another or talked in bewildered whispers.

In January I sent a first rough print of the film to Virgil
Thomson with a request for another of his great American
fugues—such as he had composed for *The River, Louisiana
Story* and *Tuesday in November.* Within a month it was done
and the Franklin National Bank had raised sufficient additional funds to have it recorded by Eugene Ormandy and the
Philadelphia Orchestra. Our next task was to find out how
our film looked and sounded under the rather special conditions in which it would be shown at the fair. Our screen was
the back wall of the large entrance hall through which the
crowds would stream into the U.S. Federal Pavilion. They
would view the film from wooden benches (several hundred
at a time), before moving on through the building that
housed the United States government's exhibits. We had
some trouble with our projection equipment, but we finally
achieved adequate acoustics and a powerful image that
proved particularly effective in the cumulative montage of
immigrant faces with which we ended the film.* Conventionally projected in black and white,† *Voyage to America* was generally admired, though it never received the technical or
critical attention aroused by the multitudinous images that
confronted the spectator on Charles Eames's IBM "People
Wall" or by the panoramic novelties of Francis Thompson's
three-paneled screen in the Johnson's Wax Pavilion. But it
fulfilled its purpose and achieved a record of sorts by being
shown to full houses more than fifty times a day (five times

* The print that is shown today at the U.S. Archives in Washington
is "squeezed" and distorted and has little of the quality and power
of the original.
† Our only color was the Jasper Johns American flag that we used
behind the titles.

an hour for ten hours a day) over a period of several months. According to one patriotic reviewer, "it should be shown every twelve minutes around the world."

I enjoyed making it, and, in my triple capacity of entrepreneur, producer and writer, I received a reasonable reward for my four months' part-time work. Yet I never quite got over the feeling that it would have been a more original and striking film if Charles Eames had been able to execute it.

Two of my other activities that winter were vaguely prophetic. One was an evening in UCLA's vast Royce Hall. It started as a lecture undertaken at short notice as a substitute for an ailing Tyrone Guthrie. It ended up as a potpourri over which I presided as master of ceremonies, relating to women's behavior in life and literature from the Middle Ages to the present day. Flanked by my team of Nina Foch, Pippa Scott and Betty Harford, I delivered what I felt was a lively and variegated entertainment that drew on the writings of Bacon, Shakespeare, Congreve, Ibsen, Elizabeth Barrett Browning and George Bernard Shaw. It marked my first appearance as a performer before a large audience and revealed a streak of exhibitionism in my nature of which I had not been aware.

This was soon followed by my unpremeditated appearance as a professional actor in a full-scale motion picture. John Frankenheimer (who, at my urging, had come to live at the beach) was directing a controversial film, *Seven Days in May*, starring Burt Lancaster, Kirk Douglas, Fredric March and Ava Gardner. It dealt with a conspiracy by a small military group to abduct the President of the United States and replace him with one of their own whom they considered more capable of running and defending the country. Over drinks one weekend Frankenheimer asked me if I'd like to play the small but telling part of a treasonous admiral. Two days later I was fitted with a suitable uniform by Paramount's costume department, and the morning after that I was on a sound stage, in my admiral's quarters, rehearsing my two scenes— one alone at the telephone when I learn that the plot has been discovered, the other when the President's special assistant, played by Martin Balsam, arrives to confront me with my treason. This created a curious situation; the last time I had worked with Marty was when, as his director, the year before, we had worked together on the hideously demanding role of Hickey, the drummer, in *The Iceman Cometh*. As a result of this curious reversal, it was Balsam, the veteran actor, who was now jittery and blowing his lines; Houseman, the amateur, numbed by his unfamiliar situation and totally concentrated on remembering his words, was cool as a cucumber. (Balsam's discomfort was aggravated by the curious behavior of John Frankenheimer, who, in imitation of some famous director, kept firing pistol shots close behind us at critical moments. Here again it was Marty whom he disturbed; knowing no better, I took John's fusillade in stride.)

My first appearance in a film passed generally unnoticed except by a few friends, who were so astounded to see my face on the body of the treasonous admiral that they remained stunned and confused and never quite believed what they had seen. Years later, after I had become accepted as an actor and *Seven Days in May* was revived on television, values were discovered in my performance that were not apparent at the time.

I enjoyed these excursions into unfamiliar areas of show business, but they were all short-term, unrelated activities which gave me no consistent sense of accomplishment or satisfaction. During the years of my success I had grown accustomed to working with the solid structure of a repertory company or of a studio production system. Both, in their different ways, called for sustained effort and gave me a sense of cumulative creation and rising power. Lacking that sense, my present life, for all my expenditure of energy, left me unsettled and insecure. Once again, as during the troubled years of my late forties, I was snatching, without plan or continuity or real satisfaction, at any activity that came my way.

Try as I will, I find it impossible to determine the exact moment at which I decided to go abroad. My departure was first verbalized to Abbott Kaplan in the spring of 1964 when he called me in New York and asked me to return to the

Theatre Group, which had overreached itself with an unfortunate attempt to bring classical repertory to Southern California with two distinguished but obscure early-seventeenth-century dramas, Lope de Vega's *Peribáñez* and John Ford's *'Tis Pity She's a Whore*. The combination of two such difficult and elaborate productions—rehearsed and performed simultaneously—proved too much for the group's actors and for its educated but still-insecure and conservative audiences. The season enjoyed only moderate success, and at its end the executive committee ruefully noted the loss of all but a fraction of the forty-thousand-dollar profit the Theatre Group had so painfully accumulated over the past three and a half years.*

I told Kaplan I would give it some thought and call him back. Two days later, I informed him that I was going abroad for an indefinite period but that, before leaving, I would undertake a production of *King Lear*.

The decision to go abroad came as a surprise to me and to everyone else. But the seeds of such a drastic and far-reaching resolve must have been germinating for months. I consulted no one and gave little thought to the consequences such a violent change would have on my own life and on the lives of my wife and children. (When I finally broached the subject to Joan, I discovered that she was, as usual, far ahead of me and had faced and accepted the prospect of total upheaval some time before.)

I was well aware of the recklessness of my move and of the great risk I was taking in throwing away my professional safety nets and giving up a security it had taken me more than half my life to achieve. But, like most of my crucial decisions (such as lingering in Argentina instead of going to Cambridge; sailing suddenly to America at twenty-three,

---

* It must be noted, in fairness, that with each successive production the economics of the group's operation were becoming less favorable. Even before inflation, costs had begun to rise, and the university was now demanding payment for many of the services that had been free in the beginning. Inevitably the group was getting ready to join the general run of subsidized, deficit-operated regional theatres.

leaving my English life behind me without thought or regret; walking penniless into the New York theatre at the age of thirty-one without experience or prospects of any sort),* this one was made suddenly and arbitrarily in response to some deep, subconscious, irreversible urge that was quite impervious to sense or reason. Once I had made it, I never had one single moment of hesitation or misgiving, even though it was not entirely clear to me or anyone else exactly what this mad migration was expected to accomplish.

Looking back, I can trace a number of motives behind my decision—some positive, some altogether negative. On the negative side, there was the growing mood of discontent into which I had been drifting over the past few years, together with the lack of commitment without which I was finding my work stale and unprofitable. This restlessness extended to my personal relationships. There was nothing wrong with my marriage or my family or the large circle of my friends; in that respect my situation compared favorably with that of most of my peers. But it lacked motion; it was predictable and monotonous. In that sense this voyage was an escape—a flight from what I felt to be the diminishing returns of my life. Also, not to be ignored, there was the dangerous exhilaration I had always felt at the prospect of destruction and dissolution—the masochistic excitement I derived from the tearing up of whatever roots I had painfully managed to put down. Finally, with my inherited gambler's instinct, I may have felt that only by some drastic and reckless move could I break the run of what I felt was my recently declining luck.

On the positive side there was one other obvious but unconvincing explanation for my departure. After so many years of stress and grinding toil, I needed, deserved and could finally afford a complete and extended holiday. But that was sheer nonsense and I knew it. If there is one thing in the world I have never needed and consistently abhorred, it is a holiday!

A more plausible explanation for this self-imposed exile

* See *Run-Through*, "Overture."

was the hope that it might finally enable me to write that book I was always talking about. Progress so far had been ridiculously slow—so confused and fragmentary that it had become depressingly clear that under existing conditions it would never get written at all. Joe Barnes's attempt to encourage me by giving me a contract with Simon and Schuster and a modest advance had not helped. It would take a complete change of attitude and circumstance to get me started. Perhaps in Europe, free of the distractions and inhibitions with which I went to such pains to surround myself at home, I might finally feel free to write the story I was so eager to tell.

This helped to fix Paris as the site of my residence abroad. During my long months of vain struggle with my material, it had become clear that my original intention, to write an objective, dramatic, factual narrative of my adventures in the theatre in the mid-thirties (with Orson Welles as its leading character), would not work. For the story to have any reality or value it must be a subjective memoir, including an investigation of the personality of the "I" whose reactions to all those strange and exciting events of the thirties were to be the subject of my book.

In that case it became necessary for me to recapture the emotional and physical atmosphere of the places in which that personality had been formed. I was confident that with the sights and sounds of Paris filling the function of Proust's *"madeleine"* it would be possible for me to go back into my past and break the logjam that had kept me paralyzed for so many months in California. The more I thought about it, the more essential and exciting my return to the scenes of my childhood became.

By late spring, my bridges had been burned: my decision to move to Paris was final, and the machinery for the liquidation of our lives in Malibu had been set in motion. This involved renting the house, getting the boys out of school, disposing of animals and automobiles, and dealing with the vast logistical problems involved in such a major migration. As usual, the bulk of this tedious and painful labor fell on Joan, for by then I was entirely absorbed in my production of *Lear*. She executed it with her usual reluctant efficiency.

Only, once in a while I would catch her looking wistfully around the rooms of our house, her eyes misting at the thought of once again leaving her beautiful home. She was convinced that she would never live in it again. And, as usual, she was right.

I believe that my resolve to do *King Lear* was directly related to my decision to leave for Europe. It too was compulsive—the response to an urgent emotional need. In view of my recent history with the Professional Theatre Group, it was important that I end our association on a note of triumph; *Lear* was my chance to go out with a bang.

The play already had a special place in my life; doing it with Louis Calhern in New York in 1950 had been an overwhelming theatrical and personal experience* which I was determined to repeat if ever the proper opportunity presented itself. Now, suddenly, it seemed that the moment had come.

I knew I could never entirely recapture the exhilaration and terror in which I had lived during the preparation and production of that first *Lear*. Yet now (when, like the mad King, I was about to throw safety to the winds and risk my entire future on a desperate whim) it seemed right to take another crack at this greatest and most dangerous of Shakespeare's plays.

To do *Lear* you must have a great King, and, by good fortune, we had one. I had seen Carnovsky's Lear at Stratford the previous summer and admired it (though, with a normal director's ego, I had found many things in Alan Fletcher's production that I would have done differently). I had run into him at a party during the winter and asked him casually if he had any desire to play Lear again. He replied that he did. Now I approached him once more and repeated my question. He said he was available and interested.

When I got back to Los Angeles I spent several hours in Schoenberg Hall, trying to decide whether that small theatre,

* See *Front and Center*, pp. 328 *et seq.*

which had been perfectly suited to so many of our productions over the past four years, could hold the immensity of *Lear*. Then I had an inspiration. I called Bill Severns, general manager of Philharmonic Hall, the Hollywood Bowl and other scenes of Los Angeles cultural activity, about the availability of the Pilgrimage Theatre. This was a medium-sized outdoor theatre on which I had long had my eye. Built into the side of the Hollywood Hills, it had a good stage, remarkable acoustics and an intimacy that was rare in outdoor theatres.* It was now the property of the county, which had taken it over from a religious group which had erected a huge electric cross on the mountain above it.

Severns said it was available and listened sympathetically to my proposal that the county join the university in the financing of a production which, if successful, might mark the beginning of an annual Shakespeare festival, of which Los Angeles was in dire need.

At my next meeting with the Theatre Group's executive committee I outlined my double project. We would present *King Lear* first in Schoenberg Hall for four weeks for our subscribers and our regular audience. (Within a week of our announcement all seats had been sold for the entire run.) Then, ten days later, we would present it in an expanded form at the Pilgrimage Theatre under the joint auspices of the county and the UCLA Professional Theatre Group.

In all my preparations and throughout rehearsals, this plan for a double engagement played an essential part in my decisions. As a result—except for Jeakins' revised costumes and Blitzstein's score, both of which I used—this West Coast production bore slight resemblance to what I had done in New York fourteen years before. The use of anything resembling Ralph Alswang's raked platform and flying "stalactites" was out of the question. In their place I ordered six massive wooden towers of abstract form which, set in a rough

---

* Max Reinhardt had used it to good advantage for the *Midsummer Night's Dream* that he produced there when he first arrived as an exile from Germany in the thirties.

semicircle at the rear of the stage, could be turned or moved to form walls, gates, battlements, a jousting ring or, simply, the ominous background for a storm or battle. They were designed and hand-painted by a young sculptor-instructor in the UCLA Art Department named Oliver Andrews, who also happened to be Betty Harford's husband. These towers, the throne and some tables and chairs were the sum of our scenery.

In my casting, I chose actors who, I felt, could be equally effective in the intimacy of our 465-seat house and on the vast open stage of our Hollywood hillside. Many were Theatre Group regulars or actors with whom I had worked before. For a rough, honest Kent I turned once again to Mike Kellin. Charles Aidman, who had become increasingly active in the group, was capable, I felt, of carrying the key role of Gloucester. For his bastard son I chose Don Harron (of Stratford, Connecticut, and Ontario). He was an intelligent, attractive and therefore doubly sinister Edmund, while Steve Joyce came into his own in his contrasting scenes as Edgar and Poor Tom. Theodore Marcuse was a sadistic Cornwall, Joseph Ruskin a subdued, sincere Albany. Bob Casper was a despicable but comprehensible Oswald. Finally, Robert Doyle, as the Fool, was lively and adequate but lacked the heartbreaking tenderness that Norman Lloyd had brought to his relationship with Calhern.

On the distaff side, Rae Allen was a powerful, unsubtle Goneril; Nina Foch, who had been our Cordelia in New York, accepted the part of Regan with some reluctance and then withdrew "for personal reasons" on the third day of rehearsals and was replaced by Betty Harford. With my Cordelia, I succumbed once again to the temptation of casting an ingenue in the part of Lear's youngest daughter. Katharine Ross was a strikingly beautiful girl who had spent a few months as an apprentice with Bill Ball's American Conservatory Theatre in San Francisco. In life she had a forthright, clear-eyed, courageous quality* that seemed entirely right

* Which made her a film star with *The Graduate* and *Butch Cassidy and the Sundance Kid.*

and which I hoped would compensate for her inexperience and her insufficiently trained voice.

My most delicate problem, the one I faced with the deepest apprehension in the days immediately preceding rehearsal, was the fact that both Carnovsky and I had done *Lear* before —he as an actor, I as a director—in productions that differed widely from each other and from the one on which we were about to risk our joint reputations. The danger would have been even greater but for the circumstance that we were very old friends, that we respected each other, and that by inviting Morris to Stratford in 1956 for his first performance of Shakespeare I had in fact changed the entire course of his professional life.

The night he arrived I handed him my acting version of the play; we spent several days going through it carefully and made certain changes at his request to conform to what, for him, were the essential elements of the part; I, in turn, laid out the emotional curves I hoped to follow. We did not always agree, but the adjustments we made then and in the course of rehearsal were not unduly painful, either for him or for me.

I had faced the fact, from the beginning, that his Lear and Calhern's would be very different figures. Neither was a master of theatrical verse but each, in his own way, had substantial stage presence and vocal power. Morris lacked the personal beauty and the decaying elegance that made Lou's declining King such a moving and tragic figure. But he had a massive nobility of his own and he made effective use of the patriarchal tradition that has distinguished many of the great Jewish performances of *King Lear.*

I had been right, too, in my feeling that rehearsals would lack the exhilarating sense of discovery that had made my first *Lear* so unforgettable. Our New York company had been made up of an astonishing collection of egomaniacs who, in facing the challenge of appearing in one of their generation's first American professional performances of *King Lear,* had fused their individual temperaments for the duration of the production into a fervent, cooperative effort. This never quite happened with the California company. There was a rigidity about Carnovsky's rehearsal habits that made him difficult to approach for those actors who had not done the play before. This was particularly true of Katharine Ross, of whom he complained, with some justice, that she was idle as well as utterly ignorant of the rehearsal process. (The truth is that she was frozen stiff with terror.) It also extended to his relations with the Fool and with Rae Allen (Goneril), with whom he had worked before, but for whom he now developed a deadly and unremitting hatred that gave his cursing of his ungrateful eldest daughter a personal and chilling quality.*

We opened triumphantly in Schoenberg Hall on June 8, though there were moments when I feared that the walls of that small, sophisticated auditorium would explode with the violence of that superhuman tragedy. Once again the Theatre Goup was hailed as having "reached the summit of its existence." Superlatives abounded: "One of the best Shakespearean productions ever to be done in America." "This great and difficult play spills on the stage with a turbulent fever." "Houseman's direction is like a controlled storm and is the force responsible for its mounting effect; Carnovsky is the mighty arch whose strength supports it.". . .

Two days later we began rehearsal on the outdoor stage of the Pilgrimage Theatre. To take advantage of our new, amazing location, I made some fairly drastic changes, particularly in entrances and exits and in the physical scope and projection of the production. To help me in this unfamiliar task I had invited Gordon Davidson to fly out from New York and join me as production stage manager and assistant director.† Another welcome reunion was with Jean Rosenthal, who hap-

---

* His rage was so great that on opening night, one hour before curtain time, he delivered, by hand, to her dressing room a handwritten seven-page letter in which he told her how despicable she was as an actress and as a person!

† He had been my stage manager at Stratford for three years and had recently returned from a season in Israel with the Martha Graham Company. He and his wife (whom he had first met in Stratford) moved into my office-apartment on Beverly Glen. It had just been vacated by Marian Fenn, who had gone off to join her husband, the stage manager of the Living Theatre, on a European tour.

pened to be in California as consultant for the new theatres being built in the Music Center, and who contributed her miracles of light to our outdoor production.

It had been my intention to truck our wooden towers over from UCLA and set them up on the Pilgrimage stage. The stagehands' union vetoed the move on the ground that the towers that had been constructed on the campus were not union-built. So a second set of structures was erected on the stage of the Pilgrimage, for which I asked Oliver to make revised designs, half as large again as the original and re-painted to blend with the Hollywood Hills.

And here, during our rehearsals, which took place by day under the burning sun and late at night after the Schoenberg performances were over, a strange, exciting thing happened. Whether it was the glow of success following our Schoenberg opening or whether a new sense of discovery and excitement developed during this unfamiliar outdoor work, the fact is that some of the fervor I had missed in our early rehearsals now made its appearance and carried the company through its long all-night rehearsals while we labored to solve the unfamiliar light and sound problems created by our new stage.

Actually, Carnovsky's finest performances were given in the Pilgrimage Theatre, and in my own memory it was this outdoor production that justified the huge effort of restaging this California *King Lear*. It gave the play a stature that could never be achieved indoors. The storm scenes, in particular, were the best I have ever seen: the small, tattered band of the King and his followers coming down the steep wooded hill, their clothes flapping and their torches blowing in the wind, is a sight I shall never forget.

Once again *The New York Times* felt it necessary to send its first-string drama critic to the West Coast:

> In a year of many Lears the finest is being performed in a dramatic outdoor theatre carved out of the side of a Hollywood hill. . . . Mr. Carnovsky's Lear, large in scope and passionate intensity when he appeared at Stratford Connecticut, last year, has become grander and more penetrating. Played against the immensity of this natural

setting, with the rock towering darkly in the background, it takes on the terror of a primeval force and the pity of the inescapably tragic human condition. Supported by a cast of high caliber, the curve of his performance is now irreproachably sustained. It moves like pitiless fate from stubborn wrongheadedness through intemperate wrath to disbelief, madness, humility and tenderness to a final redemptive strength.

(In an unusual use of a rave review, I had that half page of the *Times* of July 28, 1964 Xeroxed and used it as the background for a personal message that I wrote and mailed out to several dozen friends and acquaintances: "WITH LOVE FROM ALL THE HOUSEMANS WHOSE ADDRESS FOR THE COMING YEAR IS: C/O NATIONAL CITY BANK OF NEW YORK 60 AVENUE DES CHAMPS ÉLYSÉES PARIS, FRANCE.")

Now I had only a short time left to savor my success and to wind up my affairs in California. To the UCLA Professional Theatre Group my parting gift was the suggestion that Gordon Davidson be invited to take over the position of producing director that was left empty by my leaving. My advice was taken.*

For my own part, even if I had wanted to change my mind at the last moment, it was too late. The liquidation of my life in Malibu had gone too far. Our house in the Colony was easy to rent; a wealthy tenant was found, and this monthly income, added to the severance payments from MGM and CBS, assured us of a comfortable life in Europe for two to three years. Next came the scholastic separations: Sebastian was doing so poorly at the Montessori School that his departure could only be regarded as a mutual blessing; John Michael had moved from Malibu to a rich kids' boarding school

---

* For two and a half years Gordon Davidson headed the Professional Theatre Group and produced a series of plays that was rather more adventurous and no less successful with audiences than mine had been. At the end of that time the Theatre Group, under his direction, was offered the Mark Taper Forum downtown and became the dramatic arm of the Music Center and one of the most admired regional theatres in America.

in Ojai which he so heartily disliked that for him too the change was a deliverance.

Our numerous animals presented a more serious problem. Funnyface, the beloved female poodle, had been hit by a car and killed on the Pacific Coast Highway early in the year; Sam, her brother, a magnificent beast, was adopted by our friend Ellis Rabb, with whom he led a contented and interesting theatrical life before returning to us four years later. Joan's diminutive Yorkshire, Mousy-Cat, would, of course, accompany his mistress to Paris. That left Virgil the crazy dachshund, Josephine the basset hound, two cats (Katsky and Mimi) and two tortoises (Cecil and Grandpa). It was arranged for all of them to go and live as paying guests with Barbara, our devoted cook, who adored them all, in her new house in Oxnard, where, in spite of the love and care she lavished on them, they came to diverse tragic ends.

Our fleet of cars, four in all, was easily disposed of, except for a vintage Thunderbird to which Joan was particularly attached and which we decided to take to Europe with us. Finally, there was the dispersal and disposal of personal and household possessions. Between the things Joan felt we would need in France and the things she refused to leave to our tenants, a vast cargo of trunks, bags and crates was accumulating in our garage. And this affected our choice of transportation for our seven-thousand-mile voyage.

As soon as I began to look into the question of how we should move two grown-ups, two boys, a vast amount of baggage, one car, a mass of household equipment and a very small dog from Southern California to France without spending half of our year's income on travel, it became evident that it must be by ship. (We were in no great hurry; a leisurely decompression from one world to the other was actually desirable.) Investigation revealed that the French Line (Compagnie Générale Transatlantique) had a fleet of freighters, all bearing the names of American states and running a regular schedule between Vancouver and Le Havre.*

* I remembered having shipped wheat on them in those far-off days when I was exporting grain from western Canada.

The voyage from California to France took around three weeks, depending on the weather and stops for cargo, and their route took them down the west coast of Mexico, through the Canal, to Aruba for refueling and then across the Atlantic to Le Havre. Further investigation revealed that these ships carried few passengers and were reputed to be comfortable. The cost of a passage (four hundred twenty dollars for adults, three hundred dollars for children) was less than a one-way plane fare and included full board for the duration of the voyage. Passengers were permitted unlimited luggage, and there would be a modest charge for the car.

I booked passage on the motorship *Maryland,* due to sail during the first week of August. By the time *King Lear* opened at the Pilgrimage, we had said goodbye to the animals, buyers had begun to take possession of our automobiles, our tenant was preparing to move into the house, and our liquor (except for a few vintage wines that were put into storage) was being drunk up in a long series of farewell parties. As the date of our departure approached, like sailors' wives on their widows' walks gazing out to sea for a sign of their men, we made daily calls to the French line for news of our ship. It had left Vancouver. . . . It was loading in Seattle. . . . It was ready to leave San Francisco. Then one morning came the official notification that we should present ourselves on the dock at Long Beach together with our baggage and our automobile two days hence between the hours of 2 and 4 P.M.

Our sailing turned into something of a happening. People were no longer accustomed to seeing their friends off on ships, but, remembering New York's legendary midnight sailings of the twenties, a number of our friends were determined to hold such a ceremony in broad daylight in Los Angeles Harbor. Getting our goods and chattel to the dock was a massive undertaking: two hired trucks and a procession of cars including the departing Thunderbird carried some forty or fifty persons down the coast from Malibu to Long Beach, where the *Maryland* lay at her berth. Like pirates boarding a prize, we swarmed aboard, took possession of our cabins (one for Joan and me, one for the boys), then invaded the upper deck and opened the champagne. From there, as the afternoon wore on, we leaned over the railing and watched our possessions, including the Thunderbird, being hoisted high up in the air, then lowered into the darkness of the ship's gaping hold. * At dusk the ship's bell was rung and the last of our well-wishers was ordered ashore. We watched their unsteady descent and continued waving to them on the dock as the *Maryland* moved slowly out to sea. Soon after that, the oil wells on Signal Hill faded in the smog. But it was not until the last low hills of the Southern California coast had sunk into the sea that the full enormity of what I had done was finally borne in upon me.

* Unnoticed among the innumerable objects that were lowered into the hold was a suitcase full of socks and underwear belonging to Renate's husband, Ronnie Knox, the celebrated Ram football star, which accompanied us to France, where they were laundered and sent back.

Book Two

Book Two

CHAPTER IX

1964-1965

PARIS
THIS PROPERTY IS CONDEMNED
TOSCA

IN THIS FLAWED WORLD there may not be such a thing as a perfect month, but our three and a half weeks aboard the *Maryland* brought us closer to it than I had thought possible.

For twenty-four halcyon days the sun shone and the sea was smooth as glass. The gentle motion of the ship, day and night, became part of our lives; it rocked us to sleep at night and gave a pleasant, tidelike motion to the seawater in the canvas swimming pool that the crew had rigged on deck on our first day out and in which John Michael and Sebastian spent several hours of each day—spidery pink figures against the pale blue of the ocean.

We discovered, after our well-wishers had left the ship, that there were only nine passengers aboard, including the four of us. (Three got off at Aruba, leaving only two intruders.) We also discovered that the ship's food was delicious (French *cuisine bourgeoise* washed down with two wines at every meal) and that our crew, mostly Bretons, was made up of agreeable, intelligent men. They invited the boys into the wheelhouse for an hour every morning to steer the ship and joined us in ruthless games of shuffleboard in the late afternoon. (The sliding quoits furnished endless diversion to Mousy-Cat, who soon came to regard the ship as his natural habitat.) In the evening John Michael and the captain played backgammon (*jacquet*).

Our cabins were comfortable if not spacious, and I soon transformed the ship's saloon into a private study where I sat every morning, looking out the window as I forced myself back in time and struggled to find a form for the book to which this voyage had irrevocably committed me. It was a curious feeling to be delving into the remote depths of my European childhood while staring out at the sunlit tropical Pacific Ocean. But around that small desk in the corner of that paneled room I did manage, for hours at a time, to create a vacuum which allowed me to float free of the present and to drift back into those remote regions where my life had been formed. After three weeks I had less than a dozen pages to show for my six to eight hours of concentrated daily work. But, finally, a start had been made.

Our first port of call was Mazatlán, where the *Maryland* docked next to a mysterious black ship that appeared to be Chinese. The next was Panama, where we spent a night and a day leaning over the rail, watching the slow, careful process of taking our ship through the Canal—the contrast of the clanking machinery that hauled us through one narrow lock after another and the bright-green jungle on either side, only a few yards away, with its trees almost touching the side of the ship and the air echoing all night with the cries of invisible birds and monkeys.

Aruba, where we refueled, was our next and last stop. On this trip the *Maryland* was not paying its customary visit to Guadeloupe: all we saw of that island were some distant lights one night as we moved out of the Gulf of Mexico and across the Atlantic. Still, the weather held. It was not until our twenty-fifth day, as we approached the coast of France, that we became aware of an extreme barometric change. The first officer warned us that we were heading into foul weather: there was a storm in the Bay of Biscay, and by morning we would be in the thick of it.

All my life I have been a terrible sailor. (My entire childhood was splashed with vomit from the agonizing Channel crossings I made six times a year for more than nine years—including a war—as I shuttled between my British school and my parents' home in Paris.) I lay in fear that night as our cabin began to groan and creak and heave in the rising seas. Next morning we found it difficult to wash and dress and make our way to the dining room, where, to my amazement, I ate a hearty breakfast; then I went out to those parts of the deck that were not roped off, to admire the mountainous waves sweeping past and sometimes above us. In three weeks the gentle, incessant motion of the ship had become so much part of me that the present violent motion caused me not the slightest discomfort. Later that day I was able to rush out with the boys and two members of the crew to rescue Mousy-Cat from a monstrous wave that threatened to sweep him overboard.

As we entered the Bay of Biscay our radio picked up reports of ships in distress, and once, off to starboard, faintly through a curtain of rain and spray, I caught sight of a small ship wallowing in that awful steel-colored flood. That night we rounded Pointe de Saint-Mathieu and entered the English Channel. Late the next afternoon, in a sudden, unnatural calm, we docked at Le Havre. We spent our last night aboard without sleep; at dawn we watched our things being lifted out of the hold and onto the dock. By eleven we were through customs and in possession of the Thunderbird, in which the four of us (five, including Mousy-Cat), together with a mass of hand luggage, were squeezed into a car built for two. In our excitement at being together on French soil we ignored our discomfort as we drove south toward Paris, where we arrived at dusk and made our way through the evening traffic to the small hotel off the Rue de Rivoli in which my mother had lived ever since her return from America.

We had arrived on a holiday, the celebration of the liberation of Paris, and after dinner we made our way through the dense crowds to the Place de la Concorde. With our arms tightly linked so as not to get separated, we stood packed like sardines for two hours looking up at the sky, where an extravagant display of fireworks had been organized by General de Gaulle. This was the climax of our miraculous voyage. It was twenty-eight days, though it seemed half a lifetime, since we had left Southern California.

The next day we moved, bag and baggage (including the thirteen trunks and packing cases that arrived by road from Le Havre), into an apartment we had rented by long distance in the Rue de Prony, near the Parc Monceau. It was a quarter of Paris that had been famed in the nineteenth century as the residence of the town's most illustrious courtesans. Their *hôtels particuliers* had been replaced early in the present century by rows of substantial apartment houses of the kind that had been inhabited during my childhood by members of my father's family—except that they, being Jewish, were more inclined to live in the newer sections of Paris (the Seizième) closer to the Bois de Boulogne.*

Ours was a typically overdecorated upper-middle-class Parisian flat. Its tenants for the previous six months had been our friends the Ustinovs, who had just moved into a house of their own in Neuilly. The apartment was pretentious and expensive and not entirely suited to our needs, with its elaborate green Directoire salon which we rarely entered, its formal dining room and elegant master bedroom, all with tall windows overlooking the park. In the back, along a narrow corridor, were three small rooms that gave out on an airless courtyard. Two of these were occupied by the boys, who found them cramped and dark after their free life at the beach; the third was mine, with just enough space for a narrow bed and an oversized Empire desk.

Here we spent our first five months in a city which for each of us represented something entirely different. For Joan it

* All except my father, who had a consistent preference for midtown hotels. To the best of my knowledge, except for the big house in Rumania in which I was born and which also served as his office, my parents, in their twenty years of marriage, never once had a place of their own.

meant a return, after fifteen years, to the place in which she had spent thirty years of her life, including the bad years of the Occupation. It was a return she had dreaded but to which in fact she adjusted far more readily than she expected. Within a few weeks she had renewed a number of close friendships and her association with what was left of the Surrealist world of the thirties and forties. Though she continued to have a difficult and highly charged relationship with her Russian-Spanish mother, this too seemed to present less of an emotional hazard now that they saw each other several times a week than when they were separated by a distance of seven thousand miles. Living very much in the present and getting no reliable indication from me as to how long we were likely to stay abroad, Joan soon found herself regarding Paris, once again, as her home.

For John Michael and Sebastian, Paris represented yet another change of surroundings. Armed with what little French John Michael had acquired during his year in France and with what they had both absorbed by osmosis from Joan and me at home and, more recently, from the crew of the *Maryland*, they were soon familiar with the Parisian transportation system and roamed the city at will in total disregard of the cultural itineraries laid out for them by their two grandmothers. They found the open spaces around the Palais de Chaillot particularly suited to skateboarding, and their photographs appeared one morning in the *Paris Herald Tribune* as pioneers in this, the latest American sport to cross the Atlantic.

With the opening of school, their fine free days came to an end. Now a blue bus collected them every morning and delivered them to the American School of Paris. Situated in a suburb not far from SHAEF, it had been created after the war for the children of American Army personnel and business executives stationed in Paris and had many of the faults one might expect from such an institution. Neither of the boys has particularly happy memories of it.

Mousy-Cat, on his part, took to Paris like a duck to water. The sidewalks offered smells that were more heady and varied than those of the Malibu beaches, and the lush green lawns of the Parc Monceau seemed particularly seductive. Not even the stiff brooms with which he was threatened by certain ill-tempered concierges of the neighborhood could dampen his spirits. My own reactions were more complicated. This was not my first adult view of Paris. After my enforced absence of more than thirty years (following my conflict with the French military authorities*) I had been overwhelmed, when I finally came over in 1955 for the filming of *Lust for Life*, by the city's incredible beauty. This sojourn was different. I was no longer a two-week visitor, living it up in the international luxury of the Hotel Georges V. I was here now as a resident, for an undetermined period, with the calculated and dangerous purpose of recapturing the most impressionable years of my life.

Within a few days of our arrival, in my anxiety not to lose the little I had achieved during my three weeks at sea, I resumed the rigid work schedule I had set up on the *Maryland*. I started at eight each morning and went on until I could work no longer. Then, to clear my head after hours of painful and seemingly useless effort, I would wander, without aim or direction, through the concentric tree-lined avenues that had been laid out in the previous century by my namesake, the Baron Haussmann. Often as I walked, I had a feeling that I had been there before; the buildings and shops and trees that lined those wide, well-tended streets had the vague familiarity of a landscape in a recurrent dream. Even the street sounds, far from seeming strange, confirmed this sense of recognition.

Then, one afternoon, quite by chance, in one of those short, steep streets that link the Avenue Friedland to the Champs-Élysées, I suddenly came upon the small residential hotel in which my father and mother had lived for so many years. And instantly I understood that within this modest, not particularly attractive building lay the heart of the mystery I had come here to unravel. It was here that I had sought refuge at the age of six after running away from my cousins' day school (Les Cours Dieterlin), which I was determined not

* See *Run-Through*, p. 40.

to attend;* here, in my parents' bedroom, that my tonsils were bloodily removed the following year; here, while munching croissants dipped in *café au lait* in my parents' warm bed, that I had listened in wonder to my father reciting Corneille, Racine and Victor Hugo over his washbasin. It was to this place that my father had come home in great agitation one evening in August 1914 to announce that Madame Caillaux† had been acquitted and that France was at war with Germany. And it was here, above all, that I had created that secret universe of fantasies and desires in which my mother was queen and I was her only beloved son—that private Garden of Eden for which I had yearned so desperately throughout the desolating loneliness of my English schooldays and for so many years after that.

This discovery released such a flood of nostalgia that, for some weeks, I found myself living on two quite separate and often conflicting levels: that of our well-organized family life at 99 Rue de Prony and that other, far more exciting world I entered the moment I was alone and shared with no one: a world of sights and sounds and intimate memories that had lain buried for more than half a century and were now surfacing once again; a world in which the wheels of the dark-green double-decked streetcars on the Avenue Henri Martin were wreathed in clouds of hissing steam; in which ice-skating at the Palais de Glace on the Champs-Élysées was a fashionable teatime occupation; in which the luxurious, perfumed dressmaking establishments to which I accompanied my beautiful mother during Christmas and Easter vacations were those of Worth, Patou, Vionnet and Paquin.

(Evidence of the gulf that lay between those two worlds was to be found in the difficulty and pain I suffered as I tried to reconcile the two images of my mother: the memory of the pretty, sweet-smelling lady in three-tiered hats and pearls—the dream queen who had been at the center of my emotional

* See *Run-Through,* p. 18.
† The wife of the French statesman Joseph Caillaux had shot and killed Gaston Calmette, a newspaper publisher, who was threatening to print compromising material about her and her husband. Her trial for murder became a major political event.

life—and the reality of the slightly shrunken but still-beautiful, vain, lively, opinionated and elegant old lady of eighty-four who still used Guerlain's L'Heure Bleue as her perfume and who rarely left her bed till midafternoon, in time for her double Scotch-and-soda followed by an elaborate dinner she barely touched; who went regularly to theatres and concerts; who, after a residence of more than sixty years, still spoke fluent, ungrammatical French with a strong English accent.)

For a time my world of ghosts was more vivid and satisfying than the realities of the present. Then, gradually, as the first thrill of rediscovery wore off, it became evident that these journeys into the past were becoming an end in themselves and that they had gone far beyond the needs of the book of which they were supposed to furnish the emotional base. Within three months of our arrival in Paris my mind was so clogged with sentiment that writing had become not only an agony but an utter impossibility.

After several sterile weeks I decided to take advantage of the offer Virgil Thomson had made me just before my departure from America. He owned an apartment on the Quai Voltaire, in a building in which Ingres, the painter, had once had his studio. It consisted of a fair-sized living room, a bath with a primitive water heater, and a small kitchen and pantry. For close to two months this became my daytime refuge and hiding place, the laboratory in which I struggled to make the agonizing conjunction between the past and the present, between my childhood memories and the personal and professional events of my adult life.

Among the tons of baggage that had emerged from the hold of the *Maryland* was a massive but delicate German tape recorder with a sensitive microphone, through which I now made daily explorations of the various layers of my past. From the Rue de Prony it was a long but possible walk—along the Rue Saint-Honoré, through the Tuileries Gardens (always bright with flowers) and across the river. By the time I arrived at the Quai Voltaire and climbed the three flights of stairs I was exhausted and in a perfect mood for these subconscious excursions into my childhood.

They followed no chronological order. Each day, on my

way, I would choose one or more specific memories with which to begin and from which I wandered freely as one recollection evoked another. Sometimes I talked, without stopping, for the two hours that a tape lasted. Sometimes I fell asleep in the middle of a sentence and went on when I awoke. At other times I would fly off in an entirely different direction, following some bright splinter of memory that had surfaced during my sleep. It was a painful but enormously exciting and satisfying process that left me drained and dizzy.

Within a few weeks several dozen reels had accumulated in a corner of Virgil's room. They contained miles of narrow brown tape on which an intimate but disorganized and fragmentary account of the first two dozen years of my life had been recorded in several hundred thousand words. They might have remained in that form forever but for a fortunate accident. My former secretary, Marian Fenn, had accompanied her husband to England, where the Becks' Living Theatre was opening its first major European tour. I got an urgent call one night from London, where their premiere had been such a disaster that the company was temporarily disbanding. Did I have a job for her? I urged her to come over immediately and found a room for her in a horrendous little hotel not far from the Quai Voltaire. She was a lightning typist, and since she was being paid by the page she sat there, day after day, before a rented American typewriter, transcribing those miles of often obscure and occasionally embarrassing tapes, stopping only when her sight failed or when her fingers froze on the keys. (She has assured me since that those were among the worst weeks of her life.) When the last tape was on paper, she took her money and flew back to California, leaving me six hundred and eighty triple-spaced pages to struggle with. Much of it was repetitious, self-pitying and useless. But when *Run-Through* was finally written seven years later, the first third of it was, in fact, a corrected, reorganized and drastically edited version of that self-indulgent outpouring.

The completion of these tapes coincided with a sudden change in our lives. We had rented the apartment at 99 Rue de Prony for one year, but after five months, hearing that an

American film producer was anxious to take it over, Joan persuaded the owner to release us and moved us all to an entirely different part of town, much closer to her own former haunts. It was a smaller, cheaper, less elegant but more livable apartment, situated on the third floor of a newish *immeuble* in the heart of Montparnasse, only a few blocks from those favorite establishments of the intelligentsia the Dôme, the Rotonde and the Coupole. A few hundred yards away, on the other side, was the Montparnasse Cemetery, in whose Jewish section my father lay buried, and, a few blocks beyond that, the little house in the Rue Boulard—one of several in an enclosed garden—which had been Joan's mother's home for so many years and where Joan herself had grown up. Here we lived among local shops, cafés, seedy nightclubs (including one notorious Lesbian establishment) and run-down hotels to which the cheerful, hard-working ladies who plied their trade on every corner were in the habit of conducting their customers. Almost without exception, the girls doted on Mousy-Cat, who, in addition to these unexpected caresses, found new and infinitely varied delights among the market booths that were set up during the night, each Tuesday and Friday, right under our windows, loaded with merchandise that ranged from fruit, vegetables, fish, meat and dairy products to working clothes, hardware and minor artworks.

The move had a stimulating effect on us all. John Michael and Sebastian had recently celebrated their respective birthdays (thirteen and ten), and they too welcomed this new environment, in which they lived a freer and more colorful life than in the middle-class respectability of the Rue de Prony, where no flame-swallowers, escape artists or other mountebanks had ever appeared after dark as they did almost every evening in the Boulevard Edgar Quinet. A bus from American School still came for them, and the boys seemed to board it less reluctantly than before. (It was not until months later that we discovered that, as they sat each morning outside the corner bistro waiting for their bus to arrive, they were both fortifying themselves, like the French workingmen around them, with a brimming glass of Calvados.)

For my part, with my six hundred and eighty pages of

confession safely stowed in a suitcase under my bed, I was finally getting around to dealing with the current problems of life with Joan in Paris which, in my obsessive preoccupation with the past, I had so far ignored or evaded. If I had counted on my European background and my perfect French to temper the panic (the "new boy" syndrome) that I continued to feel, well into my sixties, each time I had to face a new and unfamiliar society, I had seriously miscalculated. Familiarity, in this case, seemed actually to increase those fears. In my excavations of my Parisian childhood, I had uncovered many of the emotions and attitudes that were at the root of my chronic alienation. Recognizing them in no way diminished their disturbing effect.

Add to this the loss of the protective structure of props and supports on which I had come to rely in America. In my deepest doldrums at home, when I felt most rejected and alone, I had only to pick up one of the many telephones that lay within easy reach and, with a few words, I could rejoin the society of which I now, finally, regarded myself a recognized and accredited member. Here, thousands of miles from my professional base, without position or function, I felt almost as defenseless and vulnerable as I had as a child.

Soon after our arrival, at my mother's behest, I had made an approach to what was left of my father's French-Jewish family. Those who had survived* or returned from abroad after the Occupation were back in their former homes and prospering in their various affairs. We had never been very close, and I knew that they had never quite forgiven my numerous tribal defections—my British schooling, my refusal to serve with their boys in the French Army, my departure for America and, in a final immorality, my abandoning an honorable and successful mercantile career for an insane plunge into show business. Our first reunion was formal and embarrassed, and I made no further attempt to bridge the gap between us.

* One aunt and two cousins were victims of the Holocaust. Their death in Auschwitz was commemorated in a plaque on the wall of the family vault in the Cimetière Montparnasse. (See *Run-Through*, p. 26.)

I was more at ease with Joan's friends—a variegated and interesting lot that ranged from Jesuit-educated school chums to poets, painters, art dealers, publishers, a celebrated analyst* and the United Nations' most respected translator from the Russian. But my contacts with them were limited to social occasions (lunches, dinners and a few weekend visits to the country), and I remained remote and timid among them —a stranger on a brief visit from a distant country about which, like most Frenchmen, they had ambivalent feelings.

I have long been aware that most of my adult relationships (except for the emotional and physical accidents of an occasional love affair) have, in fact, been professional associations —no less close and intimate for being based on some sort of working connection. It was therefore with some relief that I discovered that there were a number of my former associates currently residing in Paris. Besides the Ustinovs, there were the Frankenheimers, Evans and John, with whom I had worked on *Playhouse 90* and *All Fall Down* and who now occupied a picturesque duplex on the Île Saint-Louis. Also the Bernheims † with whom we had become friends in California and who had now formed a successful film agency in London and Paris with a clientele that included Pierre Boulle, Louis Malle, my old friend Nick Ray (who appeared in town occasionally from his Baltic island with a patch over one eye) and James Jones, at whose home, also on the Île Saint-Louis, we spent some agreeably contentious evenings. Another figure out of a different past was Lesley Blanch (my "technical" adviser on *The Wings of the Dove*), whom I found sick and depressed, following her divorce from Romain Gary, living with two cats in a small apartment in Passy.‡

---

* Jacques Lacan, with whom I spent several hours one evening trying to convince him that Kennedy's shooting was not part of a government-sponsored plot.
† On their return to France after the war they had recovered some but not all of their former wealth. Their historic *manoir* in Normandy had been admired by Marshal Goering, who had it transported stone by stone to Germany.
‡ In striking contrast to the days when I used to visit her in her suite in the French Consulate in Beverly Hills (where her husband, Ro-

Going further back, there were a number of my associates from the French desk of the Voice of America, including that bright and handsome woman Yvonne Michel, who had been executive assistant to Pierre Lazareff and who continued to hold that position on *France-Soir*. And there was red-haired, peanut-faced Lazareff himself.* Since their return to France, in the mid-forties, Pierre and his wife, Hélène, had become dominant figures in French journalism, publishing, film and television. It amused Pierre to introduce me to his partners over lunch at the Berkley as *"mon boss américain,"* and one Sunday Joan and I drove out in the Thunderbird to one of the famous lunches that he and Hélène gave in their country house near Versailles, where, in the course of a few hours, we seemed to meet every French figure of prominence from Coco Chanel to the Pompidous.

Then, too, there were Americans on their way through. We received a visit from Ellis Rabb and his assistant Jack O'Brien (on their way home after riding camels around the Pyramids), full of ambitious plans for the next APA repertory season. Other visitors were Jack Landau on a holiday and Larry Kelly with Nicola Rescigno, the conductor of the Dallas Opera, who invited me to return to Texas in November to direct Renata Tebaldi in *Tosca*. Finally, Jean Rosenthal appeared, on her way to or from Israel with Martha Graham.

I had arrived in Europe with an assignment from the theatrical magazine *Show* to write a series of articles about the French and, later, the Italian and German theatres. I had ignored it during my months of intense self-exploration, but I returned to it now with renewed energy. The shows I attended in order to document my first piece took me all the way from the stale, well-made plays and comedies of the Boulevard and the Palais-Royal (which had hardly changed since

main Gary, was consul general). She had covered its floor and walls with Persian rugs, so that she always gave the impression of living in a tent in the desert waiting for a dark horseman in flowing robes to carry her off.

* See *Front and Center*, pp. 52 *et seq.*

my precocious theatregoing during the First World War) to the Comédie-Française, where I saw revivals of *Cyrano de Bergerac* (to which my father had sent me as a child), together with two Molières, one Racine and one of the three Feydeau farces that were currently playing in Paris. I preferred the other national theatre, the Odéon, where (under the energetic, catholic direction of Jean-Louis Barrault and his wife, Madeleine Renaud) I saw plays that ranged from the controversial premiere of Genêt's Algerian play *Les Paravents (The Screens)* to revivals of Claudel's *Le Soulier de Satin* and *Le Partage de Midi,* performed with classic splendor by Edwige Feullière, as well as my first exposure to Beckett's *Les Beaux Jours (Happy Days),* played by Madeleine Renaud in its original French version. I sat through an adaptation of Arthur Miller's *After the Fall* directed by Visconti and found it even less to my taste than I had in Kazan's original New York production. In smaller theatres, I was one of an audience of half a dozen who turned out for the perennial Ionesco repertory at the Théâtre de la Huchette, and I enjoyed a performance of *The Cherry Orchard* directed and acted by the youngest of our former French broadcasters at the Voice of America, the tall red-haired Sasha Pitoeff. In preparation for my own production in Dallas I went to the Paris Opéra to see Maria Callas' vocally declining but dramatically brilliant performance of *Tosca.* That winter, finally, I was introduced to the works of Ghelderode, presented by a visiting Belgian company at our neighborhood theatre, the Montparnasse,* and found them strangely exciting—little suspecting that my own return to the theatre in America would be with two of his plays.

Finding myself back in the theatre, even as a spectator viewing plays in another language, gave me a renewed feeling of belonging and broke down some of the isolation in which I had been living for the past seven months. It was no accident that the only two new friendships I formed in Paris

---

* The theatrical home for years of the distinguished French producer-director Gaston Baty.

that year were directly related to the theatre. Both were with women and both were platonic.

Joan has never been an enthusiastic theatregoer. My frequent companion, in her absence, was Sonya Orwell, whom I had met with Virgil Thomson in New York and who now became my guide to the new French intellectual avant-garde.* It was through her that I met and formed a brief, stimulating relationship with Marguerite Duras, who was then near the beginning of her brilliant, controversial career. She was an intense and provocative companion whose colonial childhood seemed to set her apart from the general run of French writers of her generation. She was fascinated by all forms of dramatic communication, particularly theatre and films, and during the several visits we paid to her country house at Neauphle-le-Château† she gave me a number of her still-unproduced scripts to read—including a harrowing autobiographical play, *Des Journées entières dans les arbres,* which I later saw performed by Madeleine Renaud at the Odéon and by Peggy Ashcroft with the Royal Shakespeare in London.‡ My acquaintance with Marguerite Duras was brief and superficial, and I have not seen or communicated with her in more than a decade, but I remember our friendship with pleasure.

The truth is that by the spring of 1965 I was beginning to enjoy my life in Paris. At the same time I was starting to worry, once again, about money. The gloomy communications I received from my lawyer in New York indicated that our expenses abroad were running higher than ex-

* It was from her translation of an essay by the French philosopher Merleau-Ponty that I quoted a fragment on the first page of *Run-Through:* "To say that life is entirely what we make of it or entirely the data which we are given is to say the same thing. . . . We are never predetermined and we never change; we can always find in our past the presage of what we have become."
† A village near Paris that later became the refuge of the Ayatollah Khomeini during his exile from Iran.
‡ I sent it to Helen Hayes as a possible vehicle for herself, but the First Lady of the American Theatre turned it down on the grounds that it was "depressing."

pected. The three years of travel I had promised myself were reduced to two—one of which was more than half spent.

These financial concerns may have been the spur I needed. I went to Brentano's on the Rue de Rivoli, bought *Roget's Thesaurus* in its latest edition and began writing. Within a week of finishing my first theatre article and sending it off to *Show* in New York, I was deep into an entirely unpremeditated piece for *Harper's*. It was the longest I had written for them, and I mailed it to Russell Lynes with some apprehension. It described the strange manner in which Raymond Chandler had completed his screenplay of *The Blue Dahlia*, which I had produced for Paramount in 1944. *Harper's* accepted it, and it appeared (with some cuts and dramatic subheadings of which I disapproved) in the July issue and later formed part of the chapter in *Front and Center* in which I recorded my early experiences as a Hollywood film producer.

It was while I was finishing the *Harper's* piece that I received two transatlantic phone calls within a few days of each other. The first was from Ray Stark, whom I had known for years—first as one of Hollywood's sharpest and most ambitious agents, and more recently as a successful Broadway and film producer. He had formed his own company, Seven Arts, and his latest project, a starring vehicle for Natalie Wood, was a film based on Tennessee Williams' *This Property Is Condemned*. (Rather, it was a film that used the title and some of the characters mentioned but never shown in Tennessee's beautiful miniature, two-character play.) Ray was too busy with his company to give the picture the personal attention it needed. He offered me fifty thousand dollars plus living expenses if I would come to Los Angeles and produce it for him. Since he was contractually obligated to start photography by early August, the whole thing would take up no more than three or four months of my time.

I had never before taken over a film conceived by someone else, for which a script had already been written and the leading actor selected. However, it was the first offer I had received in fifteen months, and, as I pointed out to Joan, it would buy us another year abroad. She accused me, with some truth, of having been waiting for months for just such a summons to California and added that if the only way I could salvage my ego was by once again becoming a harassed big-shot Hollywood producer, then, obviously, I must accept Ray's offer. If I really meant what I said about another year in Europe, she was willing to hold the fort during my absence and to take care of the boys and their summer holiday until I got back.

I don't know how much I was swayed in my decision by another transatlantic call I received a few days later. This was from New York, from Peter Mennin, head of the world-famous Juilliard Music School. It was entirely unexpected and opened up such astonishing vistas that all I could say to him was that I would soon be in America and would prefer to discuss his proposal in person. I told Joan of the call but not of its implications. And that night I called Ray Stark in California and accepted his offer. As usual, he was in a tearing hurry, and he urged me to fly to California within a week.

In Los Angeles I found little changed—including my own first violently hostile reaction to the place. I arrived with two suitcases and a small trunk in which I had packed the first three hundred of Marian's triple-spaced pages,* together with several notebooks full of false starts and aborted fragments of my book on which I hoped to work during my solitary California evenings. I spent two nights with my friends the Lloyds, then moved into a hotel in Westwood related to the University of California which seemed to be inhabited almost entirely by African students, whose voices in the patio, speaking mostly in French, made me doubt, the first few nights, that I had really left Paris.

This sudden, unexpected transatlantic move made me conscious, as never before, of the gulf between the Old World and the New. Driving to the office through Westwood in my rented Chevy, between the pretentious new office buildings

---

* In the course of the next five years it accompanied me three times across the Atlantic and twice that many times from coast to coast.

that were rising above the movie theatres, gas stations and short-order restaurants, I found myself comparing my sensations with those I had experienced only a few days earlier, during a final, long-promised family excursion we had made in the Thunderbird to the Cathedral of Chartres.

Each of us had his own separate and personal reaction to that "most perfect piece of architecture in the world." For Joan, as a negligent but persistent Catholic, it was part of the living heritage of faith and beauty which she had acquired in her childhood. The boys were impressed by the colors of the glass in the windows and by the hundreds of candles, to which we added one for each of us. But what they enjoyed most were the carvings over the portals and the marble dogs lying at their masters' feet in the crypt. My own reaction (that of an aging man with an underdeveloped visual sense and no religious feelings whatsoever) was one of utter amazement and wonder at this incredible achievement of the human spirit: the miracle that men, living more than eight centuries ago in a dark age of violence, deprivation and sudden death, inspired by beliefs that I considered puerile and myths that I found incredible, should have created monuments of such soaring and sublime audacity and magnificence that they made our most ambitious structures look like the work of desperate earthbound megalomaniacs!

Ray Stark's Seven Arts occupied an entire floor in a new bank building in Beverly Hills. Here he operated in an atmosphere of feverish activity, and here, on the morning of my arrival, I encountered a number of familiar figures. But there was one new face—that of a dark, bearded, intense young man who was introduced to me as Francis Ford Coppola.* I learned that he was a recent graduate of UCLA's Film Department whom Ray kept locked in a small cell in the rear of the building, turning out first-draft screenplays at the rate of around one a month for a minimum wage. Our script of *This Property Is Condemned* was his.

Film finances have always been mysterious and incompre-

---

* Francis Ford Coppola achieved fame and wealth five years later with *The Godfather*.

hensible. Certain films are made with little hope of artistic quality or of popular success merely because a studio entrepreneur, for some special reason, finds it advantageous to produce them. *This Property Is Condemned* was such a film. For my own part, I had known before I went to work that I would not have much fun with it except, as Joan had unkindly pointed out, for the satisfaction of finding myself once again in the big time. And even that was limited by my awareness that all important decisions on the picture would be made by Stark, who (though he could not have been more thoughtful and pleasant) was in the habit of making them capriciously, unilaterally and often without informing anyone until long after they had gone into effect.

Since I had talked with him in Paris he had added Robert Redford to the cast and his production department had prepared a schedule that involved shooting in New Orleans, on the Mississippi Gulf Coast and finally at the Paramount Studios in Hollywood, where I had cut my teeth as a producer twenty years before.*

A few important parts remained to be cast, including that of our heroine's outrageous mother, for which I engaged that fine Canadian actress Kate Reid.† As one of the two railroad men with whom she was sleeping, we chose a powerful but still-obscure character actor by the name of Charles Bronson.

Stark was not stinting on his production. For our cinematographer we had James Wong Howe, the best in the business. To direct the picture Ray had wooed John Huston and failed. In his place, he sought my approval of a newcomer by the name of Sydney Pollack, whom I knew from television as an assistant on *Playhouse 90* and as an "observer" who had sat in on my rehearsals of *Six Characters* at UCLA.‡ He was a

---

* Its production head was Howard Koch (not to be confused with the writer), who had been our highly competent assistant director on *Julius Caesar* in 1952. (See *Front and Center*, p. 390.)

† She had an unusual contract with us that called for her to lose twenty-five pounds before the start of photography. She made it in less than a month.

‡ Later he broke through in a big way with *They Shoot Horses, Don't They?*, followed by *The Way We Were* and *Three Days of the Condor*, etc.

dark neurotic young man of considerable talent and furious ambition. No sooner had he signed his contract than he set about compulsively trying to undermine my position and to form an axis with Natalie and Redford to gain control of the film. This maneuver was facilitated by the fact that we were shooting a weak screenplay, publicly repudiated by Tennessee. In the weeks before and during shooting, as many as five writers were assigned to the script, each working for and with a different person and each trying to strengthen the film's contrived and dubious love story. While this troupe of writers was slaving away at a feckless task I took a long weekend and flew to New York for my meeting with Peter Mennin at Juilliard.

He was a composer of repute as well as a calculating executive who had concluded after much consultation that I was the man best qualified to set up and head his new Drama Division. Our first meeting was tense but positive. I came away with a number of questions still unanswered, but, with two months to go on the film, I had plenty of time to consider my decision. It was agreed that we would meet again when I returned to New York and that I would give him my final answer at that time.

Our first location for *This Property Is Condemned* was Pass Christian, a resort town on Mississippi's Gulf Coast, not far from the Louisiana state line. It had a small railroad station and a spur of track along which we could work undisturbed except for the passage of two freights a day—both driven by black engineers. Here Grimes, our red-bearded production designer, reconstructed a ramshackle yellow building to represent the railroaders' boardinghouse and here we did our first three weeks' shooting. The heat was intense, and we slept in a large, elegant hotel some twenty miles away, to which we commuted each morning and evening.*

From Pass Christian we moved to New Orleans, which I found sadly changed from the romantic, pleasant city I had

---

* All of them—hotel, station and reconstructed boardinghouse— were totally destroyed when Hurricane Camille swept the Gulf Coast in August of 1969.

lived in for several weeks in the fall of 1927 (supervising the loading of wheat shipments to Europe). We shot for two weeks in the French Quarter,* but by now our patchwork script was beginning to give us trouble. In Pass Christian the scenes with the little girl on the railroad track and most of what went on around the railroaders' boardinghouse had been derived directly from Tennessee's one-act play. In New Orleans we were on our own, trying to dramatize Wilma's decline and fall, prior to her ending up in what her baby sister called "the boneyard."

After New Orleans there was another month of studio work on the Paramount lot. By now I was so discouraged and irritated that even Pollack's continued manipulations failed to disturb me. Some of our footage, particularly the scenes between Natalie and her mother, had real dramatic quality, and Bronson lent his own special kind of energy to a scene at the water hole. But our love scenes (the combined product of five well-paid Hollywood writers) made little sense.

The film had been rough-cut as we went along. I left the final editing to Stark and Pollack, and within a few days of the end of shooting I was on my way home via Dallas, Texas, where *Tosca* was due to open in ten days. For a director *Tosca* offers less excitement than the tumultous drama provided by Shakespeare and Verdi in *Otello,* which I had directed for the Dallas Opera three years before. But there was one challenge I was eager to meet: I hoped to elicit from Renata Tebaldi (whose Tosca was, vocally, one of her most acclaimed roles) some of the dramatic energy with which I had seen a declining Maria Callas fill the role in Paris. I was warned that she was a pleasant artist, set in her ways and resistant to directorial innovations.

Except for her natural aversion to extended stage rehearsals (which she felt were fatiguing and bad for the voice) she behaved like an angel and did everything I asked her, including singing "Vissi d'arte" "quietly, almost like a prayer, stand-

---

* Including a day in the old sunken graveyard with the raised tombs that seems to have become the common denominator of all films shot in that city.

ing at a tall window to one side of the stage" and, in the last act, making her final dash up the steep, narrow steps of the Castel Sant'Angelo—though I spared her the fatal jump by bringing the curtain down quickly just before the leap.

John Rosenfeld, the local critic (who was conducting a running feud with the Dallas Civic Opera) was ecstatic about Madame Tebaldi, "who gave Puccini the optimum of vocal beauty, interpretive temperament and the resource of one of the great singing skills of the day," and polite about my staging:

> There had been much comment that this was to be a restudied and redirected "Tosca," which, happily, was an unfounded rumor. Except for the strolling worshippers during the love-duet in the Church of Sant'Andrea della Valle, John Houseman's staging was honest and conservative.

After the frustrations and aggravations of *This Property Is Condemned, Tosca* had been a rewarding activity that sent me relaxed and confident to New York for my decisive meeting with Peter Mennin.

Four days later, on the morning of my departure for Paris, the New York papers carried the news that

> Juilliard has put in its bid to join the ranks of major drama conservatories with the appointment of John Houseman to head its new Drama Division when the school moves into Lincoln Center.
> Houseman is one of the most experienced producers and directors in the country. His appointment underlines Juilliard's designation as the overall educational arm of Lincoln Center.

For the first time in many months I felt exhilarated and confident. It was not until I was halfway across the Atlantic that I began to rehearse what I would say to Joan about what I had just decided. We had spoken on the phone; she knew of the Juilliard offer, and, though I had given her few details, she could not fail to be aware of its consequences. Knowing me as she did after fifteen years of living together, she must also have known that I would accept it. So that when I informed her on the night of my arrival, over a welcoming glass of champagne, that we would soon be returning to America and that our home, for the next few years, would be Manhattan and not Malibu, she had already made her adjustment to the situation. What I did not dare to tell her until later was that before leaving New York, in my exhilaration over my new life, I had spent most of the money I had just made on Stark's film buying an apartment on Gramercy Park.

CHAPTER X

1966-1967

JUILLIARD
THE HONOURABLE ESTATE
APA-PHOENIX
PANTAGLEIZE

THE JUILLIARD SCHOOL of Music was half a century old and was generally recognized as one of the world's leading musical conservatories.* The chairman of its board, for many years, had been my friend James Warburg, and its present structure and reputation had been established in large part by William Schuman, its president for seventeen years until 1962, when he assumed the position of president of the new Lincoln Center for the Performing Arts.

When the Rockefellers decided to follow their successful real-estate operation at Radio City with the creation of a performing-arts complex uptown that would include the Metropolitan Opera, the Philharmonic, a branch of the Public

---

* Among its most celebrated recent alumni were Leontyne Price, Rise Stevens, Van Cliburn, Misha Dichter, William Kapell, Itzhak Perlman, Pinchas Zukerman, James Levine, Leonard Slatkin, etc. etc., not to mention Richard Rodgers and the Juilliard String Quartet.

Library and the sundry activities of the New York City Center (such as the City Center Opera and Ballet), they decided that they also needed an educational arm. The Juilliard School, an obvious choice, was invited to occupy what turned out to be the most architecturally distinguished building in Lincoln Center.* One condition of the move was that, in order to qualify as a conservatory for the performing arts, Juilliard must add drama to its curriculum.

Since the Juilliard building was the last to go up, Mennin, when he assumed the presidency in 1962, still had several years in which to make his decisions about the new Drama Division. He did, however, inherit a considerable backlog of thinking and planning, which generally followed two separate and incompatible lines. The first assumed that the Drama Division would be closely associated with the Lincoln Center Repertory Company, which was about to be formed, and that it would conform to the artistic principles and theatrical preferences held by whoever was chosen to run the theatre. The second took a broader and more academic view: it held that Juilliard's Drama Division, like its School of Music, should have its own independent curriculum and theatrical ideals.

A strong supporter of this second view was Lincoln Kirstein, at whose suggestion the Rockefeller Foundation sent a qualified observer to Europe for a year to cover the entire field of theatre training—in England, on the Continent and, if possible, behind the Iron Curtain. From the report Robert Chapman † gave the foundation on his return it was clear that, in his opinion and in that of most of the people he consulted, there was one outstanding figure in the field. This was Michel Saint-Denis, who had started as an actor (under his uncle Jacques Copeau, and then with his own Compagnie des Quinze) before moving to England in the early thirties

* Its architect, Pietro Belluschi, was known for his additions to the Massachusetts Institute of Technology, for the Equitable Building in Portland, Oregon, and for the chapel he designed for the monks of Portsmouth Priory.
† Playwright, member of the Harvard faculty and director of the Loeb Theatre in Cambridge, Massachusetts.

and organizing the London Theatre Studio, which had been favored by Gielgud, Olivier, Redgrave and many others. After the war (during which he served as principal French speaker for the BBC overseas programs) he, George Devine and Glen Byam Shaw had organized the Old Vic School, which had directly influenced every one of Britain's other theatrical institutions.

On the basis of this report, Saint-Denis had been invited by the Rockefeller Foundation to spend several months in the United States, observing the theatrical and academic scenes from coast to coast and making suggestions for a training program to meet the current needs and conditions of the American theatre. Before leaving, he prepared a long and detailed report on his findings together with a number of recommendations for the training of American actors, directors and designers. This came to be known around Juilliard as "the Saint-Denis bible."

On his return to Europe in the late fifties Saint-Denis, at the behest of General de Gaulle and André Malraux, had set up a number of French regional performing-arts centers, including one in Strasbourg known as the Théâtre de l'Est. He was also invited, with Suria, his wife, to organize the bilingual Canadian National Theatre School in Montreal. Soon after that, he was chosen as one of the "troika," with Peter Hall and Peter Brook, appointed to run Britain's Royal Shakespeare Theatre at Stratford-upon-Avon.

Meantime, back in New York's Lincoln Center, things were moving along—but not quite as expected. Direction of the Lincoln Center Repertory Company had been entrusted to a team made up of Robert Whitehead and Elia Kazan whose attitude toward actors' training varied substantially. Whitehead knew and admired Saint-Denis' work in Europe; in the early days of the Repertory Company (while it was located downtown in a temporary building) he had set up the beginnings of a training program that was not inconsistent with the Saint-Denis approach. Kazan, on the other hand, had been trained in the Stanislavsky "Method" according to Lee Strasberg—though he had later transcended it in his own work. Having founded the Actors' Studio in collaboration with Robert Lewis and Lee Strasberg, it was predictable, if and when a union occurred between Juilliard and the Repertory Company, that he would turn the school over to these former associates. This meant a somewhat specialized and limited form of training with emphasis on subjective interpretation and little concern for the disciplines required for the performance of the English classics.

It never came to a test, for in 1964 Kazan and Whitehead suddenly resigned as producing directors of the Repertory Company. They were replaced, after a long search,* by two young men, Irving and Blau, who had run a small, lively art theatre in San Francisco. Their initial New York production of that doomed piece *Danton's Death,*† at the newly opened Beaumont Theatre in Lincoln Center, was a resounding disaster. Since then, in their struggle to survive, Irving and Blau had been far too preoccupied and insecure to take on the added responsibility of a conservatory.

It was at this point—with the Juilliard building slowly rising out of the ground—that Peter Mennin found himself faced with the necessity of appointing a director capable of organizing a program that could go into effect by the time the Juilliard School moved into its new quarters. This was now expected to happen in the fall of 1968. Time had clarified one point: the school should be set up independently of the Repertory Company, with a strong director and a firm theatrical viewpoint of its own.

I have never known how many candidates were considered for the position nor how my name finally rose to the top of the pile. (I don't believe it was ever actually offered to anyone else.) I had certain obvious qualifications. In addition to my reputation in the mass media I had a theatrical record, going back to the days of the WPA and the Mercury, for effective production of the classics, confirmed by my four years at Stratford and my recent term as artistic director of the UCLA Professional Theatre Group. I have always believed that one

* Sitting in Paris, I had indulged in occasional daydreams that, like Coriolanus, I would be approached and begged to return and take over the Repertory Company. No such offer was made.
† See *Run-Through,* p. 377.

of the prime movers in my appointment was the unpredictable Lincoln Kirstein. (We had had our artistic and personal differences, but we shared a sense of continuity and a firm belief in the classics as a basis of training.) My recommendation was supported by the Ford Foundation in the person of McNeill Lowry, who, in his effort to promote and encourage theatre in America, was contributing substantially to the financing of the new school. He qualified his approval (so I've been told) with the warning that I was a prickly and opinionated character who would not be easy to deal with. Finally I believe that Saint-Denis, when consulted in England, spoke well of me.

For my own part, unlike many of my most crucial decisions this one was not lightly or hurriedly made. All my life, well into my sixties, I had jumped from one risk into another without serious misgivings or apprehensions—confident that there was no wrong decision or miscalculation that could not be reversed, no situation, however disastrous, from which I could not extricate myself. This was different. Whatever I decided now represented a final commitment, one that would directly and permanently affect what was left of my life.

During the two months in which I considered the implications of Mennin's offer (in Pass Christian, in Los Angeles and, finally, in Dallas) I had done a lot of thinking. Much of it was based on my reluctant assumption that as I entered my sixty-fourth year my best days in show business were over. My latest, unrewarding experience with *This Property Is Condemned* confirmed my doubts that I could ever pull myself back to the top. This made for a bleak future in which I would keep jumping from one project to another with what I was beginning to fear might be steadily diminishing results.

Juilliard represented a position of prestige and security. At the same time it could be regarded as an acceptance of defeat and a final surrender of the illusion, so dear to every man and woman in show business, that the Big Break is just around the corner. It also represented a sharp drop in income—from over one hundred thousand dollars down to twenty-five thousand dollars a year (which was the most such an academic position could command at the time). Even assuming that I could augment it with moonlighting and additional theatrical employment, it meant a drastic change in our life-style at a time when our boys were about to enter the expensive part of their education. It also meant living once again in New York, and I knew that this would create a serious domestic problem.

My decision to accept the Juilliard offer was motivated, finally, by none of these things. It was made in direct response to the challenge offered by this unexpected opportunity to attempt something quite new and different. Faced with the question of whether I was capable of creating and directing the country's most advanced and effective theatre conservatory, it became absolutely necessary for me to prove that I could.

With my usual mixture of modesty and arrogance, I tried to make a conscientious appraisal of my ability to create such an institution. As an educator my experience was limited. My functions with our embryonic school at Stratford had been supervisory and protective, with Jack Landau doing most of the work. I had some academic background—at Vassar, Barnard and UCLA—but I never thought of myself as a teacher. (I was far too impatient and egotistical and I lacked the total dedication I had observed in all the good teachers I had known.) However, conducting a conservatory, like running a theatre, called for a delicate balance of creative and executive authority and energy, and these I felt I possessed to an unusual degree. I had organized no fewer than six theatre companies; I had produced and/or directed a greater variety of professional classical productions in New York and elsewhere than anyone else in the country. And I had been involved, in one way or another, with most of the significant American theatre movements of the past thirty years.

Timing too played its part. I felt that this was a particularly propitious moment for the creation of such a school. Following the recent surprising renaissance of serious theatre in America, there were, by now, several dozen active, viable, effective theatres throughout the country (with more on the way) performing programs that included a percentage of classical works. These new companies* made entirely different demands on their artists than either Broadway or the mass media. Because of the variety of their productions they called for an ability on the part of their actors to work in a wide range of periods and styles. In consequence, one of the most important and vital functions to be fulfilled in today's American theatre was the creation of a carefully planned and developed actor-training program suited to meet these new professional needs. To create the model for such a program appealed strongly to the combination of ambition and the urge for public service that had played such a persistent part in my professional life.

I was back in Paris early in December 1965, in time for the Christmas family rituals and for the sixteenth anniversary of a marriage which, all passion spent and in spite of certain areas of chronic misunderstanding, had come to represent, for Joan and myself, the only real and durable relationship in our lives. I had been away for close to five months—our longest separation yet—but on the Boulevard Edgar Quinet little seemed to have changed. The same ladies stood on the same corners; the market booths were still set up before dawn every Tuesday and Friday; the fire-eaters and escape artists still performed during the weekend.

The family had had a good summer. Joan, Sebastian and Mousy-Cat had driven in the Thunderbird to Biarritz, where they had joined the Bernheims and the Joneses, and had then gone on with the Botsfords to Spain. John Michael had spent his vacation in England, on the outskirts of London, with his five female cousins, daughters of Joan's sister Françoise. Now he and Sebastian were both back in school, where John Michael had finally discovered a stimulating teacher—of mathematics. Sebastian was not so fortunate, and one of my first assignments after my return was a voyage to Lausanne to enroll him in a Swiss school for the rest of the school year.

* For which there was no accepted or definitive name; they were referred to variously as "nonprofit," "repertory," "institutional," "regional," "resident" and, even, "art" theatres.

He and John Michael were very loving brothers, but this had not prevented their sibling rivalries from becoming tedious and injurious. (A critical point was reached when Sebastian was found weeping disconsolately one evening because his brother, at thirteen, weighed several pounds more than he did at ten.) His new school at Vevey on the Lake of Geneva did not impress me, but it gave us a chance to spend the night together at the Hotel Beau Rivage at Ouchy, which I had visited so often as a child with my own parents.*

A more satisfying voyage was one I made the following month to Stratford-upon-Avon to visit Michel Saint-Denis, whose help I needed in formulating my plans for the Drama Division. I had not seen him in seven years (since he had lectured for us at Stratford, Connecticut), and I found him older and frailer but still full of energy and ideas. I spent two days with him and his handsome Russian wife, Suria,† in their house near the theatre (where I saw *The Tempest* and *Cymbeline* with Vanessa Redgrave as Imogen) and made two important discoveries, both of which suggested that Saint-Denis' collaboration in the organization of Juilliard's Drama Division was not as remote a possibility as I had feared.

I knew there had been problems with de Gaulle, of which I now learned the details. (With the diversion to France's atom bomb of funds originally destined for the arts, there had been severe cuts in the cultural programs that Saint-Denis had been engaged to set up. When his protests were ignored, he resigned.) I also realized, after two days in Stratford, that in the Royal Shakespeare Company's governing "troika" the two active and dominant members were the two leading English directors—Peter Hall and Peter Brook—

* The Beau Rivage had been one of Europe's most glamorous hotels. In its more luxurious rooms there were still banks of bells which communicated directly with the wing in which the guests' personal servants—maids, valets and chauffeurs—had been quartered.

† Suria Magito had studied theatre arts, music, drama and dance in Paris, Berlin, Milan and London and was first recommended to Saint-Denis by the composer Darius Milhaud. Her work combined speech, mime, the use of Nō masks, chanting and dance. She had been Saint-Denis' collaborator for many years.

leaving Michel, the respected elder statesman, to act mostly as arbiter and adviser.

When I got around to talking to him about his situation, I was pleased to find him intensely interested in my proposal that he join me as consultant director of the Drama Division of the Juilliard School. Details would be worked out later, but, with his consent, I sent a cable to Peter Mennin the next day informing him of Saint-Denis' availability. He and Suria would be going to France in a few weeks; at that time we would meet again in Paris, put our agreement into final form and discuss the structure of the new school before I returned to America.

Before that, he suggested that I spend a few days in Strasbourg observing the workings of the school he and his wife had founded there. I flew back over the Channel the next day, pleased and infinitely relieved, but more conscious than ever of my own inadequacies as compared with the total absorption and infinite experience of a man like Saint-Denis, whose whole life had been dedicated to the work that I was assuming so blithely in my mid-sixties.

Strasbourg, which I visited the following week, was the city from which my father's family had migrated after the Franco–Prussian War of 1870. I found the school small but instructive. Its director, Pierre Lefèvre (who later joined us at Juilliard), and his assistant, Barbara Goodwin, had both been trained by Michel Saint-Denis at the Old Vic School, and I found it valuable to compare the actual, practical work that was being done in Strasbourg with the theoretical precepts laid out in our Saint-Denis "bible." I also found it fascinating to conjecture what differences there would be between the French students whom I was observing and the young Americans who would be attending Juilliard.

Another, more distant voyage was one I made that spring to India at the invitation of my old, dear friend Rosamond Gilder, head of the U.S. branch of the International Theatre Institute. A theatre conference was being held in New Delhi under the auspices of UNESCO, and she urged me to accompany her there. (I think she had a secret hope that I should one day succeed her at ITI and that this Asian junket was an attempt to get me involved.) As future head of a theatrical conservatory I felt it behooved me to attend such a function; I met her in Paris and went on with her from there, with a stop in Beirut.

On the night of our arrival in Delhi, after an exhausting flight, we were driven to a ceremony held on a vast plain outside the city, of which the traditional climax was the setting alight of brightly colored fifty-foot-high wicker effigies by flaming arrows, while hundreds of thousands cheered as they collapsed and were devoured by the flames. The next night there was an exhibition of Kali dancers, bright, oversized and masked, in their slow, interminable, gyrating ritual combats ending with the fall and death of the villainess, from whose gaping mouth long reels of scarlet tape unwound and covered the stage with paper blood. But my strongest impression, finally, was not of the Taj Mahal, to which we were duly conducted over the weekend, but of the neighboring Red Palace at Fatehpur Sikri,* which, in the splendor and extravagance of its planning, made me think of the structure erected by the Sun King at Versailles a century later.

The conference itself, the first of many I attended in my new academic role, was of limited interest. The fashion that year was antiliterary—to decry the written text in favor of improvisation and spontaneous creation by actors and director. There were long speeches on the subject, of which I made one in opposition. I was introduced one evening to Madame Gandhi, and I enjoyed meeting Joan Littlewood, a lively, sentimental little woman who had just been ejected from Tunisia for behavior its government considered subversive. I also spent one day visiting Delhi's acting school, reputed to be the best in India, where classes were conducted and plays performed in both English and Hindi.†

•

* Built late in the fifteenth century by the Mogul Emperor Akbar, at vast human and financial cost, it was abandoned fourteen years later when its water supply failed.
† A group of vernacular dialects spoken and written in northern India.

The time was approaching when I must return to America —not only on Juilliard business and because it was necessary to enroll John Michael in a good school there, but also because I had agreed to direct a production for the coming season of the Shakespeare Festival Theatre at Stratford, Connecticut. I had received the offer with misgiving but accepted it for three reasons: first, at Joe Reed's personal request, to assuage the feud that had been smoldering between us for close to seven years; second, to celebrate the Festival's decision, for the first time in its history, to do what I had advocated years ago—to produce each season at least one non-Shakespearean play; third, and not least, because I needed the money.

Since the lease of our apartment on the Boulevard Edgar Quinet ran through the end of July, Joan decided to stay on, wait for Sebastian to be free of his Swiss school and then join me in Connecticut. For my own part, now that I was about to leave, I was falling in love with Paris. I had missed the previous spring, but this one was incredible; lilac was blooming in Joan's mother's garden in the Rue Boulard and along the wall of the Montparnasse Cemetery, into which I wandered with my son one afternoon to take a last look at my father's family vault.

While I was busy packing and preparing for departure, the Saint-Denises arrived from London, and we held a series of meetings at their hotel at which we laid out as much as we could of the Drama Division's curriculum. We worked hard —seven or eight hours a day—and I noticed that by midafternoon Michel would grow tired and vague and, except for an occasional sharp, emphatic interjection, would leave most of the talking to Suria. On the night following our last meeting, while my son and I were in midair over the Atlantic, Michel Saint-Denis suffered the first of a series of strokes that diminished and, finally, within three years, destroyed him.

Virgil Thomson had recommended Portsmouth Priory, the Dominican school in Rhode Island, as the most desirable place for John Michael's education. It was notoriously difficult to get into, but word finally came that he would be accepted as one of six candidates qualified to compete for the next year's last two vacancies. This meant his spending a month in Newport beginning in June. We flew on together to California, where we stayed with friends and where I made a momentous decision concerning the house in Malibu. Our present tenants were eager to buy it and were offering more than twice what I had paid for the house five years earlier. I accepted their offer. It seemed a bonanza at the time and an insurance against the sharply reduced income I would be earning at Juilliard.

John Michael stayed on at the beach till it was time for him to go to Newport. Meantime, I flew back to New York and from there to Stratford, where I went to work preparing *Murder in the Cathedral*. Since mine was the last show of the season, I had to use actors from the two plays already in the Festival repertory—except for the role of the Archbishop, in which I cast Joseph Wiseman (my Edmund in *King Lear* and the father in *Six Characters*). He was a fervent, perhaps over-intense prelate of whom it was difficult to believe that he had once been the King's hunting and whoring companion. This was more than offset by the beauty, clarity and conviction of his speech. But there were two respects in which I felt the production fell short of the one I had done in California. To accommodate the large company already assembled I agreed to let the Tempters and the Murderous Knights be played by two different sets of actors and thus lost some of the dramatic irony of the double casting. And, to please Joe Wiseman, I agreed to let his wife, Pearl Lang (who had been one of Martha Graham's leading dancers and now had a company of her own), work with me on the movements of the Women of Canterbury. This led to a polite but relentless struggle between director and choreographer which, in my opinion, reduced the dramatic effectiveness of the Women's Chorus. Nevertheless, we opened to the best reviews of the season, and, though I made a point of keeping aloof from the Festival operation, I found that much of my former rancor had dissolved.

For the six weeks of my sojourn on the banks of the Housatonic, I occupied Kate Hepburn's fisherman's shack, in which I lived alone until Joan arrived from Paris with Sebastian and her former school friend Paulette Neuville, who while I was in America had joined our household as combined housekeeper, governess and companion. She was a hyperactive, industrious, very emotional woman, a tireless worker and troublemaker in the best French manner, who had led a life of tumult and tragedy—most of it of her own making.

My reunion with Joan was marred by the visit we paid soon after her arrival to the apartment on Gramercy Park which I had acquired so impulsively the previous spring. What I had described as a glamorous duplex in one of New York's most desirable locations* turned out to be somewhat less than that. In the state in which it had been left by its former occupant (an extremely old, bedridden lady who had lived there under the care of a nurse for a quarter of a century) it looked drab, musty, cheerless and ridiculously cramped for the household of five we had become. Joan grieved for a while, then set to work and converted it within a few months, at considerable cost, into one of the most attractive small duplex apartments in New York City. But there was nothing she could do about its size, and we remained crowded and constricted throughout the three years we inhabited it.

I had promised Joan a summer in California, and, the day after the opening of *Murder in the Cathedral*, we loaded the Ford station wagon (for which I had traded our beloved, much-traveled Thunderbird) with a mass of luggage and a live cargo consisting of Joan, Sebastian, Paulette, myself, Mousy-Cat and Virgil Thomson. Our itinerary included Bryce and Zion Canyons in Utah, both of which proved to be awesome and beautiful, but the trip on the whole was not one of our happiest continental crossings. Virgil was more imperious than usual, and Joan was brooding over the imminent dissolution of her beloved Malibu home.

* No. 24 Gramercy Park had been built years earlier as an ideal condominium of some dozen apartments by a number of New York's most distinguished professional gentlemen, including Rosamond's father, Richard Gilder, editor of the *Century* magazine. What I had bought was in fact the servants' quarters for one of those apartments.

In California we moved into a modest but agreeable single-story house belonging to Joan's friend the painter Renate Druks. It was on a hilltop up the coast from the Colony, with a spectacular view of the ocean. At Joan's urging I tried to buy it at a fraction of what we were getting for our house in the Colony, but we lost it to a couple from Idaho with a previous option. We spent six pleasant weeks there, joined presently by John Michael, who had missed Portsmouth Priory by one place. However, in recognition of his good work during his trial period, the Dominicans had placed him in another, newer school, a sort of annex to the Priory—the Thomas More School in New Hampshire, which he attended for the next three years.*

The boys had a good summer at the beach—their first in many years. Joan, delighted to be back in Malibu, would have enjoyed herself even more if so much of her time had not been spent dismantling the home she hated to leave and shipping things to an apartment that was too small to hold them in a city she had always feared and detested.

Our drive back east was a nightmare. We made it in four and a half days in a heat wave that was particularly hard on Mousy-Cat, who spent most of the trip panting and choking in Joan's arms. When we reached New York, the apartment was not ready; we moved into the Gramercy Park Hotel across the square, and it was from there that Mousy-Cat was rushed one night to the only veterinarian's office that was open. He died the next day, gasping for air. He had lived with us for close to six years, and it took us fourteen years to replace him.

I spent much of my time that fall in the old Juilliard building at Claremont and 120th Street, meeting with the dean, the comptroller, the registrar and Peter Mennin, going over our budgets and setting the academic requirements that would give the Drama Division an accredited university

* Joan, though she had herself been educated by Jesuits, made quite a scene when she discovered how many Irish and how few Jewish names there were in the school catalogue.

standing. Joan, meantime, assisted by Paulette, was struggling to make the apartment habitable and to adapt emotionally to the prospect of, once again, living in New York. John Michael went off to his school in New Hampshire, and Sebastian was enrolled at the progressive City and Country School in Greenwich Village, where his principal distinction turned out to be that he was the only child in his class whose parents were not separated or divorced. It did not help matters that, early in November, I had to return to California to fulfill a commitment I had made nine months earlier from Paris by transatlantic phone.

I had agreed to put on the opening entertainment in the new auditorium designed by Edward Durrell Stone for the California Institute of Technology in Pasadena. I arrived with a title, *The Honourable Estate,* and little else except a general idea that I would present an evening about love and marriage. The next day I called Nina Foch and asked her to be Winnie in Samuel Beckett's *Happy Days,* which I had seen Madeleine Renaud play in Paris. She refused, as usual, then, as usual, agreed. That took care of the second half of my evening. For the first, I assembled relevant and lively material from Shakespeare, Donne, Marvell, Congreve, Ibsen, Strindberg, Shaw, Samuel Butler, Virginia Woolf, Queen Victoria and Dorothy Parker.* To perform it I recruited a handful of ladies who had worked with me before, including Joanne Linville, Betty Harford and Norma Crane. On the male side there was the faithful Ted Marcuse (to play the silent husband in *Happy Days*) and, as narrator and master of ceremonies—myself.

When assembled and rehearsed, the show was surprisingly coherent and actually seemed to benefit from the haste and enthusiasm with which it was thrown together.

Exquisite is *The Honourable Estate* and exquisitely played is Samuel Beckett's *Happy Days.* . . . The first is an amal-

---

* Our texts, besides Beckett's and a number of poems of various periods, included *The Taming of the Shrew, The Way of the World, A Doll's House, The Stronger, Getting Married, A Room of One's Own* and *The Way of All Flesh.*

gam of soaring poetry, brittle dialogue, witty, compassionate and moving language. The other is a wan, tongue-tied, empty string of words. The one enchants the senses, the other numbs and horrifies the brain.

So reported the *Los Angeles Times,* while the rest of the local press found the evening "delicious," "provocative," "delightfully devastating," "sometimes outrageously funny, sometimes devastatingly sad."

We sold out at every performance, and the day after we closed I flew back to New York in time to join the family in Joan's Christmas festivities, which, by now, had been celebrated in Malibu, Santa Monica, New City, Paris and New York!

My contract with the Juilliard School called for full employment beginning on January 1, 1967. Since the new edifice could not possibly be ready for a year or more, I was given an office on the ground floor of the old building on Claremont Avenue. It was a large, dark, gloomy space (normally used as a faculty room) into which I moved with Marian Fenn, who had reentered my life with the title of administrative secretary. Our equipment consisted of two desks, one table, one filing cabinet (all ancient), two telephones, busts of Beethoven and Brahms, and a huge, exploded sofa purloined from upstairs. Here I spent eighteen months working on my book, laying the foundations of the Drama Division and doing my best to prepare myself for the assignment that lay ahead.

This involved innumerable interviews and endless correspondence and phone calls to schools, universities and theatrical institutions all over the country, informing them of our existence and asking them for suggestions and recommendations. It meant humble visits to major foundations and consultations with the Department of Education in Albany; there were also visits to regional theatres and to universities and even high schools that had acquired a reputation for theatrical training. In the course of my investigations I spent three days at the bilingual Canadian National Theatre School in Montreal which the Saint-Denises had helped to create; I attended a national conference in Minneapolis at which the nation's liberal-arts colleges admitted their inability to prepare their graduating students for a professional acting career; I was in Pittsburgh for a week observing the training at Carnegie Tech and the stimulating work being done by Bill Ball's American Conservatory Theatre Company at the Pittsburgh Playhouse.

My longest voyage—undertaken once again in the company of Rosamond Gilder—was to Sweden, to attend one of a series of international theatre conferences at which members of theatre schools and conservatories discussed the problems of actor training. This, the last of the series, took place in Stockholm and had as its subject *"le bagage culturel de l'acteur"* (cultural equipment for the actor). Though, in my shyness and ignorance, I kept my mouth modestly shut during the four days of the conference, I found it absorbing, not so much for the pedagogic information I received as for the glimpses it gave me into the personalities and activities of my future colleagues on both sides of the Iron Curtain.

In Stockholm one thing was generally admitted: that acting students everywhere detested and paid scant attention to lectures or academic teaching of any sort; the trick, it seemed, was to slip cultural and historical material into their heads without their noticing it—as part of their acting training. By way of illustration there were demonstrations by students of various countries from which the Eastern Europeans, particularly the Yugoslavs, emerged with special credit for energy and imagination.

Another thing that became apparent during the conference was the position occupied by Michel Saint-Denis. It was his first international appearance since his stroke, and though he was clearly incapable of prolonged or sustained effort the speech he made, with Suria at his side, seemed to me to be the most authoritative and penetrating of the conference.

I continued my education later that spring when Rosamond once again pressed me into service at the twelfth biannual congress of the International Theatre Institute that was being held in New York. She asked me to act as organizer and supervisor of the *entretiens*, or panels, that were held over a period of three days on the general subject of "Theatre Tomorrow."* Subjects on the agenda included "The Responsibility of the Theatre to the Progress of Society," "Stanislavsky, Brecht, Artaud—Synthesis or Conflict?," "After the Theatre of the Absurd—What?" The undisputed star of the proceedings was Roger Planchon, whose theatre at Villeurbanne, near Lyon, was recognized as the most advanced in Western Europe. But though the fireworks and the eloquence were mostly Planchon's and Felsenstein's (Europe's most distinguished director of opera) and, for one evening, Harold Clurman's, I was impressed, once again, by the respect and affection with which Saint-Denis' brief appearances were received.

Both here and in Stockholm I had taken advantage of the Saint-Denises' presence to continue working on our plans for the school. His arrival in New York gave me the chance to make the formal announcement of his appointment as consultant and co-director of the new Drama Division of the Juilliard School. This brought us extensive national press coverage and a feature article in *The New York Times:*

STAFFING FOR THE THEATRE

Although the new Drama Division of the Juilliard School will not begin teaching its first freshman class until September, 1968, it is hammering out its philosophy now. John Houseman and Michel Saint-Denis, the co-directors, have gained enough experience in their extensive careers in the theatre in the United States and Europe to know in which direction they would like their school to go. Nevertheless, they are fashioning their curriculum with scrupulous care; their objective is nothing less than the training of talent capable of transforming the American theatre.

With Peter Mennin they share the attitude toward

---

* Among the participants were such international luminaries as Radu Beligan of Rumania, Roger Planchon of France, Felsenstein of East Germany and Georghie Tostonogov, director of the Gorky Theatre in Leningrad, together with local talent in the persons of Harold Clurman, Alan Schneider, Dick Schechner and Stella Adler.

professionalism that has informed the Juilliard School's work in music; they feel that training for the stage must be no less rigorous than it is for the opera or the concert platform.

Though I did not cease working on my Juilliard problems, I found myself combining them, that summer, with a number of other activities. True to my incurable habit of scattering my energies in different directions, I found myself deeply engaged in another theatrical enterprise that came to play a dominant part in the next eighteen months of my life. I became a director of the organization known as the APA-Phoenix.

My association with T. Edward Hambleton and his partner, Norris Houghton, went back to our joint production of *Galileo* in 1947, to our production of *Coriolanus* in 1953 and to the Phoenix Theatre's association with the Stratford Festival Theatre in the winter of 1956–57. Since then, I had followed their ups and downs, including the Phoenix's move from the big theatre on Second Avenue to a much smaller house on East Seventy-fourth Street, where fortune had smiled upon them with a brilliant and successful production of Kopit's *Oh, Dad, Poor Dad, Mama's Hung You in the Closet and I'm Feelin' So Sad,* which had filled the house for over a year. Since then, they had met with only moderate success.

My connection with APA had begun in the late fifties when Ellis Rabb, who had acted for me in Stratford for two seasons, combined with his wife, the brilliant young British actress Rosemary Harris, and a few friends to form a theatrical workshop known as the Association of Producing Artists. I was on their board of directors when they opened their first repertory season in 1960, including engagements in Princeton, Milwaukee and Ann Arbor, Michigan, which became their regular summer base for a number of years.

I remember sitting with Ellis and Rosemary in the Plaza Bar in New York in 1962, warning them of the perils of a New York engagement. They ignored my advice, rented an abandoned Yiddish theatre on the Bowery and presented a brief repertory season of three plays to considerable acclaim.* The following year Hambleton and Houghton invited the APA to share their theatre in a full season of jointly produced repertory.

Before leaving for Europe in 1964 I had become involved, as a long-distance pander and marriage broker, in the negotiations that led to the union of the Phoenix and the APA. The following year I was in New York to admire their first joint season, in which they presented *Man and Superman,* Piscator's version of *War and Peace* and Giraudoux's *Judith.* It was a brilliant repertory of three massive, big-cast productions, but (as with my own Pelican season in Los Angeles) their costs were far too high for their diminutive theatre.

For the APA-Phoenix to continue to produce on that scale (and Rabb would consider no other) it must transfer its operation to a larger house. Negotiations were begun with the Shubert organization, which controlled most of Broadway's theatres, including the Lyceum on Forty-fifth Street—a beautiful playhouse built and equipped at the turn of the century by the Frohman brothers as a repertory theatre. It was rarely used and the rent was reasonable.

Since the cost of operating under Broadway conditions far exceeded the combined resources of APA and Phoenix, an appeal was made to the Ford Foundation, which seemed receptive, and preparations were begun to present a season of repertory at the Lyceum. At the last moment, the grant fell through on technical grounds. This was a fatal blow, and when the company went off for its annual summer season in Ann Arbor it had virtually given up hope of a New York engagement to follow.

What happened next was a combination of showmanship and luck. Among Rabb's proven skills was a shrewd appreciation of American plays of an earlier generation and an ability to direct them in such a way as to delight contemporary audiences. Having demonstrated this with his successful revival of *The Tavern,* Rabb now turned to a hit of the thirties —Kaufman and Hart's *You Can't Take It with You.* Its produc-

* Their repertory consisted of *The School for Scandal, The Sea Gull* and George M. Cohan's *The Tavern.*

tion in Ann Arbor was received with such enthusiasm that
"T." was able to bring it into New York, into the Lyceum, for
a straight commercial run, where it became one of the surprise hits of the new season and established the APA-Phoenix
as an organization to be reckoned with in the Broadway theatre. It also loosed the Ford Foundation's purse strings (to
the tune of three hundred thousand dollars a year) and
made possible plans for a full Broadway repertory during the
1966–67 season.

The plays chosen were *The Wild Duck, War and Peace,* Pirandello's *Right You Are If You Think You Are, We Comrades
Three* (a dubious assembly of Walt Whitman material) and
*The School for Scandal.** It was a full, rich, varied season such
as New York had not known since Eva Le Gallienne's Civic
Repertory in the late twenties and the Mercury's first season
in the mid-thirties.

Since Los Angeles had now become part of APA-Phoenix's
summer circuit, Joan and I saw a lot of Ellis and the company
during their month's stay in California during the summer
of 1966. And we watched with dismay as the personal and
professional relationship between Ellis and his wife, Rosemary, began to fray and tear apart. She had been a pillar of
strength for the company, in its formation and during its
growth—a star who received consistently brilliant reviews but
who was not above moving scenery in an emergency or mop-
ping and sweeping the stage floor between performances.
For years she had been turning down stage and film offers†
in order to help hold together a company and a marriage to
which she was fully committed. When she left the company
that fall, or, rather, when she finally felt that Ellis had left

---

* The company, during those years, included among its members—
besides Ellis Rabb and Rosemary Harris—Richard Easton, Will
Geer, Donald Moffat, Nancy Marchand and her husband Paul
Sparer, Dee Victor, Keene Curtis, Patricia Connolly, Christine
Pickles, Sydney Walker, Richard Woods, Clayton Corzatte, Jennifer
Harmon, Betty Miller, James Green, Nat Simmons, Jack O'Brien
and others.
† Including a standing offer from Olivier to play leading female
roles for the new National Theatre in London.

her no choice but to leave, the APA lost not only its brightest star but an essential element of its survival.

In its current wave of success this was not immediately apparent. All the more since, overlapping Rosemary's departure, the APA had acquired an even more famous luminary in the person of the First Lady of the American Theatre, Miss Helen Hayes. To show her allegiance to the idea of repertory, she stepped into such modest parts as the mother in *Right You Are* and Mrs. Candour in *School for Scandal* before starring the following season in *The Show-Off*.

During the winter of 1966–67 both Rabb and Hambleton had wooed me, in different ways and with separate arguments, to assume a more active part in the operation of the APA-Phoenix. Tempted but concerned with the responsibility of getting my new school off the ground, I delayed giving them an answer. But all through that winter and spring I spent many hours at the Lyceum appraising the problems of a theatrical operation that I considered the best in the country but which I knew to be suffering, for all its achievements, from a number of dangerous stresses.

Some of these were inherent in the nature of the organization. From the day of its birth, much of APA's success and many of its problems stemmed from the fact that it was conceived and operated as an actors' company, in which the atmosphere was "sensitive, relaxed and loving" but which, for that very reason, lacked the firm, consistent direction that even an art theatre requires if it is to survive the stormy waters of American show business. Ellis, with Rosemary at his side, had supplied this leadership—although, from the beginning, he was given to neurotic and self-destructive withdrawals and treacheries. Hambleton, on his part, was steady as a rock but too modest and diffident in creative matters to transcend the image that Ellis tended to emphasize—of a wealthy, tenacious, benevolent amateur. It was a union of opposites between whom, during the four years of their association, communication was never fully established.

Whatever problems existed in such a hybrid organization were aggravated by the unendurable economic pressures under which it was operating and from which Ellis had unreasonably assumed Hambleton would protect him. By the middle of that first triumphal Lyceum season, it had become evident that repertory on Broadway (the way APA-Phoenix was running it) involved a deficit of a million dollars a year and that, short of a miracle, no such subsidy could be found in the United States for an independent theatrical organization. This had created an atmosphere of anxiety in which reasonable planning, artistic or fiscal, had become virtually impossible. It was consistent with my own personal history that I should choose this particular moment to join the company, first as a "consulting" and then as its "producing" director.*

Subsequent disasters and horrors should not obscure the truth that the first few months of our association were exciting and satisfying and that, after Orson Welles, Ellis Rabb remains the most creative and stimulating theatrical partner I ever worked with.

I have described my first excited encounter, in Paris, with the plays of Ghelderode. It so happened that Rabb, quite independently, had received the same impression from reading them in translation. In *Pantagleize,* in particular, he felt he had discovered the perfect play with which to open his new season. He asked me to be his co-director, and we spent two long weekends in a borrowed house at Montauk Point working around the clock, drastically editing the text of the British translation which we were trying to adapt to current American theatrical usage.

Pantagleize is described by its author as "a farce to make you sad." Its main character is an innocent Everyman whose casual remark that "it's a lovely day" triggers a revolution and projects him into the thick of a fantastic and, finally, tragic destiny. Our production was called variously an "intellectual charade," "a major work of twentieth century European drama" and "a tale told by an idiot signifying everything." And it was consistently thrilling to work on.

We held a number of readings and rehearsals during the

* For which I received the sum of fifteen thousand dollars a year.

late spring on the stage of the Lyceum. Though Ellis was generous in giving me first place on the directing credit of *Pantagleize,* the production was really his in its general conception and in most of the details of its execution. Frequently, during our early stages in New York and in the final days and nights of rehearsal in Los Angeles, where we opened, I had the eerie sensation of having suddenly gone back thirty years and of fulfilling a function that was almost identical with the part I had played during my association with Welles at the Mercury.* At that time it had been my responsibility "to protect him from exhaustion and confusion and to disentangle the essentials of his production (and of his own performance) from that obsessive preoccupation with subjective and destructive detail in which he was inclined to seek refuge when fatigue and self-doubt had finally begun to wear him down." Once again, considering my normally competitive attitude, I was surprised by the ungrudging willingness with which I subordinated myself to an associate whom I considered superior to myself in imagination and creative capacity.

Since it had been decided to open the APA's Los Angeles season with *The Wild Duck,* followed by Miss Hayes in *The Show-Off,* I did not go with the company to California. Instead—believe it or not—I spent the next four weeks in Stratford, Connecticut, directing *Macbeth,* a play I had long disliked and feared.†

Except for my two stars, my cast was once again drawn from the existing Festival Company, which was already weary from rehearsing and performing *Midsummer Night's Dream* and *The Merchant of Venice.* My Thane was John Colicos, a strong young Canadian actor who had been with us at the Festival in 1957 and '58.‡ For my Lady Macbeth I made the

* See *Run-Through,* p. 232.
† Welles made it work for us in Harlem by wrapping it up in a thrilling and theatrical atmosphere of voodoo magic. (See *Run-Through,* pp. 184–86.)
‡ He had played a raging Leontes in *Winter's Tale* and replaced Alfred Drake as Benedick in the final weeks of our Hepburn tour. More recently he had been an impressive Lear in Ontario.

eccentric choice of a beautiful young woman by the name of Carrie Nye whom I had admired as Cassandra in Cacoyannis' production of *Trojan Women*. One reason for casting her was my desire to emphasize the strong sexual attraction between that ambitious, neurotic, blood-stained couple.

It was a hot summer, and Miss Nye's rehearsal costumes were a series of pastel-colored bikinis in which she flaunted her perfect blond figure under the nose of her lecherous but frustrated and increasingly disturbed Greek-Canadian partner, who was busy masking his own insecurity under a show of contemptuous arrogance that ended by marring both his own performance and their relationship onstage. This was further aggravated by the lack of unity and purpose in the production with which I surrounded them. For my sets and costumes I turned, once again, to Rouben Ter-Arutunian, who was in his metallic, false-perspective period: the foreshortened, gleaming metal walls with which he enclosed his sharply ramped white platform were lethal and terrifying, but by midevening they had become constricting and monotonous. Our costumes, for which I must take much of the blame, were "modern" and suggestive of contemporary military and political violence.

Our opening was tense and underrehearsed, and our reviews were mixed: one critic wrote of Colicos that he played the first half of the tragedy in imitation of Laurence Olivier and the second of Ralph Richardson; another referred to Nye as the "debutante queen." Dan Sullivan, alternate drama critic of *The New York Times,** disliked almost everything about the production, while William Glover of the Associated Press found it the most direct and dramatic performance of the play he had ever seen. Since he was syndicated in papers all over the country, including the *Los Angeles Times,* his review, fortunately, was the one that greeted me on my arrival in California two days later.

Joan was there before me. She had come out as production assistant to Ellis Rabb and was staying with the rest of

* He later became drama critic of the *Los Angeles Times,* a position he has occupied for many years.

the company at my old haunt, the Chateau Marmont. *The Wild Duck* had opened the season, followed by *The Show-Off*, in which Miss Hayes had scored a great personal success. While that was running, we resumed intensive rehearsals of *Pantagleize*, and once again I found it exhilarating work.

The company was at the peak of its powers, and in *Pantagleize* almost every one of its principal actors had an opportunity to shine. The production was a demanding one: it called successively for an attic; a street; a café; a public square in which the revolution breaks out; the War Office; the apartment in which Pantagleize's beloved (a beautiful Jewish revolutionary) is murdered; a nightclub; another street; a court-martial; the blood-stained wall against which our hero, still innocent and uncomprehending, joins his friends before the firing squad. And it all had to be done with a minimum of scenery and with instantaneous scene changes. It was here that Ellis Rabb particularly impressed me.* While freely improvising, he followed a dramatic curve that had been clear in his head from the beginning, so that, for all our inventions and changes, the play never lost its form or its line. At the same time, within that complex structure, he had to deal with a second, more personal problem, that of developing and rehearsing the enormous role of Pantagleize, who appears in every scene of the play and consistently, though unconsciously, motivates its every action.

Here again, watching Ellis' difficulty in balancing his duties as director and principal actor, I was reminded of my years with Welles, of whom I had written that "suffering more than the usual actor's apprehensions, he welcomed and exploited the technical hazards of his productions as a means of delaying that hideous moment when he must finally get up on the stage, as an actor, before an audience and deliver a performance."†

Orson had William Alland (alias "Vachtangov"), whom he

---

* Working with his team of James Tilton for scenery and Nancy Potts for costumes.
† *Run-Through*, p. 237.

was in the habit of using as combined stand-in, understudy, whipping boy and personal assistant. Ellis had found such a factotum in the person of a bright young man named Jack O'Brien, a graduate of the University of Michigan at Ann Arbor, where he joined the company and soon became invaluable in that multiple capacity.* During rehearsals of *Pantagleize* he fulfilled his role so effectively that it became difficult for us to entice Ellis onto the stage!

Yet, in the end, Rabb gave an unforgettable performance which proved to be one of the high spots of his own acting career and the climax of this startling and unusual production. According to a local review:

> Baroque brilliance and slashing satire inspire as much laughter as horror. . . . You can forget the profundities completely and be deliciously swept along in the mad rush of events that sometimes suggest a Marx Brothers movie. . . . The balance between slapstick and social comment is scrupulously maintained by the directors, John Houseman and Ellis Rabb. . . . Played against a world aflame in revolution, with gunfire, riot, explosions and martial music thundering from loudspeakers, it builds into a terrifying experience, chilling in its portrayal of the modern innocent crucified in a dehumanized world. There is the throb of marching men, the waving of innumerable banners; † the stage is cloaked in acrid smoke as revolutionaries and military, pointless forces, oppose

* O'Brien was also a writer of lyrics. Our final, gruesome military chorus, "Blue Tattoo," which he and his friend Bob James created for *Pantagleize* became a "single" record in the commercial market. He joined the Acting Company as associate artistic director in 1974, directed the successful 1976 revival of *Porgy and Bess* and, later, became artistic director of the Old Globe at San Diego.
† A particularly ingenious theatrical effect: behind a nine-foot-high wall set parallel to the footlights, and some twelve feet upstage along the entire width of the proscenium, more than a hundred flags, fixed on long poles lashed to invisible market carts, were maneuvered by members of the cast, so that from the front, accompanied by suitable sound patterns, they gave the impression of an enormous and endless procession of marching and wheeling demonstrators behind the wall.

each other in a welter of meaningless violence and slaughter.

The third play in the APA-Phoenix repertory that year was Ionesco's *Exit the King*. Written during and immediately following the author's almost fatal illness, it has revealing insights into human behavior in the face of death. Richard Easton, recently returned from England, played the dying King to Eva Le Gallienne's "Old Queen." Rabb directed it, and Joan, who had been our note-taker and production assistant during *Pantagleize*, continued to work closely with him.

I played little part in the production, for I was fulfilling a brief engagement as lecturer and consultant with the California Shakespeare Company at Santa Clara.* By the time I got back to Los Angeles, *Exit the King* had begun to take shape. Mounted in black cellophane by Rouben Ter-Arutunian, it was beautiful and strange to look at, though it was my feeling that Ellis had taken a more romantic approach to the play than Ionesco had intended. Harold Clurman wrote of it later as "an extraordinarily fine play in an excellent production. It is better by far than the Paris, Warsaw and London productions I have seen of it."

It was never a popular success; the aging middle-class audiences that formed the bulk of our public found it too close to their own imminent confrontation with death to be altogether enjoyable.

I stayed for its California opening, then flew to New York, where Juilliard business awaited me. This included a lunch with Peter Mennin, who used these social occasions to impart the latest unfavorable and doleful news. This time, in the basement of the Lotus Club, he informed me that the new building in Lincoln Center could not possibly be ready for occupancy by the fall of 1968, the date on which we had been planning to open the Drama Division. This gave us two

* This was the summer operation of a lively, talented group of young West Coast actors (including Elizabeth Huddle and David Ogden Stiers). I learned more from them than they did from me.

choices: to postpone for yet another year or to open in temporary quarters elsewhere. There was no room for us in the old Juilliard building on Claremont Avenue or in any of the surrounding buildings belonging to Columbia University. But there was one possibility: International House, situated directly across the street from the Juilliard building, was a Rockefeller-financed institution for foreign youth, including a number of Juilliard music students.* Considering the Rockefeller connection, arrangements could perhaps be made for us to occupy its public rooms by day during the first year of our operation.

Mennin advocated postponement. I was emphatic and passionate in my desire to get started. I pointed to the substantial publicity we had already received and to the growing interest we were generating all over the country. I mentioned the many contacts and moral commitments I had made, and, finally, I reminded Mennin of our dependence on Saint-Denis and of the very real problem created by his deteriorating health. What I did *not* mention was my own raging impatience and (knowing the patterns of my emotional behavior) the danger that if I had to wait another twenty months to get started my enthusiasm for the project would wither and die. It was not Mennin's habit to make definite or positive decisions, but I was allowed to continue preparing for a September 1968 opening. And then late one night I got a call from Joan, with the APA in Toronto, urging me to fly up just as quickly as possible.

The Show-Off had repeated its Los Angeles success at the Royal Alexandra Theatre and was due to go on to the 1967 World Expo in Montreal before moving to New York and being replaced in Toronto by *Pantagleize*. A few days before the opening, for reasons that Joan was unable to clarify, Ellis canceled all further rehearsals and announced that he was taking *Pantagleize* out of the repertory.

---

* One of its proudest boasts was that Leontyne Price had lived there and worked in the cafeteria during her first two years at the Music School.

324

At first, when "T." and I arrived in Toronto, Ellis wouldn't see us. The next morning, at breakfast, he was pale and polite, but firm in his decision to kill *Pantagleize*. I argued with him that it was the most successful performance of his career and waved his Los Angeles reviews under his nose. To no avail. He said that he felt the show wasn't right and that he wouldn't appear in it. We decided to wait one day before canceling the Toronto performances and revising the entire New York repertory schedule. Then, late that night, O'Brien woke me up to report that Rabb was calling a rehearsal of *Pantagleize* for noon of the next day.

The crisis was over as suddenly as it had begun, and the matter was not mentioned again. I never found out what had happened—what personal misery or sudden malice, deepseated terror or mysterious inertia had seized him. But things were never quite the same between Rabb and myself, and later, when the APA-Phoenix troubles came to a head and ended in disaster and dissolution, I found myself looking back on those two days in Toronto as a warning to which I should have paid more heed.

Pantagleize opened at the Royal Alex to notices that were no less glowing than those it had received in Los Angeles. Nathan Cohen of the *Toronto Star*, Canada's leading and toughest critic, described it as an "altogether rewarding experience" and credited the APA (together with Britain's National Theatre*) with having contributed to "what is manifestly the best theatrical season Toronto has ever had."

In a manic moment in California, Ellis had proposed and "T." and I had enthusiastically agreed on the bold tactic of opening our New York season with *Pantagleize* rather than with Miss Hayes's far safer and more popular *Show-Off*. This, added to the memory of our Toronto crisis, made our Manhattan opening a particularly tense one—for everyone except Rabb, who seemed unusually calm and happy that week.

Our first two previews had gone well, both as to numbers

* Which was playing simultaneously at the O'Keefe Center in a repertory that starred Laurence Olivier in *The Dance of Death* and *Love for Love*.

and as to audience reaction. But it came as a nasty shock when Clive Barnes of *The New York Times,* on whose good opinion we were almost totally dependent, suddenly sent back his opening-night tickets and ordered seats for a matinee preview two days earlier. We had no choice but to accede to his request, then spent an hour before curtain time debating whether or not to tell Rabb and the company. I finally did, and, after a brief, violent protest, they settled down and gave an unusually relaxed and vital performance before an enthusiastic matinee audience.

Barnes's fine review appeared in *The New York Times* two days later: "*Pantagleize* is a marvelous play; the production is excellent and the whole thing is funny, thoughtful, stimulating and entertaining."

As an actor, Rabb received the best reviews of his life. His playing of the title role was hailed as "an achievement of brain, body and soul"; he was compared as a comedian to Chaplin and Tati and credited with "a performance of sweetly contrived style, beautifully calculated and including a death-scene that in its sheer athleticism might win him the envy of Laurence Olivier."

The company too was much admired,* and, surprisingly for such a strange, far-out play, *Pantagleize* was generally liked and did good business whenever it appeared in the repertory. But our most popular play of the season, predictably, was *The Show-Off,* which opened a few days later. "Unquestionably the best American play seen on Broadway for some seasons," reported *The New York Times* amid unanimous

---

* "This superb ensemble feasts on a series of bizarre caricature roles —Patricia Connolly's fiery, intellectual, mini-skirted Rachel whom Pantagleize loves for a few hours; the remorselessly menacing cop of Stefan Gierasch; Joseph Bird's inept General MacBroom; Keene Curtis as a machine-gun-waving, defiant revolutionary; Nat Simmons as the black leader of the insurrection; Sydney Walker as the educated waiter; Nicholas Martin as the hippie poet; Will Geer in a gigantic masked helmet as the Generalissimo; and Richard Woods as a bored defense counsel—the acting is flamboyant, exuberant, probing the dark currents of the drama for a sort of mindless, inhuman fun."—*New York Times*

huzzahs for Miss Hayes, whose performance was described as "a miracle of sweetly calculated charm."

Variety, in the first week of our season, reported: "The most exciting hit on Broadway is the A.P.A. Repertory. A glittering production of *Pantagleize* and now a captivating revival of *The Show-Off*." Yet, within less than two months, it had become evident that our annual deficit would once again exceed one million dollars and that, with all our successes, we were no more secure than before. Our houses continued to be good, with sellouts on weekends; but our grosses never came near what they would have been if we had been running one single "hit," while our expenses were immeasurably higher and kept increasing as we added new productions to the repertory.

(The bitter truth, then as now, is that repertory, which is accepted by New York audiences for opera and dance, runs directly counter to Broadway's entire theatrical mechanism, critical as well as commercial. The Broadway theatre lives by the creation of "hits": theatregoers, ticket agencies, advertising firms and theatrical unions, not to mention hotels, restaurants and the owners of taxi fleets, count and thrive on them. So, in a curious way, do the critics—or, rather, the theatrical reporters—whose function it is to identify and publicize these bonanzas. They may admire and praise a play that happens to appear in the repertory, but, almost without exception, they review each show by the same "hit-or-flop" standards as they do their commercial assignments.)

With the New York opening of *Exit the King* and with Eva Le Gallienne taking on the direction of *The Cherry Orchard*, my producing activities with the APA-Phoenix were over for the moment. I still spent between two and three hours a day in the subway shuttling between my home on Gramercy Park, the Juilliard School on One Hundred Twentieth Street and the Lyceum Theatre off Times Square, which I continued to visit almost every day to check on performances and to attend meetings between "T." and Ellis at which they both insisted that I be present.

Personal, financial and organizational crises continued to plague the APA-Phoenix and to threaten its survival. I did my ineffectual best to help deal with these problems, but, from now on, my energy was increasingly focused on my preparations for the opening of Juilliard's Drama Division, where my authority was complete and which I was coming to regard, with rising anticipation, as the major, final undertaking of my professional life.

CHAPTER XI

1967-1968

JUILLIARD
THE ''RETREAT''
APA-PHOENIX

"A school is a place to reinvent theatre."
—MICHEL SAINT-DENIS*

MUCH OF MY TIME that year was spent investigating the current state of actor training in the United States. I audited classes at Boston and New York Universities and at New York's Academy of Dramatic Art; I paid a second visit to Carnegie Tech and observed Viola Spolin's Theatre Games in Chicago; I appeared at Brandeis, Temple and Yale and attended conferences and made speeches before such bodies as the National Theatre Conference and the National Educational Theatre Association. Everywhere I went I encountered interest and curiosity about the new school; in

* A full treatment of the Saint-Denis theory and practice of training is to be found in *Training for the Theatre: Premises and Promises*, edited by Suria Saint-Denis and published in the United States by Theatre Arts Books.

exchange, I picked brains and tried to recruit human material.

Other activities included endless meetings at Juilliard in which I analyzed our budget and tried to establish the basis (institutional, academic and financial) on which the Drama Division might be integrated with the much older and larger School of Music. At one of our periodic lunches, Peter Mennin informed me, with grim satisfaction, that the enormous losses incurred by William Schuman's International Season at Lincoln Center had been defrayed out of funds previously set aside for the first two years of the Drama Division, which was consequently in serious jeopardy—and might never open! I had learned to discount such jeremiads, secure in the knowledge (imparted to me by my friend Lincoln Kirstein) that, no matter what happened, the Rockefellers were morally and publicly committed, for a time at least, to support the school. And gradually I came to understand and to discount Mennin's emotional, doom-laden moods, which were partly subjective and partly related to the operating tactics of this shrewd, complicated, jealous and devious man—known to some as "the Sinuous Sicilian."

My most urgent assignment that fall, to which I devoted much of my time, was the preparation of a brochure describing those elements of our training that distinguished our curriculum from those of other schools in the country. By late November I had prepared such a document, based largely on the Saint-Denis "bible." Prominently displayed was the question "What kind of an artist do we hope to train at the Juilliard School and what sort of theatre are we training him for?" And the answer:

We are trying to form an actor equipped with all possible means of dramatic production, capable of meeting the demands of today's and tomorrow's ever-changing theatre—an actor who is capable of participating in those changes and who is, himself, inventive enough to contribute to them. For, in the final analysis, whatever experiments may be attempted through fresh forms of writing, on new stages, using the latest technical devices,

everything ultimately depends on the human being—the
actor.

The rest of the brochure, aside from housekeeping details,
was an attempt to outline how we proposed to train such
actors. Spread diagonally across the front of our handsome
brochure (printed in red and black against a white architectural mock-up of the Lincoln Center complex) was a sum-
mary of our four-year curriculum. Checked and approved
by the Saint-Denises, it was mailed out to several thousand
individuals and institutions, and the reactions were encouraging. By the new year, student applications were pouring in
from all over the country and Marian Fenn was preparing a
schedule of auditions to be held in seven major cities from
coast to coast.* Early in the year Peter Mennin and I had
lunch once again, this time at the Century.

Did I really feel, he asked, that we should launch the
Drama Division in the fall? Would it not be wiser to postpone
our opening until after the move to Lincoln Center? He listened to my indignant reaction and to my proffered resignation if such a postponement occurred. Then he asked me to
express my reactions in writing, which I did with the full

* Among the many questions raised in our discussions two were
particularly controversial. The first was the awarding of a B.F.A.
degree: Saint-Denis was opposed to it on the grounds that there
were already too many theatre teachers in America and that acting
students must make a total commitment to the theatre without the
escape hatch of a degree and a teaching career. The second was the
vexed question of *age:* whether to start training acting students at
eighteen, on leaving high school, when they were totally inexperienced and malleable; or whether to take them at twenty or twenty-
one when they had acquired some emotional and worldly experience
and their commitment to an actor's life had weathered some sort of
test.

Both questions were solved for us by the Vietnam War: students'
exemptions from the draft must be applied for on leaving high
school and were granted only for educational institutions that
awarded degrees. (Ten years later, with the war long past, the average age of the Juilliard Drama Division's freshmen had risen from
eighteen to over twenty-one—with about half of them transfers
from liberal-arts colleges.)

knowledge that they would be passed on directly to our patron, John D. Rockefeller III.

This was the last of our threatened impediments. Our first round of national student auditions was set for the spring of 1968, and, while applications were being processed and divided into regions, I found time for three separate outside activities.

The first was the organization and rehearsal of a small company that I sent touring throughout the Southeast in a modified version of *The Honourable Estate,* which I had presented in Pasadena fifteen months earlier. Of the original cast only Betty Harford remained. Geraldine Fitzgerald took over the part played by Nina Foch in Beckett's *Happy Days;* other new recruits were Barbara Barrie and William Hickey, for whose benefit I added a new sketch by Jules Feiffer.

We opened at Goucher College in Maryland (where the Feiffer sketch caused some offense), then moved south, over the Great Smoky Mountains (where the bus's brakes caught fire) and into West Virginia (where the company arrived on the day Martin Luther King was assassinated). The tour lasted seven weeks, and I was profoundly relieved when it ended and my turbulent troupe returned safely to New York with no major casualty and no appreciable profit or loss.

My second activity was one that was thrust upon me. For its major production of the year Juilliard was preparing a new work, *The Mines of Sulphur,* by the young English composer Richard Rodney Bennett.* It was to be staged by another Englishman, Christopher West, a distinguished opera director who had been head of Juilliard's Opera Theatre since 1963. Soon after selecting the opera and before he had a chance to work on it, West had fallen ill with what was presently diagnosed as terminal cancer. Though his condition was deteriorating rapidly, West tried to keep it a secret, hoping against hope to complete his work on the opera before he was forced to retire. Two weeks before the start of

* One of his symphonies was to be performed in the same week by the New York Philharmonic.

rehearsals, he collapsed, and he died within a few weeks. Since sets and costumes had been assigned and most of the principals cast and musical preparation was well under way, it was difficult, at this stage, to find an outside director. Mennin asked me to take over the opera, and I agreed.

Encouraged by my operatic experiences in Dallas and anxious to establish relations with the other divisions of the Juilliard School, I plunged into production. Costumes were being designed by Hal George, with whom I had worked with mixed feelings at APA, but whose talent was well suited to the opera's baroque style. A version of the set had already been designed and made into a model by Douglas Schmidt, with whose work I was unfamiliar. It was a two-story structure, an "old dark house" designed in exaggerated perspective which I suggested be slightly reduced to permit my singers to walk upright. This caused a brief discord between Schmidt and myself, followed by a collaboration that lasted for close to a dozen years.* Musical direction was by Jean Morel, an aging, formidable Frenchman of considerable international repute. (We conversed in French and formed an alliance, not unlike my relationship with Raymond Chandler, based on our being Old World gentlemen in a world of crude and ill-mannered barbarians.)

Within a few days I had assimilated the various elements of the opera, and, after numerous playings of the British tapes to familiarize myself with Bennett's "dodecaphonic" score, I was ready to begin my staging. The work was different in every way from the star-studded grand operas I had directed in Dallas. My cast was young, eager and malleable, the opera was wild and melodramatic—perfect director's material. And, for a change, I had all the time I needed.

We opened on January 17, 1968, to reviews that expressed reservations about the music but none about the production. "Quite the best Juilliard has presented in a long time," *The New York Times* described it. "This is the modern style of American operatic acting at its best. There was not a lurch,

---

* A pupil of Ming Cho Lee, Schmidt later became one of Broadway's most successful scenic artists.

not a hint of beating breasts and eyes cast to heaven. . . . The cast was strong and everybody was in his part all the way through."

This minor triumph helped to consolidate my position at Juilliard, where, as head of a problematic, embryonic division, I had been regarded with suspicion and doubt. It was good for my morale and did much to sustain me during the Drama Division's uncertain and bewildering first year.

I did not have long to savor my success. Almost immediately I found myself caught up in another venture. My long-time friend and associate Nina Foch had married Michael Dewell, one of the founders of the National Repertory Theatre, which, after years of touring, was about to settle down as the resident company of Ford's Theatre in Washington, restored after many years to its condition on the night of Lincoln's assassination. I was invited to direct the inaugural entertainment—to be broadcast nationally over CBS and attended by the President of the United States. Remembering the difficulties of my Eleanor Roosevelt evening, I respectfully declined. Two days later I went to work.

Script and continuity were by Paul Shyre, and among the performers who had agreed to appear were such old friends as Helen Hayes (taking a night off from the APA-Phoenix), Henry Fonda, Fredric March, Robert Ryan, Andy Williams, Odetta, Harry Belafonte and his male chorus, Carmen de Lavallade and the United States Marine Band.* This time I knew there would be no time problem: since the show was to be televised, it would be meticulously rehearsed and clocked to the second. Our only real hazard stemmed from the presence in the audience of so many VIPs. Throughout the day of the show, in addition to the television crew, dozens of FBI and Secret Service men invaded the theatre and got in the way of production. During the dinner break between the dress rehearsal and the performance, Miss Hayes, Freddy March, Bob Ryan, Odetta and other members of the cast

---

* Conducted on this occasion by the musical director of NRT, a beautiful red-haired lady in black velvet pants named Lisa Redfield.

were barred from the theatre and kept waiting in the rain for twenty minutes until an authorized person could be found to identify and admit them.

The house was packed when the Secretary of the Interior appeared onstage. Facing the empty box in which Lincoln had been shot and standing roughly on the spot on which John Wilkes Booth had landed, Stewart Udall welcomed the distinguished audience on behalf of the members of the President's Cabinet and the National Park Service: "May we learn to love this place as a living memorial to a man. Here some, unhoping, will find hope; some, grieving, will discover gaiety, and many, weary, will rest. I believe Mr. Lincoln would have wanted it this way."

Our show was smooth and lively, but not without incident. Offense was caused in certain quarters by Harry Belafonte's version of "The Battle Hymn of the Republic" as sung by the men of the Union's black regiments during the Civil War. But the main surprise of the evening was the nonappearance of the President of the United States. His place was taken and his speech, between the acts, haltingly delivered by an obviously unprepared Vice-President. It was not until the early edition of the next morning's paper that we learned the cause of the President's absence; Mr. Johnson was in his office receiving the critical news of the Tet offensive, which the North Vietnamese had tactlessly launched in direct competition with our little theatrical gala.

From Washington I flew back to New York and set about making final arrangements for our national students' auditions, which I approached with hope and trepidation. On the quality of the human material we discovered and on the decisions we made in selecting our first year's students depended not only the fate of the school but, I sincerely believed, the future of actor training in the United States. It was a responsibility I was unwilling and unable to face alone. Saint-Denis, who should have shared it, was too frail for the rigors of such a voyage. Jack Landau, on whom I had counted to take his place, could not accompany me for an even more valid and tragic reason.

In the years since my departure from Stratford, Landau and I had drifted apart, but we had kept in touch and occasionally discussed projects, none of which were consummated. When I accepted the Juilliard offer he was one of the first whom I told about it and to whom I found myself turning for advice.

Our collaboration at the Festival had been close and creative—a relationship in which personal rivalry had played a surprisingly small part. I was aware of certain personality problems that might be more evident in a school than in a theatre; on the other hand, I had watched him set up and administer our Festival school under difficult and discouraging conditions with satisfying results. Also, I remembered that Landau had been a student and, later, an assistant teacher at London's Old Vic School, and this would make him a knowledgeable and valuable intermediary between Saint-Denis and myself.

To avoid premature speculation and to give Saint-Denis the courtesy of participating in our final decisions, no contracts had been signed and no announcements made concerning the new Drama Division's faculty. But, for months, there had been an understanding between Jack and myself— approved by Saint-Denis and communicated to Mennin— that Landau would be my second-in-command and our principal teacher of acting. As a result I had fallen into the habit of discussing my plans with him and of seeking his counsel on the school's problems as they came up. He lived not far from Gramercy Park, and one evening I asked him to come over and discuss some question of organization. He was currently working on a documentary series for a New England TV station and was spending several days a week in Boston, but he said he'd come by for a drink on his way to the airport. Joan asked him to stay for dinner, but he said he had a breakfast meeting in Boston and must catch the nine-o'clock shuttle from LaGuardia.

I was at the Lyceum around eleven the next morning watching an APA understudy rehearsal when someone came down the aisle and said there was a call for me in the box office. It was from Landau's agent and close friend, Barna

Ostertag. She asked if I'd heard from Jack. There had been a call from the Boston TV station; he had not shown up for his early appointment, and when they called his apartment the phone seemed to be disconnected. Forty minutes later she called again—in tears. A man from the station had gone to the apartment and found the door unlocked and Jack's body on the floor—dead from seven stab wounds and three neckties knotted in a garotte around this throat.*

Four young men were arrested in Boston the next day driving Jack's car with his TV set and two of his suits in the trunk. To avoid adverse publicity the TV station and its affiliated newspaper had the story hushed up. What was left of Jack's family came in from the Midwest and took his body home for burial. Except for a few people in the theatre who had been close to him and whose careers he had advanced, his passing left almost no trace. I missed him and knew how difficult it would be to find someone to take his place.

By mid-February the Drama Division had received over six hundred applications from students all over the country, of whom we proposed to accept no more than thirty-five. These would make up our first freshman class, and, since I was determined to make this a national rather than a New York or Eastern school, I decided to hold our first round of auditions in seven major American cities, each the center of a regional area. Later we would hold auditions on the East Coast.

I left New York on the evening of March 10, 1968, carrying a horribly heavy box that contained additional applications and two thousand appraisal forms on which to record impressions of the candidates. My companion was a tall, dark,

---

* We recalled later that in recent weeks he had seemed nervous and troubled. He had made a documentary film some months earlier on the drug scene. It had been well received, but now I remembered his telling me that there had been trouble after the show with some of the boys he had used in it, who were now claiming that they had been exploited. This might have had some relation to the fact that his New York apartment had been broken into three times in the past month and, possibly, to the manner of his death.

handsome, nervous young man named Michael Kahn, who had flown very little and who spent most of his time in the air in alternating states of ecstasy and panic. I had selected him finally after much thought and countless interviews to fill the place left vacant by Landau's death. It says something about my own taste in collaborators that they were both young, intelligent, mercurial, Jewish and basically unstable. Kahn* had a more attractive and dynamic personality but lacked Landau's cultural experience and stubborn organizing ability. This tour was a test of his competence and of our compatibility.

Auditioning candidates for an actor-training program is a delicate and tricky process. Young musicians seeking to enter Juilliard do not consider applying unless they can demonstrate a high level of technical accomplishment. The same is true of dancers. For young actors no such test is possible. Since the essence of acting is the portrayal of mature human emotions, the selection of young acting students is inevitably intuitive and subjective, an appraisal of potential quality rather than performance.

Faced with the challenge of assembling a brilliant first class for a school which was still in formation, I had decided, in making our choices, that we would set a higher value on originality and temperament than on the more obvious and conventional standards of looks and competence. Our auditioning procedure was simple. We would give candidates fifteen minutes each, during which we would meet and talk with them and they would perform two short pieces—one classical (preferably in verse) and one realistic and contemporary. If this was not sufficient to tell us what we needed to know about them, Kahn would put them through a number of simple

---

* Born in New York and educated at the High School of Performing Arts and Columbia University, he had produced *P.S. 193* for the Writers' Stage (1962) and directed Off-Broadway premieres of *The Funny House of the Negro, America Hurrah* (at Café La Mama), *The Rimers of Eldritch* and Albee's *The Death of Bessie Smith*. He had directed *The Merchant of Venice* for the American Shakespeare Festival the summer I did *Macbeth* there and had taught acting at the Circle-in-the-Square Workshop and at Brooklyn College.

exercises which, we hoped, would give us further insight into their personality and imagination.*

Our first stop was Kansas City, where Pat McIlrath, head of drama at the University of Missouri, had lent us the stage of the University Playhouse. Our applicants were a mediocre lot, but we gave qualifying marks to one ingenue, Leah Chandler, and to one plump boy with a fine voice, a Louisville bookie's son named David Schramm, who had been recommended to me by his English teacher at the University of Kentucky in Bowling Green.

The next day we were in Little Rock, Arkansas, where a performing-arts center had been in existence for two years and was now being dissolved.† Its director hoped that some of his students might qualify for Juilliard. We rated four of them as acceptable, plus a local boy of sixteen, a high-school football hero named Norman Snow, and moved on to Chicago, where we held auditions in the Jane Addams Theatre at Hull House. Of the thirteen applicants who showed up, five qualified and two were outstanding: a strange, wild girl from a convent school in Minneapolis and a nervous, bow-legged black youth, Steve Henderson, who made an enormous impression on us both.

In Dallas, where Larry Kelly helped us to organize our auditions, we had slim pickings, and we moved on to Southern California, where, for lack of suitable space in Los Angeles, we held our auditions in the Cal-Tech Auditorium in Pasadena. My notes indicate that we found no fewer than seven "possibles," of whom we qualified five, including a

* These were improvisations commonly used in acting classes: "You are going through a revolving door on your way to an important appointment and it gets stuck"; "Sing 'Happy Birthday' in three different situations: to your baby, to your lover, to your dying mother"; "As you are crossing the stage you are suddenly confronted by a huge puddle of thick black mud. React to it." This last was particularly revealing: the timid and cautious ones skirted and avoided it; others, the lively and original ones, leaped or waded in.
† Partly because Governor Winthrop Rockefeller, its principal backer, had lost interest and partly because a student play based on the hideous conditions prevailing in the local penal system had provoked the wrath of the Arkansas legislature.

beautiful, intelligent, self-destructive and troublesome girl named Quinn and a very tall, talented blonde who later left us to marry a warlock.

Our New York auditions, which were open to students from all over the country, extended over a week during which the record shows that we auditioned thirty-two on one day and forty-three on another! The majority were from New York City,* but there were also candidates from New Jersey, Virginia and the Carolinas. There was also a contingent from Florida, among whom we found one of our most unconventional and exciting students, Mary Lou Rosato.

In May we held a last-chance audition in New York City, and when it was all over we found ourselves with close to fifty young people who, in our opinion, qualified for admission. Since it had been decided that the number of freshmen must never exceed thirty-five, the next painful step was to eliminate a dozen or more of those who had qualified.

On our appraisal sheets there were eighteen who, in the joint, often eccentric judgments of Kahn and myself, rated A or A-minus. These eighteen would be taken into the school, regardless of financial or other problems. The remaining thirty were subjected to a second scrutiny, in which we were influenced by considerations that were not altogether aesthetic. We had declared in our brochure that students would be selected entirely on the basis of merit. This was strictly true among the A's, of whom the majority turned out to be indigent and in need of total remission of tuition. Considering our strictly limited scholarship funds,† there was only one way to take care of our needy A's—to accept only those among the B's who could afford to pay part or all of their way. This led to delicate and often painful maneuvering

---

* Which gave us Patti LuPone, Gerald Guttierez, Tony Azito, Ben Hendrickson and others who later distinguished themselves in the American theatre.

† These were set by the Juilliard School at thirty-three percent of the total tuition fees. Of every hundred thousand dollars collectible in tuition, one third could be remitted in the form of scholarships; it was up to each division to determine how these scholarships were allocated among their individual students.

throughout the summer until, finally, on the first day of school, we registered thirty-four freshmen (twenty-two male and twelve female*) to form what turned out to be the most variegated, brilliant and troublesome class that ever attended the Drama Division of the Juilliard School.

Between the end of our auditions and the opening of the school year there was a hiatus of more than three months in which I was able to attend to more personal matters. First, I set about investigating a rumor I had heard that spring, through a former New City neighbor, that my House on the Hill was about to come back on the market. It proved to be true; the people to whom I had regretfully sold it five years before were thinking of moving back to New York, and we now began cagey negotiations that took several months to consummate.

Meantime, in deference to Joan's determination not to spend the dog days in our cramped city apartment, we had made rather curious arrangements for the family's summer. The West had always attracted her. Now, through our friend Keith Botsford, who was living in Austin, Texas, with a new, ravishing, teenage English companion and a number of children from his first marriage, we rented from one of his colleagues at the university, sight unseen, an attractive house on a wooded hill overlooking the town. I drove the family out there in our new black VW station wagon, with stops in South Carolina and New Orleans, and spent three weeks with them on the first vacation I had had in two years.

Unlike Dallas, which I had grown to abhor, I found Austin a pleasant medium-sized Southwestern city where life was easy and peaceful except for the almost continuous hovering of helicopters over President Johnson's ranch nearby. Our son John Michael, who was vaguely considering a medical career, got a summer job in the town's most advanced diagnostic clinic (where he was presently put in charge of urine

---

* Not out of male chauvinism but because most of the plays they would be reading or performing, especially the Elizabethans, had an overwhelming preponderance of male roles.

341

analysis). The rest of the family spent its days quietly lolling around our pool under the trees. Joan, in particular, found it an agreeable and idle life, marred only by the increasing pain in her back, which had been growing steadily worse over the past three years and of which the pain had now become so constant and intense that she was reduced to tears every morning by the agony of rising from her bed. (An X ray revealed a seriously damaged disc requiring eventual surgical intervention.) For my part, I did some work on my book, attended one meeting of the National Translation Center, of which Keith Botsford had made me a board member, and then, all too soon, accompanied by Sebastian (who had to spend the rest of the summer cramming for admission to the Thomas More School), I flew back to New York and did not return.

Earlier that summer, in spite of my growing involvement with the Juilliard School, I had signed a new contract as producing director of APA-Phoenix for the 1968–69 season. It does not seem to have occurred to me that by carrying this additional burden I might be impairing my effectiveness as head of the Drama Division. On the contrary, such was my addiction to overwork that I felt stimulated by my double activity and sincerely believed that the school was, in fact, benefiting from this outside commitment.

It was never clear to me or to anyone else exactly what my functions and my authority with the APA-Phoenix really were, and this was unfortunate at a time when clear direction was badly needed. The 1967–68 season had ended with a dubious *Cherry Orchard* and a massive deficit. Miss Hayes, in a wildly generous gesture, had offered to take *The Show-Off* on the road and to turn over to the company all profits from the tour, together with the percentage of the gross receipts she would normally have received as the superstar of a commercial production.* But, creatively, the company's prospects seemed less bright than in previous years.

---

* This finally amounted to about three hundred fifty thousand dollars and helped to prolong the life of APA-Phoenix by several months.

The main reason for this was Ellis Rabb's own diminished activity. On the grounds that he was utterly exhausted and beset by continuing trouble with his eyes, he informed us that, for the first time in the history of the APA, he had no intention of directing or appearing in either of the season's first two new productions. One, Molière's *Misanthrope,* was in the skilled and experienced hands of Stephen Porter, an APA charter member. For the other, T. S. Eliot's *The Cocktail Party,* Rabb had chosen his friend Philip Minor as director; after which he had gone off to spend the summer in California while T. Edward Hambleton flew to Iceland for the salmon fishing.

Soon after my return from Austin I received a call from Ellis in San Diego asking if I could fly out immediately. He was anxious to discuss the coming season, and, more particularly, he wanted me to see a production of *Hamlet* he was staging at the Old Globe. This was news to me, and when I arrived I was taken to see a final rehearsal of a newly edited, scenically sparse production of Shakespeare's tragedy with a tall, dark, energetic junior member of the company named Marco St. John in the leading role.

It was all quite puzzling and disturbing. I found some of Rabb's staging and lighting exciting, the acting questionable and some of his inventions perverse and ineffectual. (One of these was the notion of having the Ghost played by a handsome, athletic young man, Barry Bostwick, encased in a huge silvery mask from whose depths issued Ellis' own well-modulated voice, prerecorded on tape.) * In its present unfinished version the production lacked a perceptible point of view, and I found it difficult to express an intelligent and constructive opinion on a project which I never entirely understood until it suddenly dawned on me, on my flight back to New York, that this was Rabb's devious first step toward a full-scale *Hamlet* which he intended to include in the Lyceum

* Edith Skinner, whom Ellis had brought to San Diego as speech coach, became increasingly indignant as her written notes on the Ghost's speeches were ignored night after night. She would never get it through her head that, being recorded on tape, the speeches were immutable.

repertory the following season with himself as the Prince of Denmark.

When I got home I learned that we had bought back the House on the Hill for occupancy in October and for only a little more than I had sold it for five years before. Joan, whom I called in Austin with the good news and who saw in it the prospect of yet another major move, was rather less elated than I was.

With "T.'s" return from Iceland (with several oversize salmon, one of which he presented to us) we set about preparing the schedule for the 1968–69 APA-Phoenix repertory season at the Lyceum. It had a curiously complicated shape. *The Show-Off*, starring Miss Hayes in last season's hit, would reopen in mid-August, sufficiently early to permit her to begin her tour immediately after Labor Day. Next would come a brief revival of *Pantagleize*, which, in turn, would be followed into the Lyceum by *The Cocktail Party*, following a preliminary engagement at the Royal Alexandra Theatre in Toronto. Meanwhile *The Misanthrope* would have been rehearsed and opened in Ann Arbor prior to joining the New York repertory later in September.

After that, for the rest of the season, there was a blank—with three possible entries. One was a production of Sean O'Casey's *Cock-a-Doodle Dandy* which O'Brien, Moffat and other members of the company were eager to undertake but for which they did not yet have Rabb's approval. The second was an ambitious and expensive project, suggested by a young Greek director, of Euripides' *Bacchae*. The third was Ellis' problematical *Hamlet*.

It was not a particularly reassuring program, but my own energy at this time was concentrated on the search for a faculty for the Juilliard School and on a plan that involved the luxury of carrying a staff of some two dozen teachers, many of them full-time, for a full year, to instruct a student body of thirty-four. I was convinced that this was the only way we could hope to develop the fully informed and integrated faculty on which the future of the Drama Division depended and who must be chosen with particular care—not only for their individual quality, theatrical reputation and personal energy, but also for their willingness to work as part of a long-term and closely cooperating team under the supervision of the Saint-Denises and myself.

I had done a lot of interviewing and negotiating over the past year. And by the summer of 1968 I had finally assembled what I considered a remarkable collection of teachers and theatre people from among whom our final choices would be made when the Saint-Denises arrived in this country. Before that, I made only three firm commitments: with Kahn and with two members of the crucial Voice and Speech Department.* The first was Edith Skinner, the most highly esteemed speech teacher in America—the leading exponent, if not the originator, of so-called "mid-Atlantic" speech among American classical actors. Her reputation was enormous and her presence on our faculty brought us instant prestige. My arrangement with her called for her to spend two days a week (Monday and Tuesday) at Juilliard and the rest of the week at Carnegie Tech in Pittsburgh, where she continued to teach (though she had been formally retired) and where she had strong personal and academic ties.

To deal with the problem of her limited presence, I named her head of our Speech Department, while for Voice I selected a vital young woman with excellent professional qualifications by the name of Elizabeth Smith.† She was shy, aggressive and sometimes exasperating in manner, but she was a dedicated, indefatigable teacher with a totally profes-

---

* *"The training of the voice is the most time-consuming and difficult of all our disciplines. It includes the mechanism of breathing and resonance, voice placement, articulation, diction, purity of speech and, finally, singing—all this with a view to developing a vocal quality in the actor that is clear, rhythmic and musical. Since our aim is to achieve reality in various styles, we are not after vocal emphasis or quality for its own sake; we want the actor to have at his disposal vocal resources that will permit him to work in all styles including the most elevated."*—From the "bible" of Michel Saint-Denis.

† She was a graduate of London's Central School who had taught at the Royal Academy of Dramatic Art and then, in the United States, at the Neighborhood Playhouse School, the Stella Adler Studio and, currently, the Yale Drama School.

sional attitude and no directorial pretensions. In outlining her function at Juilliard as eventual head of the Voice and Speech Department, I was quite frank with her about the difficulties of the Skinner situation, which she understood and was prepared to accept.

Michel and Suria Saint-Denis were due to arrive from Europe in early August. This would land them in America six weeks before the opening of the school and one week before what came to be known, first humorously and then historically, as the "Retreat."

I had persuaded the Rockefeller Foundation to give us a special grant of ten thousand dollars, with which I set about organizing a two-week residence in Washington, Connecticut, where we would take over the spacious premises of a famous young ladies' establishment known as Wykeham Rise. Here, while the girls were away on their summer vacation, I proposed to assemble all the teachers whom I was seriously considering for positions on our faculty. Here they would meet the Saint-Denises and each other; be confronted with the teaching methods we were intending to employ; discuss and demonstrate their own theory and practice of actor training; and, finally, test their personal and pedagogical compatibility with the other elements of the new school. To aid us in this task I had made an arrangement with Canada's National Theatre School in Montreal to lend us four of their second-year students (two male, two female) to be used as guinea pigs for demonstrations and illustrations by the Saint-Denises and others.*

Teachers' invitations had been sent out for August 16; as that date approached and as I grew increasingly nervous at the prospect of starting an entirely new career at the age of sixty-six, I found myself, for the first time in my life, resorting to a journal. Its account of the school's first months varies substantially, I suspect, from the report I would have made if I had relied, as I have elsewhere, on memory colored by hindsight:

* One of the girls became a film star; one of the young men wooed and later married our administrative secretary, Marian Fenn.

August 12. Suria and Saint-Denis arrived this afternoon from London with their Strasbourg assistant, Barbara Goodwin, ninety minutes late. I watched from the observation platform as Michel appeared in a tweed cap and came limping slowly down the steps out of the plane. Suria and Barbara tried to help him, but he knocked their hands away. He seemed exhausted and bewildered as we drove across the Triborough Bridge through a great sunset to the Gramercy Park Hotel.

August 13. Drove the Saint Denises to Juilliard to meet Dr. Mennin. Michel still vague. Then back to Kennedy, where we found the cargo area and cleared the unbelievable mass of luggage (summer and winter clothes, blankets, papers, books, inkpots, masks, pharmaceuticals, etc.). Then over Throgs Neck to Norwalk, Danbury and north to Washington, Connecticut. Tried to discuss our problems but gave up. Michel still stunned with fatigue. Reached the Mayflower Inn around five.

August 14. Worked in the morning on the schedule for the Retreat. My present intention is to let Michel Saint-Denis start us off with a brief, general introduction— then devote two days to speech (Skinner, Smith and Freed*) and movement (Sokolow, Yakim and Leibowitz). This will give the Saint-Denises time to meet the faculty and to prepare Michel's major statements.

August 15. More preparation—and today Michel seemed quite lucid and lively, but the prospect of working with him in this condition is alarming, especially in view of the protective screen of invalidism Suria has built around him—with good reason, I'm afraid. There is also the delicate problem of dealing with Suria as his intermediary and surrogate. I know that without her he could not function at all and would probably not be alive today, but she has developed a technique of mingled helplessness and intransigence on his behalf that is hard to take.

---

* Margaret Freed was a young married woman who had been one of Edith Skinner's graduate students at Carnegie; we were considering her as an assistant in the Speech Department.

After dinner we looked at 'Abd el-Kader Farrah's*
brilliant designs for "neutral" and "character" masks,
which the Saint-Denises had brought with them, and
selected eight full-face and thirty-two half-masks to be
executed over here.

August 16. In the morning I collected Woodman† and
Freed at the local bus stop; then, after three hours with
the Saint-Denises and some housekeeping at Wykeham
Rise, drove off to spend the night with Sebastian at
Thomas More School in New Hampshire.

August 17. Left for New York at 5:45 A.M.! Stopped at
Gramercy Park for a bath, then picked up Leibowitz‡
and Steve Aaron§ and arrived back in time for a reception given by the very elegant, liberal, sophisticated
headmaster of Wykeham Rise School. Drinks and buffet,
in the midst of which Smith and Kahn (with a grievous
case of piles) arrived from Stratford. All to bed at 10:30
in the young ladies' dormitories. The only complaints I
have heard so far have been of congestion in the bath-
rooms.

Not mentioned in the diary is the political turmoil that
surrounded us that summer. The Retreat coincided with the
'68 Democratic convention in Chicago. According to Marian
Fenn, "those of us who did not have transportation and
could not, like you, get away from it all, sat every night watching the riots, clubbing and violence while smoking some

---

* A well-known European stage designer responsible for a number
of the Royal Shakespeare Theatre's settings, including *Cymbeline* and
The Caucasian Chalk Circle.
† William Woodman, who had been one of my stage managers at
Stratford, had become a director and was being considered as a
member of the faculty and executive assistant to Saint-Denis and
me.
‡ Judith Leibowitz was the director of the American Center for
Alexander Technique, which William Ball had recommended and
which I was considering introducing into our curriculum.
§ A director-producer and an alumnus of the Old Vic School, where
he had worked with Saint-Denis.

very high-class hash graciously supplied by one of your staff."

August 18 (Sun.). First general meeting at noon. Bad beginning. Introduced Saint-Denis, who, very rattled, made a disastrous start, referring to notes he couldn't follow and unable to recall the simplest dates and facts. To make matters worse, his hearing aid was bust. Serious alarm and concern—especially among those who, like Kahn, are meeting him for the first time. Then, slowly, with Suria at his side, he recovered himself. Flashes of his old authority and charm returned. Between them, they outlined the various "disciplines" involved, using such phrases as "the discovery phase," "improvisation," "nondramatic reading," "speech delivery," etc.—which meant little to most of us. A few questions. ("When do we *teach* acting?" Kahn wants to know and gets an answer that doesn't quite satisfy him.)

In the evening—early dinner and off to the Tanglewood Music Festival to see *Elephant Steps.** A long, hard drive. Back at 1:30 A.M.

August 19. Today, amid protests and nerves, the faculty "demonstrations" began. All feel they are being tested, which indeed they are! They are being observed and appraised by the Saint-Denises, by their future peers on the faculty and by me—for quality and adaptability to our program. We began with speech and voice. First, Edith Skinner gave us a sample of what she has been teaching at Carnegie for so many years, outlining the seven rules for good "mid-Atlantic," Anglo-American speech (beginning with the varieties and effects of the letter *r*). She's very impressive and authoritative and vain and difficult, but I don't despair of making the Smith-Skinner axis work for a certain time.

After lunch Elizabeth Smith gave her first elementary voice-training class. She is an abrasive and hard-driving girl, but her work is excellent even though the Canadian guinea pigs' vocal capacities and resonance turned out to be surprisingly weak.

* A new musical work by Stanley Silverman and Richard Foreman.

To the bus to meet Anna Sokolow,* whom I am considering as head of Movement. She is aggressive and defensive and bristles at the very idea of talking to the Saint-Denises!

August 21. Thunderstorm in the night and awoke to the news of the Russian invasion of Czechoslovakia. Locally, things are improving. With Saint-Denis' new transistors (bought yesterday at the village drugstore) his hearing aid is working so effectively that he was following Edith's class and everything else that was said today in demonstrations and personal conversation.

In the morning Kahn, overcoming the misery of his piles, gave a lively demonstration of "theatre games" as a quick, elementary, valuable means of introducing students to each other and to the faculty in action. I'm not sure how much the Saint-Denises got out of it—in view of Suria's instinctive resistance to anything that is not part of their system.

The rest of the day spent on "body training," to which Saint-Denis attaches great importance.†

First, Anna Sokolow did a ninety-minute class with the guinea pigs that left them panting and groaning and everyone else exhausted—just from watching them! I enjoyed it, but I'm afraid it was hardly calculated to allay the Saint-Denises' feeling that Anna's work is altogether too violent, energetic and opposed to the "relaxation" that they consider so essential during the first year's training. Anna, on her part, insists she is not afraid of tension and believes in the building of strength and muscle (not so different between actors and dancers) which

---

* One of America's leading dancers and choreographers. Among her creations are "Rooms," "Lyric Suite," "Dreams"; on Broadway she choreographed *Candide, Regina, Street Scene, Camino Real* and many others.

† *"The training of the young actor's body should aim at physical harmony, balance and, above all, relaxation. It should lead to that state of physical well-being which is the basis of the actor's mental and imaginative growth and of his capacity for expression. In addition to 'Movement,' Body-Training reaches out gradually into the realm of expression . . ."*—From the "bible" of Saint-Denis.

will enable performers to "move into and sustain whatever position is technically and emotionally required of them onstage." She left for New York this evening.

August 22. The first part of the day was Barbara Goodwin's. She took us through *her* version of body training: stretching, relaxation and the beginnings of walking and running—all this at the opposite pole from Sokolow's intensity and strain. On the other hand, watching Goodwin, I was confirmed in the impression I formed in Strasbourg that there is something soft and bland about her work that will need to be fired up and "Americanized" (whatever that means) if she is to teach at Juilliard.

After that, Judy Leibowitz, working with the guinea pigs and some of the faculty, described and demonstrated the theory and technique of the "Alexander Technique."* She is secure and convincing and I could see that the Saint-Denises and Elizabeth Smith found her work compatible with their own. (For my part, as I watched her, it occurred to me that what she was demonstrating might be the very thing that would conceivably help Joan with *her* back.)

After that, late in the day, we discussed "nondramatic texts," but the demonstration was poorly organized and the Saint-Denises will have to be much more specific about the true function of this discipline.

August 24. Flew early from New York to Toronto and saw the final performance of *The Cocktail Party.* It did not make me happy. In the absence of Ellis and Minor (whom I have found idle, obstinate and inept) I did some talking to Brian Bedford and Trish Connolly, about their opening scene; to Frances Sternhagen about her first entrance, which seems unnecessarily high and harsh; to Sydney Walker, who is hurting the play with some "foxy-grampa" playing of Sir Henry.

* The Alexander Technique was introduced by an Australian actor, F. Matthias Alexander, in 1894 and is in general use in theatrical circles in England and the United States. It has been described as "an effortless mind-body exercise that unlocks the flow of physical and mental energy to achieve a higher level of well-being and effectiveness."

August 25. Back to Connecticut for the Big Day of the Retreat. In my absence there seems to have been a valuable rapprochement between the Saint-Denises and Kahn, who, having recovered from his initial shock over Michel's condition, is beginning to take him seriously.

By noon today we had twenty-six people assembled at Wykeham Rise; latest arrivals include René Auberjonois,* Bill Hickey,† and Solomon Yakim.‡ Also Brian Bedford—who flew down with me from Toronto. A thoroughly successful day. At lunch new friendships were made and old acquaintances renewed.§ Gradually the Retreat is assuming the scope and vitality it lacked during our first week. This afternoon we got around to the prime subject of improvisations. To avoid a repetition of last Sunday's disaster I read from Saint-Denis' paper for the Bucharest conference, pausing now and then for comments by Michel and Suria. This was followed by a description of more elaborate exercises such as "transformations," "dreams" and, finally, "group improvisation" and the eventual use of masks.¶

By way of demonstration, Saint-Denis himself donned one of the character masks, with sensational effect. The character he created before our eyes—half-comic, half-

* René Auberjonois (an apprentice at Stratford in 1956) had been a leading actor in Bill Ball's American Conservatory Theatre before starring in a number of films.

† William Hickey, who appeared with Shelley Winters in *Hatful of Rain* on Broadway, was one of the principal acting teachers at the Berghof-Hagen studio.

‡ Solomon Yakim was an Israeli mime and choreographer whom I was considering as one of our teachers of movement.

§ Saint-Denis turned out to be a friend of Auberjonois' grandfather, the Swiss artist who did the sets for the first production of Stravinsky's *L'Histoire du Soldat*.

¶ *"For young acting students 'Improvisation' is the basis of training and assumes the greatest importance during the whole of the first year and the first half of the second. Its fundamental purpose is to make them discover the nature and possibilities of physical expression which, related to the 'inner life' and combined with it, will produce 'acting.' Above all, it helps the student to find the relationship between the truth of his own inner (intellectual and emotional) life and the means of expression through which he can convey this reality to others."*—From the Saint-Denis "bible."

tragic—was essentially the one he describes in his book, whom he created, and named "Oscar Knie," more than half a century ago. As we watched we forgot the physical frailty and the failing brain, entirely captivated and convinced by the imaginative energy of the spirit inside that papier-mâché shell!

A pause for coffee, then off to the ballroom to watch Suria's and Barbara's first demonstration of class improvisation. With Michel's interjections and professional questions from Kahn, Bedford, Yakim and Auberjonois, the two hours were full of electricity.

Afterward, many drinks and a fine dinner of rare roast beef and Baked Alaska. General and private talks in which Michel played an active and creative part. Before long, Hovey Burgess* had half of them juggling and tumbling, while others were having mask confrontations with themselves in the mirror. Others dancing. Like a mother hen I watched all this with proprietary satisfaction and began to feel some sort of a collective, creative identity emerging.

August 26. In the cold light of this morning's dawn I couldn't help feeling that last night's minor debauch was a highly creative occasion. Auberjonois left at dawn for Lincoln Center, where he is rehearsing the Fool in *Lear.* Moni Yakim started the day with a demonstration of his version of a movement class. In view of the Sokolow situation it begins to look as though he might end up as our beginners' movement teacher.

Class work with "neutral" masks was demonstrated by Suria and Barbara, together with some observations by Saint-Denis himself about the relation between the mask and the individual and their gradual absorption into each other.

Resumed after lunch without the Saint-Denises. Michel, exhausted by his activities of the past twenty-four hours, had retired to bed, watched over by Suria. Also without Hickey, who is suffering from last night's excesses. Discussion of style and period, with a demonstra-

---

* An intellectual acrobat and circus performer whose work in circus techniques I had seen and admired at New York University and whom I intended to engage at Juilliard.

tion by Barbara of French seventeenth-century behavior —with shoes, clothes, hats, fans, etc., borrowed from APA. She knows her stuff and did well with the guinea pigs.

August 27. Michel still under the weather and Suria is nursing him. The mask work and the conviviality were too much for him. Obviously he is incapable of sustained effort; we will have to use him for guidance, advice, criticism and occasional star appearances. Meantime, we must try to arrange things so that Suria can continue to function even when Michel is out. Otherwise, in our present embryonic state, we're in trouble. (I might have created this school *without* the Saint-Denises, but I chose not to. Having made that choice, I am now utterly dependent upon their guidance.)

In the morning Hickey, back among the living, gave his version of improvisation. He is full of Method jargon, but I am impressed by the eloquence and intensity of this crazy and apparently inarticulate man as soon as he starts to teach.

After lunch a demonstration by Hovey Burgess of circus techniques. Once again I was astounded at the rapidity with which he gets beginners to acquire the skill and confidence to execute, without danger, what appear to be really difficult feats.

August 28. Final day of the Retreat. This, partly because of my own imminent departure and partly because I feel we have done all we can. Saint-Denis' failure to reappear and his consequent inability to explain and illustrate the progression from improvisation to interpretation made it pointless to hold any more general sessions at this time. Discouraging but not serious. All this will be covered at later staff meetings and in extracts of the Saint-Denis "bible" that I propose to circulate among the faculty.

Later this evening I shall drive some of the faculty into New York, then leave for Los Angeles.

So, the first hurdle—the Retreat—had been cleared. All in all, I felt we had achieved valuable results without which I could not have launched this strange, scary project of ours. It was not as successful as I had hoped, but it was not as disruptive and discouraging as I had feared it might be. For my own part I remained conscious of my own inadequacies, but less disturbed by them than before.

My flight to Los Angeles was for the purpose of attending the annual conference of the American Educational Theatre Association, where I received an award and formed part of a panel gathered to discuss the state of actor training in the United States. I made my pitch for Juilliard after lunch to a friendly but listless audience. The next morning I flew to Dallas, where I found Joan, Paulette and Michael waiting for me in the station wagon at the airport. We drove to New York over the Labor Day weekend—along the Gulf Coast and then north through Georgia and Virginia.

My first activity on my return was the planning of the Drama Division's move to International House and the organization of full press coverage for our opening. I had been promised a Sunday piece in *The New York Times,* and I sent an account of the Retreat, together with photographs, to the magazine section and spent time with the *Christian Science Monitor* and the Associated Press. They all seemed interested.

At the same time I continued to fret over the affairs of the APA-Phoenix. My journal reports that I attended a demoralized run-through of *Pantagleize* without Rabb, but that he finally appeared the next day in time for dress rehearsal and that we reopened that same night before a small but appreciative audience that included Edward Albee. It also records

a long, unpleasant meeting with T. and Ellis, filled with the usual recriminations and tantrums, in which little was settled except the liquidation of *The Bacchae* as a poor risk artistically and financially. This leaves us with nothing for the second half of the season except *Cock-a-Doodle Dandy* (which Ellis continues to ignore) and his own perplexing *Hamlet!*

That weekend I drove back up to Washington, Connecticut, to collect the Saint-Denises and bring them back to New York. The rest had done them good; I found Michel more lucid than at any time since his arrival. He remembered names and dates and had clear ideas about the problems of our first term. One of the items discussed as we drove down through brilliant sunshine was the question of students' dress. At Strasbourg all students had worn uniform black leotards for classes involving movement, and dark shirts and jeans or skirts for other classes. The opening of our school coincided with the peak of the hippie movement, and it was felt by our younger faculty members that a too-severe insistence on uniformity would be injurious. There was also the matter of beards to be settled.

When I got home I found a message to call the Lyceum Theatre and was informed that five minutes before curtain time Ellis had walked off the stage and out of the theatre. The performance of *Pantagleize* was canceled and the money —what there was of it—returned.

September 16. The move into International House continues. Today our furniture arrived—shabby but serviceable, including the exploded sofa. We have reached a compromise about clothing, and Suria and Fenn are out shopping. Suria's multipurpose skirts for the girls have been ordered.

September 17. Following a breakfast conference with the brass of International House I spoke severely to Marian and her staff, including her Canadian boyfriend, about tact and charm in dealing with I.H. staff and students.

Dined with Joan at Virgil's. Among the guests: Boulez* and his sister, the French Jesuit Père Danielou, Maurice Grosser, and Lady Penrose, who turns out to be none other than my playmate of the early thirties—Lee Miller.†

* Pierre Boulez, composer, conductor, teacher and essayist. He became one of the creators of totally serialized and "aleatory" music. In 1970 he became musical director of the New York Philharmonic.
† Lee Miller, a beautiful blonde from Poughkeepsie, New York, was a successful fashion model before supplying the mold for the statue in Cocteau's *Le Sang d'un poète,* learned photography from Man Ray in Paris, sued *Time* magazine for printing an unauthorized close-up of her navel, married an Egyptian prince and became a leading war correspondent before marrying one of the world's recognized Picasso experts, Roland Penrose.

September 19. More preparation at International House. The faculty is drifting in to sign contracts. Also a few early-bird students, looking for places to live.

September 20. Word from *The N.Y. Times* and from the Associated Press that they will be covering the opening of the school. This afternoon, as a desperate measure, I took Joan around to Judy Leibowitz and arranged for treatments which, I hope, will help her back. Anything to avoid dangerous surgery!

September 22 (Sun.). A big luncheon party at Gramercy Park to celebrate my sixty-sixth birthday: Joan outdid herself. Good talk—mostly French. Early to bed—only to be awakened by a call from T. in Ann Arbor reporting a mediocre preview of *The Misanthrope*. I was unsympathetic. All that concerns me tonight is the exciting and terrifying realization that *my school opens tomorrow!* God help us!

CHAPTER XII

1968-1969

JUILLIARD: THE FIRST YEAR
THE COCKTAIL PARTY
THE MISANTHROPE
COCK-A-DOODLE DANDY
HAMLET
ANTIGONE
THREE BY MARTHA GRAHAM

FIRST TERM: SEPTEMBER–DECEMBER *

The first year of the basic professional training course is one of preparation and discovery. Technique, imagination and initiative lead to physical, mental and vocal expression and a sense of disciplined freedom in the young actor. Time is divided between training of Body, Voice and Speech, together with Improvisation in its various phases.
—FROM THE SAINT-DENIS "BIBLE"

YEARS LATER, after the school had achieved success and I had become a film and television star, I used to refer to my first

* The Juilliard School followed the standard U.S. university year of two semesters. Since I regarded this as a wasteful division of time and because the Saint-Denis' planning was based entirely on the European system of three terms to the school year, I had set up the Drama Division's curriculum accordingly, while conforming to the opening and closing dates of the Music School.

year at Juilliard as a time of calm and to the school as a welcome academic refuge from the pressures and anxieties of show business. Nothing could be further from the truth. Personally and professionally it was a time of tension and apprehension, of financial strain, marital uneasiness and endless overwork, unrelieved by the climaxes and cathartic consummations of theatre and films.

September 23. Opening day has come and gone without disaster. All day faculty and bemused students have been drifting in and out of International House—looking around, getting acquainted and studying the schedules which are finally posted. No formal meeting until tomorrow.

September 24. Convocation at noon in the Home Room, at International House. Press and photographers in swarms together with the brass from Juilliard. After they'd left I introduced faculty and students to each other and gave my opening speech—part housekeeping, part inspirational. Then Saint-Denis spoke briefly and well. In the afternoon informal socializing and distribution of free tickets received from the League of New York Theatres.

September 25. Work began at nine with Kahn's theatre games. He was well prepared and energetic and the kids seemed lively and uninhibited. The Saint-Denises were impressed.

After lunch general meeting—mostly warnings about the Perils of New York. Then Edith Skinner kicked off with her opening speech class for the whole of Group I.*

September 26. Arrived uptown at dawn to find Freed, Woodman and Fenn already at work. At 8:55 I led Sections A and B across the street into the Juilliard building for their first "academic" class—English literature under

---

* Certain disciplines could be taught in large units, known as "divisions." Others, such as the Alexander Technique, improvisation and nondramatic texts, were best taught in smaller groups of no more than seven or eight, known as "sections." This is what made scheduling such a complicated process.

Louise Bernikow.* Back to International House for a movement class by Yakim under Barbara's guidance, followed by Alexander Technique with Leibowitz, speech under Freed (substituting for Edith Skinner) and voice with Liz Smith. Some rescheduling will be necessary on account of sound leakage between the International House ballroom and lounge. Most of the girls are already in tights and leotards; the boys are slower and more obdurate. We still haven't solved their problem of dress in the commissary. Or beards.

At noon, reluctantly, downtown by subway to the APA-Phoenix board meeting. The same dreary deficit report; the same gloomy faces of benevolent but aggrieved patrons who feel offended by our poverty; the usual lack of communication between APA and Phoenix. I was glad to return to the fresh, eager atmosphere of the school, where I found Kahn in the midst of his second games class, including some faculty. Great success—followed by near-disaster! At 4:00 Michel Saint-Denis was scheduled to make a brief clarification of improvisation and its place in the program. Instead he fumbled through one of his old "papers," losing his place, repeating himself, ending up in confusion and general embarrassment. Finally, he abandoned his text and recovered. But it was a close call.

September 27. Up at 5:30 to catch the 8 A.M. plane for Detroit. Drove to Ann Arbor, where I arrived in time for a run-through of *Hamlet,* with Easton now playing the Prince.† The production has matured since San Diego and there are the same occasionally brilliant moments of staging and lighting. Easton was solid though underrehearsed, but that's all academic since Rabb has no intention of letting anyone play Hamlet in New York besides himself!

* "We hope that in addition to their theatre training our students will take with them from the Juilliard School a cultural education equal to the best that can be obtained in our liberal arts colleges the country over."

† The program announced that Hamlet would be played on successive nights by *three* different actors—Richard Easton, Marco St. John and Ellis Rabb. By the time I got there Marco St. John had been liquidated.

In the afternoon saw a rehearsal of Sean O'Casey's *Cock-a-Doodle Dandy*. Then early to bed with a vile, neurotic summer cold. Phoned Fenn. All well at Juilliard.

September 28 (Sat.). Another run-through—this time a technical dress rehearsal with Ellis as Hamlet. He appeared, to my horror, in the platinum wig he wore years ago as the Player King and Camillo in Stratford and was deep into his nervous trick of mumbling and gabbling his lines. Between acts I persuaded him to change his wig—also to slow down his speech. But it all remains tentative and distressing. There is almost no communication with his fellow actors.

(What troubles me is that Rabb—both as a director and as an actor—is perfectly capable of an intelligent and moving *Hamlet*. Then what's so wrong with this one? And why does his threat of bringing it into New York fill me with real terror—for him and for the company? I think it has to do with the neurotic, secretive way in which he has approached the whole thing—as a mysterious, personal, emotional and defiant gesture of which he is himself in deadly fear but which he will not abandon.)

Caught the last plane out of Detroit and arrived home after midnight dead tired and discouraged.

September 29 (Sun.). Drove with Joan to New City to survey the House on the Hill. It has been well cared for, and valuable improvements have been made.

September 30. The Saint-Denises were at International House today. (Barbara Goodwin goes back to Strasbourg tomorrow.) Long discussion at lunch about the "test" (also known as the discovery phase) which we are due to start in a few days. As outlined in the Saint-Denis "bible":

> *At the beginning of the first term a play is put into rehearsal (for 2 to 3 hours a day, five days a week) during which the student goes through an early and necessarily limited experience of acting. He is made to work on a play (Shakespeare or similar scope) without yet possessing the technical equipment to do so. It is like throwing him into deep water to make him discover what he can do to keep*

himself afloat. It must in no way be considered a perfor-
mance. . . .

At the end of four or five weeks the student should have
some idea of what he lacks and what he has to work with.
The faculty, on its part, gets some idea of the needs and
capacities of each individual student.

The Saint-Denises insist they have found it invaluable over the years. Long discussion about the choice of plays. Settled on *Lear* and *Midsummer Night's Dream*—to give the girls a break.

October 2. At school, growing problems. With Goodwin's departure we depend more than ever on Suria, who, poor woman, is torn between coming uptown to supervise classes and staying at the hotel with Saint-Denis, who, when she isn't there, refuses to get out of bed.

Spent time with Kahn and Woodman casting for the "tests," then back downtown to the Lyceum for the evening preview of *Misanthrope*. Nice house, good show— particularly Easton and Bedford.

October 4. Preview of *The Cocktail Party* at the Lyceum. The audience seemed bored. Morale is low and I continue to be glum and angry over my inability to get through to that inept and obstinate director.

October 5 (Sat.). Moving Day. Two trips in the station wagon moving stuff from Gramercy to New City. Back for another, somewhat better preview of *Cocktail Party*.

October 7. Started today on the "test." Bill Woodman is taking Sections A and B in *Dream;* I'm taking C and D in *Lear*.

October 8 (2 A.M.). *The Cocktail Party* opened at the Lyceum last night—as good as it could be in the circumstances. Brian, particularly, came through, but the audience wasn't with it. Over to the Sardi Building to catch the early TV reviews, which were mixed. Then, at midnight, the crucial Clive Barnes report in the *Times,* barely comprehensible as we heard it relayed to us over the phone by a semiliterate printer's devil. But we heard enough to know it was wretched!

(11:30 A.M.). The reviews for *Cocktail Party* are not *all* bad. If *Misanthrope* shapes up we'll have enough for a decent display ad. But my gloom persists.

Today at school I got my first students' complaints about Edith Skinner's speech class. It's "too complicated." They "can't follow" her. And today I began work on *Lear* with Sam Tsoutsouvas [the Greek from Santa Barbara] reading the King, alternating with the far deeper and more emotional but insecure Henderson [the black soldier's son from Kansas City].

October 9. I am disturbed by the Saint-Denis situation. I was prepared for limited attendance by Michel. But it becomes clear that their joint input will be even less than expected. For four days now Michel has not left his bed. (A vicious cycle, since this aggravates the circulatory problem that is part of his condition.) Even when Suria is with us, she's only half there—worrying about what he's doing at home alone.

October 10. Continued rehearsal of *Lear.* A pleasant surprise with our alternate Cordelia—Cathy Culnane [the mad girl from the Minneapolis convent school]. Tomorrow, while I'm away, they must work by themselves studying text and relationships.

October 11. Once again, off with T. to Ann Arbor. Spent the afternoon watching a run-through of *Cock-a-Doodle Dandy.* It's rough but lively. In the evening a performance of *Hamlet.* Ellis had moments of elegance and beauty. But his Prince still comes through as effete, false-romantic, enervated and neurotic.

October 12 (Sat.) Flew back early and reached New City at noon. Sheer delight to be home in that bare, beautiful house. Joan and Paulette have done wonders. . . .

October 15. Lunch with Suria and tried to persuade her not to make such a mystery of the Saint-Denis "disciplines."

Then down to Lincoln Center to meet Westerman [the architect for the Juilliard theatres] and Jeannie Rosenthal, who is our consultant, to discuss details of the new

Drama Theatre. I knew she was not well,* but I was shocked by her frailty and pallor—also her evident weakness, in spite of the courage with which she traipsed around that damp concrete shell, full of practical and constructive ideas. (I've hardly seen her since Dallas and since we did the Boscobel sound-and-light show together. She breaks my heart.)

The APA's *Misanthrope* opened to generally favorable notices. This allowed us to take out a full-page display of quotes in *The New York Times. The Cocktail Party* became

"Brilliant, impressive . . ." "A magnificent play brimming with compassion, poetry and wit . . ." "A witty play with an excellent cast . . ." "A provocative evening. Anybody interested in modern theatre should see it."

For *The Misanthrope* it was easier. Clive Barnes had called it

"The best play in town . . . It is timely; its social attitude finds a mockingly telling echo in our society . . . This Molière deserves to be one of the hits of the town."

To which we added quotes from Watts and Kerr:

"*The Misanthrope* is a wonderful comedy and it is given a delightful production by the A.P.A. It is an evening of complete theatrical enchantment that brings back the joy of *words* to the theatre."

"Brighter, richer, headier and happier than anything on or off Broadway, it is the exceedingly rare spectacle unembarrassed by being a masterpiece."

In spite of this impressive display, paid for by a member of the Phoenix board, our crisis was unrelieved. Only the weekly bonanza we were receiving from Helen Hayes's tour of *The Show-Off* kept the APA-Phoenix alive that winter.

October 16. Worked all morning with Suria, planning the long-term transition from improvisation to interpreta-

---

* Early in 1968 Jean Rosenthal was taken mortally ill. Her operation for cancer was major and she was never well again, but none of us suspected how close to death she really was.

tion. Then back to *Lear*—out of Goneril's house into
Gloucester's. It's all very slow, but a few stimulating
things are happening—mainly with Henderson and Culnane.

Tonight I started two letters to Ellis and tore them
both up.

October 17. To the doctor this morning for a checkup. He
says my gut-ache is tension and *gas!*

October 18. An article has appeared in the International
House magazine, written by an outraged Hindu, which
suggests that our students are ill-mannered, illiterate,
unhygienic and totally incompatible with the refined,
scholarly air of International House. It has amused our
kids, but it muddies the waters.

October 19–20. New City for the weekend. Joan and Paulette have plastered and whitewashed the living room
and master bedroom. In the afternoon I drove in for
Virgil's concert at the Hotel Pierre, where parts of his
new opera, *Byron,* were sung for Metropolitan Opera
patrons—a ritzy, tepid crew seated at tea tables.

October 23. To Lincoln Center to Lee Cobb's *Lear.* He is
vain, self-indulgent, egotistical and lacking in power or
grandeur. He seems to have infected Freedman,* whose
direction is overloaded with irrelevant, naturalistic business in contrast to his usually resourceful work.

October 24. All morning at school, planning the critiques
of the "test." Delicate business. *Lear* (heath scenes) in the
afternoon. I shall be lucky if I get to the reunion with
Cordelia.

October 25. Rehearsed *Lear* till five, then general meeting
of the student body to hear comments and complaints
on the operation of the school to date. Most of their
concerns are trivial—clothes, cashing checks and vague
apprehensions about the future. On the whole, I was

* Gerald Freedman had directed many of Joseph Papp's Shakespearean productions in the park. He was later a teacher at Juilliard
and, for a time, associate artistic director of the Juilliard Acting
Company.

pleased and I have a sense that they understand our objectives. So far, so good . . .

October 26 (Sat.). Lavish breakfast with Keith Botsford and Roger Shattuck* at the St. Regis (champagne, melon, chipped beef) to discuss the dubious affairs of the National Translation Center prior to next week's executive committee meeting in Texas.

October 27 (Sun.). Long lunch on the Hill with Henry and Bessie Poor.† Henry is pleased at our return to the house he built for me twenty years ago with so much love; Bessie was her usual outrageous, loving, emotional self.

Drove in through Sunday traffic to Stephen Porter's party for the APA. Talking of Ellis and his recent behavior, Bedford repeats glumly that "madness in Great Ones must not unwatched go!"

November 1. Lear rehearsal, then to Newark and off to Austin, Texas, for tomorrow's meeting of the National Translation Center.

November 2 (Sat.). Long meeting from 9 A.M. to 7 P.M. Botsford and the Center have got caught up in the general conflict raging here at Texas U. between humanities and sciences. More specifically, university auditors are complaining of the loose way in which Botsford has been running the Center—peculations by a secretary, purchases of Mexican furniture, strange voyages and expenditures, including excessive entertainment. Also some of the board feel Keith has been too much occupied with other things. What the hell am I doing in all this?

November 3 (Sun.). From the airport directly to Rabb's. A long, frustrating session. For two hours nothing but evasive small talk. I love and admire him, but he drives me mad. Finally, over drinks, I try to explain how I really feel about his *Hamlet.* He listens, then changes the subject

---

* A member of the Texas University faculty and a specialist in French literature; one of the founders, with Botsford, of the Translation Center.
† The Poors were my oldest and dearest friends on South Mountain Road. See *Run-Through*, p. 89; *Front and Center*, pp. 160 *et seq.*

and insists that the Phoenix's business manager must be fired immediately!

November 4. A meeting with the Saint-Denises to review the final selection of texts to be Xeroxed in preparation for nondramatic readings. (Classes will be conducted by Freed, Woodman and Smith under Suria's supervision.) *Lear* all afternoon.

November 5. Election Day. Rehearsed *Lear*, then went downtown to vote against Nixon and by bus to New City.

November 7. Today we had our first viewing of Bill Woodman's *Midsummer Night's Dream*, followed by a faculty dinner at the local Chinese enlivened by the usual comic, well-bred hassle between Smith and Skinner over "correct" use of the broad *a*—as in "bath," "laugh," "chance," etc.

November 8. This afternoon my *King Lear* (what there is of it) was shown to the faculty. (It's absurd—in four and a half weeks, with green students—to attempt even part of that titanic work.) But I was pleased on the whole: two contrasting Lears, a decent Kent, a nimble Fool and a really touching Cordelia—how much more can one ask? Monday we start on the critiques.

November 9–10 (Sat.–Sun.). Worked on the New City house inside and out. (The drive is blocked by two incapacitated London taxis left behind by the recent occupants, together with a carved twenty-foot family totem pole they've promised to remove.)

November 11. Early to Juilliard for the critique of the "tests," beginning with *Dream.* Saint-Denis opened with a brief review of his impressions. Then we listened while students told us what they felt they had learned from the ordeal. On our side, we have learned more about these kids in a month—about their capacities and weaknesses —than we could have learned in six months of classes.

Meeting with Rabb, who informs me that Brian Bedford is taking over the direction of *Hamlet!* I accept the change and so inform T. when I get back to Gramercy. T.'s patience is monumental.

November 12. Awoke to ice, snow and high winds. An SOS from Joan in New City. The hill is iced over and she can't move, but she's taking it well. All schools disrupted and subways delayed, but at Juilliard surprisingly few absences. At 2 P.M., critique of *Lear*—rather bloodier than *Dream.* We left few stones unturned. When it was over, at their request I played my tapes of "The War of the Worlds" for the entire school.

November 14. Following the "tests" there are emotional upheavals, breast-beatings, soul-searchings. I'm getting lots of requests for interviews ("Can I talk to you?," "I'd like to discuss," etc.). Other teachers report the same.

The "tests" were the last acting they will be doing till the middle of the third term. Tomorrow we start on nondramatic texts.*

Talked with Joan in New City. She is icebound but safe, with enough food for days.

November 15. Spent most of the day at school watching the start of nondramatic texts. I detect a growing ferment and a general sense of unrest. Absences and lateness have multiplied. Yesterday I called an emergency meeting and formally announced that three absences or latenesses (not explained to my satisfaction) between now and the end of the term will result in dismissal. I'm not sure they believed me.

Off to New City for the weekend.

November 16 (Sat.). Awoke in pain and alarmed by an intense ache in my side. It may be fatigue and tension. But I wonder . . .

November 17 (Sun.). Worked all day on the hill, clearing the gutters and removing accumulated leaves, weeds and

---

* *"The purpose is to have the student read simple texts of various sorts— period and contemporary—in order to bring to life each text in its proper character and intention. At first, little demand should be made on the student, whose technical deficiencies in phrasing, diction, inflection and style may be overlooked. The student should, above all, feel the enjoyment of reading aloud to others and the emphasis should be on speech vitality."*—From the "bible" of Saint-Denis.

brambles. Exhausted but triumphant—and the pain is going!

November 19. Back to International House to meet with Julius Novick* about his theatre-history course for next term. My pain was bad again today. If this continues beyond Thanksgiving I'll have the whole region X-rayed.

November 20. Watched Auberjonois conduct the improvisation class he's taken over from Kahn. Good work but less experienced as a teacher. This afternoon an ominous wire from Shattuck confirming Saturday's emergency meeting of the board of trustees of the Translation Center at the St. Regis. At Juilliard I received yet another turndown from Mennin on scholarship money. I shall have to raise at least fifteen thousand dollars personally for student subsistence.

November 23 (Sat.). Late in the night Keith Botsford called. He was a bit tight, said the Texans were out to get him, swore he would fight to the end and begged me not to let them fire him!

When I arrived at the St. Regis this morning, I was shown his letter of resignation, which was accepted by the board, which included Auden and Hannah Arendt. (Auden seemed particularly callous—looking up once in a while from his crossword puzzle as another nail was driven into Botsford's coffin.) I found myself in the curious position, outsider that I am, of attacking the savage tone of the auditor's report. Nevertheless Keith is out. So, I suspect, is the entire Translation Center!

November 26. All day at Juilliard. Everyone is exhausted. Thank God the day after tomorrow is Thanksgiving and the holiday starts tonight. Collected John Michael and Sebastian and drove out to New City.

November 28. A lovely Thanksgiving and a celebration of our return to the House on the Hill. Virgil came out by bus and cooked the yams and carved the turkey. Paulette's Crême Brulée was delicious. Then we all drove to

---

* Drama critic of *The Village Voice* and author of several books on theatre.

the Poors and afterward to call on Burgess Meredith in Mount Ivy.

November 29. Quiet day. Virgil and the boys drove into town. Dinner by the fire alone with Joan. My pain is almost gone.

December 2. Early to school, where a number of AWOLs have been making remorseful calls. Thanksgiving closely followed by Christmas is a disruptive absurdity!

December 3. Order restored. Today I took over one of the nondramatic-texts classes. It is apparent that half these kids *have never really learned to read!*

December 4. Lunch with Martha Hill and the faculty of the Juilliard Dance Department to discuss possible collaboration. Little progress. Limón* is a saint; the sharpest brain there is Tudor's,† but what a bitch!

December 5. All day at school observing classes, especially Kahn's. A brilliant teacher when he's in the mood—I watched him use the opening scene of *Hamlet* as an improvisation exercise to develop a sense of temperature, darkness, general anxiety, and later the "armament" speech as an exercise in nondramatic texts.

December 6. To the doctor to be X-rayed. There is nothing wrong with my insides except a faint ridge of arthritis in the region of the pelvis. He recommends aspirin . . .

December 7–8. Weekend in New City. Herculean tasks—clearing leaves and silt from our drains and filling up the worst of the potholes on the hill with blacktop.

December 9. Meeting of all speech, voice and acting teachers to discuss next term's transition to dramatic readings. Our plan is to spend ten days each on three plays of different styles and periods: contemporary, Elizabethan

---

* José Limón, dancer, choreographer and director for years of his own company. He is most celebrated for his choreography of *The Moor's Pavane.*
† Antony Tudor, choreographer for Sadler's Wells and the American Ballet Theatre. His best-known ballets include *Lilac Garden, Pillar of Fire* and *Romeo and Juliet.*

and Greek. These are readings *without* movement but with a full awareness of text, period, background and dramatic structure together with the beginnings of interpretation.

December 12. New crisis at the Lyceum. This morning Ellis refused to rehearse *Hamlet*—because someone known as "Fred" had failed to serve him breakfast. What happens next?

In the evening to the opening of Juilliard's *Marriage of Figaro.* It seemed crowded and overdirected. They kept bumping into each other. My cold is getting worse.

December 17. Horrible weather. Freezing in the subway. All day at International House conducting reviews of students' first-term reports. In the evening with Joan to see Tyrone Guthrie's *House of Atreus.* Grave reservations about the production, but I enjoyed seeing the trilogy. Supper at Sardi's, where we sat next to Harold Clurman and a young woman he was "educating."

December 18. At school, general unrest and ragged nerves. Last night Ron Baker [one of the Arkansas boys] went berserk during Skinner's speech class and started smashing up the Home Room.

Tomorrow, thank God, school closes for the holidays. But it's not likely to be a particularly cheerful Christmas. I am worried over our finances. Joan takes it hard; Christmas is important to her, and the thought that she can't organize it as she would like for her family and dependents fills her with gloom and fear.

December 25. A fine Christmas after all! The boys arrived yesterday. Once again Joan has wrought miracles. In spite of our financial stress she has managed to make everything look gay, beautiful—even lavish. With me as m.c., innumerable presents were opened around the tree, to cries of admiration and gratitude accompanied by pâté, eggnog, Vouvray and a roaring fire. Christmas dinner at five. Turkey and plum pudding.

December 26. Today at 4:30 P.M., through a phone call from Jeannie Rosenthal, Martha Graham reentered my life. The Ford Foundation is giving her a quarter of a million to "record" her repertory on film—as archives. Instead, Martha wants to spend the money on a TV taping of three major works and wonders if I will help her to produce it. Of course I will . . .

December 28. Drove in for a technical rehearsal of *Cock-a-Doodle Dandy,* which is now, officially, APA's third production of the season. Then down to Jeannie's for a meeting with Lee Leatherman* on the Martha Graham project. It is still uncertain if the Ford grant can be diverted to this new concept. Jeannie looks terribly frail.

December 31. The boys stayed in town for New Year's Eve. Joan and I had a quiet and pleasant *réveillon* by the fire with champagne and foie-gras and Guy Lombardo's "Auld Lang Syne" at the Waldorf in the background. Her back continues to improve and we can dismiss thoughts of an operation for a while.

January 1. Worked all day on the book.

January 2. Went by the deserted school in the afternoon and from there down to the Lyceum, where a meeting had been called onstage by actors of the APA to discuss their future. They complain of the absence of planning and information. Brian Bedford, more outspoken than others, expressed the opinion that it was not the business management but the lack of artistic direction that was responsible for the company's plight. Ellis then announced that he was abandoning *Hamlet* in favor of Ghelderode's *Escorial* (with Barry Bostwick as the hunchbacked jester). Throughout the meeting Ellis never once spoke to me or met my eye.

January 3. Late last night Ellis called T. to say that, "since none of us trusted him," he was resigning as artistic director of the APA-Phoenix.

January 5. The holiday is over. This morning the boys, both full of good intentions for the new year, returned to school in New Hampshire. Worked all afternoon with

* For some years general manager for Martha Graham, and author of a book, *Martha Graham: Portrait of an Artist.*

Suria at the hotel while Michel slept. Visited Roz Gilder and had supper with her.

SECOND TERM: JANUARY–MARCH

January 6. School reopened with only three absences. After lunch Suria took over both divisions in group improvisation. Then at 3:30 Clurman lectured on American theatre of the thirties. An inspiring performance and a fine preparation for the contemporary American plays we shall be "reading" next month.

January 7. Unexpected, gaping absences from this morning's movement class. A big party last night—presumably with much pot.

January 8. "T." (tenacious as ever) has come up with the suggestion that Rabb appear in Alan Schneider's revival of *Waiting for Godot** as the fourth APA production after *Cock-a-Doddle Dandy*. No reaction from Rabb.

Today at school we began our first dramatic readings —*Picnic* and *Time of Your Life*—under Bill Woodman and Margaret Freed. And at lunch I found myself comforting Michael Kahn, whose next Stratford season, which looked so good, has begun to unravel. But he's tenacious and fast on his feet. Down to the Lyceum in the afternoon for a run-through of *Cock-a-Doodle Dandy*.

January 10. First group singing with Roland Gagnon. He's a horror, but he knows his stuff and even Liz Smith approves. Down to the Lyceum for an executive meeting to discuss the fourth show, for which we have taken money from subscribers and must produce. No decision reached. Went with Joan to the Minneapolis *Arturo Ui*. I wish I could have seen the other versions—Berliner Ensemble and Tony Richardson's.

January 11–12 (Sat.–Sun.). New City all day working on the book. I am through my bankruptcy in 1931 and about to enter the theatre. In the evening to the Lyceum for a dress rehearsal of *Cock-a-Doodle*, in which Ellis has agreed to appear as the "ancient Shanaar."

---

* Which he created in America in 1955.

January 13. Interviewed Liz Keen as a possible movement teacher. Introduced her to Suria, who took to her instantly. In the evening a surprisingly good preview of *Cock-a-Doodle.*

January 14. This afternoon there was a sudden drastic switch in APA-Phoenix affairs. I got a call from Ellis—the first time he has spoken to me in ten days—asking me to come over at once because he had something important and private to say to me. I found him lying in a rumpled bed in a darkened room. He said he realized he had made a criminal mistake in allowing himself to be dissuaded from his production of *Hamlet.* Like Lear ("which I played so brilliantly in Toledo") he had given away his power. But now he is taking it back! He must do Hamlet by himself in his own way! As he was taking me to the door, I noticed that there were tears running down his cheeks. Then, suddenly, with his hand gripping my arm, he pleaded with me to stand by him and to help him with the company—particularly with Easton, whom he now surprisingly wants as his Claudius. "John, I'm so frightened," he whispers as the door closes.

January 17. Meeting with Mennin. It has been decided, for reasons of space and money, not to have a scene-design department in the school for the present. I regret it, but we have problems enough as it is.

(Another course dropped from the original Saint-Denis curriculum was one in direction, to which I was opposed in an undergraduate program. Direction cannot be "taught." It was not entirely ignored, however; each year one or more selected students who might otherwise have been dropped as actors were kept on and encouraged to work—first as stage managers, then as directors of student productions. Gerald Guttierez and Gregory Mosher are examples of how effectively this system worked.*)

* Guttierez became repertory director of the Juilliard Acting Company and then a successful director in New York (*A Life in the Theatre, Geniuses,* etc.). Gregory Mosher has been artistic director of the Goodman Theatre in Chicago for several years.

374

January 18. This afternoon, true to my word, I met with Easton and passed on Rabb's request that he play Claudius. He smiled and agreed to do it. Went on from there with Joan to Arnold Weissberger's party: the usual attendance* swarming around Mama's sensational buffet.

January 20. Today Michel Saint-Denis made his first appearance at the school since mid-December to watch the reading-rehearsal of *Picnic* and, after a break, *The Time of Your Life.* Tomorrow we start reading-rehearsals of *Twelfth Night* and *Much Ado* under Bedford and Auberjonois.

January 23. APA's *Cock-a-Doodle* has opened. The press is medium to poor. There is little enthusiasm for the play and not much excitement over the production.

O'CASEY ROOSTER FAILS TO ROUSE

January 27. This morning I visited Michel Saint-Denis in his hotel and suggested that when we do our Greek reading-rehearsals he might want to give the students the benefit of his vast experience with *Oedipus.* He was pleased to be asked.

Spent the rest of the day at the Ford Foundation with the Advisory Panel for Television Programming reviewing the shows that resulted from last year's four-million-dollar grants. Do they justify the vast sums they received?

January 28. Back at Ford Foundation. The quality of last season's TV programs was only fair, with some disasters —particularly the black shows, which were so generously endowed. Hurried over to the Lyceum during the lunch break to watch Rabb rehearse the nunnery scene with Amy Levitt, then back to Ford for the rest of the day.

February 3. Meeting with Capobianco† to discuss possible cooperation between Drama and Opera. He is disgrun-

---

* On this occasion it included Anita Loos, Maureen O'Sullivan and a couple of daughters, Leo Lerman and Gray Foy, Virgil Thomson, Eileen Herlie, Martin Gabel and Arlene Francis, Barbara Tuchman, the Amorys, etc., etc.
† Recently appointed head of the Juilliard Opera Theatre.

tled; Juilliard is not what he hoped; he feels betrayed by Mennin. I think he's getting ready to resign.

At 3:30 I attended the "reading" of *Twelfth Night,* which was disappointing because Bedford had not really understood the purpose of these reading-rehearsals and had spent too much time trying to get "performances" out of inexperienced kids rather than give them an over-all acquaintance with the text and movement of the play.

In the evening saw Joseph Chaikin's *Serpent* with the Theatre of Action. Excellent work on a good text by van Itallie. Good voice work by Linklater.

February 6. Rehearsal of Rabb's *Hamlet,* followed by a board meeting of Bil Baird's American Puppet Association, of which I tend to forget I'm president.

February 9 (Sun.). Blizzard all day, but I made it to the *Hamlet* run-through at the Lyceum. Easton is solid as Claudius, but Ellis' performance remains mysterious.

February 10. Total disruption due to the blizzard. Only thirteen at school, so dismissed them. Down to Theatre de Lys for Marian Seldes' reading of her Agee anthology. Sparse house. Well performed, but the script needs work.

February 11. Got up at 4:30 A.M. to get Sebastian over to the East Side Terminal. Because of the blizzard, no plane, no bus. At school we decided to go ahead with *Much Ado.* Pleasant surprise. Voice and speech are improving; so is the ability to communicate.

February 12. Got Sebastian off and lunched with Marian Seldes, whom I invited to direct our reading-rehearsal of *Trojan Women.** Woodman will do *Oedipus,* with Saint-Denis observing and advising.

February 15–16 (Sat.–Sun.). Out to New City through the thickest, stickiest snow I can remember. Joan takes it all very calmly. A fine weekend with all fires burning.

---

* I had known Marian Seldes from childhood and admired her work as a young actress. She told me later that she wept for days before accepting my teaching offer, because she interpreted it as an assumption on my part that her acting career was over.

February 17. In today's Juilliard mail we received a five-thousand-dollar scholarship check from Ray Stark. God bless him!* Attended Greek readings, then down to the Lyceum, where Ellis is lighting *Hamlet.*

February 18. Lunch with Lincoln Kirstein and showed him a circus class and improvisation under Auberjonois and Yakim.

As I was leaving, Mennin called and asked if I would take over the U.S. premiere of Honegger's *Antigone.* I will—if I can fit it between Drama Division auditions and Martha Graham's film project.

February 20. Watched Seldes' rehearsals of Greek plays. The kids love her. And it was a good idea to invite Saint-Denis to work on *Oedipus.* He tends to fuss and interrupt, but his presence is inspiring.

In midafternoon, down to the Lyceum. Joan called during *Hamlet* rehearsal. She came close to getting killed in the VW station wagon on Forty-eighth Street, stepping out on the street side. Door smashed, but she's uninjured and no harm to her back, which improves daily.

February 21. Lunch with Irene Selznick.† I love her dearly—intelligent, shrewd, loyal and loving (but I doubt if I'll get much scholarship money out of her!). All afternoon rehearsal of *Hamlet.* Easton announced today that he is returning to England in the spring.

February 23. Today, Sunday, we held our first New York auditions for the second year of the Drama Division. Then down to Lincoln Center to a preview of Gordon Davidson's *Oppenheimer.* The acting is less mature than in the production I saw in Paris two years ago, but excellent graphics by Ellie Bunin.

February 24. Felt high all day preparing to rehearse *Antigone.* Early dinner downtown with Joan, Ellis and Eas-

* Later he told me, characteristically, that it had been a mistake and that he had intended it for the Film Division of New York University!
† Daughter of Louis B. Mayer and divorced wife of David O. Selznick, in whose success she was, in part, instrumental. She became a Broadway producer—with *Streetcar Named Desire* and *The Chalk Garden* among her successful productions.

ton at La Strada before the final dress rehearsal of *Hamlet*. No surprises, but Amy Levitt's Ophelia, though still strangely cast, is becoming interesting.

February 25. Readings of *Oedipus* and *Trojan Women* continue, but Saint-Denis' participation, alas, was short-lived. Yesterday he "caught cold" and today he's back in bed! How much of this is in the head? He was becoming emotionally involved in *Oedipus* and there were indications of the same anxiety (so painful to watch during *Puntilla* in London *) that preceded his first stroke.

Attended the first *Hamlet* preview. It went smoothly— except for a few bad laughs in the last scene. I keep giving notes and advice, but I am close to despair, nursing a project in which I have no faith at all. For all his intelligence and occasional brilliance, Rabb's Hamlet is hollow, false-romantic and lacking in cerebral or emotional vitality.

February 26. Early to Juilliard to attend Jean Morel's musical rehearsal of *Antigone*. He is ill-tempered and garrulous but totally professional and I am grateful for his presence. Staging will not be difficult once I have clarified my own ideas. Second preview of *Hamlet*—again with student audience. No laughs tonight, but I found Ellis hard to understand.

February 27. Meeting at Lincoln Center with Poindexter standing in for Jean Rosenthal, who is back in hospital for transfusions. Questions about our movable thrust, for which I want a variety of step arrangements, including a twelve-foot-wide Stratford-type pit with adjustable steps.

Back up to International House for the final reading of Greek plays. Results excellent, fully justifying the grind of the past four months. Some real talent is beginning to surface (Schramm was remarkable as Oedipus; so was Snow. Chandler, Rosato and even Quinn broke through). Nurtured and primed, the group could give

---

* A production of Brecht's play that Saint-Denis directed unsuccessfully for the Royal Shakespeare Company in 1966, and of which I witnessed final rehearsals.

us a really strong ensemble of young actors three years from now!

March 2. Met to discuss the Martha Graham project. Then, through a howling snowstorm, to the usual gloomy Phoenix executive meeting and back to the Lyceum for our final *Hamlet* preview. Ellis was audible but hollow. Did I do wrong, finally, to persuade T. and the board to let Ellis have his way? What will result from this disaster? Will it simply harden him in his perversity?

March 3. Spoke to Jeannie in hospital. She sounded cheerful, but that merely proves her courage.*

Antigone all morning, then at 3:45 the critique of the Greek plays. Tomorrow, without further ado, we move on to a rough staging of the two Wilder plays—*Our Town,* under Auberjonois, and, for those left out, *The Happy Journey,* under Margaret Freed.

Rabb opened tonight in *Hamlet.* My own impression, as I sat unhappily in that supercharged and hostile first-night audience, was one of embarrassment and sadness. It is a pointless, self-indulgent ego trip motivated by some deep, tantalizing death wish. I refused to sit up for the reviews, evaded the party and crawled into bed. But, at least, that nightmare is ended.

March 4. The reviews are as expected. They speak variously of a Hamlet that is "old-fashioned," "unusual," "off-center" and "ludicrous." Clive Barnes complains of a "Hamlet that is no longer a prince but an Oedipal figure lost in a Freudian gloom," one who "comes down to the proscenium at the drop of a soliloquy and speaks like a man confident of winning a prize for elocution if nothing else," in a production that "has no passion and no blood and therefore no life." The company—Easton and Amy in particular—comes out generally unscathed.

Spent the day at Juilliard making final arrangements for our second national audition tour. Applications slightly below last year (due to Mennin's insistence on an audition fee) but still over five hundred. I have no fears about girls; what we need are ten to fifteen strong, heterosexual boys!

* She had less than two months to live.

March 7. Spent another day on the seventh floor of the Ford Foundation distributing another four million dollars—most of it to the larger public-television stations. Once again proposals were weak on drama; music barely represented, the visual arts not at all.

March 8 (Sat.). Meeting with Martha Graham, with whom I had not spent time since we worked on *The Dancer's World* twelve years ago. What a woman! At seventy-five (or more) she is as beautiful as ever—vain, feminine, willful and full of wiles. We discussed the contents of the projected taping, which should be chosen from among the pieces performed during her coming New York season.

Home to New City, where T. called after dinner to inform me he had just received a hand-delivered letter from Ellis formally dissolving their partnership.

Our second Juilliard audition tour started in Dallas, followed by Los Angeles, where we had average luck. Next morning we flew to San Francisco, where we saw the American Conservatory Theatre's *Three Sisters*. (Some queer casting, but a sense of youthful energy and enthusiasm that recent APA productions had lacked.) Our auditions, held in the ACT basement, proved disappointing except for a rabbi's daughter by the name of Hausman.

Chicago next. One outstanding boy and one good girl from Michigan. Kahn and I were able to catch the last plane back to New York.

March 17. Rehearsed *Antigone* all afternoon, then to Ellis' apartment at his urgent request. He seemed in high spirits and apparently unaware of the havoc he has wrought. To my amazement he asked me if I'd produce and direct something for the APA's Ann Arbor season in September while he produces *Macbeth* in San Diego. This was all news to me and I said I'd have to think it over. My only reason for doing it would be the chance to produce and direct Ghelderode's *Chronicles of Hell,* for which I have developed hot pants. We shall see.

March 18. Meeting with Eugene Lesser about a teaching job for next year. Rehearsed *Antigone* all morning and again in the evening.

March 20. More *Antigone*—in both French and English.
Today one of our Southern boys, the handsome, gentle
one, went loony suddenly, roaming down Broadway,
crashing stores, removing his clothes and harassing people. One Latino pulled a knife on him.

March 21. *Life* spent the morning visiting the school and
seemed impressed. Meanwhile our mad boy's condition
worsens. Fenn and friends sat up with him all night to
prevent him from jumping out the window. At noon they
took him to St. Luke's. His collapse has had a disruptive
effect on the school and confirms those who say I am
overworking everyone.

March 23 (Sun.). Juilliard auditions all day.* One possible
boy and one vital girl whom we shall take despite Smith's
dire warning that she has an incurable lisp.

March 24. Meeting with Morel over *Antigone,* then back
to rehearsal, with Liz Keen helping me with simple
chorus movements.

March 25. The school's end-of-term "work demonstrations" have begun. Marked progress in speech and
voice. Improvisations inevitably uneven, though here
again I was pleased with the general level of energy
and imagination. In the afternoon, interviews with
our "threatened" students, then rehearsed *Antigone* till
midnight.

March 27. Easter vacation has begun. The office is abandoned—untidy and silent except for phones ringing,
mostly about auditions. Breakfast with Kirstein and
lunch at the Plaza with Robert Lantz, the agent, to find
out (in view of the APA-Phoenix debacle) if he's interested in representing me for theatrical work. (He isn't.
He spent most of lunch on the phone with Mike Nichols,
who is his client and who was on location somewhere in
Mexico.)

By 3 I was back uptown, still without an agent, rehearsing *Antigone:* our Chorus is unprepared and inadequate

* Our New York auditions were held on Sundays to permit the
faculty to attend.

FINAL DRESS

in numbers. Complained to Morel and went on rehearsing the principals till 9, when I stopped in sheer exhaustion.

March 28. Meeting about the Martha Graham taping with Poindexter, John Butler* and Leatherman. Then back up to Juilliard to work on the *Antigone* projections. I hope to Christ they work! Rehearsed till 10 P.M., then to the Chelsea Hotel for the tail end of Virgil's dinner party. Joan reported good food and fine wines. Boulez explained to me that Honegger, being Swiss, composed *Antigone* "with a *Swiss accent.*"

April 2. Lunch meeting with Leatherman and Pat Birch† to organize the Graham taping. It's too early to involve Martha, who is facing the imminent threat of her New York season.

April 3. Checked *Antigone* slides and rehearsed till 6. On the way to New City with the boys, stopped on upper Broadway to collect Russian Easter delicacies—*paska* and *kulich.*

April 5–6 (Sat.–Sun.). Joan's Easter eggs are more beautiful than ever and my forsythia is out! Put the boys to work collecting leaves, fallen trees, brush, etc., followed by a trip to the dump and a climb to the waterfall by the males of the family. A fine view of the river.

In the evening Auberjonois called. He has been summoned to California for Altman's film—*Brewster McCloud*—in which he stars, and he won't be able to finish directing *Our Town* for the School. Reluctantly but magnanimously I offered to take it over.

April 7. Joan drove me to the early bus and I was at International House before 9. By noon I was at City

---

* Butler was a former Graham dancer, a choreographer with considerable television experience, who had worked on *Seven Lively Arts* in 1957.
† Dancer, choreographer and director. She studied with Martha Graham, was "Anybody's" in *West Side Story* and choreographer of *You're a Good Man, Charlie Brown, The Me Nobody Knows* and *Grease* on stage and screen. At this time she was with the Graham Company as dance director.

Center watching Martha Graham rehearse "Cortege of
Eagles" and a new piece, "Archaic Hours," with décor by
Jean Rosenthal which she was not there to light.

THIRD TERM: APRIL–JUNE

April 8. Group I is back looking more tired than when
they left.

Rehearsed *Antigone* with orchestra and from there to
La Guardia to fly to Toledo and Bowling Green, Ohio,
working all the way, in airports and on the plane, to
finish my lecture. Arrived just in time and was driven
directly on to campus. Moderate audience, but the lecture was the best yet and one I can use in the future.

April 9. Up early, reached Newark by 10:15 and went
directly for conferences with Martha. Later, to the Met
to hear a concert performance of Virgil's *Byron*. Rudolf
Bing was there and enigmatic. Back to Juilliard for rehearsal of *Antigone,* then out to New City.

April 10. Back on the early bus, since today I had to start
making good on my promise to take over from Auberjonois, directing *Our Town.*

April 11. Work on *Our Town* and *Antigone* and to Graham's opening in the evening.

April 12. A radiant spring day with beginnings of dog-
wood. Worked on the book and in my neglected garden,
then drove in for Martha's second night. Found her in a
fearful state about her reviews (or rather, her lack of
reviews) and her own physical condition; she announced
backstage that she had no intention of doing the film!

April 13. Work on book and garden. Ellis came to dinner
with Elizabeth Ashley. (He is writing a play about the
middle age of Peter Pan in which Mr. Darling, Wendy's
father, is modeled after me.)

April 14. Drove in early to check the new slides for *Antigone.* Friday, during rehearsal, the plastic trays melted,
destroying both carousel and slides! Worked on *Our
Town* in the afternoon, then back to Juilliard for a dress

rehearsal of *Antigone*—still without slides. The girls' wigs are a disgrace and the orchestra is out of balance, but I have faith in Morel. Utterly exhausted, spent the night in my cell at International House.

April 15. Early to my office for student interviews and to receive Marian Fenn's resignation! She is going west at the end of this month with our former Canadian guinea pig. Frankly I'm only half sorry; she has been of enormous help and I'm really fond of her, sour-puss that she is. But I must stop trying to run the school entirely with my own personal team. For months now I have been in a constant state of exhaustion. I can't abuse my health forever. (Or can I?) Worked on *Our Town* and then on a full dress rehearsal of *Antigone* in two languages.

April 16. Rehearsed *Our Town* for three hours, then across the street for final check on *Antigone*. Among my opening-night telegrams, one that devastated me:

> BEST WISHES AND ALL MY LOVE. HOPE I'M THERE TO SEE IT.
>
> JEAN ROSENTHAL

Immediately after taking my bow I drove home to New City with Joan, who raged all the way about the vulgarity of the *Antigone* costumes.

April 18. The *Antigone* reviews are okay for the piece and excellent for the production, but they are overshadowed by the news from Miss Graham. Ever since her opening night, the question of her appearance in the film has been moving toward a crisis. On my return to Juilliard today there were three messages from Lee Leatherman —all urgent. The last one informed me that "Martha finally and categorically refuses to appear in the film."

I called her and we talked for forty minutes during which she ran the full range of her Tragic Muse performance. Finally she let herself be persuaded: "John, I promise you—I'll go to the country for three days and get in shape!" We discussed specifics—casting, costumes, etc. I so informed Leatherman. But when I got back to New City, there was another urgent message. Half an hour after the end of our talk, Martha had called Leatherman and screamed at him for an hour, complaining, "Houseman is forcing me! You're all forcing me!" She forbade him ever to mention the film to her again!

April 19. Leatherman called once more—at dawn. Last night's was a good performance of "Cortege of Eagles," and Martha got a standing ovation. After which, at 1:50 A.M., she authorized him to sign for the studio and go ahead with the film!

Worked on *Our Town* for three hours, then closed up the school and transported everyone by bus to Stratford to see a preview of Kahn's *Henry V.* The new, revamped stage is fine, and I feel—and hope—that Kahn may restore some of Stratford's former quality.

Drove in fog and rain to New City. And this morning I had a long talk with T., who is leaving for Europe for a month, so that the final dissolution of APA-Phoenix will take place in his absence.

April 20 (Sun.). Spent most of the day tearing ivy from the front of the House on the Hill, where it has become an untidy tenement for thousands of birds. Then drove in for the final performance of Martha's City Center season, which was well attended. Leatherman says she has veered once again; she predicts that the film will be a disaster and that she has every intention of making it one! But by 10:30, after her ovation and surrounded by worshipers, she posed backstage with Butler, Noguchi* and myself—all smiles and enthusiasm for the project. There was a party afterwards at Pat Birch's.

April 22. To school for *Our Town,* which is slowly shaping up. Patti LuPone will be nice as the girl. At night I read Salka Viertel's memoirs, of which I find the European part fascinating and the California section timid and disappointing.

April 23. Breakfast with Lincoln Kirstein, who hates Kahn's *Henry V,* and then to Graham's studio to see what has been accomplished in blocking "Cortege of Eagles"

---

* Isamu Noguchi, Japanese-American sculptor and architect. He designed many sets for Martha Graham, including "Night Journey," "Seraphic Dialogue," "Clytemnestra" and "Acrobats of God."

for television. It's two-thirds done and it looks good. Back to International House, where three bits of bad news awaited me: Cathy Culnane, the most talented girl in Group I, has fled suddenly to San Francisco; Michel Saint-Denis blacked out in the commissary during lunch and was taken home in an ambulance; Marian Seldes' ex-husband, Julian, died following a very minor operation.

Afternoon showing of *Our Town*. A pleasant surprise. Most of the kids showed more energy and imagination than they indicated during rehearsal. Afterwards, down to the Lyceum to say goodbye to the APA Company before they disband. They still await word from their leader and are bewildered by the various things they hear about San Diego, Ann Arbor, etc.

April 28. Today, almost by accident (since I came close to ignoring her application and then kept her waiting for almost two hours before I interviewed her), I found a young woman whom I shall engage as our administrator to replace Fenn. Her name is Margot Harley; she is half English, half American, a graduate of Sarah Lawrence and LAMDA.* I shall sleep on it, but my present inclination is to grab her. Then, back down to Graham, whose tireless, disciplined energy fills me with admiration. She has been on her feet for two days, ten hours a day, helping to shape "Cortege" and "Acrobats" for taping.

April 30. Today I hired Margot Harley as administrator of the Drama Division.† (Even as I did so, Fenn informed me that she would like to remain. Too late, Marian! She has resigned four times this year.)

May 1. Mickey Kinsella called early this morning to say that Jean died in the night. I knew it was coming, but it hit me like some deep underground explosion. On the surface I go on working as though nothing has happened, but far down inside me I feel that something irreplaceable has been taken from me forever.

---

* London Academy of Musical and Dramatic Arts.
† A position she occupied for more than ten years with great efficiency and unusual sensitivity to faculty and student problems before taking over as executive director of the Acting Company.

Life goes on. Spent the morning having scenes: first with Skinner and Smith, then with students over lateness and absences. In the evening to Martha Graham's fund-raising party, which she carried off in spite of the news about Jean. At supper I was seated at Graham's left and watched her, fascinated, in her new black-and-gold dress, as she played Cleopatra to Nureyev's Antony and then moved around from one guest to another making each one feel, for a moment, loved and admired. Later one of the guests broke his leg on the dance floor and was taken away in an ambulance.

May 2. Early this morning Jean's brother called and asked me if I would deliver the eulogy at tomorrow's memorial for Jean. Of course I will.

Spent most of the day with Harley, beginning her indoctrination. Then home early to New City to work on my tribute to Jean.

May 3. Up at 4:30 A.M. to work on the eulogy. (What unspeakable creatures we are! Here I am, bowed with grief, desolation and despair over Jeannie's death. Yet, this morning, all this was mingled with the almost pleasurable excitement I felt at the challenge of delivering a eulogy that will be admired, remembered and quoted by Jean's friends.)

After the ceremony I drove back with Martha to her studio for a run-through and blocking for all three of the shows we're about to tape.

Home to New City and slept fitfully, thinking all night of Jeannie.

May 5. To Astoria for the first day of the Martha Graham taping. We missed Jeannie. Some excessive, vulgar light effects had to be got rid of without hurting feelings. By early afternoon we had one good take on the warrior sequence of "Cortege," then worked until seven for an acceptable take on the opening. We'll try again in the morning and should start on "Seraphic Dialogue" in the afternoon.

May 6. Today at school I asked Edith Skinner (who has just received a Mellon Award for "preeminence in her field") if it were true she was leaving us. She denied it.

On to Brooklyn, where we taped "Seraphic Dialogue" all day. Suria sat with me in the control room for a while. (Saint-Denis has not been near the school for two weeks, and Suria comes only every other day.)

May 7. Another hard day in Brooklyn, taping "Acrobats." Martha was in great form and improved in temper and energy as the day wore on. Taped two sections by lunchtime, the last two by 9:30 P.M. (The dancers were dead but so disciplined that no fatigue showed on the screen.) Drove to New City to find Joan in a gloom over our finances. This comes at a bad time. I am tired and vulnerable and, with the demise of the APA-Phoenix, I see no steady additional income.

May 9. Last day of Graham taping. The excitement of the fresh medium has given Martha new life. I hope this works for her and that we can record a few more of the great ones—perhaps even "Clytemnestra"—before it's too late.

Following the taping I started to record the narration we'd prepared. At which point a curious and alarming thing happened. Suddenly, *for the first time in thirty years, my stammer returned!* I couldn't get past the *p* in "people"! Embarrassment and terror! I sent someone out for a glass of whiskey. Thirty seconds after downing it, all trace of my stammer had disappeared!

Home in New City by 11:20 to find a delicious cold supper awaiting me and the most beautiful tulips and lilac from the garden by my bedside with a loving note from Joan.

May 12. All morning at school cleaning up messes and meeting with Suria. Michel's condition grows steadily worse. Lunch at the Century with Joe Barnes to talk about the book and to prepare him for its inordinate length. (One of his colleagues at Simon and Schuster has already questioned whether my life really warrants more than one volume!) Back to International House in time to take a long-distance call from Helen Hayes in California. She informed me, in "T.'s" absence, that she and Jimmy Stewart are eager to revive *Harvey* on Broadway next season for the Phoenix! So, once more, miraculously, T. and his Phoenix will rise from the ashes. Not so APA, I fear. . . .

May 14. This morning Skinner sought me out to tell me, with tears in her eyes, what a wonderful class she'd just had and that, despite Carnegie's blandishments, she *will* be with us next year!

Long Chinese lunch with film critic Pauline Kael, who is doing a piece for *The New Yorker* on the authorship of *Citizen Kane* and seems highly agitated over her "discovery" of Herman Mankiewicz.* I gave her all the information I had and will send her more. (Without being disloyal to Orson I am glad that Mank's essential role in the making of that great film is finally to be recognized.) †

Back to school and another minor drama. In improvisation this morning the beautiful and touching but hopeless Woudjie Dwyer ran out of class, scribbled a note resigning from the school and was later found by the police standing in the middle of a busy street "trying to get hit by a car." The sad thing is that she is already marked for dismissal.

May 19. A turbulent day at school, ending with a faculty meeting to make final decisions on eliminations. Almost every student has his or her last-ditch defender on the faculty. Then across to the main theatre for a general faculty meeting of the entire Juilliard School, followed by the annual year-end reception onstage. Many famous faces.

May 25. Glancing over our tests in theatre history, I am appalled by their incredible illiteracy.‡ Again this raises

---

* See *Run-Through,* pp. 447–61.
† Kael's *New Yorker* pieces were later published as *The Citizen Kane Book,* which created considerable uproar in professional film circles. Her facts were correct and well researched, but, in her excitement over vindicating Mankiewicz, I have always felt she ended up underestimating Orson's contribution to the tone and quality of *Citizen Kane.*
‡ Under the guise of "doing one's thing," many students had virtually given up reading during those troubled years. I asked one bright girl, who had read a lot in high school, why she had stopped. "It might affect my thinking," she said.

the question of whether we are just an actor-training school or something more.

May 26. Back down to Lincoln Center to try to solve our sight lines problem in the Drama Theatre by reducing the thrust and slightly raising our seats. From there to Gramercy Park to meet Elizabeth Ashley, who is looking for a New York apartment. She found ours too small for her.

June 2. Visit to Roz Gilder, who is preparing to leave for the annual ITI meeting in Budapest. Then, meeting at Gramercy with Stark Hesseltine,* who heard of the apartment from Liz Ashley and is ready to buy it immediately for seventy-five thousand dollars. I might have got more, but I am relieved to be rid of it without loss (including the forty thousand dollars Joan spent on remodeling and decorating). So—yet another one of our homes is dissolved, but this will ease the financial bind that has been harassing us all year.

June 4. All day at school, meeting with individual members of Group I. The "liquidations" will be painful but salutary.

At 6 Joan picked me up and we drove across town to Gracie Mansion for the Mayor's reception for Helen Hayes. A lavish affair with fireboats spouting water, and a fine buffet. Speeches were sentimental but short, followed by dancing in a vast yellow tent. Joan danced with the Mayor; she looked lovely with her Lalique dragonfly perched on her shoulder. (Her back continues its miraculous improvement. God bless Judy Leibowitz!) Home in New City by 1:30 A.M.

June 5. Spoke to Weissberger to confirm the sale of the apartment and from there to a running of the tape of *Three by Martha Graham,* as it's now called. The room was airless and crowded with tense dancers staring at themselves on the TV monitors. It looks pretty good, and each work has its own style and mood. The color is least good in "Acrobats," which is also least successful in its translation from stage to screen. (According to Pat Birch, who

* One of New York's most successful theatrical agents.

390

rehearsed it and danced in it, "Seraphic Dialogue" is four beats out of sync throughout, but it's too late to do anything about it.) I am pleased on the whole and proud and called Martha to tell her so.

June 6–7. Off With Joan to spend the night with the Siepmanns in Vermont.* Their meadow was beautiful—so was dinner at the Inn. Then up early and off to New Hampshire to the Thomas More School for commencement, which was held outdoors in radiant weather. John Michael won a number of prizes and made an earnest, surprisingly conventional valedictory.†

June 9. The school, in its final week, is bristling with tensions—the main one being the imminent "separations." This afternoon we saw the final exercise of the year—*Winter's Tale* directed by Woodman. Encouraging on the whole, especially speech and voice. Some awkwardness in stage movement and in their spatial relations to each other. This is not surprising, since (as Kahn keeps pointing out) they have had no real "acting" lessons all year.

This morning I had a painful session with Suria. The doctors who have been examining Michel Saint-Denis have alarmed her over his condition—mentally and physically. They speak of irreversible brain damage following the last two strokes. The decision must now be made whether to stay in America or to take Michel back to England for good. All I could do was reassure Suria that this would in no way affect our financial arrangements, including the royalty payments that should take care of their financial needs for some years. What it means for the school is that from now on we must resign ourselves to getting no further help from Michel, except through the intermediary of Suria. It's a blow, but it comes as no surprise and I think we are capable of adjusting to it.

* My oldest friends in the world. Charles Siepmann and I had known each other since 1909 at Clifton!
† Surprising because, in his last semester at Thomas More, he and two friends had put out a disorganized and vaguely subversive publication they called *Black Flag* which advocated an emotional form of anarchism.

June 11. "Work demonstrations" all morning. In the afternoon I began my end-of-year interviews—the easy ones—with admonitions and encouragements. The grim ones start tomorrow.

June 12. More work demonstrations, followed by the critique of *Winter's Tale.* Quite bland; everyone is dead tired and can't wait to get away.

Afterward I resumed my students' interviews—most of them painful. Some pretend to be shocked and astounded at their dismissal; usually it is those who have been the most idle and incorrigible who are the most abject and insistent. Altogether, a harrowing experience which left me limp. Slept fitfully, for the last time, in my cell at International House.

June 13. This morning I conducted a tour of our premises at Lincoln Center, sprinkled champagne over the stage and toasted its future.

This has been an amazing and generally satisfying first year, but I'm glad it's over.

June 14. New City. Stormy weekend with rain and Hudson Valley thunder. Worked all afternoon using the new-fallen rain to check my new ditches. Heavy, brutal pickax and spade work, but I love it!

June 15. More rain. Joan's friend Zoe-e Woolfolk, the celebrated astrologer, drove out for lunch. She assures me that after seven years of unremitting menace Saturn and all other adverse planets are finally moving out of my ken. Beginning next year my future looks absolutely radiant!

CHAPTER XIII

1969-1970

JUILLIARD: THE SECOND YEAR
THE CHRONICLES OF HELL
THE CRIMINALS

FOR A FEW WEEKS, during the early summer of 1969, our family was reunited on the hill in New City. Sebastian, charming and idle as ever, spent most of his time playing with the girls in the valley below and evading the homework he had been assigned over the long holiday. John Michael, having chosen Brandeis over Harvard (in a sudden awareness of his part-Jewish heritage), decided to spend the second part of his holiday hitchhiking through the Midwest. Before departing he received a communication from his draft board, to which he replied with a long, self-righteous letter in which he explained that, on religious and moral grounds, he found it quite impossible to accept their invitation to register for the draft.

This letter, which he read to us with considerable pride, became the subject of heated family discussion. Joan, whose mother had been a student "revolutionary" in her Russian girlhood and who had herself been involved in the French Resistance, was divided between her satisfaction over her son's spirit and her horror at imagining him in prison. For my part, I was not displeased by his activism, but, since his admission to Brandeis assured him of an automatic deferment, I regarded his letter as a gratuitous and self-defeating bid for martyrdom.

Otherwise, it was an unusually peaceful time, in which the House on the Hill was finally allowed to exercise its magic—especially on Joan, who found herself sharing a pleasant exurban existence with a few of her neighbors on the South Mountain Road. For my own part, for the first time since leaving Paris I was able to set up and follow a routine for writing (beginning between five and six each morning and going on into the late afternoon) and to hold to it through most of the summer. By the end of July *Four Saints, Panic, Valley Forge* and *The Lady from the Sea* were behind me and I was about to enter into my association with Orson Welles.*

In my preoccupation with the past, I did not cut myself off entirely from the present. Between my hours of writing and the energetic but unskilled gardening with which I filled the latter hours of those long summer days, I continued my participation in the separate affairs of the APA and the Phoenix. Of the two, the latter was in far better shape; James Stewart and Helen Hayes had confirmed their intention to appear in *Harvey,* and a Broadway theatre had been booked for them in late January. The APA, in the person of Ellis Rabb, faced a more desperate future. For all the horrors of the previous winter and in spite of what I considered his betrayal of his company, our personal relations remained close. In June, to escape New York, he had retired once again to the Old Globe in San Diego, where he was directing *Macbeth,* with Richard Easton as the Thane and Sada Thompson as his lady, in a summer season that included *The Comedy of Errors,* directed by Jack O'Brien. To satisfy the University of Michigan's demands for the three shows that APA still owed them for the

* See *Run-Through,* pp. 185 *et seq.*

394

1969 season, Rabb had agreed to move *Macbeth* to Ann Arbor at the close of its San Diego run. Also on the Michigan program was a production of *Private Lives* starring Brian Bedford and Tammy Grimes which was being directed in New York by Stephen Porter.

Since Rabb had not the slightest intention of going near Ann Arbor himself, he asked me to produce and direct the third of the season's Michigan offerings. My enthusiasm for *The Chronicles of Hell* was greater than ever and I agreed to direct and produce it as an APA production, sponsored by the University of Michigan. Since it would run only a little over an hour, I suggested to Jack O'Brien that we add Beckett's three-character *Play* using members of the Ghelderode cast, which presently included Christopher Walken, Peter Coffield and (from my Stratford days) Patrick Hines as the monstrous bishop, Laquedeem.

Late in August I drove with Joan to Ann Arbor, where she became my indispensable production assistant throughout rehearsals of that violent and morbid play. It was an absorbing experience, heightened by the excitement of the student discontent that was rising all around us. The University of Michigan was in the forefront of that year's antiwar movement, and our reviews, when they appeared, were printed between reports of disturbance and protest.

Both plays were well received. O'Brien had done a sensitive and skillful job of phrasing and pacing Beckett's stylized adulterous middle-class intimacies, but, inevitably, it was the Ghelderode that received the critics' main attention. Under the headline "Death, Decay and Demons" it was hailed as a "macabre masterpiece" and "a hellish spectacle that might have leapt from a canvas of Hieronymus Bosch. . . . It disgusts, it appalls; it carries the stench of decay, of death, of corruption, but its timelessness seizes the present with a grip of steel."

Jules Novick covered it for *The New York Times* in a report headed "APA Is Alive and Well—in Michigan." He described *Chronicles* as "rotten-rich and festering with gruesomeness" and its acting as "solid and strong—rather more so than APA acting has usually been in the past." At the end of his review he asked the inevitable question "What happens to the Company now?" Like jesting Pilate, he received no answer.

I was proud of *Chronicles of Hell* but it was a very special piece that could survive only as part of a strong repertory. Failing that, it played out its week in Ann Arbor and died. And with it died the only first-class American repertory company of that generation. It saddened me that I had not been able to do more to save it. As to Ellis Rabb, with whom my friendship has continued over the years, he has miraculously recovered and gone on to a number of independent successes —as an actor and a director.

My association with the Phoenix lasted some months longer. Soon after my return to New York from Ann Arbor I lunched at the Century with T. and his co-founder of the Phoenix, Norris Houghton,* to discuss the future of the organization they had established sixteen years earlier, and that had played such a valuable part in the New York theatre. I made one short-term proposal. I had recently come across a three-character play, *Los Assassinos*—known in translation as *The Criminals*—by a Cuban playwright, José Triana. Though somewhat derivative of Genêt, it was a strong, exciting piece, and its low-cost production would give the Phoenix the attractive parlay of an "experimental" play opening Off-Broadway at the same time as it was presenting the commercially infallible *Harvey* uptown. I made it clear that I would not be available to direct it but agreed to supervise its production.

Meantime I continued to work on my book. By Labor Day, in spite of interruptions, I had recorded my experiences with the Federal Theatre of the WPA: my fifteen months with the Negro Theatre in Harlem, followed by the formation, with Welles, of the Classical Theatre (Project 891), where, following *Doctor Faustus*, we had produced Marc Blitzstein's controversial labor opera, *The Cradle Will Rock*.†

It had been a satisfying and productive but lonely summer,

---

* Houghton, like me, had turned academic and had accepted the position of dean of the Theatre Department at the new State University at Purchase, New York, of which my former associate Abbott Kaplan was now president.

† *Run-Through*, pp. 173–279.

and it was a relief, by the end of September, to find myself back in the restless, gregarious, overcharged atmosphere of the school.

In the second year emphasis continues on Improvisation—on planting the roots of the young actor's invention at the deepest possible level. In mid-year a juncture begins between the technical and improvisational work and those problems in interpretation to which these disciplines have been an introduction and a preparation. Considerable time is devoted to the reading and rehearsal of plays of the past and present in as many different styles as possible.—From the Saint-Denis "bible."

In the decade I spent as head of Juilliard's Drama Division, 1969 and 1970 were the years in which I devoted myself most intensely and single-mindedly to the task of guiding and developing the delicate and complicated organization which I had helped to create and which I continued to administer with paternalistic authority.

Our second year began without the Saint-Denises. Since Michel was physically incapable of making the long journey to America, it had been agreed that Suria would fly over in mid-November to observe and appraise the work that had been done during the first part of the term and help us to organize the rest of the school year. It was clear by now that we would never again see Michel at the school. This was a tragic loss for the students and faculty and, above all, for myself. Our occasional difficulties with him and Suria during our first year were as nothing compared to the assurance and inspiration we had derived from his presence among us. Built on the firm foundation of his long European experience and adjusted to my own sense of the changing American theatrical scene, we had set up a structure that was to survive, without appreciable change, for more than fifteen years. It was sad that one of its principal creators should be unable to watch its development and enjoy its great success.

With a total of fifty-five registered students, our time was now divided between the twenty-one returning members of what was still known as Group I and the thirty-four freshmen

397

who now became Group II.* New members of the faculty included Margot Harley (administrator), Eugene Lesser (acting) and Elizabeth Keen (first-year movement). But the most far-reaching difference between this and the previous year was the fact that we had finally moved into our new home in Lincoln Center.

What a splendid structure it was—inside and out! The ground floor was occupied by the main lobby, which led to the thousand-seat Juilliard Theatre, complete with good backstage space, scenic workshops and dressing rooms, prop rooms and musicians' quarters underground. Also on the street level was the concert hall (donated by Alice Tully and bearing her name), which was operated independently, with a separate entrance and lobby on Broadway. The second floor housed the school's executive and administrative offices, a sumptuous boardroom and an elegant, wood-paneled concert hall (Paul Hall) intended for chamber music, solo appearances and organ recitals.

The third floor was the school's principal working space: it held our six drama studios, together with the offices and studios of the Balanchine-Kirstein School of American Ballet and a vast acoustically treated hall for Juilliard's orchestral rehearsals. Our own offices and those of the Juilliard Opera and Dance Departments were on the fourth floor, together with a large rehearsal room for the Opera Department and the Music Department's complex of cells and rehearsal spaces (in which many of the Juilliard's two hundred pianos were housed). The fifth floor was occupied by the library, more music cells and the classrooms used by the Academic Department.

As we took possession of our offices, classrooms and studios, it became apparent that we had been presented with one of the most spacious and luxurious theatre training plants in the world. Surrounding our two-hundred-seat Drama Theatre (the best-designed small theatre in New York

* This nomenclature had been suggested by the Saint-Denises and proved simpler and more convenient than the usual shifting references to freshmen, sophomores, juniors and seniors. It allowed each group to retain its identity throughout its time at the school.

398

City) we disposed of six studios. Number 304, on the north-
west corner, was the largest but the worst-shaped, with pillars
at one end. It was used mainly for large classes in movement
and in group improvisation. Next came two modest rectan-
gular spaces (303 and 302), usable as classrooms or intimate
rehearsal rooms, in which Leibowitz and Skinner conducted
their operations. Beyond that was 301, a well-shaped, acoustically admirable space with a small balcony and a grid for
lights which we proposed to use as a second theatre or *Kam-
merspielhaus* for productions unsuited to our main Drama
Theatre. On the south side of the building we had two more
large studios, used for classes in the morning and for rehearsals and performances in the afternoon and evening. All this
was more than we required during our first two years,* but it
was ideally suited to our future needs when, with the addition
of two more "groups" and two sets of advanced students, our
enrollment would rise to close to one hundred—working on
four entirely separate schedules.†

For the present, we had our work cut out adjusting to
the immediate problem of teaching two groups instead of
one.

It takes time—months, sometimes years—for a class to assume its final identity. But already, halfway through this
year's "tests" (*Antony and Cleopatra* and *The Merchant of Venice*),
it had become clear that there was a decided difference of
quality and behavior between our first two groups. Considering that they had been recruited in the same manner and by
the same people (Kahn and myself), this divergence, which
grew more marked with each passing month, was astonishing
and called for somewhat different attitudes and methods in
their teaching.

(Our first impression of our new Group II was, as I recall

---

* At the time of our move to Lincoln Center the School of Music
had close to six hundred full-time students, Dance around fifty,
Drama fifty-five.
† Broken down into divisions and sections, this meant that there
were often between eight and ten classes being conducted simultaneously on the premises.

it, a favorable one. Its members seemed calmer than their predecessors and gave less trouble, individually and as a group. Also, they seemed to adjust more readily to the hazards of the big city and to those rules and disciplines that Group I had consistently questioned and resisted. As a result, our attitude toward them was that of parents toward a second child. Group I, our firstborn, remained the main object of our preoccupation, since, in a very real sense, we felt that we had created the school together and that our future was irrevocably identified with theirs. For four long years we alternately loved and loathed them, spoiled and persecuted them and gave them a consistently disproportionate share of our concern and affection.)

Generally our program continued to develop along the lines we had planned, except that during the winter of 1969–70 a new and unpredictable element was added. By then, the student unrest that had been sweeping the country for close to two years had finally penetrated to the ivory towers of the Juilliard School. This was demonstrated on October 15 when a national "Moratorium" was proclaimed to protest against the Vietnam War and, for the first time, members of the Juilliard School participated in large numbers in a national student demonstration.

October 15. No work today. All morning the streets around the Center were dark with disciplined crowds. Then at noon a Juilliard orchestra appeared and started to play in front of our building—the *Eroica* slow movement and the Brahams *Requiem.* At the same time dancers and drama students came out in their rehearsal uniforms—black jeans and blue denim shirts—with their faces painted dead white, and performed an improvised Dance of Death. At the end, the dead arose, joined hands and led the crowd in singing "All we are saying is, Give peace a chance!" as they moved into Lincoln Plaza and gathered around the fountain in front of the Met. Later most of them moved across town to the United Nations Building. Drama was well represented, but I was curious to see who participated and who didn't. (Absent were *all* our black students. I wonder why and whether they are following orders from somewhere.)

October 16. Back to normal, but emotional vibrations persist.

October 17. Drove with Joan to Bradford, Massachusetts, for my lecture. An old-fashioned girls' college (Methodist, I think), where we were kept awake half the night in our guest quarters by young ladies being visited by their swains in the parlor or so-called "fishbowl" next door.

October 18. On to Boston and Brandeis, where we had arranged to meet John Michael. No sign of him. I made my way on foot through quadrangles and labyrinthine corridors and found him asleep in a basement cell which was fetid and piled with junk. He arose and joined us— unwashed, unkempt, three-day growth, in dirty pants, crumpled shirt and flowing black cape! He looks pale and tired and coughs a bit. His current academic interest is philosophy rather than medicine or science. He is deeply involved in student protest and has drawn an early Selective Service number which puts him on a collision course with his draft board. After lunch we drove into New Hampshire. The countryside is glorious—maples ranging from yellow to crimson. We found Sebastian waiting for us in Dublin, where, during dinner, he made a considerable effort to amuse and divert us. He lacks any consuming ambition or drive, but he *is* a charmer.

October 19. Breakfast with Sebastian, then started for home, stopping at the Siepmanns' in New Canaan for lunch. Eliot Noyes and his wife were there.* Pleasant hours except for the shocking news that Joe Barnes is in Harkness with what seems to be a recurrence of cancer —this time abdominal.

October 21. Early to school to watch Anna Sokolow's first movement class with Group I. They emerged aggrieved and groaning but uninjured. Dined alone in a deep

---

* Noyes (a brilliant architect) and my friend Eames were close associates and longtime design consultants to IBM.

gloom following a long talk with Betty Barnes: an operation was performed on Joe this morning at Harkness and ended with incomplete removal of the malignancy. No treatment is contemplated; radiation won't help. Clearly it is terminal and hopeless.

October 22. Great agitation at school this morning over a female member of Group II with a positive syphilis test. Margot handled it promptly and efficiently and assures me that the reprobate has slept with no one in the school and will be cured within a fortnight. Today the Music Department supplied us with a volunteer orchestra of seven "period" instruments to play during our "style" movement class. A welcome first step toward collaboration between departments!

October 24. Preparations for Suria's imminent visit, followed by two hours in our Drama Theatre with consultants from Jean Rosenthal's Production Service and Pacitti* checking the installation of the movable "thrust" stage I planned with Jeannie last summer. It is flexible and handsome, with good entrances and exits.

October 25–26. Weekend in New City filling new flower beds all around the house with the topsoil that was delivered earlier in the week. Rested briefly, then drove in with Joan for the formal opening of the Juilliard building. Very grand and festive—except that Mrs. Nixon, on a tour of the premises, was trapped for eight minutes in one of our elevators.† Supper afterward at the Running Footman with Leo Lerman,‡ and home.

---

* Joe Pacitti was an endearing, passionate but disorganized Sicilian with a handlebar mustache who had recently been appointed technical director of the Juilliard theatres. As such he was in charge of the construction and technical operation of all our plays and operas. He later came to play a vital part in the formation of the Juilliard Acting Company.

† Mrs. Mennin, who thought ill of the Drama Division's social behavior, was inclined to blame us for the breakdown, which was caused, in reality, by the excess weight of the Secret Service men who surrounded the First Lady.

‡ Lerman was a former associate from the Federal Theatre who became literary editor of *Mademoiselle* and *Vogue* and author of a book about the Metropolitan Museum of Art.

Suria Saint-Denis arrived in November, tired and nervous over leaving Michel alone in London. She was with us for less than three weeks, but she arrived in time to participate in a controversy that now broke out among members of the faculty. This was part of a long-standing disagreement over the nature of acting-teaching and it came into the open as Group I moved out of the elementary disciplines of its first year into the field of interpretation.

It began with a complaint by Kahn, supported by Lesser, that none of the improvisation work on which we had spent so much time during the first year showed in the performances of Group I's recent "exercises"—*Misalliance* and *Fanny's First Play*. They had been far too concerned with memorizing and phrasing Shaw's pithy English dialogue to pay attention to the essence of acting—which is the portrayal of human behavior. As a result, their performances had been amateurish and superficial—a backward step in their development as actors.

While I did not disagree, I was aware that this was a basic issue affecting the future direction of the Drama Division's teaching methods. Determined not to be diverted from one of the basic tenets of the Saint-Denis doctrine, I found myself quoting the "bible" to the effect that, at this stage, rehearsals must be treated "lightly" as exercises and not as mature performances:

> *Students must go through successive phases of reading and rehearsal with explanations of the play, examination of its form, texture and period, of its characters, its sense and meaning, the "blocking" of the play as a whole and its individual scenes; they are learning how to memorize a text, train their memory and come gradually to a general understanding of play production before they are finally able to give a full, public performance.*

Finally—and this was at the heart of the matter—I reminded them that Saint-Denis had repeatedly expressed his objection to the "scene classes" which I knew that Kahn and Lesser were eager to introduce into the curriculum.* Suria

* "Scene classes" might give both teacher and student a sense of

supported me in what turned out to be a constructive and valuable debate. When it was over we had agreed to a schedule of dramatic exercises for the rest of the year.

For Group II and their dramatic readings we chose two Elizabethan plays, *All's Well That Ends Well* and *Two Gentlemen of Verona;* two Greek, *Agamemnon* and *The Libation Bearers;* and four contemporary, *Another Part of the Forest, Bus Stop, Six Characters in Search of an Author* and *Pillars of Society.* And, for the final, staged exercises of the year, *Tartuffe* and *As You Like It.*

Group I had an even more extensive schedule designed to satisfy both the Saint-Denises' insistence on "plays in many styles" and Kahn's demands for more emphasis on acting. For our next production we would do Brecht's *Caucasian Chalk Circle* with the entire group, which would then divide again, after Christmas, for productions of *Richard III* and *The House of Bernarda Alba.** After that they would unite once again to rehearse Feydeau's *Hotel Paradiso* under René Auberjonois as part of their second-year study of comedy.

Overlapping all this, as a compromise with the advocates of "scene classes," we scheduled a number of one-act plays, to be rehearsed intensively in small groups simultaneously with our major productions. These too were chosen for their diversity: Brecht's *The Measures Taken* (director, Lesser) and *The Jewish Wife* (Seldes), Kafka's *Metamorphosis* (Sokolow), Schisgal's *The Tiger* (Aaron), Ionesco's *The Lesson* (Houseman), Williams' *The Lady of Larkspur Lotion* (Marchand †), Horowitz' *The Indian Wants the Bronx* (Lesser), Williams' *This*

---

accomplishment, but they were dangerous if used too early because they tended to "force-feed" the student, who should acquire his sense of character and situation gradually by exposure to a variety of complete plays rather than through intensive work on short, climactic scenes.

* Euripides' *Trojan Women* and Lorca's *House of Bernarda Alba* are frequently used in drama school to redress the injustices suffered by female students in the classical repertory.

† Nancy Marchand was a rising young actress and a longtime associate at Stratford and with APA. Later she became nationally known as Mrs. Pynchon in the TV series *Lou Grant.*

Property Is Condemned (Marchand) and Pinter's *The Lover* (Aaron).

For the final productions of the year we would present two full-length Chekhov plays, *The Sea Gull* and *The Three Sisters*.

It was a formidable program, which we fulfilled with varying degrees of success over the next six months and to which we added Fugard's *Bloodknot* and LeRoi Jones's *The Great Goodness of Life,* both of which gave us an opportunity to deal with the special problems of our black students.

The Caucasian Chalk Circle was the first of our shows to be rehearsed in our new Drama Theatre. I had decided to direct it myself—partly because it is necessary, now and then, for the father figure to expose himself, and partly because I dearly loved the play.* It had the advantage of requiring a large and varied cast; also, since it is in two distinct parts, it was well suited to the double casting of the main roles which we still found necessary at this stage of our development.

We played it in exercise clothes augmented by acres of burlap and fragments of borrowed finery; our only scenery was one small central revolving structure of plain raw wood designed by Doug Schmidt which, at different angles, became the palace, a number of shacks and huts and, finally, the gallows and the court of law in which Azdak dispenses his eccentric justice.

"Breakthrough" was a term we frequently, and sometimes thoughtlessly, used in discussing our students' development. But I believe *Chalk Circle* did, in fact, offer wider theatrical experience than they had encountered thus far. David Schramm, as Azdak, showed clear signs of that power and intelligence that made him a strong and eloquent Lear eight years later. Steve Henderson, the alternate Azdak, was hampered by his psychological handicaps (what Judy Leibowitz called "the problems of his inner image"), but he used his

---

* Which I had first seen with "T." and Eric Bentley, its original translator, in a modest production at the Hedgerow Theatre in 1948 and then again, years later, in Peter Hall's brilliant production with the Royal Shakespeare Company in London.

confusions and frustrations as a provincial black in New York City to express Azdak's anarchic anger in the latter scenes of the play. Mary Lou Rosato, who had faced serious problems of adjustment during her first year, brought to the Governor's wife a stylized energy that was our first clear indication of the talent that eventually led her to play Mother Courage for the Juilliard Acting Company. Sam Tsoutsouvas was the doomed Governor and Tony Azito the sinister Prince Kasbeki, while Ron Baker and Ben Hendrickson were our singing narrators. Patti LuPone doubled as the Governor's wife and as a "member of the band" in which she performed with enthusiasm and skill on a tuba almost as large as herself.

As rehearsals progressed I found myself disrupting the school's schedules to a degree that I would not have tolerated in other teachers. Several times a week we rehearsed so far into the night I found myself sleeping in the small, agreeable but still bare apartment I had recently taken in Lincoln Towers overlooking the river at Seventieth Street, five blocks from the school. But, for students who spent two hours getting to and from their homes in Brooklyn and Queens and who were expected, under pain of expulsion, to show up for their 8:30 A.M. movement class, these night rehearsals created a hardship that, in my directorial enthusiasm, I was inclined to ignore.

There was another feature of my direction that disturbed the faculty. For my opening and closing crowd scenes and for the combined wake and wedding, I decided—contrary to all rules—to add Group II to the cast. For the final week of rehearsals, the entire student body (all fifty-five of them) was working together onstage and often far into the night. I justified this on the grounds that it gave them valuable theatrical experience; it also gave me an opportunity to test the scenic and acoustical values of our new stage.*

In mid-December we gave two dress rehearsals and two performances of *Chalk Circle*. The critique that followed was

---

* Because of its amphitheatrical form it called for more projection than would normally be required in a theatre of that size. For a student workshop this was an asset.

constructive but painful. In my limited time, following my usual practice as a director, I had been more concerned with the rhythm, action and clarity of the piece as a whole than with the intimacies of individual relationships. The faculty—particularly our teachers of acting—did not fail to point this out, and I noted once again, this time through bitter personal experience, that these academic critiques, necessary and valuable though they might be for students and faculty alike, were more difficult for a director to accept than the harshest and most cruel judgments of professional critics. (After so much grueling work it is hard to sit by while your students' inexperience and individual weaknesses are used against you as weapons in the power plays that characterize faculty relations—no matter how close, affectionate and loyal they may be.) Even at my age and with my ego, I found the critique of *The Caucasian Chalk Circle* a distressing ordeal.

Suria left for London early in December with an understanding that she would be back in the spring to review our entire year's work. I think that, on the whole, she was favorably impressed by what she had observed. For my part, brief as it was, I was grateful to her for her visit. She remained the high priestess of the doctrine on which our institution was founded; she was our conscience and, in her strict adherence to her husband's theory and practice of actor training, she helped to counteract the deviations attempted by the zealous and occasionally contentious Young Turks on our faculty.

If I had one general complaint about this courageous, dedicated and elegant lady, it was that she has very positive and opinionated on small, and sometimes personal, matters but vague and indeterminate on such complicated Saint-Denis disciplines as group improvisation, character masks, advanced speech delivery, etc., on which we needed more specific and detailed instruction and guidance.

It was our policy (and one of the virtues of having our school in New York City) to encourage both faculty and students to attend as much contemporary theatre as possible. The winter of 1969–70 saw the arrival of several visiting companies, two of which were of special interest to anyone concerned with the training of actors. The first was William Ball's American Conservatory Theatre, which was now firmly established, with its own theatre and school, in San Francisco. For his opening show, Bill presented his own excessive version of *Tiny Alice*, followed by a stylized and mechanical version of Feydeau's *A Flea in Her Ear*. The New York critics treated ACT even worse than they had the Minneapolis Guthrie Theatre the year before, and it went home with considerable loss of money and reputation.

Far more significant was the season presented by Grotowski's celebrated Polish Laboratory Theatre. Of the first visit I made, with Peggy Freed and Michael Kahn, to the old Washington Square Methodist Church where they were performing, I recorded that "we were kept waiting for some time in a light rain and then, for close to half an hour, in a bleak, unheated vestibule and on steep stairs leading to the balcony, from which around a hundred of us who were finally admitted were permitted to look down onto the gutted arena below." I found myself wondering whether these delays were due to incompetent management or, more likely, formed part of a deliberate attempt to shock us out of our normal theatregoing complacency and to prepare us for the arduous and almost religious ordeal to come.

Of the three productions I saw, *The Constant Prince, Akropolis* and *Apocalypsis cum Figuris,* the first (for that reason perhaps) made the deepest impression. An adaptation of a seventeenth-century Spanish play by Calderón, it was described in the *Times* the next morning as "a formal story of martyrdom and moral integrity." The action was not always clear, but its cumulative emotional impact was overwhelming. *Akropolis,* their next offering, with its unmistakable references to the death camps of the Holocaust, achieved a more direct empathy. Its ending, the procession of victims following a soiled rag doll and ending with their final dive, one after another, into the dark box that engulfed and annihilated them, became almost unbearable.

(I think, overall, we reacted more to the energy, virtuosity and dedication of Grotowski's actors than to the plays, which we found obscure and alien. We were filled with professional admiration for performances which, in their disciplined violence, transcended the limits of what we had come to expect in the theatre but which, finally, were not generally applicable to our own problems of acting.)

Other performances I recall from that winter are those of the two companies with which I was still, in some measure, involved: the Phoenix and the APA. The latter was indirectly represented by the *Private Lives* which Stephen Porter had put together during the summer with Brian Bedford and Tammy Grimes. David Merrick had picked it up in Ann Arbor and brought it to Broadway, where it received good reviews and became a moderate commercial hit for which Tammy Grimes received a Tony Award.

The Phoenix, on its part, was represented by two plays, of which the first, *Harvey,* was a predictable smash. The second was a dark, tumultuous piece, *The Criminals,* with which I was directly concerned as producer. My initial choice for director had been José Quintero, who liked the play but whose agent persuaded him that he should no longer work for Off-Broadway wages. Our next was David Wheeler, a sensitive, if somewhat permissive, director, who ran a small theatre company in Boston (of which Al Pacino had been an early member).

For such an intimate and subjective play I felt it essential for the director to select his own cast. For the girls Wheeler chose two young actresses with whom he had worked before: for Beba, the younger and more aggressive sister, an undisciplined blonde with large features and a wild imagination by the name of Penelope Allen; for Cuca, the older, an outwardly conventional but equally emotional brunette named Linda Selman. Their male sibling gave us more trouble. Wheeler's first choice was a rising young actor, D. J. Sullivan, who had a previous engagement with another show. In his place we engaged a talented and dynamic actor named Barry Primus, an active member of the Actors' Studio. With such a cast we were in for trouble, and my journal confirms this:

January 25. Jesus! Such rehearsal habits! They talk, quarrel, giggle and waste time—their own and the director's. In their attempts at "interiorization" they spend hours jabbering about events in their own lives that are not even remotely or emotionally related to their emotional situation. The warnings I received about Wheeler's permissiveness are borne out. . . .

January 26. Attended a rehearsal of *Criminals* which finally begins to make sense, but they're still all over the place. I'm tempted to talk to them, but Wheeler begs me to let them alone for two or three days more. He says I "awe" them.

Early in February we moved into the Sheridan Square Playhouse, where we set up the small, ramped platform that constituted our single setting. Here, in what became their second home, our three actors, in defiance of Equity rules, spent between eight and fifteen hours a day in rehearsals of which I wrote that "there was lots of talk and argument and some tears but not enough work on the play." On February 13 we gave our first preview, followed by a symposium, mostly for Phoenix subscribers. Gordon Davidson, whom I had invited, complained of lack of specific background and location; Marian Seldes hated the acting.

February 17. Another preview of *Criminals*. The best yet, but that's not saying much. There were still a number of walkouts.

February 19. Tonight, a shameful preview of *Criminals*. (They tell me last night was "wonderful.") Barry Primus was all over the place—self-indulgent and self-satisfied. In the intermission I had a bad scene with Wheeler on the sidewalk in front of the theatre. Afterward I went back and yelled at the actors about their work habits and their obligation to their audience and to the play. To my charge that he was giving only one decent performance in three, Barry blithely replied, "That's art, John. You have to fail most of the time." On my way out, Wheeler thanked me. For what? My hopes for *The Criminals* sink by the hour.

As the dread night of our opening approached, the usual uncertainty persisted as to whether Clive Barnes or Mel Gussow would cover us for the *Times*. For a far-out piece like *The Criminals* (with a history of successful international performances) I was eager to have Barnes, whose heavy schedule was complicated by the fact that two Phoenix productions, *Harvey* and *The Criminals*, were opening on successive nights. At 12:05 P.M. on Sunday the twenty-third (three days before our official opening) the *Times* called and announced that Mr. Barnes would be attending that afternoon's preview.

February 23. Panic, confusion and a mad, last-minute scramble to fill the house with lively young people, including two dozen shanghaied from Juilliard and rushed downtown. What Barnes saw this afternoon was an untidy show with the usual missed lines and ad-libs but high energy and the best audience reaction yet. After the final blackout he was treated to a bit of additional drama by our lunatic cast: as Penny and Barry were leaving the stage in the dark she lunged at him across Clive's nose and yelled that if he ever threw water at her again onstage she'd "cut his fucking heart out!"

Barnes's review came out three days later:

Phoenixes, of course, rise from the ashes by definition. The Phoenix Theatre appears to be well-named and at present it is kicking around a most lovely lot of ashes. . . . The night before last it weighed in with a surefire but excellently primed hit in a starry revival of *Harvey*. Last night it completed its gestural double-header with a strange, yet strangely effective Cuban play.

It was a long piece, in which he described the games played by those three young people in their attic:

Terrible, lacerating games in the course of which they slip between identities, between what they are and what they are acting. . . . They play them to a terrible infinity where the end judgment is never in doubt. Who are they? Did they kill? Are they trying to explain their past deed? Or are they trying to justify their future actions? . . . It is a very odd work, yet I urge you to see it. It dares and it dares effectively. It is a weird, wild play.

In conclusion, as though to reproach me for my lack of faith, he described the performances of Barry Primus, Penelope Allen and Linda Selman as "the best I have seen this season," adding, "They are communicating on a special level of reality that makes most normal acting irrelevant."

His was, in fact, the only good review we received. The TV reviews were particularly hostile, though the weeklies (*New Yorker, Cue, Village Voice*, etc.) all took the play seriously and some of them praised the performances.

The Juilliard audition tour on which I set out early in February with Michael Kahn covered the same cities as before: Chicago, Dallas, San Francisco and Los Angeles. Group III, which would be formed from these auditions, turned out to be an unusually good one, but we had no way of knowing that at the time. The spread between hopeless and talented seemed about the same as in other years, except that we seemed to be stronger than usual in males. The main difference between this and our previous audition lay in the fact that, for the first time, we were also recruiting the advanced students whom we had described in our third-year Juilliard brochure:

> For the academic year 1970–71 the Drama Division will accept a few ADVANCED applicants between the ages of twenty and thirty in a special TWO YEAR course. They will be drawn from the following categories:
>
> 1. Graduates of the Theatre Arts Departments of Liberal Arts colleges who have had acting experience in University or Resident companies.
> 2. Young professionals who have worked in the theatre as actors or journeymen and who are seeking additional training in the disciplines included in Juilliard's basic actor-training course.

Recruitment was made more difficult by the fact that we ourselves had only the vaguest idea of how these advanced students would be absorbed into the school and how money would be found for the scholarships they needed.*

* The three we finally accepted all turned out remarkably well. David Ogden Stiers was a tall, resourceful, intelligent young actor

I was in the air, on the way back from Chicago to New York, when Joan got a call from John Michael at Brandeis in which he informed her in a lugubrious voice that Sebastian was with him, having just been expelled from the Thomas More School for possession of mescaline. Sebastian denied it, but it became quite clear, when I called the school that night, that he was guilty as hell and had behaved so foolishly when caught that there was no alternative but to sack him. I asked John Michael to put him on a bus to New York and from there I drove him to New City, where I placed him in the reluctant custody of his mother. Then I called Allan Laufman (his and John Michael's former tutor at Thomas More), who was now teaching at the Storm King School at Cornwall-on-the-Hudson nearby. He had heard of Sebastian's plight and offered to try to get him into Storm King. This called for a personal visit and a copious consumption of humble pie by Sebastian and myself. I noted in my diary that on March 8 I delivered him, "together with a check for $1,350, looking clean and sobered but not crushed," to his new school. He had been a prisoner in the House on the Hill for two weeks, during which he split several cords of wood and he and his mother enjoyed the close and pleasant relationship they seemed to develop every time they were left alone together.

whom I had encountered in California two years earlier; he had played a number of classical roles including Lear but felt the need for additional training in voice and movement. Kevin Kline was an actor-musician, a highly recommended graduate of the University of Indiana at Bloomington. The third, Mary Joan Negro, we auditioned in Chicago under the impression that she was a graduate of the Theatre Department of the University of Michigan at Ann Arbor; in reality, she had virtually no theatrical training, but Michael Kahn and I were so struck by her intelligence and beauty that we took her anyway and never regretted it. All three joined the Juilliard Acting Company on graduation and, after several years on the road, went on to outstanding success in the entertainment business: Stiers as Charles Winchester III in *M*A*S*H;* Kline as a Tony Award winner in *Twentieth Century* and *The Pirates of Penzance;* Mary Joan Negro for her performances in films and the New York productions of *Wings, Modigliani,* etc.

John Michael's trouble, which came later that month, was more serious. In line with his self-righteous letter to his draft board, he had ignored his number when it came up. Now an agent visited him at Brandeis with a subpoena instructing him to appear as a "witness" before a grand jury in New York City in connection with a matter of "conspiracy." The Civil Liberties Union lawyer with whom we got in touch told me that he was puzzled and disturbed by the "conspiracy" aspect of the case. Much of the weekend that John Michael spent in New City before his appearance in court was devoted to a discussion of his situation. He himself was divided between apprehension and anticipation, torn between fear of prison and a vision of himself delivering a historic antiwar oration before an awed and admiring judge and jury. Recalling my own observations of HUAC and other such inquisitorial bodies, I assured him that that was not the way it worked. He would be asked certain loaded questions which he must answer; all attempts at eloquence would be ruthlessly and legally squashed. His lawyer told him the same thing.

I was out of town on the day finally fixed for the hearing. (Considering my own long and supposedly subversive record, this was probably just as well.) Michael was kept waiting in court for a day and a half before being called to the stand. After he had taken the oath and answered some routine questions about himself, the prosecutor (for reasons no one ever understood) suddenly thrust a sheet of paper before him and—over the objection of his lawyer—told him to write his name *ten* times. He was on his fifth signature when an attendant burst into the courtroom and announced that there was a bomb in the basement. The case was recessed, then postponed till the next day and, finally, dismissed. John Michael returned to Boston, richer by one hundred seventeen dollars—representing his per diem and the expenses he had incurred as a subpoenaed witness. The mystery of his "conspiracy" was never solved, but when he faced a routine hearing for draft evasion some weeks later he received a suspended sentence of one year, which was expunged from his record two years later.

By the end of that spring we all seemed to be involved, in

one way or another, in some form of unrest. For months tempers had been rising in campuses throughout the country with protests against the war and also against the academic structure in general, sharpened by charges of racism and collusion with the military-industrial establishment. In its extreme form this discontent found expression in violent explosions such as those at Berkeley, Ann Arbor, San Francisco State, Columbia and Kent State. Juilliard, as a professional conservatory, was never in the vanguard of student activism; but by midspring of 1970 the gathering storm could no longer be ignored, even in a stronghold of privileged culture such as Lincoln Center. It manifested itself in a growing number of bomb threats, all of which proved false, and in two major disturbances. The first was a spontaneous explosion of indignation during which several hundred bodies— of students and faculty alike—lay as dead for an hour in the noonday sun on the pavement of Lincoln Center Plaza in a symbolic protest against the bombing of Cambodia and the violence at Kent State. (I remember lying there surrounded by members of the school, with Margot to the left of me and Jean Morel, who was aging and sick and about to retire, on my right.)

The second was longer-lasting and more disruptive. Just as the most effective instrument in the creation of the CIO in the thirties had been industrial sit-in strikes, so now the most effective weapons of the New Left were the paralyzing student strikes organized with varying degrees of effectiveness on the country's leading campuses. Juilliard was among the last to be affected, but throughout that spring a growing number of hirsute young men and intense girls in battle dress appeared among us, evading the security guards and mingling with the students of all three divisions to promote strike action. They had little effect at first. Of our musicians, dancers and actors the majority were apolitical and obsessively and egotistically concerned with their own artistic and professional future. What appeal the agitators succeeded in making to our own acting students was to their dramatic instincts rather than to their political sense.

A national student strike had been called for late April,

and, as the weeks went by, the gap began to widen between pro- and antistrike elements in the Drama Division. The latter (headed, as I recall, by Patti LuPone and her fellow Italian Mary Lou Rosato) maintained that they were studying to be artists and that these external disturbances represented an unwelcome threat to their training. Those who favored the strike did so almost entirely for histrionic reasons. It was not the arguments of the organizers that won them over so much as the prospect of an exhilarating, dramatic activity in which they saw themselves playing leading roles. Knowing almost nothing of the national and academic issues involved, a number of our students got themselves elected (for their energy and dramatic sense) to key positions on the various committees and delegations which began to conduct negotiations with a bewildered and outraged Dr. Mennin and his aides. Using the lessons (the "improvisations" and "adjustments" and the "choices") we had taught them so assiduously over the past twenty months, they soon revealed highly effective and colorful personalities that had remained unsuspected till now. Quinn, for instance, changed overnight from a tense, stiff, inhibited California beauty into a flushed, wild-eyed, utterly exasperating version of La Pasionaria—a local firebrand urging her laggard associates to acts of reckless audacity. Schramm, the talented but indolent Kentucky bookmaker's son, did some hurried research into *Ten Days That Shook the World* and emerged in a black jacket, a new-grown Trotsky-style goatee and a bright-red scarf knotted about his arm, to lead the people's armies against the forces of reaction.

Mennin, supported by his board and a generally conservative music faculty, took a firm stand and announced that if Juilliard were closed by a strike it might never reopen. Nobody believed that, but things went so far that one final, critical meeting of the entire school was called in the main Juilliard Theatre, in which the strike issue was to be put to a decisive student vote. Drama students spoke on either side, with Schramm and Quinn among the most eloquent advocates of a strike, which was blocked at the last moment through the efficient, hard-nosed parliamentary maneuvering of an associate dean.

A week later everyone was quietly back at work. Neither Quinn nor Schramm took any further interest in the affairs of the school or the nation. But I have always believed that this brief, superficial exposure to political passion played a vital and highly valuable part in the theatrical development of Group I. No matter which side they were on, the crisis furnished them with an emotional experience of which the calmer and more complacent classes that succeeded them never had the benefit.

These scenes of turmoil, with all the emotions they touched off, caused surprisingly little disruption in the routine of the school. My journal, that winter and spring, is filled with reports of meetings, confrontations, decisions and minor crises that seemed serious at the time—as when one of our more hysterical girl students reported that she had been abducted and raped within a block of Lincoln Center; or when a fairly valuable Rowlandson drawing from a theatrical collection lent to us by Lincoln Kirstein was found missing one morning from the wall outside my office; or, worst of all, when Tony Azito had himself photographed for his ID card in full makeup and drag!

After the blasts of publicity that had greeted our opening and our move to Lincoln Center, I was doing my best to keep a low profile for the Drama Division and not to invite comparison with the flashy activities of our competitors at Yale, NYU and Cal-Arts.* However, the general curiosity about us persisted, and the flow of guests, job applicants and foreign dignitaries who came to admire our premises and observe our work continued throughout that year and the next. Italians, East and West Germans, Yugoslavs, Rumanians, Russians and Scandinavians were given the grand tour; so were visiting theatrical VIPs, among whom I remember John Giel-

* A new liberal-arts college founded in Southern California with Disney money.

gud, Irene Worth, the Barraults, Zoe Caldwell and Jacques Lecoq (the high priest of mime). Many of them stayed and talked with our students, on whom Gielgud and Worth made a very special impression.

Recorded in my journal is a steady succession of business lunches in which specific subjects were considered.* More regular and casual luncheon companions were T. Edward Hambleton, still trying to work out the future of his floundering but indestructible Phoenix; Pat Birch, whom I had been seeing since the Martha Graham film and who was among those struggling to keep that organization alive; Lincoln Kirstein, whom I met frequently for strange meals of pancakes and ice cream. On one occasion he was accompanied by our former associate Joseph Verner Reed, from whom I extracted an annual scholarship for the Drama Division and of whom I noted that he had changed very little over the years, "except that his attention span seems shorter than ever." I was not aware that he was terminally ill—the latest in the long succession of deaths that were becoming part of my life.

My first awareness of death had come to me at the age of seven in Lucerne, Switzerland, induced by the paintings in the overhead panels of the ancient covered wooden bridge that I had to cross twice a day on the way to and from the hotel where my mother and I were spending the summer. It was a traditional, medieval Dance of Death depicting several dozen scenes of public and private life, in each of which there

---

* With Mark Schubart and June Dunbar of the Lincoln Center Education Program, to plan our next year's New York City school tour; with Herbert Blau, newly appointed head of theatre at Cal-Arts, to compare notes; with McNeill Lowry of the Ford Foundation, to support my request for a grant to help me finish my book; with Nick Ray, recently returned from Chicago, where he was filming the trial of the Chicago Seven; with Jean Darcante, head of the International Theatre Institute; with Louise Bernikow, to whom I had given the first three hundred pages of my book to read and edit, and whose notes were detailed, severe and valuable; and with Luciano Berio, the serialist composer, to discuss the production of a musical piece "with actors" on the Juilliard stage.

appeared a cloaked and grinning skeleton with a scythe, preparing to carry off some unsuspecting citizen to the boneyard. With the coming of night the memory of these scenes,
mingled with the misery I felt at being abandoned in my hotel
room by my beautiful mother, had set up a pattern of terror
and sadness that was as strong and deep as anything I can
remember feeling before or since.

It was not the fear of dying that distressed me. At the age
of seven my own death seemed infinitely remote and, with
my loose cosmopolitan upbringing, I was not burdened with
religious fears of hell or purgatory. What I remember feeling
was an overwhelming sense of despair at the idea of annihi-
lation: of utter desolation at the thought that all living things,
including my mother and myself, were inexorably doomed to
extinction and must disappear utterly and for all eternity,
into a black void of nothingness.

These childish terrors lasted no more than a few weeks and
never returned in their full force.* My father's death when I
was fifteen filled me with sadness but no sense of awe; I
passed virtually unscathed through two wars; my own later
brushes with sudden death (one on U.S. 5 between New
Haven and Hartford when I fell asleep at the wheel one
winter evening, and, again, a few months later, in my bed at
24 Gramercy Park, of virulent septicemia) had not revived
my child's dread of mortality. But now, gradually, as I approached my seventieth year, the Man with the Scythe was
moving back into my life—no longer a figure in a remote
costume drama, but an immediate and insistent reality from
which there was no escape. He was present in the crowd at
the public deaths of that decade—at the Kennedy assassina-
tions, at Kent State and at the shooting of Martin Luther

* They showed signs of reviving a few years later while I was receiving religious instruction prior to confirmation into the Church of
England, but my teachers' obsessive preoccupation with masturba-
tion soon drove all thoughts of eternity out of my adolescent head.
When my appendix burst that spring, just as I was receiving the
consecrated wafer at the hands of the Bishop of Bath and Wells, my
own close contact with death left me relieved and grateful for my
recovery but spiritually unmoved.

King. And, all the time, he was coming closer to me, moving in among my friends and associates, picking them off one after another with a regularity that gave me an eerie feeling of being, if not responsible, then, in some way, related and involved in their deaths.

The list was formidable. It had begun soon after my departure from Stratford, when Lawrence Langner, my longtime antagonist, died suddenly while, several thousand miles away, Edd Johnson, my close associate at the Voice of America, perished in a Mexican plane as he was taking his dog to the vet at Cuernavaca. They were followed, in rapid succession, by my beloved friend Judy Holliday; by Edna Giessen, my agent, who was found dead at her desk one morning with one of my lecture contracts in front of her; by Ted Marcuse, with whom I had worked so often in the theatre and who found the violent end he was seeking on his third attempt on the Hollywood Freeway; by Hallie Flanagan, my dynamic and fearless chief in the Federal Theatre of the WPA; by beautiful blond Constance Dowling, found dead in her Bel-Air bedroom; by Norma Crane, whose intelligence and energy were destroyed by a malignant brain tumor in her late thirties; by Marc Blitzstein, murdered on a Caribbean island; by my longtime partner Jack Landau, lying dead on the floor of his Boston apartment; by my dear friend Henry Varnum Poor, who had designed and built my House on the Hill and whose great heart had finally given out one night in his own stone house in New City.

With Jean Rosenthal's death, which shocked and diminished me more than any of the others, I hoped the long death march might be ended. But within a few months I was to suffer another devastating loss.

Joseph Barnes was a friend and associate with whom I had worked closely and long without ever feeling a trace of that dark, secret, competitive rage that has conditioned so many of my male relationships over the years. From the day I met him, my feelings for him were of admiration and gratitude. While I worked under him at the Voice of America, surrounded by power plays and political infighting of which Barnes was frequently the center, he remained a loyal and generous collaborator in whom I had absolute personal and professional trust.

After the war, as editor and co-publisher of the short-lived *New York Star,* he had surprised and delighted me by offering me a weekly "op-ed" column on the performing arts, which I wrote for three months until the paper folded. Last but not least, he had risked his status as senior editor at Simon and Schuster by giving me a contract and a substantial advance on a book which I might never finish and in which no one else had the slightest interest or faith. These were the emotional debts I owed him. Beyond that there was the stimulation and pleasure I derived from his company and a strange sense (which I had about very few men I had known) of inherent goodness.

In mid-February I left a rehearsal of *The Criminals* and walked over to the Barneses' apartment in the West Twenties. I had lunched with Joe at the Century some weeks earlier and been saddened by his appearance. But what I now saw lying in pajamas and a dressing gown in the fetal position under a blanket on the couch of his living room was the figure of death. The skin of his face and hands had the unmistakable copper color of terminal cases; his voice was little more than a croak. Without a word or gesture he gave out a sense of endless, unbearable pain. Worst of all was the fixed look of abject resignation I saw in his eyes.

It was our pretense that I had come to report progress on the book we both knew he would never see. With his usual courtesy, in what amounted to an apology for dying, he thanked me for coming "on such a feckless mission." Presently our talk drifted back, as it usually did, to our mad days at the Overseas Branch and to Edd Johnson, who had been our close friend. We also spoke of the beavers that had appeared in Joe's stream the previous summer and about his daughter who was becoming active in black urban politics. Also about my school. Sensing his exhaustion, I got up to leave. As she was seeing me to the door Betty told me what I already knew—that it was only a matter of days.

That same week I received news that our handsome, gentle

Southern student, who had suffered a second breakdown and had to be sent home, had seriously injured himself. One night soon after being discharged from the local hospital where he had been receiving shock treatment, he had stabbed himself deep in the stomach, trying to dig out the microphone that he said had been planted there by a member of the Juilliard faculty!

Through all this, the work of the school continued and we were treated, once in a while, to a pleasant surprise.

March 15. Good news for a change! Group II's *Bus Stop,* which we saw this afternoon, is the best first-year exercise we've had since we started!

March 16. This morning, with six students from Group I under Marian Seldes, we tested the vocal acoustics of the big Juilliard Theatre. Kleinholtz, the imported German expert, was not unhappy with the results, except for the constant hum of the air-conditioning, which drives him nuts!

In the afternoon I accompanied "T." to a Phoenix board meeting, where there was much gloating over the latest figures: with *The Criminals* breaking even and *Harvey* a massive hit, the Phoenix that week showed a net profit of $35,000. This will make it easier for "T." to pursue his latest plans for a "young" theatre, starting with Duffy's production of *The Persians,* by Aeschylus, in St. George's Church downtown.*

In the evening with Joan to Ter-Arutunian's elegant exhibition of stage designs at the Research Library, then to Fellini's *Satyricon,* which I found fascinating, perverse, overlong but never dull. Afterward across the street to Piraeus My Love for ouzo and a Greek supper and ran into Manos Hadjidakis,† who lives in exile on the floor above and seems to have alienated both sides in the cur-

---

* Other notions for a "young" theatre that year included a "happening" in Schechner's "Garage Theatre" and the takeover of an abandoned ferryboat for traveling performances, which never took place.
† See above, p. 233.

rent Greek political ruckus! He was charming as ever and, on the subject of *Satyricon*, surprisingly erudite.

March 19. Early to Juilliard, where I found a delegation from Group I with complaints about their rehearsals of *Hotel Paradiso* and bitching, as is their wont, about their director, René Auberjonois.

René isn't our most experienced or organized teacher-director, and I know he went into this somewhat unprepared, but Group I is taking advantage of this to work up the same confusion and discontent as they did early in the year in Liz Keen's movement class! On the other hand, some of their troublemaking comes from eagerness and a strange perfectionism that makes them the remarkable group they are.

I promised to attend their rehearsals for the rest of the week. And I will—all the more since I feel partly to blame for this crisis. For lack of suitable teachers we have failed to implement the Saint-Denis second-year program of Advanced Improvisation and Character Masks. Now we are asking Group I to face the difficult problem of playing farce before teaching them the basic elements of comic acting. No wonder they're upset.

Home to New City by bus, disturbed and more tired than I can remember ever being in my life! Felt better after a drink with Joan before the corner fireplace.

March 20. All afternoon at *Paradiso* rehearsal. They are nowhere near ready for a performance—or even an "exercise." To help things along I did a lot of yelling at everyone—singling out Sakren, Tsoutsouvas and Quinn for special abuse for not watching rehearsals when they were out of a scene.

March 21. I detected a spark of life today at the *Paradiso* rehearsal, but mostly it remained ragged and deadly. They continue to act aggrieved and sulky.

March 23. At 10:30 in Room 304, a run-through of *Paradiso* for the faculty, with Group II as audience to supply laughs. Everybody very nervous. The first act was better than yesterday but still stiff and tedious. Then, five minutes into Act II, they suddenly took off and made up for all the toil and misery of the past four weeks. Farce situations were played broadly but skillfully and there were some genuinely comic characterizations, especially among the males. If only Michel Saint-Denis were here and functioning, what wonders he could perform with this lunatic group!

By mid-April Saint-Denis' condition had improved and Suria arrived from London in time to observe a considerable body of work and to give us her reactions. Though I didn't agree with all her comments, it was useful for me to evaluate our progress through eyes that were more experienced and objective than my own. She got to see Group II's *Pillars of Society* and *Six Characters in Search of an Author,* followed by rehearsals of *Tartuffe* and *As You Like It.* She also saw Group I in multiple performances of one-act plays with widely varying but generally fascinating results.* These overlapped the year's-end productions of Chekhov's *Sea Gull* and *Three Sisters,* both of which were so strangely disappointing that their failure could only be ascribed to the fatigue and gloom that inevitably followed the agitations and overexcitements of the spring.

Even more important and significant than these acting exercises were the classes that Suria observed during her stay. Overall, things had not changed appreciably since her last visit or since her extended sojourn the previous year. Despite substantial additions to the student body and the faculty, the form and structure of the Drama Division remained pretty much as we had established it during our Retreat at Wykeham Rise. Kahn, despite his emotional caprices and his frequent absences (as artistic director of Stratford and later of Princeton), remained our most creative teacher of acting and our faculty's most intelligent and farsighted educator. Aaron,

---

* My own experience directing Ionesco's *The Lesson,* with David Schramm as the murderous professor and Patti LuPone as his doomed pupil, was entirely satisfying.

Lesser, Seldes, together with the recently added Boris Tumarin,* formed a strong supporting staff,† on which Bill Woodman played a valuable double part as director and as my executive assistant in charge of the enormous and complicated labor of scheduling.

Our disciplines continued to develop along predictable lines under their respective heads. Voice and Speech—under the still-strained joint leadership of Skinner (with her authority and wealth of experience) and Smith (with her dedication and overwhelming energy), supported by Robert Williams of Columbia University and by Margaret Freed, with her valuable sense of the contemporary American student climate— was probably our most consistently effective department. Movement fluctuated with its changing teachers: Sokolow remained a storm center and a catalyst; Yakim was energetic but erratic; Liz Keen was a welcome addition but inclined to impinge on emotional areas that our teachers of acting regarded as theirs. Leibowitz, on her part, maintained a steady level of constructive and invaluable work with her first- and second-year classes in Alexander Technique.

Secondary but fascinating activities such as judo, folk dancing, circus acrobatics and choral singing were conducted by part-time teachers; there were also classes in art appreciation, theatre history, costume, makeup and style, to which must be added a number of reluctantly attended academic courses required for the B.F.A. degree. All this led to constant complaints (supported by certain members of the faculty but consistently ignored by me) that our schedule was overcrowded and exhausting and did not give our students time to "think" (*sic*).

Finally, there was our small but efficient and devoted administrative staff headed by Margot Harley, who, with her astonishing energy and her passionate concern for the problems of students and faculty alike, was coming to play an indispensable role in our organization.

* A Russian actor and director who, for eight years, until his death, was one of the most accomplished and inspiring director-teachers on the Juilliard faculty.
† Of which it is worth noting that it was almost entirely Jewish.

There remained two areas, however, in which, after nearly two years, I felt we remained deficient. One, already mentioned, was the area of advanced improvisation, including the mask work which had so impressed me when Michel wrote of it in his "bible" and demonstrated it personally at Wykeham Rise. I discussed this with Suria and appealed to her for help. I was prepared to bring someone from Canada or Europe. Her first suggestion was that we send for Barbara Goodwin (which I was reluctant to do). She then offered to approach Pierre Lefèvre, one of Saint-Denis' outstanding disciples, who had recently resigned as head of the Strasbourg school. (He did in fact join us the following fall for a limited stay of three months and became one of our most valuable visiting teachers over the next ten years.)

There was one other area of failure that distressed me even more. In view of my own extensive work with black theatre people over the years, I found it particularly galling that our experience with black students in the Drama Division should have been so disappointing. I had helped to bring integration into the American theatre (in the Federal Theatre and with *Native Son* and the Ellington–La Touche *Beggar's Holiday*) and had proved long ago (with *Macbeth* and *Four Saints in Three Acts*) that blacks were every bit as qualified to work in classical theatre as their white colleagues. Furthermore, the Juilliard Music School, though low in black instrumentalists, was proud to list such black singers as Leontyne Price and Shirley Verrett among its illustrious alumni. Yet, of our four black students who had qualified for the Drama Division during its first two years, only two had achieved even modest progress.

One, Jim Moody, came to us from the integrated High School of the Performing Arts. A conscientious if not a brilliant acting student, and a native New Yorker, he avoided most of the pitfalls facing black students during those troubled years.* The other was a more tragic case. He was one of

* On graduation he became the first black actor to join the Juilliard Acting Company, and later he became a successful teacher of acting and a featured actor in films.

the most gifted students ever to enter our school, yet when he left us suddenly, near the end of his second year, he had so deteriorated that his entire future, as an actor and as a man, was in serious jeopardy.

Partly, this had to do with his personal difficulties, as a vulnerable Midwesterner from an indigent family, in adjusting to the tense climate of New York in the late sixties, including the worsening drug scene. Even more bewildering and destructive were the problems he faced as an educated, sensitive, idealistic Negro who now found himself under attack by his own people for attending a fancy white school and for devoting himself to the study of the white classics and "mid-Atlantic" speech rather than to the use of black idiom and the creation of "black theatre." Chief among these disrupting influences was that of the black playwright LeRoi Jones* (now known as Imamu Baraka), in whose "Spirit House" in Newark, New Jersey, the young man sought refuge and made a brief, unhappy sojourn after he had left us.†

(Eventually, as the racial and social ferment of the late sixties subsided, so did the problems of black students in the Drama Division. By the mid-seventies the ratio of blacks in the school had risen substantially, together with our ability to deal with them and theirs to profit from our instruction.)‡

Suria flew back to England just before the end of our school year. This was always a tense and difficult period—a time of winding up, of tests, appraisals and dismissals that brought out the students' most neurotic and the faculty's

---

* Author of *Dutchman, The Toilet, Slaves,* etc., and later a member of the Black Political Caucus.

† When I saw him again, eighteen months later, in Kansas City, where he had a teaching job, he seemed to have recovered his health and some of his self-confidence. He was carrying a volume of the Koran, which he laid on the table in front of me to make quite sure that I saw it.

‡ Later still, during the Juilliard Acting Company's 1980–81 season, there were three black actors, all Juilliard-trained, among its eighteen members, playing such parts as Oberon, Titania, the Mistresses Pinchwife and Squeamish in Wycherly's *Country Wife* and leading roles as garrulous male and female Venetians in Goldoni's *Il Campiello.*

most contentious behavior. Edgy and tired from eight months of intense commitment to a group of young people for whom they had developed strong professional and personal emotions but on whose individual merits they often held wildly divergent views, teachers fell to arguing and intriguing among themselves—particulary on the critical subject of dismissals. That the verdict had to be unanimous added to the intensity of these discussions; that the final act of execution had to be performed personally by me added to my own distaste for the final days of the school year.

These purges were a form of pruning from which it was generally believed the survivors emerged stronger and better for their ordeal. It is certainly true that, in an acting class, where the work is largely collective and involves intimate collaboration and mutual dependence, a weakness in one or more students can prove seriously injurious to the progress of the entire group. It is also true that the threat of dismissal creates a state of continuous apprehension which, while stimulating to some, can have a harmful effect on insecure and sensitive students.

There were English theatre schools in which purges took place at the end of every term. With us they occurred only once a year and fell into three main categories. The first and largest affected freshmen and students of whom it was generally felt that they should never have been accepted in the first place. This implied errors or oversights by Michael Kahn and myself—the ignoring, during auditions, of physical or psychological defects which, in the faculty's opinion, rendered the student unfit for a productive career in the theatre. These deficiencies or an evident lack of commitment were generally detected during the first year and resulted (as it had with Group I) in a purge that averaged up to one third of each new class.

The second, later and more controversial dismissals included those of students who had qualified physically and emotionally in their first year but about whom it was felt, after a second year of instruction, that their capacity and temperament would prevent them from ever rising above a mediocre level of theatrical achievement. These were the most painful of our executions—a delicate area in which unanimous and objective judgments were difficult to obtain.*

The third and smallest category of dismissals included some of our most creative and original students, who we never doubted would have a brilliant future but about whom we felt, for one reason or another, that there was little more we could teach them and that, for all their evident talent, they were not suitable material for the acting ensemble which we regarded as the major objective of our fourth year.†

This final category did not concern us in the spring of 1970, when we had only Groups I and II to deal with. The past school year had been a particularly trying one, from which Group I—what remained of it—emerged tempered and tried in fire. Those who survived were the ones who, with the addition of our first group of advanced students, eventually formed the Acting Company that achieved such fame in years to come.

Group II had its normal share of misfits marked for liquidation, but its general level seemed more uniform and stable than Group I had ever been. For that reason I anticipated fewer tragic scenes than in the final days of the previous year. In planning my last few days of the school year I allotted two days to Group II. The last day would be devoted, as usual, to executions; on the first I would utter words of wisdom and exhortation which I would sweeten with congratulations, of which the principal recipients would be the two girls, Sherry Rivers and Kayla Spillson, who had emerged during the spring as the unquestioned stars of the group.

Sherry was a small, quiet, blond ingenue from a good, conventional background, with a terrific temperament which she

---

* A number of those liquidated on this basis had successful careers which proved our judgment mistaken. But of those whom we retained out of kindness of heart or because one teacher held out for them with particular obduracy, only a few justified our indulgence.
† One such student was Robin Williams, whose dynamic comic talent was never in doubt but whom we never considered a likely member of our Juilliard Acting Company. He left, by mutual consent, after his third year and has never ceased to express his gratitude for the teaching we gave him.

revealed only in her acting. Kayla was a rangy, handsome girl whose father owned a hotel in the Midwest. She had a warm, open personality and unusual authority as a performer. Both were model students—yet it was at their hands that I now received two of the most shattering blows dealt me during my whole time at Juilliard. They delivered them separately, on the same morning, sorrowful but determined, their eyes brimming with tears. Both were highly motivated, both were directly affected by the fevered emotional atmosphere created by the Vietnam War. And, with both, sex played a determining part in their reluctant but irrevocable decision to leave the school.

In Sherry's case it took the form of an escape through religion from the violence and horror of the contemporary world. She had found a young man who shared her views; they were getting married and would live a simple, dedicated life in a mini-bus with a canoe on its roof. Kayla's case was simpler and more urgent. She had been living for some time with a young man who, as a conscientious objector, was being forced to seek refuge, like so many others, in Canada. She had decided to follow and was leaving to join him in a few days.*

I sympathized with them personally, but, for the school, it was a low blow on which I put the best face I could. I would have been even more upset if I could have foreseen the devastating effect their leaving would have, within a few months, on the precarious balance of the group of which they formed an important and, as it turned out, an essential part.

The closing of the school left me with feelings of sadness and emptiness. Then, within a few days, my priorities began to shift. In the fall I would return to the task of running an institution to which I was wholly committed and of which I

---

* Three years later I received a letter from her from Vancouver, B.C., where she had given birth to two children and achieved some success in local theatre. Now she was inquiring about the possibility of returning and completing her training at Juilliard. I replied that we'd be glad to take her back but I never heard from her again.

was increasingly proud. But, for the rest of the summer, I once again found myself changing my focus.

Joe Barnes's death had been a double loss. It meant the absence of a dear friend; it also meant the end of what seemed my only hope for the printing of a book into which I had poured ten years of sporadic but intensely emotional effort. So it was with surprise and renewed hope that I read a letter I received from Simon and Schuster, with whom I had a contract to publish my book:

> I know how distressed you must be about Joe Barnes —as I am. I've known him for thirteen years as a friend and a colleague, and I have always thought of him as a link to sanity in a crazy world and loved him as one of those rare men who manage to be both gentle and strong at the same time.
>
> For obvious reasons, this isn't the time to discuss business, except that writing a book isn't business, it's an emotional commitment. For reasons that are equally obvious, I don't want you to feel that you are cut off from your publisher and have no one to talk to in Joe's absence. . . . Since I know your book is nearly finished and since I think you must now be worried about its fate (and quite rightly), I would like to reassure you and do whatever I can to make you feel that you are being published by someone who knows what the book is, who you are and what it's all about. . . . Would you like to 'phone me so we can talk?
>
> Yours,
> MICHAEL KORDA,
> Editor in Chief

I wrote to thank him for his kindness, but it was some weeks before we met and months before I felt ready to send him what there was of my book.

Toward the beginning of June, I summoned up sufficient courage to carry a large package of typescript to the twenty-eighth floor of the building in Rockefeller Center where Simon and Schuster had their offices. I added the two articles that had been printed in *Harper's* ("The Men from Mars" and

431

my account of Ray Chandler's writing of the script for *The Blue Dahlia*) and enclosed a letter in which I described the existent material and indicated what was still missing.

Korda's reaction was prompt and encouraging. He urged me not to worry too much about the shape or length of the book but to go on writing and to make it as personal as possible.*

My gratitude to Joe Barnes was undiminished, but the realization that my book was now under the control and subject to the judgment of a stranger with whom I had no old ties of affection and loyalty had a strangely galvanizing effect on my writing and drove me forward at an accelerated tempo.

Throughout the summer in New City, I led a strange double life, stretched between two entirely different worlds—between the short-lived Mercury Theatre with its anxieties and triumphs of thirty years ago and the calm, pleasant life Joan and I were leading on the hill that summer. For part of the time we had a house guest, a lovely red-haired English girl of sixteen, my wife's niece, who lay in decorative patterns on the terrace beneath my study and kept Joan company during my long voyages into the past.

The boys were away much of the time—Sebastian in a summer camp in Nova Scotia, John Michael at Brandeis, performing his tedious and thankless duties as caretaker for the radical student organization of which he had become an active member the previous winter. His disillusion was gradual and was aggravated by the arrest—following an aborted holdup in which a guard was shot to death—of a girl with whom he had been associated during the winter.

This marked the limits of his radical associations. They were replaced by a mounting interest in comparative religion,

* Years later, after the great success of his own book about the Korda family, Michael told me of his ambivalent reaction to the first part of my book; he had found in my description of my polyglot Eastern European childhood and my subsequent move to England many elements that were surprisingly close to his own family experiences and to the subject of the book he was himself in the process of writing.

including the Hebraic studies* in which Brandeis was particularly distinguished. These in turn led indirectly to a growing interest in anthropology, which he eventually made his life's work.

For my part, I was back to the twelve-hour-a-day routine which alone made it possible for me to make appreciable progress on my book. I was writing now about those wild months in the mid-thirties during which the Mercury had been conceived and turned from a desperate venture by two irresponsible young men into the season's outstanding theatrical success. I found once again (as I had in Paris) that the only way to achieve credibility in describing those events and the atmosphere in which they were formed was to immerse myself totally in my own memory of that period. This called for a daily voyage into the past and involved intense concentration and a willingness to move the center of my life out of the present into another time and another place.†

I had done it before, in Paris, during my daily visits to Virgil's apartment on the Quai Voltaire. At that time I had been groping, in almost total darkness, through a past of which I remembered little—a childhood I was trying to re-create out of hearsay, circumstantial evidence and emotional echoes. Now, in describing the rise and fall of the Mercury Theatre, I had access to data, including press files, personal recollections and the research done by a UCLA student for his thesis. These helped me to keep the facts of my story straight. But this was only the frame. The real story, the only one worth telling, the anxieties and insane dreams, the spasms of hope and terror, the alternating exhilaration and despair through which we lived during those fateful eighteen months, and, above all, the intense personal relations that had swayed our lives during that time—these could be

* Under Nahum Nahum Glatzer.
† These time games have led me occasionally into curious and convoluted situations—as when I found myself, in the mid-seventies, sitting on my hill in New City, describing a time when I was sitting on my hill in 1968 trying to recapture the emotions I felt when I had first lived in New City in 1933!

evoked only by feeling them once again in something of their original intensity. And this, in turn, could be achieved only by those daily journeys into the past which made me a strange and scary companion for my wife, who found herself living all summer with a man whose emotional energies were centered on a time that was more than thirty years in the past and who seemed to find this recreated world more vivid and absorbing than the current satisfactions of life on the hill. It is also true that these voyages through time left me drained and weakened—suffering from the emotional jet lag that was deeper and more distressing than that induced by mere physical motion!

By late August I had recorded the Mercury's miraculous first year and I was preparing to move into our disastrous second season, in which "The Men from Mars" was a lurid but welcome interlude. I had written about it twenty years earlier, and I was able to absorb my *Harper's* piece into my narrative almost without change.

By mid-September the time had come to move back into my school world. However, with the impetus I had gained over the summer, I continued to write throughout the fall and winter, so that by the spring of 1971 I had finished with *Citizen Kane* and *Native Son* and was in sight of Pearl Harbor, which I had set as my goal for the first part of my memoir.

CHAPTER XIV

1970-1972

> *Work in the third year centers on interpre-*
> *tation, to which all other elements of*
> *training now converge. A number of plays*
> *in various styles are performed before a*
> *limited audience in the Drama Division's*
> *Drama Theatre and in the New York pub-*
> *lic schools.*
> —FROM THE "BIBLE" OF MICHEL
>   SAINT-DENIS

THE THIRD YEAR of the Drama Division was marked by two major changes. The enrollment of yet another class (Group III) added to the range of our curriculum and to the complexity of our schedule. But the main difference was the arrival of those advanced students whom Michael and I had auditioned the previous spring. Their number was small, but their presence made an entirely new set of demands on our faculty, which was faced with the problem of assimilating young professionals who were at a different (though not necessarily at a higher) level than our own third-year students.

This assimilation was aided by the program of performances we now undertook for the educational arm of Lincoln Center. For some years, ever since the creation of the Performing Arts Center, educational programs had been offered by its various constituents: instrumental groups, soloists, singers and small companies of dancers had been performing forty-five-minute shows during the lunch hour throughout the New York public-school system. Now, as the Drama Division entered its third year, dramatic entertainment was added.

This new assignment was not taken lightly by faculty or students. Much time and thought was devoted that fall to selecting plays that would prove comprehensible and entertaining to school audiences of varying ages and social levels, all of which had one thing in common—that few of them had ever seen or heard of live theatre.

For Group I it was a tough but valuable way to begin their acting careers. In schools that were predominantly black or Latino they faced audiences that were perplexed, unruly and hostile to the point where our young performers frequently became targets for open paper clips and other more substantial missiles. It became their assignment to give performances that would overcome this initial hostility and, within a limited time, transform these suspicions into participation and enjoyment.

Our choice of plays, after much debate, fell on two quite different shows. The first was Molière's classic and infallible farce *Les Fourberies de Scapin,* in a version prepared and directed by Pierre Lefèvre, who had joined our faculty that fall. He included in his production many of the things he was teaching Group I in its advanced improvisation and mask classes—thus finally fulfilling our avowed goal of closely meshing our curriculum with our performances. The *Scapin* translation never entirely satisfied me, but, with its simple and universal farce situations and routines and its bright, witty costumes by Carrie Robbins, it was particularly suited to the audiences before whom we played it five times a week in high and junior high schools throughout the five boroughs and later, in the spring, as far afield as Binghamton, Rochester and Buffalo. It was well cast and directed and had among its performers such talented actors as Stiers, Kline, Schramm, Sakren, Hendrickson, Rosato and, in the role of Zerbinetta, Patti LuPone.

I have always regarded these school performances as a valuable and essential element in our Juilliard training; I believe they were largely responsible for the ease and self-assurance with which our Juilliard Acting Company eventually faced the hazards and hardships of repertory touring.

Though I had fewer outside interests than usual that winter, it would have been unlike me to restrict my activities to my two main projects, running the school and writing the book.

The APA was dead, but the Phoenix went on its persistent way and I continued to bear the title of producing director. "T.'s" youth gambit had run its uneven course, and the Phoenix was back at the Lyceum with a successful production of Molière's *School for Wives,* directed by Stephen Porter, with Joan Van Ark and Brian Bedford, who received a Tony Award for his performance as Arnolphe. Later in the season the Phoenix became associated with Gordon Davidson and Leland Hayward in the New York production of Berrigan's controversial *Trial of the Catonsville Nine,* which Gordon had first presented at the Mark Taper in Los Angeles.

A more emotional involvement, that winter, took me into an altogether different area. After many months, *Three by Martha Graham* had been shown on public television and received generally enthusiastic reviews. According to Anna Kisselgoff of *The New York Times:*

The program was extraordinary on two levels—the first being that Miss Graham, whose reluctance to film her dances in the past has been well known, has finally consented to have three of her late works recorded and made available to the general public. The second is the confirmation that, given intelligent adaptation, Miss Graham's dramatic pieces—with their typical flashbacks and restructuring of chronological sequences—have an affinity with today's film techniques (which in some ways she foreshadowed) and are particularly well-suited to filming ... To say that the dancing throughout the entire program is excellent would be an understatement. Graham dancers are all "acrobats of God."

This praise was echoed throughout the country. Boston's *Christian Science Monitor* reported: "Miss Graham looks marvelous, even in closeup, refuting the argument of some who urge her to retire." Others described the color of the film as "transcendent" and the filming as "the best yet seen of ensemble dancing on a grand scale."

It was a pleasure to have the film come out as well as it did. However, this did not solve Martha's recurrent personal crises nor diminish the growing threat of dissolution faced by the Graham organization. Following my work on the film I had kept up my association with the company, particularly with Lee Leatherman and Pat Birch. Martha herself had not been in the best of health, and I knew that the question of her own continued appearances with the company was a constant and agonizing problem for her. It was more than a year since her last, dubious season at the City Center, and still Martha could not make up her mind whether, at seventy-six, she should step down as a dancer and let others take over the great roles she had created and with which she was internationally identified.

It was at this point that Birch, Leatherman and others in her harassed entourage approached me in desperation and suggested that I take over the presidency of the Martha Graham Dance Center. I hesitated, but, in what I now regard as an outrageous piece of meddling, I offered, in view of our old friendship, to have a meeting with Martha in which I would try to obtain a clearer view of her own feelings about her future and that of the company.

I went to see her one afternoon in her apartment on East Sixty-third Street and immediately I had the feeling, as I always did when I was alone with her, of being in the presence of greatness—a greatness frayed, at this moment, by rage and despair. She knew why I was there, and she must have hated the sight of me. Yet, for our first hour together, she was her usual seductive, manipulative female self. There were occasional interruptions, brief visits to a back room from which she returned each time with brighter eyes and seemingly heightened energy. On learning that I was on the currently fashionable high-protein diet, she produced three slices of delicious corned beef and pressed them upon me; she showed me a sea shell that, she declared, "perfectly combines art and homemaking"; finally, she presented to me a striking photograph of herself in "Acrobats of God." Each of these gifts called for a trip to the back room, and her speech had begun to thicken a little when she finally got around to talking about herself.

"I'm a proud, vain, spoiled woman, John, and have been for forty years. . . . My analyst tells me I'll realize one day that I'm not a goddess."

These were among the phrases I remember as, gradually, layer by layer, the full depth of her distress was revealed. I couldn't blame her. For close to fifty years, much of the time by herself, she had fought and struggled to create, with her brain and her muscles, a body of entirely personal and dangerously original work. During that time she had assembled a company of high quality and held it together under terrible conditions of deprivation and public indifference. Finally, in middle age, she had achieved a measure of success that she had built gradually into general acceptance and international fame. Now, in her mid-seventies, with her spirit undaunted and her creative powers at their peak, she was facing the horror of her own inevitable physical deterioration. Gradually her own dancing—the essential instrument of her creation—was becoming a liability to herself and to her company. Better than anyone else she was aware that critics and audiences were being tolerant of her failing powers out of respect and admiration for her past achievements; aware, too (and it hurt and angered her), that there was a growing feeling, among audiences and even among her own people, that it was her artistic obligation to herself and to her company to let younger women replace her in the great dancing roles which she had created for herself over the years but which it was still emotionally impossible for her to accept could be danced by anyone else.

"There is no reality in this piece except the inner reality of feeling eternal in all of us." So she had written in her published notebooks about one of her works. And this is what she felt now. It was not a question of ability or quality, nor even a matter of vanity. (She knew that in her day no one compared with her and that nobody would for years to come.) I believe she was convinced that without her presence these intensely personal creations of hers would cease to exist or, rather, that they would lose their "reality" if they were separated from her own physical and spiritual identity and the personality that had made them famous.

When I spoke to her of the repertory and of the irreparable loss it would be to the world if it were not kept alive, I had the impression that, in her present mood, she would just as soon pull the temple down about her head and perish in the rubble!

I gave Martha's trustees a tempered account of my interview. Most of them were old, faithful believers who had lived with her through earlier crises and who now refused to accept defeat. Flattered by their insistence and in a vague hope that, in one way or another, I could help to keep the company together, I agreed to become caretaker-president of the Martha Graham Dance Center. It is not a term I remember with pride or pleasure. Classes at the Martha Graham School continued under the company's leading dancers with irregular and occasionally brilliant incursions by Miss Graham herself. And in the winter of 1970 there was a brief, poorly attended season at the Brooklyn Academy of Music in which Martha did not dance but sat in the wings glowering at her demoralized dancers and waiting grimly, and not entirely without satisfaction, for what appeared to be the inevitable dissolution of her life's work!

I would hesitate to record this painful episode were it not that the story had a completely happy and triumphal ending.

On June 20, 1975, about two years after her own close brush with death and sometime after I had resigned from the presidency of the Martha Graham Center, *The New York Times* devoted an entire page to "one of the season's great galas of show business"—the first of the annual Graham apotheoses that have followed each other with such regularity over the years. Clive Barnes, reporting this celebration of the company's fiftieth anniversary, described the historic curtain call "with Dame Margot Fonteyn and Rudolf Nureyev—the living embodiment of classic ballet's public suffrage—flanking the divine Martha, the incorruptible and true spirit of modern dance."

That evening's main artistic attractions were a speech by Miss Graham and the premiere of her new work, "Lucifer," performed by Fonteyn and Nureyev, for whom it was specially devised and of whom Barnes reported that Nureyev "moves with a naturally pantherine, Grahamesque grace" while Miss Fonteyn "looked Oriental and gorgeous"—both of them in costumes designed for the occasion by Halston.*

The program also featured revivals of an early Graham solo, "Lamentation," and two Graham classics: "Seraphic Dialogue" and "Diversion of Angels," danced by a new company among whom few of the Graham company of five years ago were to be found but of which Barnes reported that they were "vibrant with youth and energy."

It was left to another reporter to add: "Despite the success of the fund drive and the acclaim for Miss Graham and her company, there was one note of sadness the eighty-two-year-old dance pioneer touched on in a recent comment: 'I'd much rather be dancing than choreographing,' she said. 'I'll always miss it.'"

---

* "According to Miss Graham's aides, the costumes worn by Mr. Nureyev and Dame Margot were heavily laden with gold, platinum and silver, and the baubles that glittered from the stage were true diamonds and rubies. The precious metals and jewels were donated for the costumes made gratis by Halston. One estimate by Miss Graham's associates was that the costumes were worth more than $100,000."

Nineteen seventy-two was a significant year for me: it marked the first stage of an entirely unexpected new life— one filled with a series of surprises that does not appear to have ended yet. This did not become apparent for the first half of the year. Besides the book, on which I continued to work with additional zeal now that its end was in sight, Juilliard still occupied most of my time and concern, which I divided unevenly between the three groups that made up our student body. It was too early to appraise Group III, but it was evident that Group II, bereft of its two best members, had started on its long and depressing process of disintegration. Group I, on the other hand, seemed to have shaken down and to be moving forward with a steady and exhilarating motion.

With their successful school season behind them, they settled down to rehearse two new productions. One, our most ambitious to date, was Middleton's *Women Beware Women*, directed by Michael Kahn. A Jacobean tragedy is among the most difficult of all theatre pieces to present with young American actors,* but it was something that Kahn had long wanted to undertake and for which he was well prepared. It worked remarkably well and formed the basis of the repertory season with which we surprised New York City ten months later. Three of the girls for whom there were no parts in *Women* consoled themselves with a finely honed production (presented on our small stage) of Genêt's *The Maids*, which gave them opportunities for intense and violent acting.

Other productions rehearsed that winter and spring by various groups included Ed Bullins' all-black *New England Winter*, *The Three Sisters*, *Thieves' Carnival*, *Tartuffe*, *You Can't Take It with You*, *The Orchestra*, *The Indian Wants the Bronx*, *Chips with Everything*, *Room Service*, *A View from the Bridge* and *Suddenly Last Summer*, none of which I directed, since I was busy downstairs in the main Juilliard theatre staging the premiere of a new work for the Opera Center.

The Losers was a contemporary piece that had been commis-

---

* As I had learned to my cost during my production of *The Duchess of Malfi* in 1957.

sioned by the Music School from an alumnus named Farberman, the recently appointed musical director of the Oakland (California) Symphony. Its libretto dealt with the violent and sadistic behavior of a motorcycle gang operating in the style of California's highly publicized Hell's Angels and vaguely resembled Marlon Brando's film *The Wild One*.

But, for me, this whole production was a thrilling experience, made particularly attractive by its wonderful cast of young and enthusiastic singers and dancers and by the presence at my side of a highly creative and stimulating collaborator in the person of Pat Birch, to whom I owed much of the credit I received for a production that was essentially alien to me.* Once again Doug Schmidt came through with brilliant, atmospheric settings perfectly suited to our rather complicated needs; the costumes, a satirical use of denim and black leather, were by Jeanne Button. (Motorcycles were "by courtesy of Ghost Motorcycle and Harley-Davidson of Manhattan; fuel pumps courtesy of Humble Oil Refining Company.")

I had worked with "serial" music before, but this was something else again. I remember looking down into the pit as the musicians were finding their positions, and being startled to discover that our orchestration consisted of two pianos, fourteen percussionists armed with miscellaneous contrivances, and one violin! These were augmented onstage by a jazz combo and two body-miked and highly amplified pop singers acting as commentators and chorus.†

As our opening approached, we all became more and more saturated in violence—musical and theatrical. (One of Pat Birch's most vivid memories is of our repeated rehearsals of the gang rape, during which she says I kept shouting, "Rapists upstage right! Rapees downstage left!") At the same time

---

* Her choreography for the unspeakable "initiation" ceremony and the motorcyclists' dream sequence was based on elaborate research and with help from a former Hell's Angels initiate who happened to be working as a stagehand at Lincoln Center.
† One of these, a beautiful black girl named Barbara Hendricks, a favorite pupil of Jennie Tourel, became an internationally celebrated soprano.

I detected growing nervousness on the second floor, climaxed by a phone call (of which it was never discovered whether it was genuine or a hoax) from the New York branch of Hell's Angels, announcing that they would be present in force on opening night to break up what they considered a libelous attack on their order. This, added to the goings-on he had witnessed at our first preview, was too much for Dr. Mennin, who suddenly discovered that he had an important out-of-town engagement that evening. Nevertheless, the opening took place as scheduled on the night of March 26, with some added police protection.

According to Harold Schonberg of *The New York Times:*

FISTS AND SEX ABOUND
IN HANDSOME STAGING

It's relevant, *The Losers* is, if motorcycle gangs, violence, a gang-rape and other assorted gore can be considered relevant. It's also an opera and there is a motorcycle ballet, just like the Bacchanal in *Faust.* . . .

Mr. Faberman's score is avant-garde. His vocal lines use the favored wide skips so beloved of the post-serialists. The orchestra is noisy and violent with some very stylized post-serial jazz. Mr. Faberman is nothing if not doctrinaire and he has used every stylistic cliché in the idiom. His dissonances are fine for making angry noises and squealing commentaries on life. But the result is a dreadful musical monotony. . . .

The production by John Houseman is brilliant and by far the best thing I have seen from Juilliard's Opera Center. . . . But I still think *The Losers* is, in a crazy kind of way, American kitsch.

Other reviews followed the same pattern of controversy over the music and shocked admiration for the production. The correspondent of the *Kansas City Star* wrote that "this story of robbery, rape and murder with an interlude of gang-ritual barbarity and a ballet reminiscent of a 'Walpurgis Night' is an outstanding achievement of the current operatic season." *The Village Voice* called it "the most relentlessly violent theatre work I have ever seen."

444

There was disagreement among the nation's leading music critics. Bernheimer of the *Los Angeles Times* reported:

The American Opera Center at Juilliard must command one of the most virtuosic ensembles of young singing actors in the world. And the neo-realistic physical production by John Houseman, designed by Dougles Schmidt, must represent a landmark in enlightened opera theatre as far as New York is concerned.

Alan Rich, in *New York* magazine, in a general attack on the Juilliard Opera Center, described the work as "a piece of vile, garish uncomprehending exploitation . . . just another testimonial to the idea that Americans neither want, understand nor are capable of producing Opera."

Group I of the Drama Division, meantime, was rehearsing its second major production, *The School for Scandal*, under the direction of Gerald Freedman. We were not repeating our error of the previous year. Before embarking on Sheridan's celebrated comedy of manners, members of Group I had worked all fall with Lefèvre on advanced improvisation and on character masks and complemented their classwork with the comic performances with which they toured throughout the New York school system. They had also done considerable work on seventeenth- and eighteenth-century style followed by a full month of master classes in the more subtle aspects of high comedy, conducted by Gerald Freedman.

This careful preparation showed in the three performances they gave in a formal and very elegant setting by Doug Schmidt, wearing gorgeous costumes by John David Ridge, with a cast that included Patti LuPone and David Schramm as the Teazles, David Stiers and Kevin Kline as the Surface brothers, and Mary Lou Rosato as Lady Sneerwell.* It was seen by the faculty, by friends of the cast and by a few invited guests and benefactors. After that it was put in mothballs for the summer, with the intention of adding it to *Women*

* A role for which she received a Drama Desk Award the following year.

Beware Women in the repertory we were forming for public exhibition in the fall.

On July 31, 1971, Michel Saint-Denis died in London, and we mourned his passing. We had worked together for less than two years, but what he had given us, directly and through Suria, was the accumulated wisdom and experience of a life dedicated to actor training. We might have had a Drama Division without him, but it would have been a very different and, without question, a less valuable one.

Before retiring to my hill for the summer I had agreed to spend one month in a Midwestern city in which I had resided years before. I returned to Kansas City, Missouri, at the invitation of Patricia McIlrath* as the first occupant of a newly established Chair of Theatre at the University of Missouri, which called for a series of three lectures and the direction of one play for the Missouri Repertory Company.

For the opening of its summer season I once again staged my production of *Measure for Measure,* with its usual success. According to the *Kansas City Star:*

> There are delights that gain a special zing for being so unexpected. What surprised us last night was not the company's strength (this has been evident for some time) nor was it John Houseman's acumen as a Shakespearean director—a fact well established through his long career in the American theatre. Rather it was the pleasure and sense he and his cast were able to wring from this most astringent and obscure of Shakespeare's comedies.

It was a strange feeling, between rehearsals, to find myself living within a few hundred yards of the hotel in which I had spent two miserable summers half a century ago, racked by heat and loneliness and the agonies and ecstasies of unrequited love.†

* A woman of unusual courage, energy and dedication who, against overwhelming odds, had created, first, a theatre department at the University of Missouri in Kansas City, then a viable regional theatre company and, finally, one of the finest university performing-arts centers in the United States.
† See *Run-Through,* "Overture."

These memories were particularly vivid just then as the result of an unexpected setback I had suffered with my book. On my rereading the seven hundred pages of typescript I had finally handed in, it had become horribly clear (to me as author and to Michael Korda as editor) that the book was in two parts that did not hang together. The first two hundred and fifty pages (the sum of so many years of false starts, self-examinations and taped confessions) were an emotional investigation of my childhood, my education and the tensions of my early manhood. They contained much of the book's most intimate and sensitive writing, but it was all highly personal and subjective and bore little relation to the theatrical and historical events which constituted the body of the book and which, in my opinion, alone justified its publication.

For this reason I rejected Korda's generous offer (which I was never quite sure he meant) that we make two books of it. Instead, I undertook the hard and repulsive task of reducing the first third of my book—all the events preceding my entrance into the theatre at the age of thirty-one—to the proportions of an overture, which I subtitled "The Education of a Chameleon."

This drastic cutting became my assignment for the summer. It was a tedious and painful chore in which no one could help me, for it meant going back through all those memories that had been dredged up and organized into some sort of pattern, and which now had to be torn apart once again and reduced to a brief fragment of their earlier form. I worked at it, patiently and miserably, first in Kansas City and then in the House on the Hill, till, by the time school was ready to reopen in mid-September, I had completed and delivered a new version of the book that was now just over five hundred pages long.

There remained the question of the title. I had a working title I loved, *The Chimes at Midnight,* * but no one else cared for it, and Korda, who favored a theatrical title, came up with

* By a not so curious coincidence this was the title Orson Welles had given to his film version of *Five Kings.* The phrase "the chimes at midnight" occurs in the great scene of reminiscence between Shallow, Silence and Sir John Falstaff in *Henry IV*, Part 2.

447

Front and Center, which I rejected as being too egotistical.*
Finally, going through a long list of theatrical terms, I chose
Run-Through, which seemed appropriate and was generally
approved.

Before I was finally done with the book I was exposed to
one last emotional trauma when I spent several days assembling photographs and graphic material of the past, some of
which had been moldering in boxes and faded albums for
more than fifty years. I selected the ones that seemed relevant and delivered them personally one morning to Michael
Korda. As I walked out of his office I felt suddenly and finally
free of an incubus with which I had been living for more
than twenty years.

* I used it later for my second book, to which it seemed more applicable.

CHAPTER XV

1971-1972

JUILLIARD: THE FOURTH YEAR
REPERTORY
THE COUNTRY GIRL
FALSTAFF
LORD BYRON

> *The emphasis is now on performance.*
> *While continuing their studies, fourth-*
> *year students of the Basic Course, together*
> *with Advanced Students in their second*
> *year, collaborate to present three or more*
> *productions in different styles. These are*
> *performed in Juilliard's Drama Theatre*
> *before being played on a tour of Univer-*
> *sity and Community theatres and, finally,*
> *in Repertory.*
> —FROM THE SAINT-DENIS "BIBLE"

AS THE DRAMA DIVISION entered its fourth year, I continued
to fluctuate between anxiety and pride, heightened by brief
moments of triumph when it seemed, for a few days, that all

our doubts and troubles were over. December 1971 was such a time.

The school was running at full strength now, with four groups in operation, amounting to a total enrollment of slightly under one hundred students. Group III had suffered the usual defections and dismissals, but these were not nearly as grievous as those of the unfortunate Group II. Group I stood steady at twenty (including three advanced), and it was with them and with the achievements of their final year that I was now principally concerned.

Encouraged by the unusual quality of their third-year productions, I had decided, during the summer, that the time had come for the Drama Division to throw off its wrappings and reveal itself to the world. The most effective—as well as the most dangerous—way to do this was to present Group I in a full-scale New York repertory season open to the public and the press.

Part of such a repertory already existed. *The School for Scandal* and *Women Beware Women* had been seen as student productions in the spring. For our projected season I added two shows of completely different periods and contrasting styles. One was a double bill of two short, powerful contemporary plays: *Interview,* by van Itallie (of which we had performed a fragment during our public-school season), and *The Indian Wants the Bronx,* by Israel Horowitz—both directed by Gene Lesser. For our fourth we chose, by way of contrast, Gorky's *Lower Depths,* directed by Boris Tumarin. All four were large-cast productions calculated to show off the group's versatility and its capacity for "ensemble" playing that I considered its principal virtue.

After they returned from their long summer vacation, members of Group I resumed daily classes in voice, movement and other disciplines, but the main emphasis was now on performance and on preparation for the fateful repertory season on which I had decided to risk our reputation as America's leading theatrical conservatory. Considering the chance we were taking, everyone remained surprisingly cool.

With four different directors,* it was possible to rehearse all four productions simultaneously—depending on available space and the stamina of the company. For the first part of the term, priority was given to *Lower Depths,* which was previewed in late October before a limited student audience. Our three other productions were then taken out of mothballs and rehearsed all over again, profiting from what we had learned during our previous performances. By late November all four plays were ready. (For good measure, eight of the company, on their own time, were also preparing Paul Shyre's dramatic version of Dos Passos' *U.S.A.*)

Early in the term we had sent out several thousand mailings in the red-black-and-white format we had established for our brochures, announcing our repertory and dedicating the season to the memory of our beloved co-director, Michel Saint-Denis.

We had apparently underestimated the general curiosity about our work, for by mid-November we had sold two thirds of our tickets for a season that was still several weeks away. Later that month a press release was sent out with background information about the Juilliard Acting Company, its repertory and its members. And I wrote personal notes to the New York drama critics explaining that we did not expect them to review us but that we would be happy if they would drop in and appraise the work we had been doing at the school over the past three and a half years.

We began our dry run on the first of December with previews for members of the Music and Dance Divisions and invited guests. The company took its repertory in stride, and, backstage, Doug Schmidt and Pacitti seemed to make their difficult scene changes with reasonable ease. We opened our season with *The School for Scandal* on December 7 and closed —following our announced schedule—on the night of December 16 after twelve performances.

The next morning, in *The New York Times,* we read the first

---

* Kahn, Freedman, Lesser and Tumarin.

and possibly the most important review ever received by the Acting Company.*

THE JUILLIARD COMPANY—
A SCHOOL FOR STARS

Anyone worried about the future of the American theatre should have seen the new Juilliard Acting Company in action, presenting a season of true repertory and doing it splendidly. . . .

It occupied four full columns and ended with a question:

This is a repertory that would challenge any company and it does, but each reveals, in performance, a first-rate ensemble of actors. Why can't we keep them here intact as a permanently expanding company, performing great plays in repertory?

There were other reactions—some printed, some in the form of personal letters. From Henry Hewes of the *Saturday Review:* "Thanks for inviting me to one of the best evenings I've had in the theatre this year." From Zelda Fichandler, artistic director of Washington's Arena Stage: "The training is unrivalled. You are bound to have a seminal effect on acting throughout the country." From Norris Houghton: "It fulfills itself totally and proves the rightness of the conclusion that an intensive program of training can indeed result in a superior product." It all seemed too good to be true.

Our *New York Times* review set off an immediate demand for our repertory in a number of Eastern and Midwestern universities. To satisfy these unexpected requests, we hurriedly set up logistical services for which we were totally unprepared: between January and the end of April we presented our repertory—whole or in part—at Harvard's Loeb Theatre; at Princeton; at Urbana, Illinois; at Toledo, Ohio; at Ann Arbor and Flint, Michigan; and at the University of Indiana in Bloomington.

* It was written by Mel Gussow, alternate drama critic of the *Times,* who has followed the Acting Company's progress from then to the present day.

Everywhere the reaction was the same: "Juilliard Delivers with Honors"; "Polished and Promising Talent"; "Talent Abounds in Juilliard Company"; "Dazzling Student Actors." Boston went further: our Harvard performances were covered by the town's two leading drama critics.

> The Juilliard Acting Company is, without question, one of the most endearing and talented groups I've ever seen. . . . *The School for Scandal* is rollicking, high-spirited and graceful as a minuet. On the considered level of the company's many merits, including a handsome set, superb costumes, atmospheric lighting, they should be welcome just about anywhere.   [Kevin Kelly, *Boston Globe*]

> *The Lower Depths* is in many ways extraordinary. . . . Boris Tumarin has made something of a miracle: American actors rarely get so close to the truth about Russian drama.   [Elliot Norton, *Boston Herald-American*]

And a local magazine asked the question "If Juilliard turns out a comparable crew every year, which seems likely, can the renaissance of the American stage be far behind?"

Some months had gone by since the astrologer lady had thrown her celestial bombshell into my life, and the beneficent effects of Saturn's retreat were becoming clearly apparent. Nineteen thirty-seven had been a wonder year. So had 1947. Nineteen seventy-two promised to be another.

While I continued to regard the conduct of the Drama Division as my primary concern and the crowning achievement of my life in the theatre, there was a part of me that had never ceased to regret the agitations of show business, where, for so many years, I had strained and struggled and occasionally triumphed. Following my vain attempt to interest a serious theatrical agent in my career, I had made no further move in that direction. So it came as an agreeable surprise when one morning, in New City, I received a call from Peter Witt* (whom I knew from having engaged him,

---

* Peter Witt started life in Germany, where he was a violinist and a champion tennis player. After the war he set up as an independent theatrical agent in New York. Later he became a successful producer in London and New York.

during the war, to work on the German desk of the Voice of America). He asked me if I knew Clifford Odets' *Country Girl* and if I liked it. I answered yes to both questions. Two days later he called again. One of his clients, Jason Robards, was about to play it in Washington, D.C., in the first production to be presented by the Kennedy Center in its newly opened Eisenhower Theatre. Other actors already signed were Maureen Stapleton and George Grizzard. Would I be interested in directing it? Robards had approved me; so had Maureen and George. Roger Stevens, the producer, was uncertain. Then, a few days later, Peter Witt called again to say that Stevens had come around and that contracts were being prepared for rehearsals to begin in early October.

I doubt if it is possible for a layman to appreciate the significance of this offer. It is a commonplace that everyone in the theatre is perennially convinced, between engagements, that he or she will never work again. In my case, this feeling was justified by the bitter knowledge that in four years I had not received one single serious professional offer. Kansas City had been a crumb; here, suddenly, was the whole loaf! At Kennedy Center and with that cast, I was back in the best of the commercial theatre and working with three of the most highly regarded actors in America.

Then, with the ink scarcely dry on my contract, a call reached me through Juilliard from the Washington Opera Society asking if I would consider directing Verdi's *Falstaff* (which happened to be one of the operas I love best in the world)! As further evidence of supernatural intervention I discovered that the dates were so spaced that I could direct both the opera and the Odets play and thus enjoy the extraordinary distinction of having two major productions running simultaneously in different theatres at the Kennedy Center!

This turned my next few weeks into a crazy, magical time. I spent mornings and evenings at Juilliard watching rehearsals and supervising preparations for the Acting Company's repertory season; the rest of the day was spent rehearsing *The Country Girl,* except that occasionally, in the lunch hour or late at night, I also met and auditioned singers who were being considered for *Falstaff*. For the final ten days of rehearsals, which were held on the virgin stage of the Eisenhower Theatre in the Kennedy Center, Joan and I moved to Washington and lived at the Watergate.

The Country Girl is not a difficult play to stage. I had seen it in the theatre with Uta Hagen and on the screen with Grace Kelly. But with Maureen Stapleton in the role of Georgie the play took on a different quality. There was little I could add to Robards' very personal and credible interpretation of the alcoholic actor; but the relationship between his wife (Maureen Stapleton) and his director (George Grizzard) needed to be adjusted to the personalities of the actors who were playing the parts. I faced the problem and succeeded in dealing with it—no great trick with three actors of such intelligence and sensitivity.

> Among these three exists a common attitude toward style. All have the ability to convey intensity of feeling, presenting a superficiality of naturalness beneath which taut springs are about to break from control. Usually one finds this particular accomplishment limited to a couple of players. Here one relishes watching three actors with roles of equal balance reacting to each other's nerve-ends.
>
> Director John Houseman recognizes this unanimity of approach by letting his players take over as though they were not being "directed" at all. . . . They are immensely satisfying in their unanimity of style.

So wrote Richard Coe in *The Washington Post*. The *Star* was equally enthusiastic. So was Clive Barnes, who came down to review it for *The New York Times* and described it as

> a most delicate production in which Maureen Stapleton —despite remarkable acting opposition—is totally, indelibly memorable. Mr. Houseman seems to have placed her in the very center of the play and she revels in it. It is a lovely performance, one of the finest things Miss Stapleton has ever given us. . . . I am not usually an advocate of what is all too easily known as all-star theatre. But I must admit that here all the stars glittered.

For me, the main satisfaction of the production lay in the reassurance it gave me that, far from having deteriorated during my four years at academic grass, I seemed to have gained a security and an authority I had not had before.

I did not have much time to bask in my success, for the day after our Washington opening I was in New York, shuttling between Juilliard and rehearsals of *Falstaff*. Ten days after that I was back in Washington on the stage of the Opera House in Kennedy Center, conducting dress rehearsals of Verdi's opera, of which it would be pleasant to report that it was another triumph. For a number of reasons, some of which were beyond my control, it ended up very close to a disaster.

The errors I made were mainly for lack of preparation; the mistakes that ruined the production of this glorious work were most of them made before I came on the scene. In my eagerness to direct the opera, I chose to ignore them.

The musical director recently appointed by the Washington Opera Center was a French pianist whom I had heard playing the Brahms *Liebeslieder* waltzes for George Balanchine at Lincoln Center. He was a good pianist but a weak and enervated conductor. What was worse, throughout the preparation and performance of the opera we seemed to be engaged in musical intrigues of a mysterious and dangerous kind.*

Our Falstaff was his choice—and an unfortunate one. If there is one thing required of Shakespeare's "fat knight," it is physical and vocal authority. Ours had neither. He was a light French-Canadian baritone of limited stature. To make up for his lack of mass he hopped and fidgeted around the stage in a frenzy of meaningless, exasperating and banal activity which I did not check firmly enough. We had a powerful Ford, John Reardon, a touching ingenue, Benita Valente,

---

* One that directly affected us involved Washington's leading music critic (the one President Truman had threatened to thrash for his denigration of his daughter Margaret's voice). Three days before we opened, I was shown the text of the disastrous review he had already written about our production.

and an experienced and lively Mistress Quickly, Lili Chookasian.* But that did not suffice.

I made my own mistakes. I had been spoiled by the total support I was used to receiving from Larry Kelly in Dallas and by the lavish rehearsal time I had enjoyed at Juilliard. Now, as the production began to unravel, I had neither the experience nor the time to correct it. In a hopeless attempt to give some style and energy to the final scene in Windsor Park, I persuaded Pat Birch to fly down and give me a hand with the fairies. She did her best, but, for lack of time and faced with the exasperated ineptitude of our conductor, even she couldn't help me.

Our reviews were ghastly, but I didn't have time to brood about them. The day after *Falstaff* opened I was on my way to Paris to visit my mother, of whom Joan's mother was sending me increasingly disturbing reports. I spent four days with her in her hotel off the Rue de Rivoli. At ninety-one, except for her rage at the arthritis of the spine that made it painful and difficult for her to walk and interfered with the routine of her Paris life, she seemed comparatively well and surprisingly unchanged and beautiful. She spent most of the day in bed reading; had lunch—usually of Quaker Oats; bathed and began to make up at three; went out at five and made her slow way to Rumpelmayer's down the street, where she met friends and had tea and her first Scotch-and-soda before moving on to a well-chosen dinner at one of the better restaurants in the neighborhood. She tired easily, and, after she had gone to bed I spent one late night with the Frankenheimers on the Île Saint-Louis and an evening with Marguerite Duras in Montparnasse. On my way home to America I spent sixteen hours in London, where I had tea with my old friend Lee Miller, a drink with Sonya Orwell, dinner with John Russell Taylor † and saw one act of the Royal Shakespeare Company's production of Sartre's *Kean*.

* She played it for Zeffirelli in his successful Metropolitan production the following year.
† Drama and film critic for the *Times* of London and author of many books on theatre, films and the art world.

In describing the events of 1972, as in other manic periods of my life, I have difficulty in following my movements and in understanding how I could have found the energy and the time for all the activities in which I participated. In addition to my two Washington ventures and my continuing duties as head of the Drama Division and as impresario and press agent for the Acting Company, I was president of the National Theatre Conference and the National Puppet Council, and sat on the jury and took part in the distribution of the DuPont–Columbia Awards for the best television and radio journalism of the year. I participated with Gordon Davidson and the Phoenix in the production of Conor Cruise O'Brien's *Murderous Angels** and was an organizer and master of ceremonies of Virgil Thomson's seventy-fifth-birthday celebration, held in the Grand Ballroom of the Plaza Hotel.†

Also, throughout that year, I was doing a covert job for the Ford Foundation, observing and evaluating the television programs of the Public Broadcasting System, which were being supported in part by the foundation. The constant theme of my reports, throughout that year and the next, was the lamentable state of television drama in the United States and its shameful neglect by networks and public television alike. I complained of "our continued colonial status" at a time when American TV drama was "in its oxygen tent, gasping to survive," and lamented the virtual monopoly held by British drama on U.S. public television. Week after week I urged the foundation, in collaboration with the Corporation for Public Broadcasting, to do something to correct the situation.

In early March, following its successful run at the Kennedy Center, *The Country Girl* arrived in New York and had to be

---

* An interesting but uneven play about the crisis in the Congo and the deaths of Lumumba and Dag Hammarskjold.

† When I informed Virgil that I had accepted this assignment, he said, "That's fine! You can kill two birds with one stone. You can say noble things about me and read funny passages about us out of your book!"

rehearsed and tuned up for its Broadway opening. Barnes repeated his compliments and gave credit to

> a director who had sense to realize that this play, to suc-
> ceed, would have to be acted three times larger than life.
> It is and it does. Broadway is illuminated with these ob-
> vious but thrilling fireworks.

Walter Kerr headed his Sunday piece "An Old Champion Is Still Winner" and described it as a "vigorous, flashy, emotionally satisfying revival." The rest of the press was unanimous in its praise.*

This Broadway accolade, which I would have welcomed at other times as a significant triumph, was taken almost for granted on the roller-coaster ride that my life had become.

This breathless and jumbled account of my professional activities during the first half of 1972 does not include the most important and startling event of all—the publication of *Run-Through*. Throughout the previous fall I had spent hours in the offices of Simon and Schuster selecting photographs and going over my typescript with the copy editor, the art director and the legal department. The page proofs of *Run-Through* had been my Christmas present from Michael Korda, and I had received them with strangely mixed feelings.

It was exciting and satisfying, after so many years of frustration and false starts, momentary exhilaration and utter despair, to see those hundreds of thousands of words reduced to a few hundred neatly printed pages enclosed between covers of a book. At the same time it represented a finality that I found quite frightening. This thing with my name on it that was about to be issued to the world—was it a book or an ego trip? Was it something people would read

---

* *The Country Girl*, in spite of its great reviews, was never a solid hit in New York and moved in early summer to Los Angeles, where it received fine notices but achieved only modest financial success. It did, however, earn me an L.A. Drama Critics' Achievement Award in the Area of Distinguished Direction.

with interest and sympathy? Or would it be exposed as a huge chunk of self-serving nostalgia, a futile attempt to convince the world and, particularly, myself that my life had not been entirely wasted?

The first reassurance that I had done something more than rid myself of a gigantic load of self-doubt came in a brief note from Christopher Isherwood, to whom, on an impulse, I had sent one of my precious page proofs with an apology and a request, if he felt like it, to give me his opinion of the book. He was an old acquaintance but not a close friend, and I had chosen him, objectively, as a kind of literary litmus paper. His prompt and favorable response was a certificate of quality that was of infinite comfort to me in the anxious weeks before publication.

Early in February 1972 I was summoned to meet Dan Green, head of promotion for Simon and Schuster, who led me into an office where, piled in boxes, like Ali-Baba's treasure, I beheld several hundred copies of my book awaiting my signature.

It was a fantastic moment of unqualified bliss. For half a century I had dreamed of being a writer. I had come close to it at twenty-one,* only to have it snatched away and buried under years of business and travel.† Following my bankruptcy at the age of twenty-eight, when life once again offered me a chance to realize my writer's dream, I had been horrified to discover that I had absolutely nothing to write about. Now, forty years later, by a long and complicated route, it had come true. Here I was, in a small, cluttered office high up in Rockefeller Center, surrounded by copies of a thick, shiny book that bore my name and my picture in profile on the back cover together with complimentary comments by Christopher Isherwood, Russell Lynes, Brooks Atkinson and Virgil Thomson!

In the last week of February I was sent out by Simon and Schuster on the usual author's tour of major cities—Boston,

---

* When Leonard and Virginia Woolf had considered publishing a small book of mine at their Hogarth Press.
† *Run-Through*, "Overture."

Washington, Chicago, Minneapolis, San Francisco and, finally, Los Angeles, where the Lloyds and Jennifer Goldwyn
threw a huge and splendid party for me that was distinguished by one of the rare social appearances of Alfred
Hitchcock and, even more, by the fact that it was the very last
occasion on which Oscar Levant played the piano in public.

Back in New York, a week later, overwhelmed and exhausted, I attended a party given by Simon and Schuster in
Virgil Thomson's apartment at the Chelsea Hotel. It was similar, I imagine, to dozens of literary parties given each year
by publishers to launch their authors' books, but for me it
was a unique and historic occasion. When it was over and the
glasses and canapés had been cleared away and I had
thanked Virgil for the loan of his apartment and the two
efficient and decorative girl students from Juilliard for pushing the drinks, Joan and I took a cab uptown and stopped at
the newsstand on Times Square to pick up the early edition
of *The New York Times* on the off chance that it might contain
a review of my book. It did—and it was fine!

The following Sunday, to my amazement, the entire front
page of *The New York Times Book Review* was occupied by Walter Kerr's review of *Run-Through*.

> Such an entertaining book that it could be read, more or
> less shamefully, for the backstage gossip alone. But the
> fun and games are the least of it. "Memoir" is too slight
> a word for this substantial, satisfyingly detailed, grace-
> fully written account of an exciting period of American
> theatre.

The *New York Post* described it as "one of the most brilliant
volumes of theatrical reminiscence I've ever read," and Robert Kirsch in the *Los Angeles Times* found it "so good on so
many counts that by the time one has finished reading it, that
overused and exploited adjective 'great' does not seem an
exaggeration." There was a similar tone to the dozens of
clippings that began to pour in from San Diego, Oklahoma
City, New England, Seattle, Minneapolis, Miami, etc. They
were accompanied by reviews in the weeklies. According to
Saturday Review:

Run-Through is a big book, a sprawling, rousing book—a welcome gift in today's theatrical wasteland. Add to these welcome qualities the author's extraordinary talent for total recall, together with a style almost feverish in its intensity and the result is a work whose impact is as immediate as its contents are compelling.

Walter Clemons in *Newsweek* described it as a

tense and brilliant performance, at opening-night pitch, with the theatrical virtues of pace, sharp lighting and perfect articulation. . . . As the sardonic, personal history of a complicated man, it should interest even the unstage-struck. He makes us envious that we weren't around and young, exactly when he was.

And *Life* called it "the truest chronicle of the American theatre . . . the best show in town."

Reviews were no novelty to me, but, even in my bewildered delight, I was able to appreciate the difference between the critiques I was used to receiving as a producer or director and the ones I was now getting as a writer. Beyond the pain or pleasure of having one's work condemned or admired and the material consequences of such appraisals, I was now exposed to the personal risk that comes from having one's name on the cover of a book. Beneath the reviewer's judgments of the texture, structure and subject matter of a book there lies the personal reaction to the writer and the inevitable confusion between the story that is being told and the personality of its author.

What came to fascinate me about the critical reception of *Run-Through* was the portrait of myself that emerged from the sum of those reviews. The book had been written in a calculated attitude of modesty which seemed to perplex and disturb certain critics. One of the most intelligent and perceptive of them concluded his favorable review with this observation:

People are going to read *Run-Through* for the history it covers and they are going to relish it for its vivid portraits, its entertaining anecdotes and, above all, its marvelous picture of Orson Welles. ... But, for all its theatrical sugar and spice, what remains most curious is its portrait of the man who remains the collaborator, the behind-the-scenes organizer, the vital supernumerary. ... It's all great fun, to be sure, but also sad and unresolved—a run-through without the excitement of a polished performance or the applause of the final curtain.

I would have liked to explain that a "run-through," in theatrical parlance, takes place during rehearsal and does not call for a "finished performance." *Run-Through* was a memoir written in mid-career; it covered a period of my life when, for all my frenzied activity and the steady growth of my ego, I remained totally insecure and continued to take refuge in an attitude of anonymity that was deliberate and self-protective. As to the "final curtain" whose absence he regretted, it was still more than a quarter of a century away!

Run-Through made the "New and Recommended" but never the "Best Sellers" list of the *Times*. Within a fortnight of publication I received a note of congratulations from Michael Korda in which he informed me that we had gone back for a second printing. However, any risk I might have run of having my head turned by the combined successes of the Acting Company, *The Country Girl* and *Run-Through* was sharply reduced by the next venture of that crowded spring.

Lord Byron, which was presented on April 20, 1972, in the Juilliard Theatre by the American Opera Center under my direction, was Virgil Thomson's first new opera in twenty-five years and his first without the collaboration of Gertrude Stein. It had long been a subject of conversation between us. With Gertrude gone, he had spent years looking for a suitable libretto. Following my Phoenix production, he had seriously considered *The Duchess of Malfi* but decided that Webster's magnificent theatrical verse was too strong to be fitted into the requirements of an operatic score. In a complete turnabout he had next considered Faulkner's melodramatic novella *Wild Palms*. Having abandoned that, he had heard Gore Vidal say one day that he was thinking of writing a play about Byron. "I told Vidal that the life of Byron would make a fine opera subject and suggested that he write a libretto. He said he might try."

When nothing came of that he had turned to other poets of his acquaintance, among them Robert Lowell and Robert Penn Warren. They all said it was a fine idea but did nothing about it. Around 1962, while he was in California visiting Joan and me, he made the acquaintance of a young poet, Jack Larson, one of whose plays he had liked, and suggested that he try his hand at *Byron*. Larson hesitated. He felt that it presented problems he had no idea how to solve. "Any characterization of Byron would have to compete with the legendary glamor and brilliance of the man. How could a stage Byron be made convincing? He would have to be shown as a great poet. How could a sufficient amount of Byron's poetry be included to make it a natural presence in the opera?"

Finally he had found what he believed to be a solution to these difficulties. After the poet's heroic death in Greece, the libretto would follow the attempts of Byron's relatives and friends to obtain for him the honor of burial in Westminster Abbey. An added, historically authentic intrigue would be created by the existence of a scandalous autobiographical memoir that had survived the poet but that no one had read:

> Believing that Byron is not to be trusted with his own posthumous reputation, the heirs manage to burn the memoir while they are waiting for the official decision about burial in the Abbey. I felt I could create a libretto out of that, using the intrigue among the heirs and their fear of what might be in the memoir to dramatize Byron's life and their relationship to him and to each other. I imagined a continued interplay between the present and the past.

Within not too long a time Larson had produced, along those lines, the first version of a libretto that Virgil approved and began to set to music. At this stage a commission was obtained from New York's Metropolitan Opera, with funds furnished by the Ford and Koussevitzky Foundations.

This highly publicized Metropolitan commission had what

I have always believed to be an unfortunate effect on the opera. In Virgil's own words, "We were of course delighted and, in view of the possibility of performing in so large and grand a house, Larson and I set about amplifying the work." These amplifications involved certain changes: the Met favored three acts and two intermissions, and this meant substantial modifications in what had been conceived as a two-act work. Also, physically, since set changes were now available in the lavish tradition of the Met, it was no longer necessary to develop the subtle, "fluctuating changes of time and place between the Abbey and the characters' memories" that were originally intended. Later still, under the spell of the Met's grandeur, Virgil decided to insert a full-scale ballet into the last act that was totally irrelevant to Larson's libretto.

At Virgil's behest I was present at two of several auditions the opera received during the late sixties. Both were attended by Rudolf Bing, but by 1970 it had become evident to Thomson and everyone else that the Met had no real intention of producing *Lord Byron*.* Virgil was chagrined and annoyed that "the opera seemed not to have been quite turned down and because the Met sat on its career of neglect so lightly." When, a few months later, Peter Mennin offered to produce *Byron* at Juilliard's Opera Center, Virgil accepted without hesitation:

> I liked the idea because they've been doing awfully good productions there lately and they have good singers and a first-class orchestra. Also the idea of John Houseman producing it pleases me enormously. We've done so many shows together that I welcome the opportunity of working with my old friend again.

My personal and artistic association with Virgil Thomson went back forty years to *Four Saints in Three Acts*, which had brought me into the theatre as director and producer and changed the course of my life. Since then, we had worked together in a continued collaboration that had been of great

---

* Any more than they had ever seriously intended to produce Blitzstein's *Sacco and Vanzetti*, which they had also commissioned.

mutual benefit and had gone far beyond the use of his music. We had been together on Leslie Howard's *Hamlet,* on the Federal Theatre of the WPA, on the Office of War Information film *Tuesday in November* and at the American Shakespeare Festival, where he had composed music for no fewer than five of our productions. All this had resulted in a strange and unusually close working relationship in which I was often his employer and superior but in which Virgil, with his artistic experience and brilliant intelligence, played the role of elder statesman and guru while I acted as his energetic and worldly disciple.

Now we were about to work together once again on an opera of Virgil's composition—one which never inspired the sudden wonder I had felt from my first hearing of *Four Saints in Three Acts*—one on which a number of irreversible artistic decisions had been made and for which a definite and not too distant opening date had already been set. This happened at a time when my creative energy was stretched to the limit with *Country Girl, Falstaff,* the repertory season of the Juilliard Acting Company and the publication of *Run-Through.*

I have often wondered how much difference it would have made if I had been less occupied and more available for discussion and preparation. For reasons it took me a long time to understand, my collaboration with Virgil, which had taken such varied and fortunate forms in the past, was, on this occasion, completely unsuccessful. These reasons reached far back into the past. On *Four Saints,* when he had first invited me to work with him, Thomson had, in fact, been composer, impresario and artistic director. The opera's designer, director, choreographer and conductor had all been chosen by him, and we all worked together to give him exactly what he knew he wanted. It had turned out wonderfully well. So it was only natural that I should revert now to that earlier state of mind: *Byron* was Virgil's opera on which he had labored for more than ten years and on which I felt he deserved the same artistic autonomy as he had exercised so successfully on *Four Saints.* In my determination to give it to him I surrendered much of the authority that was needed to bring off this difficult undertaking under altogether new conditions. And in so doing I betrayed him as well as myself.

Around Juilliard I had acquired a reputation for decisive and, sometimes, overbearing behavior. Throughout the preparations for *Byron* I astonished everyone by being accommodating to the point of weakness. It was an error from which we all suffered. The truth, which I failed to see at the time, was that the problems of *Four Saints* and *Byron* were entirely different, and nowhere was this divergence greater than in Virgil's own state of mind. His total and unswerving security on *Four Saints* was obscured, on *Byron*, by layers of artistic and personal doubt for which his disappointment at the Met was in part responsible.

From his expectations of Metropolitan grandeur Virgil brought over to Juilliard certain artistic and material attitudes that had already affected the libretto and which were unrelated, if not positively harmful, to the sort of production we could give him at the Juilliard Opera Center under a setup which I had helped to create and which, by Virgil's own admission, had been unusually successful in recent years in the performance of new operatic works.*

If, throughout the production of *Byron*, Virgil and I failed to achieve the sort of artistic collaboration we had so often enjoyed in the past, it was due, in part, to my own fatigue and, even more, to the fact that throughout the preparation and rehearsal of *Byron*, Virgil was in a state of nervous anxiety that I had never encountered before and that made it impossible for anyone to reason with him. He was adamant on one subject: *Lord Byron* was *grand opera*. Grand opera was what he insisted on having and what we mistakenly did our best to give him.

Most of the musical decisions on the opera were made by Thomson and Mennin together. The Opera Center was rich in good singers that year, and an adequate cast was found within its ranks—with the exception of Lord Byron himself. As Virgil had written it, the part called for an exceptionally

---

* *The Mines of Sulphur, Antigone, The Losers* had all received productions that had been generally admired.

high tenor, for which he insisted we bring in Grayson Hirst, who had sung it at the various Metropolitan auditions. And it was Thomson's and Mennin's joint decision to entrust the musical direction to Gerhard Samuel, associate conductor of the Los Angeles Orchestra.

My own first serious disagreement with Virgil arose over the scenery for his opera. This time we had no Stettheimer or Ashton to set the unique and brilliant tone of our entire production. In a concession to Virgil's Metropolitan notions, I engaged a rising young designer, David Mitchell, who had recently executed a much admired *Mefistofele* for the Met.

The first and the last scenes of *Byron* take place in the Poets' Corner of Westminster Abbey. Since they call for the presence of numerous characters and a massive chorus, first of citizens and then of poets' ghosts, plus a life-size statue of Byron to be wheeled in and unloaded from a cart, they required a large, impressive set that would convey a recognizable impression of that historic location. Before long Mitchell came up with a stunning, fairly realistic scenic version of the Poets' Corner which, in spite of its vast size, was deemed buildable on our stage by our technical director, Joe Pacitti.

At this point a conflict arose that went far beyond the concrete matter of stage scenery and affected the entire mood, action and staging of the opera. To satisfy the original concept of "a continual interplay between the present and the past," I had visualized a production of which the permanent setting was an atmospheric, all-encompassing Abbey background—a frame within which it would be possible to suggest, with light changes and a minimum of realistic scenic movement and delay, the various locales and remembered scenes evoked in the libretto. These were (1) a morning party at Lady Melbourne's; (2) the victory ball at Burlington House; (3) simultaneously, a room at Lady Melbourne's and a room in Byron's club; and (4) Mrs. Leigh's country house. Virgil stuck stubbornly to his Metropolitan dream and refused to consider any suggestion of what he contemptuously called a "unit set."

Wavering between these two concepts, what we ended up with was a series of semi-realistic settings laboriously flown or wheeled into the center of the Poets' Corner. Designed and executed hurriedly and without love, they turned out even worse than I feared and caused Harold Schonberg to write in *The New York Times* that, while the opening and closing scenes in the Abbey were handsome, "the rest of the opera had some of the tackiest, scrappiest, ugliest sets seen hereabouts in a long time." Besides being ugly they were almost impossible to work in.

The dramatic flashbacks were the parts of the opera in which, in my opinion, the libretto and music were at their least secure and needed the most help from director and designer. The cramped sets in which I was forced to stage them emphasized their weakness. One exception was an imaginative double scene in which the future Lady Byron, surrounded by girlfriends and relatives, is apprehensively dressing for her wedding while, contrapuntally, on the other half of the stage, Byron and his cronies are bawdily celebrating their last alcoholic bachelor's breakfast. But an important confrontation at the victory ball following the Battle of Waterloo, which contains the main love scene of the opera, was played with insufficient atmosphere downstage of a rigid, old-fashioned backdrop. What I did with it stands out in my memory as one of the worst-staged scenes in my entire operatic experience.

Another serious disagreement was over the ballet, which had not originally figured in the opera but was part of the *folie des grandeurs* induced by the Metropolitan connection. Musically, it was an elaboration of an earlier Thomson composition (his Second String Quartet) and contained some of the evening's most melodious music. But it had no place in the opera. I resisted it as long as I could, on the grounds that it was dramatically irrelevant and unrelated in style and that it added length to a work that was already dangerously strung out.* Virgil insisted that it remain and it did. It was danced adequately by members of Juilliard's Dance Division to

---

* Years later, after he had removed its ballet from the published version of the score, Virgil reproached me for not having opposed it more strongly in the first place!

choreography by Alvin Ailey and featured the close relationship between Byron and Shelley, who did not otherwise figure in the opera.

Rehearsals were not happy. Juilliard student orchestras had a reputation for high musicianship but undisciplined behavior. Gerhard Samuel's attempts to deal with this were not aided by the consistently testy and frequently harsh and contemptuous manner in which Virgil treated him in their presence. This behavior extended, to a lesser degree, to my own stage rehearsals, in which Virgil frequently intervened to give not only musical notes and readings to the cast but also general and particular instructions on stage behavior and style with which I did not always agree. As a result, and due to my own extreme enervation, I'm afraid I directed *Byron* without the imagination it needed to come off as a viable operatic performance.

The deeper we got into rehearsal, the higher grew our tensions. After one violent scene in which I finally lost my temper, Virgil stayed home for two days, and that didn't help. What should have been the crowning experience of a long and loving collaboration was turning into a strained and unpleasant ordeal of which everyone felt that the sooner it was over the better. When we opened finally before an audience "that seemed to be made up exclusively of composers, performers, singers and music critics," it was in an atmosphere that was utterly unlike our thrilling and triumphal Hartford premiere of *Four Saints*. That it did not permanently destroy our long association is evidence of how deep and loving that relationship had become.

Lord Byron's reception by the national press was mixed:

It is hard to imagine Mr. Thomson writing a conventional opera but with *Lord Byron* he has nobly succeeded.

A genuinely satisfying evening of opera.

A singularly empty work.

An opera for singing—not a strong dramatic piece, but lyric and sensitive.

It is precious, contrived and lacks any definite personality.

It is a masterpiece—a genuine musical entity of great beauty.

In *The New Yorker* of January 17, 1977, Andrew Porter wrote of *Byron* that it was generally underrated at the time of its first performance. "While it must inevitably disappoint anyone expecting a romantic, heart-on-sleeve, emotionally Byronic opera . . . [it is] an elegant and cultivated piece that affords pleasures akin to those of witty, lively, precise, shapely conversations on an interesting subject."

These qualities of intelligence and wit are what I failed to bring out in my production; and I did little to solve the opera's inherent problem—the interrelation of realism and fantasy. Its emotional effect went far beyond my feeling of guilt for its dubious reception. Unlike my recent reverse with *Falstaff*, which was almost immediately forgotten, this left personal and professional scars that have never entirely healed. (I'm sure this is equally true of Virgil Thomson.) Yet I continue to believe that *Lord Byron,* produced for its lyric, rhetorical and stylistic values and stripped of the appendages it collected during its abortive Metropolitan sojourn, could still emerge as a highly satisfying operatic experience.

The unkindest cut in Schonberg's *New York Times* review was his opening statement that "Gertrude Stein, everybody will be saying, was to Virgil Thomson what W. S. Gilbert was to Arthur Sullivan—and everybody will be right." I'm not so sure about that. For all our sakes (if I were not growing so very old) I would dearly love to have a second crack at *Lord Byron* and prove "everybody" wrong.

CHAPTER XVI

1972 (continued)

DON JUAN IN HELL
FIRST SARATOGA SEASON
CITY CENTER ACTING COMPANY
AT THE
GOOD SHEPHERD—FAITH CHURCH
THE PAPER CHASE

I WAS STILL recuperating from the disappointment of *Byron* when I realized with some alarm that the school year was drawing to an end. Group I was back from its successful university tour and had just added two more plays to its repertory—Paul Shyre's "concert version" of Dos Passos' *U.S.A.* and Brendan Behan's *Hostage,* directed by Gene Lesser. It was a fine, rambunctious, loose-knit show, with lots of singing and outstanding roles for several members of the company who had not previously had a chance to shine.* Its good reviews and the success of our spring repertory season

---

* Particularly Dakin Matthews, who held a curious but valuable position with the company. He was not a student but a Group I member's (Anne McNaughton's) husband, to whom I had given certain teaching functions at the school and who finally became part of the group as an actor.

merely added to the difficulty and urgency of a decision that had to be made immediately and by me alone. It concerned the fate of Group I.

I had two alternatives. My first and easier choice was to let its members graduate and find individual theatrical employment. In view of their proved quality, they would have little difficulty finding work in regional theatres or even, if they chose, in New York or Los Angeles. In this way we would have fulfilled our function as a conservatory engaged in the successful training of actors for the professional theatre. But what this meant was the dissolution of something we had spent four years creating with sweat and tears—a skilled and cohesive acting ensemble. Did we have the right to do that? Having created such a precious theatrical instrument, could we then turn around and destroy it?

The answer to that question raised an acute personal problem. Over the years I had been involved in the birth of no fewer than six theatrical organizations (not counting the APA and the Phoenix), from my two WPA theatres and the Mercury to Pelican Productions, through the Shakespeare Festival to the UCLA Professional Theatre Group. Each had presented its own special difficulties, which had been, to a greater or lesser degree, overcome; each had been valuable though short-lived, and I was proud of my connection with all six of them. But now, at the age of seventy, I needed a seventh—with its inevitable anxieties, personal crises and financial and artistic hazards—like a hole in the head!

I can see, looking back, that the issue was never really in doubt. I had accepted my academic backwater with a reluctance that had been heightened by my unexpected success with *The Country Girl* and the Juilliard Acting Company's sensational repertory season. Here suddenly was an opportunity to enjoy the best of both worlds! Offered the chance to achieve professional theatrical success while retaining the security of an academic career, how could I possibly turn it down?

My final decision was precipitated by a proposal received

473

late that spring from the Saratoga Arts Center.* Its artistic director, Richard Leach, was offering us a four-week repertory season as part of a performing-arts festival that included, among its performers, the Philadelphia Orchestra and the New York City Ballet. How could we refuse to appear in such company? Especially since the terms he offered us were sufficient to cover all our costs, based on full union scale for the company and its technical crew.

It was a gracious gesture of Peter Mennin's to invite me to deliver that year's Juilliard commencement address. Four years earlier, at the 1968 convocation, I had celebrated the creation of the Drama Division; now I was able to congratulate members of our first class on their graduation† and to announce the formation of the Juilliard Acting Company, for which I expressed the hope that, in its own field, it might one day equal, in quality and reputation, the world-famed Juilliard String Quartet.

The Housemans did not spend much time together that summer. The boys were off in different directions and Joan was busy working as a production assistant to Ellis Rabb, who was back in form, directing plays at the Vivian Beaumont Theatre in Lincoln Center. She enjoyed the work and proved a very effective assistant.‡ (Rabb came to rely increasingly on her judgment and taste as they worked together through much of that year and the next—on Gorky's *Enemies*§ and, later, on his productions of *The Merchant of Venice* and *A Streetcar Named Desire*, both at Lincoln Center and both starring his ex-wife, Rosemary Harris.)

* In which I once again detected the fine Italian hand of Lincoln Kirstein.
† Thirteen of them received B.F.A.s. The rest (including three of our best actors) had to settle for diplomas.
‡ Not unnaturally, she found it easier to work with others in that capacity than with me. We had a good time in Ann Arbor on *The Chronicles of Hell*, but it was the only show we ever did together.
§ Many of the visual aspects of that production and of its later filming for television were based on Joan's family photographs of life in Russia at the turn of the century.

For a few days in June I lived in New City, resting from my labors, tearing and hacking away at the vines and bushes that kept invading my garden, and reading and answering the many letters I had received about *Run-Through*. There were still some weeks before the opening of the Acting Company's Saratoga Season, and before that I flew to California to meet with the producer and cast of a piece I was suddenly being asked to direct.

Don Juan in Hell is the third act of George Bernard Shaw's *Man and Superman*, and it is so long and self-contained that few productions include it. In the early fifties Charles Laughton, while developing his new career as director and public reader, had obtained Shaw's permission to perform it as a separate piece with a cast that consisted of Charles Boyer, Sir Cedric Hardwicke, Agnes Moorehead and himself. They had toured it for months with great success, and now, years later, an entrepreneur by the name of Lee Orgel was proposing to revive it with Ricardo Montalban as the Don, Edward Mulhare as the Devil, Paul Henreid as the Commander and, in her original role, Agnes Moorehead as Doña Ana.* Attracted by the quality of the text and the promise of continuing royalties from what promised to be a long tour, I agreed to direct it—reproducing the original setup of four music stands and high stools set in a semicircle in the style of a chamber-music quartet. Agnes was there to remind us of how it had been done before, and my ego did not demand any appreciable changes.

Don Juan in Hell opened to a black-tie audience in Fresno, California, then started on a long tour which I followed from a distance: to Chicago (where it was well received); to Boston (where it was described in the *Globe* as "a rare and distinguished evening in the theatre"); to Toronto (where it made a fortune in the huge O'Keefe Auditorium); to Washington (where it arrived in a deluge of rain in the midst of an elec-

* I can see her still, in both engagements, in a lilac gown of her own designing, with a small gold crown set atop the flaming red hair that made her the equal, in authority and presence, of the three tall, handsome, formally clad males with whom she appeared onstage.

tion). From there, against my emphatic and frequently repeated advice, an impatient backer* insisted on bringing it into New York, where it ran head on into Clive Barnes's irrational detestation of Shaw and all his works. As a result I had the dubious thrill of seeing my name in lights for a week over the marquee of the Palace Theatre on Broadway and the annoyance of receiving one of the worst notices ever given to a production in which I was involved.†

Our first Saratoga season opened in mid-July, and, for members of Group I, now known as the Juilliard Acting Company, it was a wonderful combination of work and holiday. Four major productions, performed seven times a week plus one weekly children's matinee, kept them fully occupied but did not prevent them from attending occasional ballet and concert performances or from sunning themselves around the swimming pool that was situated a few hundred yards from the theatre.

First to arrive in Saratoga had been our able stage manager, Tom Warner, together with Joe Pacitti and a swarm of stagehands, who spent days and nights down in the basement, up in the ceiling, and crawling like human flies around the walls of the pleasant but somewhat dilapidated four-hundred-fifty-seat theatre ‡ that was to be our summer home. Over the years it had handled the skimpy scenery of sundry summer companies; now it had to accommodate four full-scale productions with massive scenery and elaborate light plots created in Juilliard's modern and well-equipped Drama Theatre. It was a huge task that Pacitti handled with his usual brawling and disorganized efficiency.

---

* He was, I was told, the world's most successful promoter of roller derbies.
† Orgel, with admirable tenacity, reopened it the following year with Myrna Loy as Doña Ana and Kurt Kasnar as the Commander. It toured, mostly college towns, for close to six months.
‡ With the rest of the Arts Center and the Hall of Waters, it had been built during the Great Depression by WPA labor and was now operated by the New York State Department of Parks and Recreation.

Next to appear were the actors. Herded by Margot Harley and Elizabeth Smith, they were billeted in a new dormitory building recently vacated by the young ladies of Skidmore College. It was perfect in every respect except that it had not yet been air-conditioned and that the heat that summer was infernal.

This was not my own first visit to Saratoga Springs.* I had spent three weeks there at the age of thirteen when my mad parents brought me over from England for my summer holidays across a submarine-infested ocean less than three months after the torpedoing of the *Lusitania*. Living in splendor at the fabled Grand Union Hotel, I had accompanied my father to the racetrack by day and danced at night in its lantern-lit garden with my mother and the daughters of her friends.

Now the Grand Union Hotel had vanished without a trace —a victim of changing fashions and termites—but there were certain things about Saratoga that remained untouched by time. One was the awful summer heat. Another was the way of life of America's racing rich, whose summer homes my mother had viewed with such curiosity and envy fifty years before. Many of them were now unoccupied and abandoned, but some remained, and it was in one of them that I spent the first two weeks of my present stay in Saratoga.

Situated on Main Street, it was one of several houses owned and occupied, for a few weeks each summer, by the Phipps family, whose name had long stood for the finest in American horseracing. Lillian Phipps, wife to Ogden, was a handsome gray-haired lady who, in addition to personally owning one of the country's most celebrated stables of steeplechasers, was, together with the Whitneys, one of the main supporters of the Saratoga Arts Center. Most graciously she invited Joan and me to stay in her home during the opening weeks of the company's residency.

It was a moderately sized but luxurious establishment,

* Nor my last. Ten years later, after the Acting Company had discontinued its summer residency, Joan and I spent two months in Saratoga in the dead of winter while I was shooting a film there. The temperature, throughout our first week, was twenty below zero.

filled with flowered cretonne and attended by a multitude of suave and competent servants, including a gentle but awesome English butler and a blond Scandinavian ladies' maid. Joan went back to town after a few days, but I stayed on till the end of the month, when the approach of the main racing season and Ogden Phipps's imminent arrival from Long Island drove me back to more modest quarters with the company. Ten days later I was invited to dine at the Phipps house and noted with surprise and chagrin that not one of the servitors I had known and grown to like during July was to be seen. After dinner, as I was driving with Mrs. Phipps to the theatre, I commented on this. She smiled indulgently. "Those were *my* servants," she said. "*These* are *Ogden's.*"

We opened our Saratoga season with *The School for Scandal,* which was well received and was followed by a hurriedly assembled production of the Anouilh-Fry *Ring Round the Moon* which we had substituted for *The Lower Depths* in deference to the supposedly conservative tastes of the spa's summer visitors.* For the rest, we repeated our repertory of *Women Beware Women, The Hostage* and *U.S.A.* Though they had all been played before, each production received a full week of daytime rehearsals, a Sunday dress rehearsal and a Monday preview. For each, the show's director came up from New York and worked with the company through opening night while Elizabeth Smith continued to work on their speech.

Even though we had a guarantee from the Arts Center, Margot and I were intensely concerned with the financial outcome of this, our first full-fledged commercial engagement. Attendance was fair at the start in a community that had known almost no theatre for several years. It grew steadily from week to week till it reached an average of sixty to seventy percent of capacity on week nights and full houses on Fridays and Saturdays. This pleased and surprised us all, but the true value of our Saratoga summer lay in the oppor-

* A cursory investigation, based on a questionnaire in our program, revealed that most of our audiences were permanent residents of Albany, Troy and Schenectady. The racing crowd occasionally wandered into ballet and concerts but rarely came near the theatre.

tunity it gave our young company to settle down, find its identity and prepare itself for its transition from a brilliant graduating student class to an ensemble of professional actors.

It was typical of the paternalistic attitude with which I had been conducting the Drama Division for four years that I had never really consulted members of Group I about their transformation into a permanent company and that they, on their part, were prepared to follow me unquestioningly into the treacherous, uncharted waters of institutional theatre. This blind faith was touching, but it aggravated the sense of responsibility with which I faced the hazards that lay ahead and to which, in the first flush of our success, I had, as usual, failed to give realistic consideration.

Now, as the weeks flew by, the problem of the Acting Company's future was becoming a pressing one, and I found myself thinking of little else during the many hours I spent that summer on the New York State Thruway, shuttling several times a week between Saratoga Springs and New York City. Our summer season was due to end in mid-August, at which time members of the company would receive their final paychecks from the Arts Center and all connection with the Juilliard School would cease once and for all.

This reflected a serious miscalculation on my part. From the first moment in which I had considered the possibility of a continuing Acting Company, Juilliard had formed part of my thinking—not merely as a prestigious name but because the school's artistic and institutional status made it an essential element of my plan. I had made no secret of my intention to use the Juilliard name: in personal conversation with Mennin and publicly, in my commencement address, I had drawn a parallel between our future activities and those of the world-famous Juilliard String Quartet.

The analogy was false—and I knew it. It did not take a financial genius to detect the vast difference between the operation of four musicians traveling with their scores and instrument cases and that of a theatrical group of thirty (including technicians) ranging by bus across the continent, accompanied by two truckloads of scenery, hundreds of valuable costumes and much elaborate equipment. Nothing in Juilliard's charter justified the school's participation in such a massive and hazardous enterprise, and, on a more personal level, happy as he had been to share in the kudos that the Drama Division had brought to the institution of which he was president, Dr. Mennin was temperamentally and neurotically opposed to any activity which he himself did not personally and absolutely control.

Thus it had become clear by the beginning of summer that Juilliard would be lending the Acting Company neither its institutional support nor its name. And this made my task of launching the company infinitely more difficult—so much so that by the end of July I was beginning to have serious doubts about its future, accompanied by a rising fear that, in my enthusiasm, I might have led its members into a dead end that would delay rather than aid their careers in the professional theatre.

Margot Harley was the only person with whom I could, at this time, honestly discuss our future, since Joan, quite rightly, saw in my creation of the company nothing but a source of renewed anxiety and overwork. Together we had come to the grim decision that one month from the end of the Saratoga season must mark the final limit of our uncertainty. If our future had not been settled by then and if we were not in production with the company back on the payroll by mid-September, we must face the shameful necessity of calling off all plans and letting Group I scatter.

Even in the depths of my anxiety I remained quite clear about our general strategy. My experiences with the Mercury and the APA (not to mention my observation of the fate of Eva Le Gallienne's Civic Repertory in the late twenties and Jules Irving's hopeless struggle to survive at the Beaumont) had convinced me that repertory in New York City was a prohibitive and hopeless undertaking. Yet repertory was the key to the Acting Company's existence and our only hope for a viable and creative operation. The steadily growing interest in our productions on the part of universities and community groups had convinced me that our best chance of survival and our only valid function in the contemporary American theatre lay in creating and operating a traveling repertory company of established quality and reputation that would tour the year round and perform guaranteed engagements wherever and for as long as it was in demand. Thus we would be fulfilling a unique and much-needed double function: we would be bringing distinguished theatre to places that did not habitually have it, and we would be giving our twenty young American actors a chance to appear in great plays, in repertory, before constantly changing and widely diversified audiences the country over.

Already, following our brief university tour in the spring, we were receiving encouraging inquiries and requests for bookings. But these were not yet sufficient in number or in guaranteed income to permit the formation of a consecutive national tour. To achieve that, we still needed a final and decisive consecration—something that would establish us, once and for all, as a professional classical-repertory company with national recognition. And this, I believed (much as I feared and hated the New York theatrical scene), could be acquired only through the publicity and press coverage attendant upon a successful repertory season in New York City. Our student season at Juilliard had been a first step; this was the next, infinitely more dangerous and difficult move.

The older I grow, the more frequently I find myself engaged in what I feel to be repetitions of the past. As I hustled around New York that summer, desperately seeking a hospitable doorstep on which to deposit this, my latest infant, I could not help recalling my attempts to launch the Mercury thirty-five years earlier. For all their variations of time and place, the two projects were strangely alike: both were based on unlimited and dubiously founded ambitions; both were improvised and utterly reckless. And neither of them had one penny in the bank!

Yet, historically, the circumstances of their birth could not have been more different. The Mercury came into being in the depths of a major depression in what was still a world of free enterprise, where "deficit financing" was unheard of and "funding" was an unknown word. Foundation support was still twenty years away, and it would be another ten years after that before the need for state and federal subsidy for the arts was belatedly recognized in the United States.

For a maverick like the Mercury, things had been tough but simple. Having incorporated in Albany at a cost of less than two hundred dollars and provided myself with a pocketful of nickels, I began to make phone calls in which I begged, bullied and blackmailed individuals of my acquaintance for a total of ten thousand dollars, with which Orson Welles and I took over a derelict Broadway theatre and put on *Julius Caesar*.

By the early seventies the situation was more auspicious for the arts but far more complicated. Foundation and federal funds were now available, but access to them was restricted and formalized. Before applying, it was necessary to qualify officially (under 501C3) as an established and recognized nonprofit, tax-exempt organization that had been in existence for two years or more. For an embryo group such as the Acting Company this was an utter impossibility. Through ingenuity, goodwill, luck and a little larceny, we managed to pull it off!

One stroke of luck lay in the discovery that a member of the Juilliard faculty, Steve Aaron, happened to be an officer in a defunct theatrical organization, the New Theatre Workshop, that had suspended operations but was still officially qualified for tax exemption. With Aaron's concurrence we merged and became known fiscally for the next two years as Group One–New Theatre Workshop.

Using this technicality, I was able to approach the Rockefeller Foundation, which had been partly responsible for the creation of the Drama Division in the first place, and which soon came up with twenty-five thousand dollars toward the organization of a New York repertory season. Our first move after that must be to convert our actors from a student group to a professional company by having them join the union— Actors' Equity. This was not difficult except that it cost money (two hundred fifty-six dollars apiece, which we had to advance them) and presupposed the existence of an established theatrical employer to sign their contract and put up a bond that amounted to close to eight thousand dollars. To fill this new and urgent need I now approached Richard Clurman,* the ambitious new president of the New York City Center,† and suggested to him that he adopt the Acting Company as his dramatic arm. He was startled but receptive to the idea.

Early in our negotiations it was made clear to me that if I was looking to the Center for substantial financial aid I was barking up the wrong tree. I said I was aware of that and made it clear that what we needed from the Center was the use of its name and a sum equal to that supplied by the Rockefellers. I also made it clear (and this was something of a sticking point) that, for financial as well as artistic reasons, I had no intention of launching our young company on its first professional New York season in the vast and extravagant reaches of the City Center Theatre on Fifty-fifth Street.

After a few days of maneuvering we reached an agreement: the Acting Company would change its name to the City Center Acting Company‡ and become one of the Center's active constitutents, beginning with a repertory season to be presented in New York City early in the fall of 1972. All artistic decisions would be exclusively ours, and we would determine both the program and the location of our first and subsequent seasons. In exchange, the City Center would match the Rockefeller contribution and cover the Equity bond. This agreement was signed and announced to the company and to the press two days before the day Margot and I had set as our deadline.

•

* A ranking executive of the Time-Life organization and a nephew of Harold Clurman.
† Created during the Great Depression, while Fiorello LaGuardia was Mayor, and using the huge city-owned Fifty-fifth Street theatre (formerly a Shrine auditorium) as its base of operations, the Center had long played a vital part in New York's cultural life. Both the New York City Opera and Ballet Companies had started and flourished there together with several theatre companies, none of which survived. At this time the Center boasted eighteen constituents including a children's theatre and the Ailey and Joffrey dance troupes —but no dramatic arm.
‡ We retained that name for two years. Then, for various reasons, we went back to "The Acting Company."

Having turned down the oversize City Center Theatre, we had to find a more suitable place in which to present our season. I felt strongly that it should be modest in size and tone; yet it must be well located and, unlike most Off-Broadway houses, possess a stage capable of receiving our four substantial productions in a style that was not noticeably different from that of our own Drama Theatre. By a minor miracle, the perfect place was available. That it happened to be located within one hundred yards of the Juilliard School was an unexpected bonanza.

The Good Shepherd–Faith Church was a survival from a time before Lincoln Center, when the West Sixties formed part of a deteriorating neighborhood, a slum once known as Hell's Kitchen. With the construction of Lincoln Center the church had lost much of its congregation but continued to function under its progressive pastor as a social center rather than a place of worship. For two years I had passed it every morning on my way to work without ever being aware of its theatrical possibilities, until Gordon Davidson discovered them when he and the Phoenix were looking for a modest place in which to present *The Trial of the Catonsville Nine*. With the choir and organ loft serving as the jury box and the space before the altar as a courtroom, Gordon had made it work remarkably well, and I remembered its social hall on the ground floor as a spacious and convenient rehearsal space.

Besides the advantages of being cheap and perfectly located, the Good Shepherd–Faith Church had exactly the right tone of calculated modesty and eccentric distinction which I was trying to create for our young company. The absence of a real stagehouse might create scenic problems, but since our productions had, in fact, been designed for an open stage, this was something Doug Schmidt, Joe Pacitti and I felt we could deal with and still retain much of our original look.

Since the church was literally penniless, the negotiations with its pastor were brief and pleasant; a six-week lease was signed for six hundred thirty dollars a week. The next morning, with a reckless haste that was again reminiscent of the early days of the Mercury, the New York papers, under the heading "6 Shows In 4 Weeks," carried the announcement of the City Center Acting Company's first professional New York repertory season.

For economic and physical reasons it was impossible for us to present our program in "revolving repertory," changing shows every day, as we had in our own Drama Theatre. As in Saratoga, our productions would be presented successively— each for seven performances, including one matinee. Sunday would be used for changeovers, Monday for dress rehearsals and previews. We also promised two children's matinees during our run and, over our final weekend, two special performances of a new play, to be announced.

In preparing our budget, John Bos, our company manager, estimated our probable attendance at sixty-five percent of our two-hundred-thirty-seat house, and that's just about what we got. But we underestimated the overtime we had to pay our stagehands for the weekend scenic changes from one production to another under horrendous conditions. Doug Schmidt and Joe Pacitti, between them, had done a brilliant job of adjusting our massive scenery to the rudimentary conditions of the Good Shepherd Church. By raising and extending the platform on which the altar once stood, they created a stage that was smaller but not unlike that of the Juilliard Drama Theatre and gave an audience that was seated in stiff, narrow and quite uncomfortable pews perfect sight lines and tolerable acoustics. Our main problem was that the church was on the mezzanine and had no storage space whatever. This meant that every prop and piece of scenery had to be dragged by hand up and down a cramped and twisting stairway, often by Pacitti himself. The same was true of our switchboards and lighting equipment, which had to be affixed to the walls and ceiling of a building that was about to collapse from age and neglect.*

* It is necessary to repeat that without Joe Pacitti there might have been no Acting Company. Not only was he a man of inexhaustible energy and resource; he was also a lunatic who was willing to undertake and execute tasks on which no man in his right mind would have ventured. Also, there was an element of sloppiness and larceny about him for which I was intensely grateful. Long after we had

I hoped that playing in such an unconventional location would provoke talk—and it did. It also created special problems which kept surfacing as opening night approached. One came from the New York Police Department, which felt that this unaccustomed activity in and outside the Good Shepherd–Faith Church might complicate its task of guarding the Chinese delegation to the United Nations in its sealed building across the street. Since our license to operate as a theatre was dubious at best, it was necessary to calm their fears, which I did with several dozen theatre tickets and an assurance that our audiences were made up of disciplined and cultivated people.

More serious was that fall's massive picketing of the Juilliard School by stagehands and members of the scene designers' union, who threatened, for a time, to include us in their picket line.* We were spared at the last moment through the intervention of friends among the scene designers who convinced the pickets that we were unrelated to the school and that we were paying our crew union scale and over.

But our most urgent problem was one of which we became aware only two days before we opened. The Good Shepherd–Faith Church had two toilets, and both were located in the space assigned to the actors as dressing rooms. What of our audience during the long stretches and intermissions of our classical repertory?

We considered routing them to Juilliard down the street but felt that Dr. Mennin might not appreciate such a sordid use of his conservatory's facilities. Nor were the delegates of

---

formally severed our connection with Juilliard, he continued to lend to the company the scenery, equipment and costumes to which we had no right but without which we could not have maintained the quality of our productions.

* This picketing lasted for several months and represented a determined effort by the International Alliance of Theatrical Stage Employees to penetrate educational theatre all over the country. Juilliard, being located in Lincoln Center and highly exposed, seemed a suitable target. The school, with some justice, maintained that unionization of its stages would drastically reduce opportunities for the student productions that were an essential part of its curriculum. After several months the union withdrew its pickets.

the Chinese People's Republic likely to welcome our theatre-goers into their well-guarded building. Finally someone (probably Pacitti) came up with the brilliant idea of renting four portable toilets from the construction company that was building a school across the street. A deal was made, and one of the special attractions of the City Center Acting Company's repertory season was the row of four maroon portable chemical outhouses neatly lined up in the parking lot behind the church!

On September 24, 1972, *The New York Times* gave us a precious gift in the form of an eight-column photograph of the company in its *School for Scandal* costumes at the top of the front page of the Sunday entertainment section:

A LOVELY "SCANDAL"

They began as acting students at Juilliard. When, last season, they modestly staged four plays to show their work, they got the kind of reviews stars might envy. Now this same group of 20 young people is winning permanent status. As the City Center Acting Company they initiate their first season with *The School for Scandal* on Thursday at the Good Shepherd-Faith Church, 152 West 66th Street, the first of six productions to be offered through October 28.

Among those who attended our first preview were the students and faculty of the Drama Division of the Juilliard School, which, coincidentally, had started on its fifth school year on that same day. Three nights later, on Thursday, September 28, the Acting Company formally opened its repertory season—a season that has lasted without interruption and without failing energy or quality for more than ten years!

What I hoped for on this occasion was a generally welcoming press for the company and particular praise for our opening show. We got both.

A first-rate repertory theatre company in New York is good news. *The School for Scandal* is the wittiest show in town. Be good to yourself and rush to buy tickets.

On with the new. . . . This is a well-knit unit of young and proficient players who tackle Sheridan with confidence and relish.

Sheridan was a wonderful playwright and his *School for Scandal* is an enchanting comedy. It was good to have the enterprising City Center Company inaugurate its new season with it and to find it as fresh and warmhearted as ever.

The City Center Acting Company has had the good sense to open its brief season of repertory with a play so strong and radiant that it sheds light on everybody in it.

The birth of a repertory company is headline news and the birth of such a fine one deserves page-one play.

As usual, it was to *The New York Times* that we looked most anxiously, and we rejoiced to discover that Clive Barnes had found our *School for Scandal*

in many respects a better performance than that being currently given by Britain's National Theatre. . . . This is not one of your mothball productions carrying reverence for a classic to tedious excess, but it also has a proper regard for the play's delicacies. . . . I enjoyed myself and what is more I enjoyed the prospect of a new repertory company that New York can grow up with. Welcome, but let no one expect them to fly all at once. Subscribe now!

Singled out for their performances were Patti LuPone, "an unusually sweet and vulnerable Lady Teazle whose vixen nature was never more than skin-deep," "the bluntly likeable" Charles Surface played by "forthright, easy and debonair" Kevin Kline, and, best of all, Ogden Stiers as Joseph Surface —"a paragon of hypocrisy, a prince of deceit."
The School for Scandal was our flashiest and most unanimous

success, and it won us national notice. It never had the explosive commercial success enjoyed in its day by the Mercury's *Julius Caesar*, but we never expected that and we gave it no time to build. Within a week we had opened our second show, *The Hostage*.

> Brendan's back and brilliant in a rousing revival performed brilliantly by the best repertory in town.

> Behan is always bawdy and boisterously beautiful company and the young City Center Acting Company has made *The Hostage* very alive and a pleasure once again.

> The City Center Acting Company continues to grow in interest and appeal. It does very well by *The Hostage*.*

So, now, by the first week of October, the Acting Company was really in business. We still had to present *Women Beware Women* and *The Lower Depths*, but the reception of our first two productions had turned the tide. The New York State Arts Council came through with an offer to finance a three-week, nine-city tour of the state, and the Locust Theatre in Philadelphia offered us a guaranteed two-week engagement that would keep the company occupied till Christmas.

Meantime, our New York season continued causing general astonishment at the size and diversity of our repertory. *Women Beware Women* was well received, but *The Lower Depths* seemed to have a more general appeal. Richard Watts in the *New York Post* was surprised to discover

> what a beautiful play Maxim Gorky's *Lower Depths* really is. The play is filled with striking characters and everyone in the cast is in the best of form. David Schramm, a mainstay of the Company, is especially fine as Luka and

---

* This time members of the company singled out were Dakin Matthews, Mary Lou Rosato, Norman Snow and Mary Joan Negro as the young lovers, Cynthia Herman as the outrageous Miss Gilchrist, and, in the role of "Monsewer," David Ogden Stiers, of whom one critic reported that he "was fiercely, furiously energetic. Even in looks, this would seem to be a takeoff on John Houseman—an affectionate spoof of the man behind this excellent company."

Boris Tumarin's staging is expert. I never knew how
much I liked *The Lower Depths.*

Mel Gussow had already reviewed it for the *Times* during
the school season but felt that it had acquired a new firmness
and confidence. Even the egregious John Simon finally gave
us condescending recognition in a piece headed

SLOUCHING TOWARD REPERTORY

One's attitude toward the City Center Acting Company will vary according to one's tolerance for well-
meaning amateurs whose general effect is still more
enjoyable than not. . . . The Group is off full steam on
the right track; like our railroads they need saving.

We gave two matinee performances of *U.S.A.,* and then,
on the last weekend of our season, we received a surprising
and welcome bonus.

I had seen James Saunders' *Next Time I'll Sing to You* in
London in the early sixties, and I had suggested it to Marian
Seldes the previous spring as an interesting rehearsal exercise
for five members of Group I.* When we saw it performed we
all liked it so much that I suggested we add it, for special
weekend performances, to our first professional season.
There it was seen by only a handful of people, including the
critic of *The New York Times,* who found it

one of the most fully realized and entertaining works in
the troupe's repertory. . . . The actors, expertly directed
by Marian Seldes, are all splendid but they must take
collective second place to Miss LuPone.
Delivering a hilarious monologue on the fatalistic aspects of premarital sex or just saucily swinging with a
feathered boa, she reveals herself as a comic actress with
enormous personal flair.

Things were moving fast now. Within a week of the close
of its Manhattan season the City Center Acting Company set

* Ben Hendrickson, Norman Snow, Patti LuPone, David Schramm
and Jared Sakren.

out on its New York State tour* with a reduced repertory consisting of *School for Scandal, U.S.A., The Hostage* and occasional school performances of *Scapin*.

Early in December, with their first tour behind them, they arrived in Philadelphia to open a two-week run of *School for Scandal* at the Locust Theatre, where they were described by Ernest Schier, the leading local critic, as "YOUTHFUL ACTORS TRIUMPHANT."

Right in the middle of the company's New York repertory season something happened which, at first, seemed just another personal diversion to which I was far too busy to pay serious attention, but which was eventually to change the course of what was left of my life.

The agent of this transformation was a young man from Paris, Arkansas, whose first play (in which Joan had played the part of a genteel barfly) had been performed in a small theatre in Los Angeles in the early sixties. His name was Jim Bridges and he had come to work for our UCLA Professional Theatre Group as a stage manager until I recommended him to Norman Lloyd, producer of the Hitchcock suspense series. There he wrote eighteen scripts before moving into motion pictures, where he soon established himself as that valuable commodity, a writer-director. At the time of *The Paper Chase*, Bridges was a young-looking man of thirty-five, boyish and balding, full of charm and affection and very shrewd and tough and determined underneath.

(One of the most endearing things about him was his combination of sophistication and regional naïveté. He once told me that at the age of twelve he had run home from school—a distance of several miles—during his lunch hour to get a glimpse of his elder sister's beau, who, it was rumored, was a *Jew*. He had never seen one and was determined not to miss the chance.)

Bridges and I had stayed in touch over the years and he

* Which took it to Albany, Potsdam, Fredonia, Brockport, Jamestown, Troy, New Paltz, Middletown and the Bronx. In New Paltz, a university town, we gave one performance of *Next Time I'll Sing to You* and lost half our audience at intermission!

had kept me informed of his personal and professional progress. Then, in the spring of 1972, he called one day in great agitation to tell me that he had just signed a contract to write the script and direct a film about Harvard Law School, based on a novel by John Osborne, who had written it during his last year in Cambridge. He had already engaged Timothy Bottoms (the young star of *The Last Picture Show*) for the leading part of a freshman law student and was hoping to get James Mason to appear opposite him as a formidable dean of the Harvard Law School. He sent me the script, which I liked, and we dined together when he came to New York to audition young actors for the roles of the law students.* He called me joyfully soon after that to tell me that he had engaged Gordon Willis, one of the industry's great cinematographers, as his cameraman. Then, as the weeks went by, I detected a growing anxiety over his inability to cast the essential role of Professor Kingsfield. Mason had disappointed him; so had Edward G. Robinson. Having tried and failed to get Melvyn Douglas, John Gielgud and Paul Scofield, among others, Bridges laughingly observed that I might end up having to play it. Early in August, while I was in Saratoga, Bridges called New City and spoke to Joan. He asked her how she thought I would react if he seriously suggested to me that I play the professor. Joan quite properly replied that I was the one to answer that question. When I spoke to him the next day I told him that I'd be delighted but that if he were foolish enough to mention the idea to the studio he stood a good chance of being thrown off the picture.

During the first week of our New York repertory season Bridges and his *Paper Chase* crew were moving into Toronto, where the film was to be shot.† He still lacked a Kingsfield and he was still suggesting that I play it. (In fact, I was begin-

---

* His final choices included Ed Herrmann, Graham Bechtel, James Naughton, Regina Babb, Craig Nelson and a young woman by the synthetic name of Lindsay Wagner, who later achieved fame as the Bionic Woman.

† The Harvard Corporation had categorically refused him permission to shoot on its campus. They had granted permission once, they explained, and the result had been *Love Story*!

ning to suspect that he was turning down the studio's casting suggestions in order to create a crisis situation in which I would be his last and only choice!) Finally I suggested that, since he now had his crew and his cameraman with him, I might fly up to Canada for a day and quietly make a test. If it stank we'd burn it. If it was at all satisfactory he'd be in a better position to talk to the studio.

I flew to Toronto the day after we opened *The Hostage*, carrying two dark suits, a selection of sober bow ties and some Xeroxed pages of one of Kingsfield's scenes. When I got there Jim said he also wanted to shoot the professor's opening address to his class.

I sat up half the night with a bottle of champagne and Winky, Jim's production assistant (who also happened to have been Pollack's assistant on *This Property Is Condemned*), memorizing my speech, which I delivered with great eloquence the next morning to a class consisting of the crew, Winky and a second assistant director:

> The study of Law is something new and unfamiliar to most of you—unlike any schooling you have ever been through. We use the Socratic Method here. I call on you, ask you a question, and you answer it. At times you may think you have reached the correct answer. I assure you that this is simply a delusion on your part. You will never find the ultimate, correct and final answer. In my classroom there is always another question—there is always a question to follow your answer. You teach yourself the law—but I train your mind. You come in here with a skull full of mush and you leave thinking like a lawyer!*

This and my other scene were both shot by midafternoon, so that I was able to fly back to New York and the Company that same evening.

Two days later Jim called in great agitation. He had just seen the test and it was "fabulous"! This was also the opinion of his two young producers, Bob Thompson and Rodrick Paul, and of Gordon Stulberg, head of production for 20th

---

* Part of this speech was used each Tuesday night over the opening title of the television series of *The Paper Chase* four years later.

Century–Fox, who had seen it at the studio and identified my behavior with that of his own contracts professor who had terrorized him years before when he himself was a law student.

Within a few days a deal had been made for me to play the role of Professor Kingsfield in *The Paper Chase,* for which I would receive fifteen thousand dollars and equal second-star billing, with a starting date of November 12. Bridges said I should have held out for twenty, but during the negotiations I was out of the country and several thousand miles away.

Two days after my return from Toronto I had received a disturbing call from Paris about my mother: she had fallen during the night and lain for nine hours on the floor of her hotel room, where she had been found half conscious by the maid who was bringing her breakfast. She had been moved to the American Hospital in Neuilly and was resting comfortably without serious aftereffects when I arrived. But it was evident that she couldn't live alone any longer, and, since she refused to admit her incapacity and seemed determined to stay in her beloved Paris, Joan's mother and I spent two days making the rounds of the city's better nursing homes to find one into which she might presently be moved.

I was back in New York for the opening of *The Lower Depths* and the confirmation of our upstate tour by the New York State Arts Council. After months of worrying about the fate of the company and of the school, I could finally sit back and relax. And this relaxation followed me to Toronto when I flew up there early in November to play the role of Professor Kingsfield in the film of *The Paper Chase.*

I had been in and around show business for forty years, and the idea of becoming an actor had never, even for a moment, entered my head. For that reason, perhaps, and because it had all happened so quickly, I went to work on *The Paper Chase* without a trace of the panic that normally accompanied the start of a new venture. I had a few secret misgivings over my ability (in my seventy-first year and without previous experience) to memorize the long speeches uttered by the professor. But once I realized that these presented no serious difficulty, I found playing the scholarly curmudgeon an agreeable and easy task, in which I was helped by the special circumstances of my engagement. This was no ordinary actor–director situation. Bridges and I had known each other for years in a teacher–disciple relationship that was not altogether unlike that which existed in the film between Kingsfield and Hart. Since we were equally committed to making my performance a success and to justifying Jim's reckless casting of me in the part, we worked as close allies— carefully, deliberately, trusting each other and in total agreement as to what he hoped to achieve.

It felt strange, of course, after so many years of producing and directing, to find myself suddenly on the other side of the camera. But I soon got used to it, and throughout the shooting of *The Paper Chase* I found my experience and my accumulated knowledge of theatre and film a constant help to me in my performance. I was privy to the strategy by which Jim and his cameraman (who sat in the bar every night planning their next day's work) were intending to heighten the initial impact of the formidable professor. Throughout my early classroom scenes I was to be consistently photographed in close-up and at angles that gave me weight and stature, in contrast to the long shots and diminishing lenses through which young Hart and my other helpless victims were introduced. I'm not sure how much my playing of those scenes was affected by this knowledge, but the use I was able to make of it unquestionably added authority and color to the relationship between the charismatic, deeply committed professor and his terrorized but worshipful students.

Also, because we knew each other so well, Bridges and I were able to play games, the best kind of theatrical games, in which the truth is understood but never entirely or positively stated. (An example of this was the elevator scene near the end of the film, in which Hart never quite knows whether Kingsfield has really recognized him. Jim and I had discussed it but had never come to a decision. During rehearsal he would let me play it first one way and then another; we all, including Timmy, enjoyed the equivocation, and no one ever tried to force me to an answer. In consequence I have always regarded that scene, as it finally appeared in the film, as one of the very few subtle and surprising things I have done as an actor.)

Owing to the lateness of my engagement for the film, I had done very little research into the legal aspects of my role.* I talked to a number of lawyers about the relations between law professors and their students, and I did what reading I could about "Bull" Warren, the Harvard professor who was generally believed to be the principal model for Kingsfield. But my performance would have been far less authoritative and credible without the help of John Osborne,† our author and legal consultant, from whom I learned not only the details of the Harvard Law School routines and the workings of the so-called Socratic Method, but also some of the philosophy that lay behind the dry legal facts and the tyrannical classroom behavior.

The relations between Kingsfield and his students, the reality of which I considered the main challenge of my performance, coincided with a curious personal problem I faced during the shooting of *The Paper Chase*. From the first day, and increasingly as we moved deeper into the film, I was conscious of the contrast between the relationship of the professor to his class (which vaguely resembled my relations with the students of the Drama Division) and my own personal feeling about the young actors with whom I was working. They were aware of my accomplishments—the long list of my films and plays—and this created an aura of professional respect, amounting to awe, of which I took full advantage in the scenes we played together. Yet they were also very much aware (at least, I felt they were) of my total inexperience as an actor. This gave me an uneasy feeling (a strange stirring of old fears) that, for all my venerable age and my established reputation, I was once again the "new boy"—the outsider yearning to be accepted into a society to which they, for all

* The actors playing the students had done weeks of personal research and had lived for days in a dormitory of the Harvard Law School.
† He was descended from a long line of lawyers; John Jay, the nation's first Chief Justice, was his great-great-great-grandfather.

their youth and obscurity, naturally and professionally belonged.

This did not prevent my work on *The Paper Chase* from being a wholly pleasant and exhilarating experience. Jim and I lived in a small hotel frequented by theatre people, the Windsor Arms, which had one of the best restaurants in Toronto and which was used for certain scenes in the film. We also shot in a block of abandoned university buildings and in a two-stage modern studio in the suburbs, in which our designer had created an exact reproduction (including hand marks on the walls) of Harvard's Langdon Hall. This was populated for several days by several hundred students from various local universities—including, in a small, featured part, one of the female guinea pigs from our first Juilliard "Retreat."

Bridges was shooting fast, and I found filmmaking hard work—especially the memorizing of my long speeches. But, in keeping with my character of Kingsfield, I made it a point of honor to be first on the set in the morning, prepared and word-perfect. Jim professed to be delighted with my performance, and I was agreeably surprised by the quality of the first rushes he allowed me to see. Yet my heart remained five hundred miles away on Sixty-sixth Street in New York, and every evening, when I got back to the hotel, my first act was to call Margot in New York to find out what had happened that day at the school and with the Company.

Looking back, I am astonished to find how little time I actually spent in Toronto. My contract called for me to start work early in November, for four weeks. I came up, shot for four days and then flew back to be with Joan in New City for the weekend. I was back in Toronto on the nineteenth and worked through the twenty-fifth, when (with Jim's permission but unbeknownst to the studio) I flew to Philadelphia to do advance publicity for the Acting Company's engagement at the Locust Street Theatre. The next day I was back in Toronto shooting my final scenes, including the night work in Kingsfield's home, climaxed by my inopportune return to find Hart in bed with my daughter.

I was back in Philadelphia three days later for the company's opening night there and missed the film's "wrap party" in Toronto* while I attended to my minimal duties as president of the National Theatre Conference, which was once again holding its annual meeting in New York City.

The week before Christmas I made a personal appearance on the stage of the City Center Theatre to introduce a children's matinee performed by the Acting Company before three thousand New York school kids and their parents. We did Chekhov's indestructible *Bear, Scapin* (a little worn and tired after two years) and *The Apple Tree* (based on a text by Mark Twain, with book and lyrics and Harnick and Bock), which served as a musical vehicle for Patti LuPone and Kevin Kline and marked the start of their long personal relationship.

Later that week I officiated at the Drama Division's term-end "exercises" and, for the last time, conducted the dismissal interviews I found so distressing. From then on, since the faculty made the decisions, I decided it was only fair that they should also assume the unpleasant task of executing them. But, looking back, I realize that this was only one example of a tendency that was becoming increasingly evident in my running of the school. By handing over to the faculty many of the decisions and obligations for which I had insisted on assuming sole responsibility during the early years of my tenure, was I being a wise and thoughtful administrator or was I, in fact and perhaps unconsciously, once again subtly preparing my exit?

* Bridges still had a few scenes to shoot elsewhere, including an ice scene for which he had to go far north and a beach scene he shot in Malibu. But this was the end of his work in Toronto—and with me.

CHAPTER XVII

1973

RUN-THROUGH IN LONDON
MACBETH
THE ACTING COMPANY:
FIRST MIDWESTERN TOUR
SARATOGA: SECOND YEAR
SECOND NEW YORK
REPERTORY SEASON

BECAUSE OF WHAT HAPPENED later, there is a strange warp in my memory that sometimes makes 1973 seem like a blank year—a fallow time during which I hung in a state of suspended animation between two lives. In reality, it was a busy, hard-working year like any other, crisscrossed by the usual pressures, distractions and temptations. I had been thrilled by my experience with *The Paper Chase,* but I still thought of it as an isolated and irrelevant adventure (not much different from my day's work, almost ten years earlier, on *Seven Days in May*) and a welcome diversion from my obsessive absorption in the affairs of the Company and the school. Of the two, it was the Company, predictably, that presented the obvious and major crises, but it was the school that continued to require the more constant attention.

This was especially true in the organization of our interpretation courses and in the handling of our directors and teachers of acting, among whom the frequent and inevitable turnover created situations that required constant readjustment. With René Auberjonois lost to films and Michael Kahn increasingly occupied (with Stratford in summer and Princeton the rest of the year), we had added several new director-teachers to our staff. These included such experienced theatre men as Harold Stone, John Stix, Ed Payson Call and, among the young hopefuls, Garland Wright, David Hammond and Jack O'Brien, all of whom made their personal contributions to the astonishing variety of plays which, following the Saint-Denis precepts, our students performed in diverse styles and amazing numbers throughout that year.*

In the essential disciplines neither the faculty nor the curriculum had changed appreciably since our opening. There had been a few novelties and superficial modifications, but nothing basic. In the spring, during Suria Saint-Denis' visit, I thought it desirable to organize, over one long weekend, what came to be known as the "Second Retreat" with the purpose of reviewing our achievements and of considering possible improvements. It turned out to be a rather dull gathering with a few personal conflicts and no apparent desire for major change.

One thing was clear: the school had greatly benefited from the success of our New York season. Group I's dramatic emergence into the theatrical limelight was having an emulating effect on the entire student body, each of whom now looked forward to one day qualifying for the Company. And, from our 1973 auditions, it was evident that we were now getting the pick of the nation's theatrical aspirants. A further

---

* During the school year of 1972–73 these included:

Group II: *The Servant of Two Masters; Happy Ending; Epitaph for George Dillon; La Ronde; The Bear; The House of Blue Leaves; The Knack.*

Group III: Scenes from Pinter and Ionesco; *The Balcony; The Kitchen; In the Summer House; Henry IV*, Parts 1 and 2; *Juno and the Paycock; Six Characters in Search of an Author.*

Group IV: *Moonchildren; The Days and Nights of Beebee Fenstermaker; A Doll's House; Major Barbara; Arms and the Man; Midsummer Night's Dream; Bus Stop; Charley's Aunt; The Matchmaker; Ivanov; The Storm,* by Ostrowsky.

Group V: *Hamlet; Oedipus; Agamemnon; Picnic; Our Town.*

valuable consequence of our success was its effect on our position in the Lincoln Center constituency, where our stock took a sudden, sharp rise. In a letter to his board of directors, Amyas Ames, the chairman of Lincoln Center, mentioned "the great success of the Drama Division and its recent graduates as the best indication that our payments to Juilliard represent one of Lincoln Center's best investments."

The truth is that, of all the major constituents of Lincoln Center, the only two that did not seem to be in some sort of difficulty that year were Juilliard and the New York City Ballet. Particularly troubled was the ill-starred Beaumont Theatre, home of what was still erroneously called the Lincoln Center Repertory. For some time I had watched Jules Irving, its artistic director, being pushed to the wall by his board. (His program was not an inspired one, but, with the addition of Ellis Rabb's recent productions, it had achieved some distinction and near-capacity audiences.) Rumors had long circulated about a change of management at the Beaumont.

Early in 1973, Irving resigned and meetings were called at which a number of theatre people were invited to submit suggestions for the future of the theatre at Lincoln Center. Mine was a far-reaching proposal that called for a year-round collaboration between Lincoln Center, the Stratford Festival, the Acting Company and the Juilliard School. It was quite evident, however, from the attitude of the bankers to whom I outlined my projects, that these meetings were nothing but a screen for a decision that had already been made. Two weeks later it was announced that Joseph Papp (who had made such a brilliant success with his Public Theatre, Shakespeare in the Park and, more recently, *A Chorus Line*) was taking over the Beaumont's two theatres with new infusions of public and private money far greater than had ever been available to any previous management. Unfortunately, he had no consistent artistic program and quit in disgust eighteen months later, leaving the Beaumont empty and desolate.

Another constitutent that was in a state of flux and in whose affairs I found myself briefly involved was the Metropolitan Opera. I met several times with Schuyler Chapin, who, following the sudden tragic death in a motor accident of the opera's great white hope, Goeran Gentele, had been named provisional administrator and artistic director. It was his notion (which I found flattering but which I never took too seriously) that I become theatrical consultant and, eventually, director of production and staging for the Met—working with Rafael Kubelik, its newly appointed musical director. I was aware that Chapin's own position was none too secure, but while our discussions lasted I enjoyed several elegant lunches at Le Poulailler and a number of free opera tickets for Joan and myself. (Before long Chapin was replaced by Bliss, and Kubelik by Levine, while John Dexter assumed the position for which I had been briefly considered.)

My own operatic activity that spring took the form of a production in the Juilliard Theatre of Ernst Bloch's *Macbeth*, composed many years ago but never performed in America. It was a massive, somewhat turgid work which, unlike Verdi's, adheres closely to Shakespeare's text and, for that reason perhaps, incurs some of the curse that traditionally dogs that ill-fated play. On an impressive, moody set by a young American painter named Yodice I staged it rather better than on my previous attempt in Stratford. But, once again, I ran into witch trouble. Bloch's supernatural music was static, untheatrical and interminable. I tried to deal with this by having the Weird Sisters sing offstage while "three mute hags," choreographed by Liz Keen, "moped and mewed" around the cauldron. It was not entirely successful. I also made cuts (some recommended by Bloch himself) for which I was severely criticized in certain quarters. "Though the abridgement of long works is common enough in professional houses, one expects integrity of a school performance that puts such expedient surgery to shame."

On the whole, *Macbeth* was respectfully received—perhaps more as a tribute to its deceased distinguished composer than for its operatic qualities. Schonberg of *The New York Times* conjectured that "it is altogether possible that *Macbeth* is a much greater work than this listener thinks it is."

After that, I spent some days with the Acting Company, which was on a tour of five states and twenty-two cities, including a residency in West Virginia, where, for the first time, we had added master classes in speech, movement, interpretation of texts, and mask work to our regular performances. But by far my longest journey that spring was to London, for the British publication of *Run-Through*.

Its sales in America since its publication the year before had been respectable but not enormous,* though it had been nominated for a National Book Award and voted the best theatre book of the year by the Theatre Library Association. Now that it was about to come out in England, its publisher, Allen Lane, invited me to come over to do promotion and to attend a simultaneous retrospective of my films arranged by the National Film Theatre.

I spent a week in London giving interviews on radio and television and making appearances at runnings of my movies, which included *They Live by Night, Letter from an Unknown Woman, Lust for Life, Executive Suite* and *The Bad and the Beautiful*. The series ended with an onstage interview with Dilys Powell, longtime film critic of the Sunday *Times*. During the evening, among other clips, we showed the pursuit sequence from Nick Ray's *On Dangerous Ground* and invited Bernard Herrmann, who had composed the score and had long maintained that it was his most effective piece of film music, to join us onstage to talk about it.

While I was in London an extract from the book appeared in the Sunday *Times*, and I read the first English reviews† before moving on to Paris to visit my mother. Installed in her *clinique*, in what had once been one of the Rothschild town houses and which Joan's mother described indignantly as "a real bandits' nest," I found her well cared for but increasingly incapacitated—also bored and restless. She was finding it hard to read and was seeing fewer of her surviving friends, who were less inclined to visit her in the depressing atmosphere of a nursing home than over afternoon tea and whis-

* Between twelve and thirteen thousand, I believe.
† They were as good as or better than those I had received in the United States, but the book, whether through inadequate marketing or because the subject was so essentially American, died like a dog and was soon remaindered.

key at Rumpelmayer's. Mrs. Courtney felt strongly that my mother would be better off in America and closer to me, but May herself was reluctant to make the move. When I left for New York after two days the subject was still undecided.

Soon after my return from Europe I was invited to lunch by Fred Friendly and David Davis of the Ford Foundation, for whom I had continued to write gloomy reports on the present state of public television. On March 19, 1973, under the joint auspices of the Ford Foundation and the Corporation for Public Broadcasting, a two-day "American Television Drama Seminar" was to be held at Tarrytown, New York. They were asking me to be its chairman, and it would use as its basis for discussion an article on the sad state of TV drama in the United States that I had published in *TV Quarterly*.

Present were many of the men and women historically associated with the best in U.S. radio and television—writers, directors and producers; also representatives of the Public Broadcasting System, the Corporation for Public Broadcasting and the Endowments for the Arts and Humanities. Present, too, was the head of TV drama for the British Broadcasting Company and leading representatives of American regional theatres. The day the conference ended I received a note from the Ford Foundation:

> Thank you very much for your work on the seminar. You are the one that caused it to happen—because of your nagging over the past few years and because your paper provided the proper stimulus. . . . We think we now have something we can work with.

I could not share their enthusiasm. I found this seminar that I "caused to happen" low on creative ideas and riddled with intrigue and maneuvering by special interests. It finally resulted in the setting up of one single major dramatic program, *Visions*, produced by Los Angeles' KCET under the direction of Barbara Schultz, one of the industry's most esteemed producers, who did her best to make of it a workshop for new writers and directors. It cost four million dollars and gave birth to a few valuable shows. But, as a force to rejuvenate American television drama, it was misconceived and futile, besides being sabotaged by its own members, the stations of the Public Broadcasting System. *Visions* never gained audience support, and its disappearance after eighteen months went almost unnoticed and unlamented.

The Acting Company's second summer season was due to begin early in July. This gave us a little over two months in which to give our exhausted young actors a vacation and to rehearse our program for the coming season. Our preparations differed from those of the previous year in one major, unhappy respect. Until now, since all of the shows we presented in our first season had been created as student productions, our sets and costumes had been paid for by the school and all our rehearsals conducted on Juilliard time. Now, though our relations with the school remained cordial, we faced the grim necessity of paying for our own productions and rehearsing them at full Equity salaries. That sent our budget soaring, and our general manager, Porter Van Zandt,* estimated the production costs for our new year's repertory of three plays at close to two hundred thousand dollars, all of which would be incurred at a time when we would be receiving no income at all. This created a cash-flow crisis that has never entirely abated during the dozen years of our operation and which, after the first glow of triumph over our unexpected success, has made the management of the company a source of continuing and agonizing financial anxiety from which I would often have given the world to free myself.

To help us deal with our present crisis we appealed to our various sponsors and benefactors and our two major contributing foundations, the New York State Council on the Arts and the National Endowment for the Arts,† all of whom were

* He had been with me on *Country Girl* and was considered the finest production stage manager in New York.
† Because she felt we were fulfilling a unique and invaluable function as a classical repertory company touring in unaccustomed places, Ruth Mayless, who headed theatre operations for the Endowment, had set aside the Endowment's rule of supporting only companies that had been in existence for two years or more.

generous in their understanding of our problem. By antici-
pating the date of their grants they made it possible for us to
make the necessary commitments for our new season, in
which we were further aided by advances from the Saratoga
Arts Center.

Saratoga was expecting three new productions from us of
which we could afford only two. We decided to repeat *The
Hostage** and threw in, as an additional attraction, Ann Jelli-
coe's *The Knack*—a light but flashy piece with four characters
and a minimal set.

Our other productions included Chekhov's *Three Sisters,* of
which I had happy memories and for which I felt our company was particularly well suited (and which remained in our
repertory longer than any other production). Our three sisters were Mary Lou Rosato, Mary Joan Negro and Patti
LuPone, and it was beautifully directed by Boris Tumarin.

Also, since it seemed desirable to include a Shakespearean
play in our program, I decided, rather than attempt one of
the major tragedies, to repeat my production of *Measure for
Measure* that had been so consistently successful. It fitted well
into the repertory—though I always had a feeling that members of the company would have preferred a show created
especially for them and that, partly for that reason, it never
quite recaptured the sharpness and wit of its original production.

Our second Saratoga season was generally considered
equal or superior in quality to the first. As a result, we were
invited to remain and play for two additional weeks during
August. That suited us perfectly, for it allowed us to rehearse
and break in our third production at Saratoga's expense.
This was Gay's *Beggar's Opera,* directed by Gene Lesser and
featuring, among others, Patti LuPone as Lucy Lockit and
Kevin Kline as MacHeath.

For a reason that I cannot recall (probably the installation
of air-conditioning), Skidmore College could not lend us its
new buildings that summer but billeted us in a decrepit, abandoned dormitory in the center of town with washrooms that

---

* Of which we also gave a performance in the local Comstock Prison.

had to be shared by both sexes. We lived there without air-conditioning for close to ten weeks, and I have sometimes wondered if this had anything to do with the curious "streaking"* fever that came to possess the Company toward the end of that long, hot summer and caused a minor scandal in the community.†

Before the start of the Saratoga season the Housemans had enjoyed a brief, welcome reunion in the House on the Hill. Sebastian had scraped through Storm King and graduated. John Michael's final year at Brandeis had been a good one, and he ended up on the dean's list for academic achievement. In his final semester he had taken a graduate course in anthropology which had so excited him that he had enrolled in a field trip organized for the summer by the University of Delaware in the mountains of Haute Savoie, in eastern France. He was preparing to go off on that, while Sebastian, having decided, with my consent, not to apply for college, was getting ready to see the world in the form of a visit to a lady of his acquaintance, a nightclub stripper in Miami, Florida—where he spent the next few months incommunicado except for the occasional arrival in the mail of surprisingly detailed and beautiful drawings of imaginary landscapes in the Doré style.‡ Joan spent some time with me in Saratoga, but much of her time was spent working on the taping, for public television, of Gorky's *Enemies*, which Ellis Rabb had directed for Lincoln Center the previous fall.

Later that summer an event occurred that, for a few days, sharply interrupted my own professional activities. Passing through New City one morning on my way to New York, I

---

* "Streak—to run naked through a public place as a humorous and defiant act"(*American Heritage Dictionary*). Streaking became a national habit that year.
† These "Naked Runners for God," as they called themselves, claimed me among their number, but I have always emphatically denied it.
‡ Gustav Doré, 1832–83, French artist best known for his highly imaginative and dramatic illustrations of La Fontaine's *Fables*, Rabelais, *The Divine Comedy*, etc.

found a letter in my mother's unmistakable, bold and still firm handwriting (except that now the end of each line sagged slightly) in which she informed me that, all things considered, she was finally resigned to leaving her beloved Paris. Coming to America seemed the sensible thing to do—all the more since it would bring her closer to me. But she was worried about the trip. I spoke to her on the phone and told her that I'd come right over (before she changed her mind) and that we'd make the flight back together.

I spent two days in Paris, mostly with my son John Michael, who had grown a lot in three months. Haute Savoie had been a great experience for him—so much so that he had come to a double decision: to remain in Europe and to study anthropology at the University of Nanterre, near Paris. He seemed not at all alarmed at the prospect of living alone in France; he had no language problem and had already, with the help of Joan's mother, found a part-time job in the Paris office of the Organization for Economic Cooperation and Development, where he started as an office boy and presently became a junior statistician.

With my usual social timidity, I had dreaded the embarrassments of a transatlantic flight with my ninety-three-year-old mother in her frail and half-paralyzed condition. Contrary to all expectations, the flight turned out to be a delight. May had always been an enthusiastic traveler, and the excitement of a long journey after six months spent in the boring seclusion of a French nursing home helped to bring about a startling transformation in her condition. It was a long and beautiful summer's day; everyone was sympathetic and kind; *Air-France*'s food was excellent, champagne flowed, and, in the eight hours it took to cover the distance from Orly to Kennedy, she and I found ourselves closer than we had been in years. We seemed to recapture, for a few hours, some of the charmed relationship we had shared during the European voyages we had taken together during my summer vacations more than half a century earlier.*

At Kennedy a Rockland County ambulance was waiting to

* See *Run-Through*, pp. 16 *et seq.*

508

take us along the familiar Hudson River route to Spring Valley. By late afternoon, with the sun still shining, May was installed in her room at the nursing home in which she continued to live for the remaining six years of her life. Three days later she was having lunch with Virgil Thomson and Bessie Poor in our House on the Hill (where she had helped to plant the rock garden more than twenty years before) and following her habitual regimen of two long Scotch-and-sodas and half a pack of Pall Mall cigarettes before and during lunch.

A few days after that I drove into Manhattan one evening for a reason that was totally unrelated to my usual shuttling between the Acting Company's New York office and the Arts Center in Saratoga.

It would be untrue to say that I had forgotten all about *The Paper Chase,* but so much had happened since the previous December that the film had lain dormant in my consciousness except when my interest was revived from time to time by emotional long-distance calls from Bridges in California.

The first studio running of the rough cut had been a dubious one. One of those sophisticated female advisers who are to be found lurking in the back rooms of motion-picture studios had written a five-page single-spaced violently disapproving report. Her main dissatisfaction had been with the character and performance of Professor Kingsfield, of whom she felt there was far too much in the film. Stulberg, the head of the studio, had sent her memo to Bridges without comment. Since then there had been two previews, in Santa Barbara and San Francisco, both of which had gone reasonably well. Now, on July 18, *The Paper Chase* was being sneaked for one night in New York City at the Sutton Theatre on East Fifty-seventh Street.

I cannot remember with whom I sat, but I do recall that word of the sneak preview had got around and that there seemed to be a number of friends in the house. As a spectator, I enjoyed the film and felt that, except for the very end, which I found soft and disappointing, Bridges had done a fine job of filmmaking. The performances (particularly those of Timmy and Lindsay, who surprised me with her independence and charm) all seemed fine, but it was Professor Kingsfield who really jolted me.

I had been puzzled and slightly contemptuous when Joan Fontaine told me, years before, that she threw up every time she had to look at herself on the screen. Now I understood. I sat there, staring up at the giant reflection of myself engaged in actions with which I was familiar (since I had played them) but that had no relation whatever to the *me* that sat frozen in my seat in the darkness below! One hour and forty minutes of being whipsawed between these two visions of myself left me limp and exhausted and quite incapable of exercising any kind of objective judgment about my performance. When the picture was over and the light had come back, I sat there for a while, drained and incredulous.

It was Irene Selznick, I think, who first uttered the words "Academy Award." They meant little to me at the time beyond Hollywood jargon, but I respected her judgment and I was pleased that she approved. I remember that Cicely Tyson hugged me on the sidewalk and that I was surprised by the number of friends who were present and by the excitement they seemed to share. By the time I was back in Saratoga the next morning, I was over my shock and Margot was waiting to embroil me in the Acting Company's latest crisis, which revolved around rehearsals of *The Beggar's Opera.*

Gene Lesser was a dynamic teacher and director who tended to push students (particularly the girls) beyond the limits of their endurance. Group I had long suffered under him. As students they had been helpless, but now, as actors, toughened by a year of arduous life on the road, they decided halfway through rehearsals of *Beggar's Opera* that they'd had enough. Insensitivity, favoritism and sadism were among the charges that the company (led by Patti LuPone, David Schramm and Mary Lou Rosato) gave as their reasons for refusing, ten days before opening, to go on rehearsing under him. In a severe test of my authority I persuaded them to go back to work in exchange for a promise that they need never work with him again. I kept my word,* though there were times, in the next few years, when I found myself regretting the absence of the neurotic energy he had injected into his shows.

It was soon after the opening of *The Beggar's Opera* that *The Paper Chase* began to take over my life. Early in September Jim Bridges, Timothy Bottoms, the producers and I, escorted by a platoon of public-relations people, male and female, descended on Atlanta, Georgia, where a dubious film festival was in progress. In their desperate anxiety to secure the world premiere of a major Hollywood film, its promoters had made a not-so-secret deal with 20th Century–Fox by which they guaranteed that *Paper Chase* would be awarded the Golden Phoenix and a number of other prestigious awards, which we accepted with appropriate gratitude in the presence of the Governor of the state, Jimmy Carter. This was duly reported in the press: "20th-Fox Takes Seven Awards to Sweep Atlanta Festival."

While we were in Atlanta, the Hollywood trades came out with their reviews of *The Paper Chase*. Over the years I had learned to regard these appraisals with suspicion and skepticism, but, for Jim and his producers, they were all they could have desired. The *Reporter* called it

> witty, affectionate and intelligent entertainment—a spirited and touching film that firmly places writer-director James Bridges among the disciplined filmmakers transforming Hollywood into the creative film center it used to be.

The entire cast got superlative reviews, but it was quite evident, by this time, who was the dominant figure in the film.

> Professor Kingsfield embodies every important teacher who ever terrorized and/or inspired his students to serious engagement with learning and its moral force.... Houseman seems the essence of humor, wisdom and

* Lesser continued to work at the school, where he remained one of our most vital teachers of acting for another six years.

pompous folly all at once and his masterly comic performance is destined to become a classic.

Variety was equally favorable but, with its usual realism, suggested that the film, because of its unusual quality, would "have to find its market slowly and gingerly."

The studio was aware of this and, over the next two months, gave *The Paper Chase* the unusual benefit of a carefully designed campaign. Long before its scheduled opening they were running the film all over the country for special audiences in law schools, universities, PTAs and even high schools.* Wherever it played it seemed to win approval of a special kind and to generate a warm sense of identification not only in law schools but in general among students and teachers.

In connection with those showings I was asked to make a number of personal appearances in New York, New Haven and Cambridge. I began with trepidation but soon discovered how much I was beginning to enjoy my new identity as an actor. The real test came in October, just before the formal opening of the film, when I spent ten days in jets and limousines visiting Chicago, Cincinnati, Toronto, Boston, Los Angeles, San Francisco and Washington, making continuous appearances on news and talk shows. In many of these cities I found myself repeating, as an actor, the television and press interviews I had given fifteen months earlier as the author of *Run-Through*. Only, this time, the interest seemed to be mostly in the actuarial phenomenon of a man who is starting a new career at the age of seventy-one.

Unlike the reviews of a play, of which the results are known overnight, the national press coverage of a film is spread over a period of several weeks. For *The Paper Chase* the reviews were generally favorable. But there was one aspect of the film on which there seemed to be no disagreement whatever, and that was the character, personality and potency of Professor Kingsfield.

* There was a joke around the studio that, after so many invited runnings, there would be no paying customers left in the country.

Dazed and incredulous, I read in *Time* magazine of "a for-bidding, superb performance catching not only the coldness of such a man but the patrician crustiness that conceals deep and raging contempt"; in the *Los Angeles Times* of "one of those uproarious, all-stops-out, fiendishly expert, domineer-ing and exhilarating performances which come along once in a blue moon of movies"; in *The New York Times* of "a brilliant, irascible old professor of contract law marvelously well played by the theatrical and film producer-writer, John Houseman." Even John Simon, in *New York* magazine, con-ceded:

> John Houseman, the experienced producer and direc-tor, makes his belated starring debut as a fine Kingsfield who teaches by the Socratic Method and rules his stu-dents with a rod of irony. . . . He exudes the proper amount of icy intelligence and fastidious prissiness and subtly suggests the underlying alienation.

What I found most surprising and what later became typi-cal of the national reaction to myself as Professor Kingsfield was the intense empathy he seemed to evoke in audiences—among whom my own personality became hopelessly con-fused and entangled with that of the character I was playing. A curious example of this surfaced in Pauline Kael's *New Yorker* review of the film. In her opening paragraph she con-centrated on the

> Houseman who carries the weight of his years and the stiff elegance of his personal authority and brings to the picture his own authenticity. He has an ineffable air of eminence. I am not sure where it comes from—having as a kid (when I was more sensitive than I am now) vom-ited after seeing a play he directed.*

* I wrote to Miss Kael for clarification and inquired if her vomiting had been the result of admiration or revulsion. She replied that she had seen *Anna Christie* in San Francisco and had been outraged by the fact that Ingrid Bergman played the part in patent-leather shoes! (See *Run-Through*, pp. 480–81.)

A more sober attitude prevailed among my own students in the Drama Division. Some days before the film's release I invited the entire student body to a running in the large projection room at 20th Century–Fox. Their behavior was exemplary; they arrived on time, laughed in the right places, applauded politely when the film was over, thanked me and left in silence. The next morning at school I waited for their reaction. I had been giving severe critiques of their performances for years, and I felt it only fair that they have a chance to do the same for mine. Nothing happened. Not a word. On the second day I waited for the lunch break, when they would be gathered in their dressing rooms and passages, and appeared among them. Still nothing. Finally I could stand it no longer and confronted a group of them.

"Well, you sons of bitches—how was it?" I inquired.

They played it cool. They said they had enjoyed the picture and they had liked Timothy Bottoms.

"What about *me*?" I insisted. "What did you think of *my* performance?"

"Performance?" they said. "That was no performance. That's the way you behave around here."*

Years later, after television had turned Professor Kingsfield into a familiar national figure, the question was still being asked: How much of the distinguished, cantankerous professor was the creation of the writer and how much was a reflection of the personality of the actor who played him?

Any effective interpretation by an actor of a powerful character inevitably raises this doubt; it poses the question of whether, in the course of performing it, the actor does not eventually assume, in his own behavior, some of the singularities of the character he has been playing.

---

* A different view was held by my mother, who had been taken by a friend to see *The Paper Chase* in Paris and who categorically refused to recognize or acknowledge me, declaring that the dreadful old gentleman on the screen was an impostor and bore absolutely no relation to her beloved son—whom she still thought of as being in his middle thirties.

In the past decade I have appeared in films and television as an archangel, the head of the CIA, Winston Churchill, a couple of grandfathers, a senile parish priest, the Patriarch of Venice, three captains of industry, two judges, the owner of a hotel chain, an ancient mariner, the conductor of a symphony orchestra, a mad scientist bent on the destruction of the Bionic Woman, and a talking computer in *Mork and Mindy*. I have also made commercials for medium-priced automobiles, the oil of sunflower seeds, and an esteemed financial institution—not to mention innumerable announcements for organizations that include bar associations, the American College of Surgeons and the American Heart Association. In each of them, Professor Kingsfield has been consistently and inescapably present.

In the winter of 1973, for all my rising agitation over *The Paper Chase*, my main concerns continued to be for the school and for the Acting Company, whose second national repertory tour was taking it, before Christmas, to Wichita Falls and Austin, Texas, then on to Denver, Baton Rouge, St. Louis and Atlantic City, and to Attica, New York. After that, in the four weeks immediately before and after the holidays we were scheduled to give our second New York repertory season at the Billy Rose Theatre on Forty-first Street.

This was an engagement to which I had been initially opposed—partly because of its excessive cost, and partly because I knew and feared the fickleness of New York audiences and press and the heavy odds against rekindling the enthusiasm we had aroused (despite our uncomfortable pews and outdoor toilets) during our first adventurous sojourn on Sixty-sixth Street in the Good Shepherd–Faith Church. However, it was generally felt that a second New York season was desirable and that this time it should be given in a full-sized, legitimate Broadway house. This was now made possible through the bounty of the Billy Rose Foundation, which contributed twenty thousand dollars (to be matched by the City Center) besides giving us free use of the theatre it owned one block south of Times Square.

The availability of that particular theatre may have been one of the reasons I agreed to this second New York season.

The Billy Rose Theatre (formerly the National) held a very special place in my affections: it had been the home of the Mercury early in 1938 during the four months of our dizziest success; twelve years later it had housed the *King Lear* I directed for Louis Calhern during the nine weeks of its New York run.*

What we now announced was a four-week season (from December 19 to January 12) for a total of thirty performances: *The Three Sisters* (ten), *Measure for Measure* and *Beggar's Opera* (eight each), *Next Time I'll Sing to You* (only three), and *Scapin* (one children's matinee).

Among the many differences between this and our previous season was the size of our theatre: the Billy Rose had around eleven hundred seats, compared with the Good Shepherd's two hundred and thirty. In order to avoid playing to half-empty houses, we made an arrangement to sell a third of our seats at reduced prices through the Theatre Development Fund, and, aided by my new fame as an actor, we conducted a brief but intensive publicity campaign on TV and in the press.

Three Sisters, our opener, was our most successful production. It gave Clive Barnes, in the *Times,* an opportunity for a rousing institutional review of the company as a whole and of *The Three Sisters* in particular:

> The beautiful agony of Chekhov's *Three Sisters* with all its humors and sighs arrived at the Billy Rose last night in a lovely performance, slow-paced at first, a little overmelancholy perhaps but soon getting into Chekhov's stride and ending exquisitely. . . .
>
> Don't go expecting to see the Moscow Art Theatre. But do go—and go expecting not only one of the greatest plays in the world but also an emergent native drama company with the beginnings of a style all its own.

Our second offering was *The Beggar's Opera,* which fared less well. Richard Watts in the *Post* found it "a likeable romp in a properly lively production," while the *Daily News* found it "a good-natured, workmanlike but rather dull evening."

* *Front and Center,* pp. 344–47.

516

Barnes came through once again with some reservations about the production but none about the company:

> Do not miss this company in its springtime. It will get better with age but it may also get more staid, and there are few deeper pleasures in the theatre than seeing gifted young actors experimenting with these gifts before your very eyes.

I was not particularly sanguine about *Measure for Measure,* having seen a wretched performance of it during a visit I had paid the company in Austin some weeks earlier. But, with added rehearsals, it seemed to be back in shape and its critical reception was generally favorable.* According to Doug Watt of the *Daily News,*

> If the Company had offered nothing else during its brief stay here, this would have made the visit memorable. . . . It is the wonder of the production that it succeeds on its own lively and melodramatic terms in doing Shakespeare full justice and making *Measure for Measure* seem so true. Don't miss this one.

I myself missed some of our New York performances when I flew to California in response to an urgent call I received late one night from two men, neither of whom I had ever met. One was Mike Merrick, whom I knew as Harry Belafonte's manager; the other was a successful writer for television by the name of David Rintels. They told me they had been in rehearsal for ten days with a one-man show about Clarence Darrow starring Henry Fonda. Now Fonda seemed to have lost faith in their young director and in the script and was talking of quitting. Would I fly out, diagnose the trouble and, if I thought it was curable, take over the show?

I was attracted by the possibility of working with Fonda, and this was the first theatrical offer I had received in more

---

* I was pleased by the reception given David Schramm in a role that was different from anything he had played before. He was described as "verging on brilliance as the passionate and inhibited Angelo," "a man obsessed with his own saintliness who intelligently shows us the character's awakening to sensuality."

than a year. I agreed to fly out, watch a run-through and talk to Fonda before making my decision.

I had known Henry Fonda very slightly ever since that distant day in 1945 when I had offered him a perfectly terrible film at RKO. I knew of his reputation as a perfectionist and of his habit of becoming depressed and discouraged halfway through rehearsals when things were not measuring up to his hopes. Sitting for two and a half hours the next afternoon with Rintels and Merrick in a shabby little Hollywood theatre, I found *Darrow* an interesting and dramatic show, and it was quite clear to me that with some trims, a few structural transpositions and, above all, a change in climate, it stood a good chance of becoming one of the outstanding performances of Fonda's long and distinguished career.

I talked to no one after the run-through. But that evening, in Fonda's house high in the Bel-Air hills, I told them all, as honestly as I could, how I felt about the show. The idea of replacing someone else was repulsive to me, but if they were determined to get rid of the present director (who, I felt, was getting a raw deal) I was willing to take over the production. That night I took the red-eye flight back to New York, and I returned three days later and went to work.

We had less than three weeks before our out-of-town opening, but that was enough. The script which Rintels had put together from Irving Stone's *Clarence Darrow for the Defense,* with additions from Darrow's own writings and from the court records of the time, was filled with eloquent, colorful and sometimes humorous material. We did some editing, changed the act ending and worked on the domestic scenes of Darrow's first marriage that had been bothering Fonda. I think I gave him confidence and I was of some value in bringing variety and movement to his two-hour soliloquy. But such was Hank's intelligence, his sensitivity and his own flawless taste that my main use to him as a director, during our final rehearsals, lay simply in my being out front and in supplying him with a trustworthy, living mirror in which he was able to see his own reflection and check the truth of his performance.

That I found this exciting and rewarding was due to my

sense that, once again, I was encountering theatrical genius. His was the kind of acting of which I had little personal experience and which I had been inclined to lump in the limiting category of "naturalism." As such, it was quite different from what we were teaching at Juilliard. Yet, to my surprise, I found that in its results when practiced by an actor of Fonda's stature it conformed in every respect to those standards of "reality" and "style" which were the final goal of our instruction.*

In mid-January we all flew together (Hank and Shirlee Fonda, Mike Merrick, Rintels, his beautiful girlfriend and I) to Louisville, Kentucky, which had been selected as the place for our dress rehearsals and out-of-town tryout. It was my first sight of Louisville since my lovesick visits to Henrietta Bingham forty-two years before,† but I was too absorbed in *Darrow* to have much time for nostalgia. Poindexter's unit set presented no difficulties or lighting problems; our only delays were in the delicate adjustment of the new radio mikes we were using, with which we finally reached the point where the audience was unaware of their existence.

We had two dress rehearsals and four performances in Louisville, then moved on for our opening in Chicago, which was, in a very real sense, Darrow's town—his residence for most of his life and the scene of his first identification with labor. (I remember, on opening night, meeting men of var-

* In a follow-up piece written after our New York opening, Walter Kerr wrote of Fonda's performance in terms that perfectly define the miracle of his acting and explain the wonder with which I observed his rehearsal habits: "Mr. Fonda has never been much of an *impersonator*. He has looked like himself, talked like himself, tailored troublesome parts to himself. In *Darrow*, he enters in no disguise; he has not even aged as much as he'd like to pretend. Evocation of that famous trial lawyer seems limited, for a while, to a certain grumpy thrust of the jaw, a gritty tensing of the facial muscles, the bothersomeness of a gray forelock that won't quite stay in place. Then, before long, you find yourself remembering, with a start, what Darrow really looked like; newspaper photographs pop into your head once more quite unbidden. A subliminal Darrow usurps the Fonda personality and the game is won, not by charm or easy skill but by intellectual metamorphosis."
† See *Run-Through*, "Overture."

ious ages who had known and worked and fought with and against Clarence Darrow at different times of his life.) Our reviews were ecstatic and we could have stayed in Chicago forever, but we were booked into Washington, where our opening became the occasion of a big American Civil Liberties Union benefit attended by several Supreme Court justices and by Jane Fonda (whom I was seeing for the first time since our strange, unfortunate stay in Greece and London).

Darrow opened in New York in the last week of March at the Helen Hayes Theatre. We had a brief, terrifying flare of trouble with the sound system on opening night, but our triumph, Hank's in particular, was complete and unqualified. There was praise for David Rintels' script, and I was credited by Clive Barnes with directing the play "with enormous skill."

As to Mr. Fonda it would be difficult to think of praise too high. Watch the way he visibly ages as the evening moves on, the way he snakes out with Darrow's sly and country humor, the way he never shrinks from sentiment and yet never stresses it. And listen to the voice— never too much inflected, never coarsely characterized yet always easy and lyrical. And the face—too quizzical to be heroic, too self-aware to be smug and with the laughter lines of a man who rated compassion higher than justice. If Clarence Darrow was not like this, he should have been . . . just plain wonderful.

CHAPTER XVIII

Metamorphosis

When, in his seventies, John Houseman finally found Professor Kingsfield—he found himself.
—GARRICK UTLEY, NBC-TV

You can't be what you were
And what you are.
No one can have everything.
It's forbidden.
—"The Soldier's Tale"*

THERE WAS A TIME, after I first came to Juilliard, when I felt
that in accepting my appointment as head of the Drama Division I had settled for a future of limited opportunity and
slow professional death. Now, seven years later, I could look
back with stupefaction on a series of utterly unpredictable
achievements, of which directing Henry Fonda in a Broad-

* A fairy tale of Russian origin, best known for its brilliant score by
Igor Stravinsky. (The quotation is from the translation by Jack Larson.)

way smash hit marked the climax but which also included the creation and administration of the country's most advanced theatre school, the publication of a book, a starring role in a major Hollywood film and the formation of an acting company that stood alone in the contemporary American theatre.

All this should finally have satisfied me and allowed me, in my mid-seventies, to rest on my laurels and enjoy the fruits of so many years of unrelenting toil. Instead, I was about to be subjected, without premonition or warning, to the most far-reaching and unexpected shock of them all.

I was conscious, and even took a certain pride in the fact, that luck had always played an overwhelming part in my affairs. I was also aware of the furious effort and incessant manipulation to which I had resorted over the years in order to take advantage of these repeated accidents of fortune. What was different and curious about this latest tremor was the apparent apathy with which I received it.

Early in February of 1974, just about the time the Acting Company was setting out on the final stage of its second national tour and Henry Fonda was making his move with *Darrow* from Chicago to Washington, the names of those nominated for the 1973 awards of the Academy of Motion Picture Arts and Sciences were made public. Mine was among them—for my performance as Professor Kingsfield in *The Paper Chase*.*

In order to appreciate what happened to me during the next few weeks it is necessary to understand the workings of the unique and monstrous machine that is set in motion each spring for the greater glory and continued profits of the American film industry. It has a motion so vast and so far-reaching that everyone in our profession is, to some degree, caught in its wake.

The Academy Awards function on two levels. Artistically they give creative members of the industry a chance to receive the tribute of their peers on the basis of professional

---

* The others were Vincent Gardenia for *Bang the Drum Slowly,* Jason Miller for *The Exorcist,* Randy Quaid for *The Last Detail* and Jack Gilford for *Save the Tiger.*

quality rather than box-office returns.* At the same time they represent a highly organized and commercialized attempt to publicize the American film business and to stimulate a worldwide demand for its product. With the advent of television and with the world's entire communications system behind it, the annual presentation of these awards reaches an international audience estimated at half a billion people; through sheer mass of numbers it takes on a glamor and an importance that sometimes transcends the contents and artistic qualities of the films and individuals that are being honored.†

This was not my first involvement in these awards. In an outburst of professional boastfulness I had announced in 1953 that the four films I had made at MGM over the previous two years had received twenty-eight Academy nominations and eleven awards! That was when I was a producer for a major studio. Being nominated for an award as an actor made everything suddenly and entirely different. For the first time in my professional life I was no longer "the collaborator, the behind-the-scenes organizer, the vital supernumerary"; suddenly the protective armature I had carefully built around myself over the years was blown away, leaving me naked and solitary, to be judged no longer by the results of my careful planning and maneuvering, but for myself alone—on the basis of my own individual performance.

None of this occurred to me at the time. My first reaction was one of incredulity and vague pleasure, followed by a certain sense of embarrassment at the realization that, whereas for most actors (particularly those in the supporting category) an Academy Award, or even a nomination, comes

* The present voting procedures were devised to prevent the undue influence of major studios or pressure on the voters through costly advertising and promotion.
† There is a perennial argument as to whether the winning of an Academy Award is truly beneficial to an actor's career. An example frequently cited is that of Luise Rainer, who won for two years in a row and never worked again. That was before television. Today a major award automatically adds several million to the receipts of a film and a substantial increase in the earning power of an artist.

as the hard-earned culmination of a long and dedicated career, mine was the reward for ten agreeable autumn days spent with a friend in Toronto!

I was like a man who has contracted an infectious disease but continues to go about his business for a time, unaware of his condition. My first real recognition of what was happening came to me in a curious way—during a long-distance call I received one night from my well-informed friend Norman Lloyd, who reported that Nick the Greek in Las Vegas had lowered the betting odds against my winning the award from five-to-one to three-to-two!

This was followed by a steady increase in the number of interviews and TV appearances set up by the studio to publicize *The Paper Chase*—to all of which I submitted, reluctantly at first and then with rising competitive excitement. The image of myself as the "septuagenarian novice" was one that was giving interviewers something different to work on.* Having, until then, carefully avoided all thought and mention of age, I was beginning to enjoy this new situation that was suddenly opening up a whole fresh area in which to exercise my ego.

The one person who might have kept me sober during those fevered weeks was not around. Joan's obstinate, almost fanatical refusal to become emotionally concerned with the more squalid and competitive aspects of show business would have been invaluable during those final, lunatic days of elaborately and deliberately contrived suspense. Unfortunately she had taken advantage of my departure for California for rehearsals of *Darrow* to pay an overdue visit to her family and friends in Europe.

I did my best to keep myself occupied—with the school, with the Acting Company and, above all, with the New York opening of *Darrow*. Then, one morning, my peace was shattered by a call I received from the president of the Hollywood Foreign Press Association inviting me with suspicious ur-

---

* "Late Bloomer," "Birth of a Star at 72," "Father of American Rep Turns Actor," "Theatre Dean Transformed" were among the phrases employed.

gency to attend its annual Golden Globes ceremony in Hollywood on the following night.* I was far too busy with *Darrow* and asked Jim Bridges to take my place. He called the next day and said he had my Golden Globe on his desk and what the hell should he do with it? The next day in Vegas my odds went to even money.

On April 1, I made an embarrassing appearance with two of my rivals on one of the early-morning shows, where, with hypocritical smiles, the three of us wished each other success. That evening I packed my black velvet jacket (the one with the scarlet lining that I had acquired in Provence during the filming of *Lust for Life* and that I kept for special occasions), and I left the next morning at dawn for Los Angeles. Installed in my first-class seat, with a glass of champagne by my side, I wrote a letter to my wife that I mailed at the airport:

> *En l'air* between
> Denver & Los Angeles
> Tuesday, April 2

DEAREST BOOBY,

I'm thinking of you and wishing you were with me to guzzle champagne in the nose of the 747 that is carrying me to Oscar-Night. Suddenly, in the middle of the night, I was seized with a most violent revulsion at the idea of sitting in that huge red theatre waiting, *les fesses serrées* [with clenched buttocks], for some goon-lady to open an envelope and announce whether I had been chosen for what would, in my case, constitute a most dubious honor! But I soon got over that and here I am, 90 minutes from L.A., where a long and black limousine will carry me to the place of execution.

Tomorrow, no matter what happens tonight, I shall rise at 6 A.M., catch a plane back to New York and arrive just in time to be present at the second night of the Drama Division's Spring Repertory Season. What a loony life it is—and how long can it go on?

Late last night, I was aroused by a call from Sebastian in Florida—ostensibly to wish me luck. He seemed

---

* The Golden Globes Annual Awards are generally regarded as reliable indications of the final Academy voting.

cheerful enough but after he had hung up and his voice lingered on for a few moments in my head, I suddenly got the very strong impression that what he was really telling me was that he was lonely and unhappy and that he would like to come home.

I'll do something about that as soon as this rat-race is over and we're settled once again in New City. Last Sunday I drove May over to lunch on the Hill. No change there. We had our usual *fin-de-saison* snowstorm last week: 6 inches in one night. As usual I was safely in New York!

I do hope you're having some fun and please give my love to Françoise and your mother and, above all, to Michael! I miss you and I'll be happy when you're back. All my love and *mille baisers*,

JOHN

P.S. In case you haven't heard—*Darrow* opened four days ago and is an enormous success!

In Beverly Hills' three major caravansaries, madness reigned. Arriving nominees were installed in suites and were set upon by packs of ferocious reporters, few of whom had done their homework and most of whom kept asking the same ridiculous questions. When I could stand it no longer I called down, pleaded fatigue and canceled all further interviews. Then I went quickly through my growing pile of telegrams and messages, and made some telephone calls to friends and to my escort for the evening. I had given much thought to whom I should invite to share this dramatic moment. Finally I had the brilliant notion of inviting an old, dear friend—the widow of my beloved collaborator Herman Mankiewicz—for whom I hoped the occasion would revive happy memories of the night her husband had been honored for his screenplay of *Citizen Kane!*

Because of the time difference with the East, we had been instructed to be in our seats by six-thirty. This gave me two and a half hours. I undressed, slept for ninety minutes and was awakened by a call from the lobby from someone whom I had not seen or thought of in a long time—a lovely lady whom I had desired for years but with whom it had never seemed possible or appropriate to consummate my lust. We opened one of the bottles of champagne with which the suite was littered and talked until it was time for me to get ready for the ceremony. We said goodbye and I retired to shave and bathe. When I came back, the lady was lying in my bed smiling—with a glass of champagne in her hand. "For luck!" she said, and we spent the next twenty minutes, without sentiment or pretense, engaged in the sheer, eager, impersonal pleasure of making love.

There were several dozen limousines waiting below, and one of them drove me to Brentwood to pick up first Sarah Mankiewicz and then James Bridges* and Jack Larson, and then downtown to the Chandler Pavilion, where we arrived in broad daylight and made our way past screeching bleachers and through minefields of cameras and microphones, immediately behind Linda Lovelace,† who had arrived in a bright-red hansom cab and a white lace dress. I was seated next to Bridges and in the same section as Timothy Bottoms, Paul Newman and George Roy Hill (nominated for *The Sting*), my friend Stewart Stern and several beautiful young persons and their escorts, whom I did not know. I was quite numb by the time the show started and only dimly aware of what was going on as presenters, award winners and musical numbers followed each other relentlessly on that huge, overlit stage and Burt Reynolds, who had been pressed into service as m.c. at the last moment, fumbled his uncertain way through the evening. As in a nightmare, I kept repeating in my head fragments of the various acceptance speeches I had been composing for days—alternately praying for an Oscar and dreading the moment when I might have to go up there and receive it.

There was a brief, welcome interlude when that year's inevitable "streaker" made his bid for fame—a pitiful, pale,

---

* Because he had bitterly opposed the executives' last-minute attempt to change the title of the film to *All the Bright Young Men,* Jim Bridges was in disgrace with the studio and was being punished by being denied a limousine, even though he had been nominated for a writing award!

† The year's porno queen, the star of *Deep Throat.*

knock-kneed nude who was soon interrupted and dragged away. After that I lapsed back into my torpor until, feeling Sarah tugging at my sleeve and looking up, I became aware of a dark, squat man and a ravishing blond girl* in a low-cut dress approaching the stage-left podium, and I realized with horror that the moment had come and that these were the presenters of the award for the best performance by a male actor in a supporting role. I could see their lips moving as they listed the names of the nominees, and heard their voices coming from what seemed to be an entirely different place. Finally the girl in the low-cut dress held up the envelope and unsealed it. Her mouth opened. "The winner is John Houseman," she said.

I woke up then, rose to my feet and made my way, in what felt like slow motion, past Sarah Mankiewicz and Jim Bridges and Paul Newman and Joanne Woodward and Stewart Stern and the girls with the escorts I didn't know, down the aisle and in the direction of the stage. As I started up the steps I heard a sound behind me that remains my most vivid memory of that night.

What happened next was not an egomaniacal fantasy: it can be verified in decibels on the tapes of that night's proceedings and in the next day's press reports. All through the evening, each successive win had been greeted by a salvo of applause that varied in volume and quality with the nature of the award and the popularity of the victor. The announcement of my name had started the kind of reaction that could be expected to greet the announcement of the first of the evening's major awards. But then, as I completed my climb up the shallow carpeted steps, turned and started on my long, self-conscious walk across the stage, the sound of applause, instead of dying down, seemed to rise and spread. What had begun as an automatic reaction to the surprise victory of a septuagenarian dark horse was turning into a minor ovation —a spontaneous expression of personal recognition and affection.

There were thirty-three hundred people in the Chandler

* Ernest Borgnine and Cybill Shepherd.

528

Pavilion that night—most of them professionals, of whom at least one quarter were men and women with whom, at one time or another, directly or indirectly, in one way or another, in theatre, radio, films or television, I had collaborated over the past forty years. What I believe they were applauding at that moment, over and above my fluky victory, was their own sentimental memory of the work we had done together.

The next thing I knew I was being handed a gleaming brass figure, which I found larger and heavier than I expected. Then, as the applause finally died away, I found myself standing all alone, staring out over that sea of faces with not one word left in my head of all those sincere and elegant phrases I had been preparing for days. I opened my mouth and, according to the official record, this is what came out:

"For the first time in a long and tumultuous life I find myself almost incapable of speech. I cannot begin to describe to you the emotions with which I receive this great honor at your hands. I do, however, have a few personal gratitudes I need to express: first, to all those who worked with me on *The Paper Chase*, for the great kindness and generosity with which they accepted the presence of a mysterious and inexperienced intruder in their midst; second, to Gordon Willis, whose extraordinarily dramatic camera work did so much to help me create the character of Dr. Kingsfield; thirdly, fourthly and fifthly, to my dear friend Jim Bridges, as the writer, the director and as the extraordinarily reckless young man who had the unspeakable gall to select an aging and obscure schoolmaster to play this perfectly glorious part in his picture."

As I started offstage, escorted by my keepers and still clutching my Oscar, I remember wondering if Orson Welles was watching the show and thinking of an interview I'd read on the plane that morning with one of the craftsmen who created the trophies and whose principal reaction was one of indignation at the sloppy way in which the winners held their Oscars in their sweaty hands and, in a few seconds, ruined the flawless satin sheen it had taken so many days to achieve.

Politely but firmly I was led to an elevator and up to where the serious business of the evening was taking place—an entire floor turned into a Tower of Babel in which scores of reporters and crews from dozens of countries were struggling to secure and record personal interviews with the night's winners. Tatum O'Neal was there (for her performance in *Paper Moon*). Aged ten, cool as a cucumber, she was brightly parrying the idiot questions with which she was being harassed. I did less well but managed to give four interviews —one in French, one in rusty German and one in execrable Argentine Spanish.

All this took close to forty minutes, and when I finally got back to my seat, still clutching my Oscar, Kate Hepburn was onstage presenting the Irving Thalberg Award. After that Jack Lemmon and Glenda Jackson received their acting honors, and the seats around us were suddenly emptied as *The Sting* carried off the best-director and best-picture awards. When it was all over, on our slow way to the limousines, a harassed girl ran up to me, snatched the Oscar out of my hands and said it would be mailed to me after it had been engraved.

The cars took even longer than usual to appear, and Sarah was tired after so much emotion and asked to be taken home. So I went with Bridges to the Academy Ball and spent an hour waiting to assuage my ravenous hunger and receiving congratulations from people to whom I had not spoken in years. When I got back to the hotel, in addition to local calls there were telephone messages from the Fondas and Rintels in New York, from Margot and the Acting Company in Washington, and from Bishopstone in England. It was too late to speak to the East Coast, but I called back the overseas operator and spoke to Joan, who was having her morning tea in bed in Sussex. She had been unable to see the show, but our friend Easton had called from London at dawn with the news. She said she'd be home soon. After that I turned off the light, tried to get some sleep and failed. It is never entirely dark in Beverly Hills, and I lay in bed in the half-light reliving the events of the night and feeling much as the frog must have felt just after he'd been kissed by the king's daughter and turned into a prince!

Postscript

IN THE FAIRY STORY by the brothers Grimm the transformation from frog to prince was total and instantaneous. Mine has been more gradual and complicated.

It took three years for *The Paper Chase* to become an admired but controversial television series and two years after that for Professor Kingsfield and myself to attain our joint national level of credibility. Without attempting to equate the magic of the princess's kiss with the ephemeral distinction of an Academy Award, it is a fact that my career as an actor and my identification with the formidable professor (both of which were established that evening on the stage of the Chandler Pavilion) have brought about changes in my life which, though less miraculous, have been just as drastic and far-reaching as those that followed the frog's move from the pond to the palace.

This is the second metamorphosis in my life. The first—

reported in *Run-Through*—took place in the thirties when Jacques Haussmann, the hybrid, halfhearted European grain merchant, was transformed into John Houseman, a rootless, desperate novice in American show business, and was formally confirmed in his new identity by the U.S District Court for the Southern District of New York. The second, occurring almost half a century later, marked my professional transformation from a respected but neglected veteran in the theatre to one of the most sought-after and highly paid aging male performers in the mass media. On a personal level, its effects have been no less decisive. When, in my mid-seventies, I stumbled into the celebrity and opulence for which I had yearned and struggled in vain for so many years, the most conclusive evidence of my alteration was the prompt disappearance of those anxieties and terrors that had haunted my adolescent and adult life and which have played such a continuous and obsessive part in this narrative.

Memoirs are normally undertaken in the latter part of a life, when most of the returns are in and the final outcome can be predicted with reasonable accuracy. Mine have been thirty years in the writing and have been produced under conditions of constant uncertainty and incessant change. Except for my latest metamorphosis, most of the adventures in which I took part have been recorded between ten and twenty years after they occurred. Inevitably, those accounts have been conditioned by the moods, pressures and circumstances of the changing present during which they came to be written.

Whenever possible, I have tried to record the emotional effects as well as the material realities of the main events of my life without the dubious benefit of hindsight. Throughout, it has been the process of personal and professional change and growth that concerned me rather than the final result. For that reason the conception and development of the Juilliard Drama Division and its Acting Company have been described with all the fears and uncertainties that surrounded their difficult birth and without the comforting assurance that, within a decade, they would both become acknowledged leaders in their respective fields. Conversely, I have tried not to tarnish the bright hopes and fervors of our first three Stratford Festival seasons through the unhappy awareness that, before long, the entire operation we had worked so hard to create would crumble into failure and dissolution.

Over the years I have found these excavations of my past an occasionally painful but a consistently exhilarating experience. Not everyone gets the chance to live his life twice over or has the good fortune to be born into a world of such violent motion as the one in which I have managed to survive for more than eighty years.

J.H.

'Do you realize that, lately, you have been on TV almost as much as John Houseman?''

LOS ANGELES TIMES, APRIL 17, 1982

Acknowledgments

My thanks to Marian Barnett for her work on the first part and to Diana Fleishman for her indefatigable typing of the many versions of this entire book.

For reading it and for pointing out my numerous inaccuracies and errors I am grateful to Norman Lloyd, Margot Harley, Marian Seldes, Gordon Davidson and Alan Hewitt.

For their selection and arrangement of the illustrations I owe renewed thanks to Vincent Virga and Edith Fowler.

Index

535

Outstanding Paperback Books

☐ **Front and Center**
by John Houseman
A riveting account of Houseman's wartime involvement with the controversial *Voice of America,* his career in Hollywood and Broadway and his experiences during the 1950s blacklist era. He recalls his relationships with Raymond Chandler, Nicholas Ray and Joan Fontaine among others in what The Chicago Sun-Times calls a "mature, shrewd and richly enjoyable book."
41391-0 $9.95

☐ **Run-Through**
by John Houseman
A lucid and fascinating account of the beginning of one of the most brilliant and diverse careers in the American theater. He tells his own story, from 1902 to 1941 with entertaining and formidable insight into his own time, offering candid portraits of such important contemporaries as Alfred Hitchcock and Orson Welles.
41390-2 $9.95

☐ **Four Screenplays of Ingmar Bergman**
"Bergman...is essentially the artist, as much writer as he is filmmaker." (Saturday Review) This quartet of screenplays for his most distinguished films reveals, for the reader, Bergman's creative process as well as his love of words.
20353-3 $9.95

☐ **The Craft of the Screenwriter**
by John Brady
Movie buffs, students, writers and filmmakers will find these six interviews with America's best screenwriters entertaining as well as an essential source of information. Brady gets the best of Neil Simon, William Goldman, Paddy Chayefsky, Ernest Lehman, Robert Towne and Paul Schrader in what Rex Reed describes as "a 'must' for the film library shelf."
25230-5 $8.20

☐ **The Art of Dramatic Writing**
by Lajos Egri
A clear, jargon-free approach to the literary creation of drama, emphasising the essential aspects of premise, character and conflict. In a direct dissection of the development of truth through human behavior, Egri provides the basis needed by the playwright or any creative writer.
21332-6 $7.95

☐ **Towards a Poor Theatre**
by Jerzy Grotowski
A controversial and compelling theatrical force, Grotowski, in writings collected here for the first time, reveals his profound understanding of theatrical tradition, literature and psychology, and his powerful commitment to existential humanism.
20414-9 $10.95